THE
OLD MAN
TOLD US

Excerpts from Micmac History
1500–1950

Ruth Holmes Whitehead

Foreword by
Dr Peter Christmas

NIMBUS
PUBLISHING LTD

Nimbus Publishing Limited
P.O. Box 9301, Station A
Halifax, Nova Scotia
B3K 5N5

Design: Kathy Kaulbach, Halifax
Cover photograph: Courtesy Nova Scotia Museum

Photograph credits: p. 3 (tracing, R.H. Whitehead), 4 (tracing, R.H. Whitehead), 9 (photo, Olive Kelsall), 15 (photo, Olive Kelsall), 113, 161, 171, 181, 195, 215, 251, 257, 270, 273, 279, 298, 305, 323, 337, courtesy Nova Scotia Museum; p. 35, 41, 53, 65, 69, courtesy The Champlain Society; p. 89, cover, Maps & Books, St John's, Nfld.; p. 263, Public Archives of Nova Scotia; p. 289, courtesy Queens County Museum, Liverpool.

Canadian Cataloguing in Publication Data

Whitehead, Ruth Holmes

The old man told us

Includes bibliographical references and index.
ISBN 0-921054-83-1

1. Micmac Indians—History. 2. Indians of North America—Maritime Provinces—History. I. Title.
E99.M6W54 1991 971.5'004973 C91-097523-X

Printed and bound in Canada by Hignell Printing Limited

FOR

PETER HULL

"The old man told us of the curious method he used in obtaining his fox-skins. He would go off alone into the moonlit forest, to the edge of some little barren, which the foxes often cross, or hunt round its edges at night. Here he would lie down and wait patiently until the dark form of a fox appeared in the open. A little shrill squeak, produced by the lips applied to the thumbs of the closed hands, and the fox would at once gallop up with the utmost boldness, and meet his fate through the Indian's gun."

—*Campbell Hardy*—

CONTENTS

FOREWORD

ON A COLD AND DREARY NOVEMBER AFTERNOON, an exhausted Ruth Holmes Whitehead stepped out of a Sydney courtroom. "Peter," she said in an unusually angry tone of voice, "this has nothing to do with justice, reconciliation, or human dignity. It just has to do with winning. At times, I felt as if I were on trial."

"Welcome to our cultural club," I tried to console. "Now you know just how the Micmac have been feeling for the last five hundred years."

Ms. Whitehead had just been strenuously and vigorously cross-examined on her qualifications as an expert witness on Micmac ethno-history, in defence of fourteen Micmac who were charged for participating in the 1988 moose hunt, contrary to provincial law. The Micmac argued that under the terms of the 1752 treaty with the Nova Scotia colonial government, they "have free liberty of hunting and fishing as usual." It was a line of defence used previously by another Micmac from the Shubenacadie Band who had been apprehended in September 1980 for having in his possession during a closed hunting season a shotgun and shells, not permitted under the Lands and Forests Act. He was convicted by the Nova Scotia Provincial Court. A subsequent appeal to the Supreme Court of Canada rendered a 1985 judgement in his favour. Ruth was now part of our "historical jigsaw puzzle."

It was only recently—in the mid-seventies—that a young Eskasoni Reserve couple removed their children from a provincial school to protest the use of a textbook, *Bold Ventures,* which contained a quote describing Jacques Cartier's first impression of the aboriginal people in the New World. Ironically, in 1974, the Human Rights Commission, in its "textbook analysis" report, gave this history book a good evaluation because, it said, "Indians were not presented as savages, but as people with a strictly defined way of life." The report continued, "There is no attempt made either to apologize for the manner in which Indians treated the newcomers nor to play up the various Indian wars and raids." Despite the positive rating, the Nova Scotia Department of Education removed it from the Grade-7 Social Studies program.

Equally ironic, Ms. Whitehead selects a similar 1534 quote from Jacques Cartier as one of the first "bits of broken mirror-glass" to begin this historical anthology. This selection, however, contains a derogatory reference to Micmacs as savages. In fact, Cartier named a landmark in northern Cape Breton "Cape Savage." As you read the historical passages, you will discover numerous discriminatory and offensive words and phrases which tend to develop or reinforce negative perceptions about us. Words like "squaw" appear so often that you almost become inured to them, and that's the danger.

Ms. Whitehead, however, conveys that one cannot change history, but one can moderate the events by presenting the other side or by giving the Micmac a sense of "humanness." This she cleverly does with juxtapositions of recorded oral Micmac history. Ms. Whitehead understands how sensitive the Micmac are to biased and prejudicial references in any publication. Long before Pope Paul III declared us human beings in 1537, we had already acknowledged that fact by calling ourselves *Lnu'k*, meaning the 'People.' By expertly and ingeniously interleafing written and oral excerpts, Ms. Whitehead has provided the Micmac with a more level field of human history.

What does the Indian want? This was a very popular question in the 1970s as the First Nations became more politically active. Now, going into the twenty-first century, the added question is, "How do we achieve what we want?" The Indians' renewed interest in their history, culture, and tradition was sparked by the 1969 Canadian government document entitled *Statement of the Government of Canada on Indian Policy, 1969*, commonly known in Indian circles as the White Paper.

It began: "To be an Indian is to be a man, with all the man's needs and abilities. To be an Indian is also to be different. It is to speak different languages, draw different pictures, tell different tales, and to rely on a set of values developed in a different world."

It continued: "To be an Indian is to lack power to act as owner of your own lands, the power to spend your own money, and too often, the power to change your own condition. Not always, but too often, to be an Indian is to be without—without a job, a good house, or running water; without knowledge, training, or technical skill and, above all, without those feelings of dignity and self-confidence that a man must have if he is to walk with his head held high. All these conditions of the Indians are the product of history and have nothing to do with their abilities and capacities. Indian relations with other Canadians have been with special treatment by government and the society, and special treatment has been the rule since Europeans first settled in Canada."

The Introduction concluded with the ominous note: "To be an Indian must be to be free—free to develop Indian cultures in an environment of legal, social, and economic equality with other Canadians."

That's what the federal government wanted. But at what cost to the Indian? While the rhetoric appeared palatable at first, the realization of the government agenda suddenly hit. The policy meant that the fiduciary responsibility of the Crown towards Indians would be abolished with the repeal of the Indian Act. It would finally and effectively enable the provinces to assume the sole responsibility for the Indians, with a promise to achieve legal, social, and economic equality. The Indians would lose their special status and historic relationship with the Crown. Their treaties and aboriginal rights extinguished forever! Such was, is and will continue to be the hidden policy of the federal government. Only through the political mobilization and intense lobbying did the Indians save themselves from cultural and political genocide, much to the consternation of the federal government and the bewildered general public.

History will not repeat itself if we understand the past. Ms. Whitehead readily concedes that there are hardly any personal histories about the Micmac—diaries, biographies, accounts of personal deeds, adventures of personal heroes are practically non-existent. She does not apologize for the "homogeneous" treatment of the Micmac in history. Rather she concentrates on what little is available in order to achieve her goal to redress the balance. And within those oral stories, court documents, records of Micmac meetings with government officials, orations, folklore, and legends, one can find clues to the human specifics. Why did the Micmac hate and distrust the British so much? Why did missionaries condone the torture of enemies in some instances and condemn it in others? Why did Micmac women refuse to take the surnames of their husbands? Why leave food at gravesites? What did the Micmac think of clerical celibacy? The reader will gain insights into these and other questions about our way of thinking, which has basically remained the same throughout time.

There are Micmac petitions and court proceedings in this source-book which provide an insight into what the Mi'kmaq wanted, then and now. Consider, for example, the vignette in 1849 taken from *The Acadian Recorder*, Halifax. The excerpt details the meeting of several Micmac Chiefs and Captains with the Lieutenant-Governor of Nova Scotia. The event is quite significant in that the Micmac bring a signed petition requesting what at first appears to be a hand-out because of a reference to begging. Upon closer examination, however, the petition is asking the government to fulfil its promises and commitment made in the 1752 treaty. The preamble to the petition is a history lesson in itself. The Chiefs describe their utopian life before the coming of the white people, "... we had plenty of good land, we worshipped 'Kesoult,' the Great Spirit, we were free and we were happy."

To be an Indian must be to be free. The Chiefs in 1849 wanted freedom to develop their own resources and govern them accordingly. Monsignor M.M. Coady, of the famous Antigonish Movement, wanted no less for the present-day farmers and fishermen. Father Coady echoes the same philosophy expressed by these Chiefs, "... give a beggar a dinner and he is a beggar still." Today, the Micmac is still pursuing freedom through self-government. The definition and the method of realizing this goal seem to be a dilemma for Canadian society.

Another vignette describes the court proceedings of *The King vs Sylliboy* in 1928. This case is interesting to me personally because my late grandfather, Joe Christmas, and my late father, Chief Ben Christmas, testified on behalf of Grand Chief Sylliboy, who was charged for hunting muskrats out of season. His defence, again, was based on the 1752 treaty. The judgement declared this to be a non-treaty offence, and the verdict was guilty as charged. The penalty and costs were waived because the Crown felt that our Grand Chief was ignorant of the current law, which had in 1927 extended the ban to November 15. Grand Chief Sylliboy had been apprehended and charged on November 4, 1927.

Do you want to conduct Micmac oral history? Do you want to write personal Micmac stories or our modern history? Do you want to cross-refer your family tree? This source-book will have unlimited uses whether you are in the teaching or the legal profession, in the Indian or non-Indian governments, in social work, in university, in public schools, in media, in independent research, in genealogy, or are simply interested in the Mi'kmaq. *The Old Man Told Us* will be an excellent foundation for your introduction into our society. It will spark your interest to seek further knowledge.

Above all, as we go forward in the next five hundred years, positive attitudes about us will be taught in the schools, promoted in the society and fostered in the home. Truly, then, you can assist us in being "Masters of our own Destiny."

Dr Peter Christmas
Micmac Association of Cultural Studies
Sydney, N.S.

INTRODUCTION

THE MICMAC PEOPLE HAVE BEEN LIVING IN THE LAND now called Atlantic Canada for at least two thousand years or more, and yet the written history of this area gives them minimal coverage at best. There are still almost no biographies of Micmac men or women available, and almost nothing to present to the rest of the world their feelings on the matter of the latest five hundred years of their residence here.

The bulk of published accounts about this region devote only a few paragraphs to the aboriginal population. The Micmac are treated as a homogenous mass, and presented as statistics. This book, therefore, is an attempt to counterbalance such works, by restoring to our collective memory— whether we are Micmac or not—a sense of the individual and specific. It is also an attempt to show, where possible, the Micmac view of events.

After fifteen years of research and collecting, the Nova Scotia Museum has compiled most of the existing sources which mention specific Micmac persons or families by name, and has entered them chronologically onto a single database. Aboriginally, Micmac persons might be given a number of different names during the course of a lifetime. In the seventeenth century, for example, a boy might be called by a diminutive of his father's name, or of an older brother's. Upon the elder person's death, the boy might assume the name by dropping the diminutive, or he might take another name altogether.

Names were generally descriptive, usually verb phrases, rather than nouns. Examples are 'born on the way' or 'he sends.' After Micmac bands began to convert to Catholicism in 1610, the people were given French names at baptism, and introduced to the concept of a first name and a surname. Surnames were created by taking the original Micmac name as a last name. Children took their father's Micmac name, and girls kept it, not taking the husband's name at marriage. This nomenclature became quite complicated when children began taking their father's first Christian name as their last name. Thus, there are many Micmac families with surnames such as Peter, Paul, Joe, Tony, etc., many of whom are not related to others with the same family name.

Further complications in tracking an individual resulted from the changes brought to a French name by a Micmac speaker. Joseph became 'Sosep,' for example; Etienne became 'Ekien.' More confusion was added by English speakers attempting to reduce names to something understandable to them. The name André became 'Antle' in Micmac, and was often rendered by the English phonetically as 'Handley' or 'Hadley.' Phonetic spellings made tracking individuals even more difficult.

Using the database, however, one could cross-reference ten different spellings, and realize that each actually referred to the same individual. (Name-variants are displayed in brackets in the text where appropriate.) This laying out on a single table, so to speak, of pieces of a historical jigsaw puzzle clarified much of the misunderstanding inherent in the archival material.

Although this is indeed a historical jigsaw puzzle, this book is not meant to be a comprehensive survey of Micmac history. It is rather a display of fragments, bits of broken mirror-glass in which one can see moments in the lives of particular people. This is a source-book, a book of readings, from whatever scattered documentation has survived. Yet the information presented herein does in itself generate certain themes and continuity as one encounters individuals at different stages in their lives, and subsequently catches sight of their descendants over the generations which follow. There is a surprising richness to it.

Aknutmaqn is a Micmac word for oral histories, 'news.' The text of the book consists of a series of "news items," beginning with four stories of the world before the arrival of Europeans around 1500 A.D., and then running chronologically from 1500 up to 1950. They are taken both from Micmac tradition and from historical documentation.

Written records, both French and English, have been included in the text under a date heading. Such sources include newspapers from three centuries, census material, autopsy reports, merchants' account books, court cases; the journals and letters of missionaries, settlers, the military, politicians; reports of Indian Agents; and oral histories collected from non-Micmac persons. Interleaved with this material are segments in boldface. These are Micmac accounts, or accounts which include Micmac speeches, or the Micmac perspective on the matter under discussion, collected as oral histories from the Micmac from 1604 up to the present day. Folklore is also entered in boldface. In some cases, such as in the letters by the Micmac writer Joseph Cope to Nova Scotia Museum curator Harry Piers, these traditions have been remembered and written down by the Micmac themselves. Some editorial notes have been added in brackets, where further information or clarification has become available. These segments in boldface, largely oral tradition, are not introduced by year, as often no precise date is known. Dates, when available, appear in the body of the quote, or in the credits at the end of each entry.

Many of these excerpts and anecdotes from the Micmac past are very moving. Some are extremely funny examples of Micmac wit and humour. Certain oral histories provide clear glimpses into the minds and hearts of the People. It must be remembered, however, that the bulk of the information coming down to us, even in a collection such as this, is being recorded by outsiders, French and English writers. The majority did not speak Micmac, certainly did not share the same world-view, and almost universally regarded themselves as culturally superior. Conversely, until some time in the twentieth century, most Micmac did not speak fluent French or English. They did not share the world-view of the European settlers, and they in turn regarded their way of life as superior. Historical research certainly provides one with an insight into the vested interests of those reporting events, and into the bias of their times. Much of the time, that bias is severe. And it has almost universally been the European bias which has gotten into print.

Nevertheless, it must be kept in mind that the histories of individuals, like the histories of nations and races, are never entirely black or white, but a mixture: acts of cruelty and forbearance, of generosity and ugliness. Included in this work are examples of each—good and bad—from all the parties and cultures concerned, because these actions and events are what happened. They are as close to the truth of the past as research enables us to come. At the same time, the very real gift these documents give us is a sense of the *humanness* of all the people who created our past here in Atlantic Canada. Ultimately, my hope is that this collection will redress the omissions, the biases, and the errors of published histories when speaking of the Micmac—the People, who have been the longest dwellers in the land. May it also help us to look without bias at the past, regardless of whom our ancestors were.

Ruth Holmes Whitehead
Assistant Curator in History
Nova Scotia Museum, Halifax

IN
THE
BEGINNING
BEFORE 1500 A.D.

THE HISTORY OF THIS LAND DOES NOT NECESSARILY begin in 1500, with the arrival of the Europeans with their alphabet, their pens and their parchment. Others were here before them. Over the centuries during which the Micmac People roamed sea and land and learned them well, history was encoded in stories and chants, passed down by word of mouth, taught through dance and song and dreams.

A Woman, Long Ago
There was a woman, long, long ago
She came out of a hole.
In it dead people were buried.
She made her house in a tree;
She was dressed in leaves,
All long ago.

When she walked among the dry leaves
Her feet were so covered
The feet were invisible.
She walked through the woods,
Singing all the time,
"I want company; I'm lonesome!"

From far away a wild man heard her
From afar over the lakes and mountains
He came to her.
She saw him; she was afraid;
She tried to flee away,
For he was covered with the rainbow;
Colour and light were his garments.
She ran, and he pursued rapidly;
He chased her to the foot of a mountain.
He spoke in a strange language;
She could not understand him at first.
He would make her tell where she dwelt.

They married; they had two children.
One of them was a boy.
He was blind from his birth,
But he frightened his mother by his sight.
He could tell her what was coming,
What was coming from far off.
What was near he could not see.
He could see the bear and the moose
Far away beyond the mountains;
He could see through everything.

"The old Indian woman ended this story by saying abruptly, 'Don't know any more. Guess they all eat up by *mooin* [Micmac *muin*, 'bear'].' She said that [this chant] was only a fragment. If you could have heard her explain what the characters said, and describing

2

how they looked, and anon singing it again, you would have got the *inner sense* of a wonderfully weird tale. The woman's feet covering and the man's dress *like* a rainbow, yet not one, which made their bodies invisible, seemed to exercise her imagination strangely; and these were to her the most important part of the story." (Anonymous Micmac woman to Louise Brown)

Louise Brown [Mrs Wallace Brown] to Charles Leland. In *The Algonquian Legends of New England*, by Charles Leland. 1884:309-310.

[By the internal evidence, Mrs Brown apparently collected this tale from a Micmac.]

The Sun Wept with Grief

They say that when the sun ... created all this great universe, he divided the earth immediately into several parts, wholly separated one from the

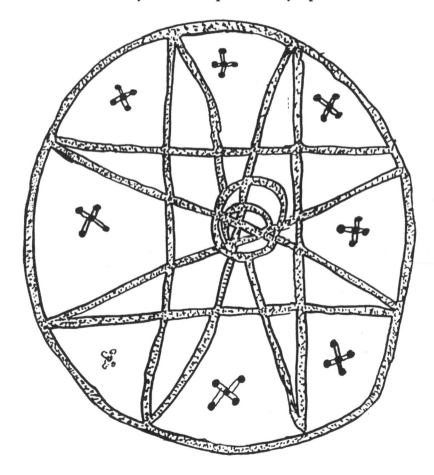

Micmac rock art, possibly pre-European, Bedford, N.S.

other by great lakes: that in each part he caused to be born one man and one woman, and they multiplied and lived a very long time; but that having become wicked along with their children, who killed one another, the sun wept with grief thereat, and the rain fell from the heaven in such great abundance that the waters mounted even to the summit of the rocks, and of the highest and most lofty mountains. This flood, which, say they, was general over all the earth, compelled them to set sail in their bark canoes, in order to save themselves from the raging depths of this general deluge. But it was in vain, for they all perished miserably through a violent wind which overturned them, and overwhelmed them in this horrible abyss, with the exception, however, of certain old men and of certain women, who had been the most virtuous and the best of all the Indians. God came to them to console them for the death of their relatives and their friends, after which he let them live upon the earth in a great and happy tranquillity, granting them therewith all the skill and ingenuity necessary for capturing beavers and moose in as great number as were needed for their subsistence.

Collected by Chrestien LeClercq (Récollet priest and missionary to the Micmac on the Gaspé Peninsula, 1675-1683). In *New Relation of Gaspesia,* by Chrestien LeClercq. 1968:84-85.

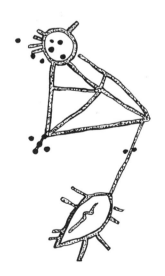

We Are the Birds of Fire
We are the stars which sing,
We sing with our light;
We are the birds of fire,
We fly over the sky.
Our light is a voice;
We make a road for spirits,
For the spirits to pass over.
Among us are three hunters
Who chase a bear;
There never was a time
When they were not hunting.
We look down on the mountains.
This is the Song of the Stars.

In *The Algonquian Legends of New England,* by Charles Leland. 1884:379.

[This tale was apparently collected by Mrs Wallace Brown from a Micmac; the Micmac symbolism of three hunters chasing the bear of Ursa Major was recorded by missionary Chrestien LeClercq in 1677.]

The Big Water Came and Drowned the Whole World

There was a man named Sebanees. It doesn't mean anything. It was just a name. Sebanees. It was in the el-time.

Sebanees was a quiet fellow. He was always thinking very deep. He lived by a lake and he used to sit there and think and dream. One day there was a big Voice out of the Sky. Says, "Sebanees, there is going to be a big water. Big water will come up over everything, drown everything. This is because people do not believe your dreams."

Sebanees said, "Am I going to be drowned too?"

The Voice said, "No. You will be saved, and all the people who believe what you say, and all the birds and fish and animals that you want."

Sebanees said, "How?"

And the Voice out of the Sky said, "Like this. There is going to be a big storm. Big flood. Now, you must watch the sky, Sebanees. You must gather all the people who believe in you, and all the birds and fish and animals, and you must watch the sky. You must gather here by the lake. When the sky right over your head turns colours like rainbow, only just red and kind of yellow, then you must do this. You must wade out into the lake and take this whistle." And he gave Sebanees a whistle made of wood. "Now, Sebanees, you must take this whistle and wade out into the lake, and put the end of the whistle down into the water, and you must blow it. As you blow, there will freeze up out of the lake a boat made of ice. The more you blow the whistle, the boat will grow bigger. You must blow the ice boat up big enough to hold all your people and birds and animals. You don't worry about the fish, because they will be frozen up in the ice the same time you blow up the boat. Then you must blow the whistle on all the birds and animals, and they will go into the boat. Then you must put in all the people who believe in you because they will believe what you tell about the Big Water coming and they will believe in your boat."

Sebanees did all these things. When the sky over his head turned red and kind of yellow, he began to blow his whistle, and the ice boat formed in the lake. And Sebanees went in the boat with the birds and animals and his people. And the Big Water came and drowned the whole world.

Well, they sailed around on the Big Water for a whole year. Then the water began to go away. The ground began to appear. The sun came back again, and melted the ice boat, and all the fish and rocks and ground that had been frozen up in the ice boat stayed in that place. And that place was what you call Prince Edward's Island. And that is the story of Sebanees.

Now, there is proof of this. Have you ever been to Prince Edward's Island? If you go, you will see that the rocks and the ground are different from the rocks and ground any other place. That is because they were brought there in the ice boat of Sebanees. Now, the Micmac name today for Prince Edward's Island is 'Abegweit' [Epe'kwitk]. That means like 'the-side-of-a-boat-when-you-see-it-a-long-way-off-and-it-seems-to-be-low-in-the-water.'

But there is another, older, name for Prince Edward's Island among the Micmac people in the el-time. That is 'Ookchiktoolnoo' [*kjiktu'lnu*], and it means, 'our great boat.'

"Information given to T.H. Raddall in August 1933 by two old Micmac men at Broad River. They were William Benoit Paul [probably William Peminuit Paul] and Mike Mo-ko-ne or 'McCooney.' Paul was at one time chief of the Micmac band on the Shubenacadie reservation, but during the summers he rambled about Nova Scotia, visiting 'my people.' Mo-ko-ne (his own pronunciation) had a little shack on the left bank of Broad River, about a mile above the highway bridge. He lived there with his squaw, a wisp of a woman, slowly dying of tuberculosis. She was highly intelligent, with a remarkable memory for Indian names and legends. When the two old men were at a loss for a name or a meaning, they often referred to her.... Paul often used this word 'el-time' frequently as a synonym for 'olden time.' Mike Mo-ko-ne and his wife ... agreed that Paul told the story correctly. The name was pronounced SEEbaneez." (Thomas H. Raddall)

Chief William Benoit Paul to Thomas H. Raddall, August 1933. Thomas H. Raddall MS, Raddall Papers, Dalhousie Archives, Killam Library, Dalhousie University, Halifax.

THE
SIXTEENTH
CENTURY

1500 TO 1599 A.D.

THIS CENTURY SEES THE START OF EUROPEAN expansion into the New World. European explorers, fishermen and traders produced the occasional logbook, letter or published manuscript, with notes on what and whom they encountered. The Portuguese are thought to have established a settlement in Cape Breton Island by 1521, with Micmac place-names appearing on Portuguese maps by 1550. By the end of the century, much of the Gulf of St Lawrence, and even the Atlantic shores of the Maritimes, had been visited by Basque whalers from Spain or France, and by the English and French. While there were encounters, both friendly and hostile, with the Micmac, descriptions of these original inhabitants of the New World are sparse—only one individual name is recorded. It was a century of action more than of the written word—many of the newcomers probably couldn't even write their own names. For example, the Basque Captain Savalet, who had made annual voyages to Nova Scotia between 1565 and 1607, apparently never penned a line about his experiences. What little Old World documentation there is, however, is here interspersed with Micmac oral tradition, musing on what life was like before these European disruptions began.

Our Fathers were hardy
We knew no want
We were the only owners of the land

When there were no people in this country but Indians, and before any others became known, a young woman had a singular dream.... A small island came floating in towards the land, with tall trees on it, and living beings. [The shamans] pondered the girl's dream but could make nothing of it. The next day an event occurred that explained all. What should they see but a singular little island, as they supposed, which had drifted near to the land and become stationary there. There were trees on it, and branches to the trees, on which a number of bears ... were crawling about.... What was their surprise to find that these supposed bears were men.

Josiah Jeremy to Silas Rand, 26 September 1869. In *Legends of the Micmacs*, by Silas Rand. 1894:225.

1534

And the next day, the last but one of the month [of June], the wind came south, a quarter south-west, and we sailed westward till sunrise on Tuesday morning, the last day of the month, without seeing still less exploring any land, save that toward evening we caught sight of a land which seemed to be two islands, which lay about nine or ten leagues behind us towards the west and south-west. And on that day we sailed westward some forty leagues till sunrise on the day following. And while holding this course we perceived that this land which had appeared to us like two islands was really the mainland [of Prince Edward Island], lying to the south-east and NNW, as far as a very fine cape named Cape Orleans. All this district is flat and low-lying, and the most beautiful imaginable, full of goodly trees and meadows; it is true that we could find no harbour, for it is all full of sandbanks. We landed at various places with our boats, and among these entered a beautiful but shallow river, which was therefore called Boat River; especially as we saw some boats loaded with savages who were crossing the river, and had no further knowledge of these savages, because the wind was blowing from the sea and beating upon the coast, so that we were compelled to withdraw to our ships.

We sailed north-east till sunrise of the next day, July 1st, when a fog and storm arose, for which reason we struck sail till about two hours before midday, when the weather cleared and we caught sight of Cape Orleans, and of another seven leagues distant from it lying north, a

Micmac rock art of an early European vessel, Kejimkujik National Park, N.S.

quarter north-east, which we called Cape Savage. On the north-eastern side of this cape, about half a league off, is a very dangerous ledge of rock. While we were near this cape, we perceived a man running behind our boats, which were coasting the shore, and making many signs to us to turn back toward this cape. Seeing these signs we began to approach him, but on seeing our coming he took to his heels. We landed, and laid before him a knife and a woollen belt on a stick, and thereupon returned to our vessels.

Jacques Cartier. In *History of New France*, by Marc Lescarbot. 1968, Vol. II:41-42.

"What did you do, my children, before the arrival of the Europeans in this region? How did you occupy yourselves? How did you spend your time?"

"Father, before your arrival in these parts where God decreed we should be born and where we have grown like the grasses and the trees you see around you, our most constant occupation was to hunt all sorts of animals so as to eat of their flesh and to cover ourselves with their skins. We hunted both small and large game-birds, and chose the best and the most beautifully feathered birds to make ornaments for our heads. We killed only enough animals and birds to sustain us for one day, and then, the next day, we set out again. But never think that our hunting was as arduous as it is today. All we needed to do in those times was to leave our wigwams, sometimes with our arrows and spears, and sometimes without, and at a very short distance from our village we would find all we needed. If at any time we did not wish to eat meat we would go to the lakes or rivers nearest to our village, or to the nearest sea-shore, and there we would catch all sorts of fish to eat. Eel was our favourite catch as it is even today. It mattered not one bit to us whether the meat was cooked or raw, and, if we found we had only tough meat at any time, we would cut and tear it into strips which we would pound on broad flat stones, and thus we were able to chew and swallow it easily. We would leave solid-fleshed fish, like sturgeon and halibut, to rot for a time, after which we ate it like all other food. At night when we met together, we would feast on meat roasted on a fire, a fire we lighted by briskly rubbing sun-dried pine-wood in our hands for a long time. Sometimes, if the fire did not start as soon as we wished, we would go to the seashore to gather those white pebbles that are so abundant there. We would each take two of these and strike one against the other over powdered rotten dried pine wood. We had fire then, without fail."

Micmac Shaman-Chief Arguimaut [L'kimu], interviewed by the Abbé Maillard, Prince Edward Island, *ca* 1740. See "Lettre à Madame de Drucourt," n.d. In *Les Soirées Canadiennes,* by Pierre Antoine Simon Maillard. 1863:299-301. Translated for this publication by Margaret Anne Hamelin.

[This interview is the only existing record where a specifically named native person discusses what life was like before the arrival of Europeans, or where we hear his actual words. The name L'kimu occurs over and over in historical documents into the nineteenth century, spelled variously Ulgimoo, Alegemoure, Algimault, Alkmou, Alguimou, Argimooch, Arguimaut, Argimeau, Argunault, etc. The earliest mention of the name is a "Pierre Arguimeau," born in 1618.]

1534

And during the time that we were there [Port Daniel, north shore of the Bay of Chaleur], on Monday the 6th [July], after hearing Mass, we went in one of our boats to explore a cape and point of land seven or eight leagues to the westward, to see in which direction this coast tended, and when we were half a league from the point we saw two groups of boats, filled with savages, who were crossing from one shore to the other. There were more than forty or fifty boats, of which one group approached this point, and a great number of these people leaped ashore with a great shout, and made signs to us to land, holding up skins on the ends of sticks, but as we had only a single boat we resolved not to approach, and steered toward the other group who were afloat. Seeing us flee, they ordered two of their largest boats to follow us, to which joined themselves five others of those who were coming from the sea, and all drew near our boat, leaping and making signs of gladness and of their wish for friendship, saying in their tongue, *Napeu ton damen assur tah* [possibly *nape'w*, Micmac for 'man,' 'cock'; *tú dameu acertar*, Portuguese trade-pidgin], and other words which we understood not. But having only a single boat, as we have said, we resolved not to trust to their signs, and gave them to understand that they were to retire, which they refused to do, but came towards us with such fury that in a moment they surrounded our boat with their seven. And since they refused to withdraw in spite of signs which we made them, we shot two fire-lances over their heads, which frightened them so that they retired towards the said point with great noise, but after remaining there for some little time, began again to approach us as before, so that when they came near the boat we shot two of our fire-darts among them, which so frightened them that they took to flight in great haste, and would not come near us again.

Jacques Cartier. In *History of New France,* by Marc Lescarbot. 1968, Vol. II:45-46.

To preserve the fire, especially in winter, we would entrust it to the care of our war-chief's women, who took turns to preserve the spark, using half-rotten pine wood covered with ash. Sometimes this fire lasted up to three moons. When it lasted the span of three moons, the fire became sacred and magical to us, and we showered with a thousand praises the chief's woman who had been the fire's guardian during the last days of the third moon. We would all gather together and, so that no member of the families which had camped there since the autumn should be absent, we sent out young men to fetch those who were missing. Then, when our numbers were complete, we would gather round and, without regard to rank or age, light our pipes at the fire. We would suck in the smoke and keep it in our mouths, and one by one we would puff it out into the face of the woman who had last preserved the spark, telling her that she was worthy above all to share in the benign influence of the Father of Light, the Sun, because she had so skillfully preserved His emanations.

Arguimaut [L'kimu] to the Abbé Maillard, Prince Edward Island, *ca* 1740. See "Lettre à Madame de Drucourt," n.d. In *Les Soirées Canadiennes*, by Pierre Antoine Simon Maillard. 1863:300-301. Translated for this publication by Margaret Anne Hamelin.

1534

On the next day, a group of these savages came with nine boats to the point and entrance of the spot whence our vessels had set sail. And when apprised of their coming, we went with our boats to the point where they were, but as soon as they saw us they took to flight, making signs that they had come to barter with us, showing some skins of little value, wherewith they clothe themselves. We likewise made signs to them that we wished them no harm, and in sign of this two of our men landed to approach them, and bring them knives and other ironware, with a red hat to give to their captain. Seeing this, they also landed carrying these skins of theirs, and began to trade with us, showing great and marvellous joy to possess this ironware and other said articles, dancing continually and going through various ceremonies; among others they took sea-water in their hands and threw it on their heads; in so much that they gave us all they had, keeping nothing back; and were compelled to go away stark naked, making signs to us that they would return on the next day with more skins.

Jacques Cartier. In *History of New France*, by Marc Lescarbot. 1968, Vol. II:46.

Then we would dance around the fire, and this is what we would sing: "Oh Fire, light our pipes and grant that, by sucking in Thy goodness, under cover of the smoke that hides Thee from our eyes, we may become strong and vigorous and always able to know our slave-women and the wives of our bed. May you stay forever in our hearts so that we may never know what it is to flinch when we are face to face with those who wish to end our days. Grant that we may laugh and sing and dance when alien executioners wish to dismember us alive. Grant that hunger, thirst and illness may never overwhelm us to the point where we are no longer as indifferent to those ills as we should be. Thou, woman, by thy care, by thy vigilance, by the great attention thou hast paid to the preservation of this spark of fire, have thereby become the principal wife of our chief, if thou art not so already. And we now summon this chief, who has broken so many heads, both human and animal, to come forward, and here in our presence he will stretch out his great fur, and thou, woman, will lie under it first and he shall follow thee. But if thou art but a concubine, leave thy master now and seek among those gathered here which young man thou wishest for a husband. This shall be thy honour and reward."

If the woman was the chief's principal wife, the assembly would bestow on her the honour of making a feast for the men, of being present at the feast with as many women as she should choose to bear her company, of being the first to speak after the feast was done, of presenting his pipe to her husband, lord and master, of being the first to get up both to dance and to sing as she wished while she danced. And all these things were done just as I have told you, Father.

Arguimaut [L'kimu] to the Abbé Maillard, Prince Edward Island, *ca* 1740. See "Lettre à Madame de Drucourt," n.d. In *Les Soirées Canadiennes,* by Pierre Antoine Simon Maillard. 1863:301-303. Translated for this publication by Margaret Anne Hamelin.

1534

On Thursday, the 8th of the month [actually 9 July], the wind being unfavourable for going out with our ships, we made ready our boats to explore this gulf, and on that day we ran up it twenty-five leagues. On the day following the weather was fine, and we sailed till midday, by which time we had explored a great part of this gulf, and found that above the flats rose other lands with high mountains. But seeing that there was no passage we began to return, coasting along this shore, and while sailing saw some savages on the edge of a lake which lies upon the flats. They were making several fires; we went thither, and found that there was a channel from the sea running into this lake, and we moored our boats at one side of this channel. The savages came to us with one of their boats, and brought us the cooked flesh of seals, which they placed on pieces of wood, and withdrew, giving us to understand that it was a present. We sent men ashore with mittens, knives, necklaces, and other such wares, in which they took infinite delight, and to the number of more than three hundred, men, women, and children, came at once with a rush to the side where we were with their boats, bringing skins and other articles to exchange for our goods. And we saw a group of women who did not come across, who were knee-deep in the sea, dancing and singing. The others who had crossed over to where we were came freely to us, rubbing their arms with their hands, and thereafter raised them to heaven, leaping and making many signs of gladness, and grew so intimate with us that they ended by bartering all that they had from hand to hand, in such wise that they kept back nothing save their stark naked bodies, for they gave us everything which they had, though its value was but small. We recognised that this folk could easily be converted to our faith. They roam from place to place, living on fish. Their country is hotter than Spain, and the most beautiful a man could see, level and flat, and every smallest spot is covered either with trees, even though it be sandy, or with wild wheat, which has an ear like rye, and a grain like oats. The peas are as thick as though sown and cultivated, red and white grapes with the white blossom on them, strawberries, mulberries, red and white roses, and other flower of a pleasant, sweet, and agreeable smell. There are also many fair meadows and good grasses, and lakes full of salmon. In their language they call a mitten *Cochi*, and a knife *Bacon*. We called this gulf *Golfe de la chaleur* [Bay of Chaleur].

Jacques Cartier. In *History of New France*, by Marc Lescarbot. 1968, Vol. II:47-48.

We used the fire-spark which had been nursed [through the three moons of winter] to light a big pile of wood which had been gathered and piled up for the purpose, and then pulled from it the fieriest-burning pieces on which we would lay all sorts of meats. Dried meats were sprinkled with seal oil, or sea-cow oil, or with pieces of whale blubber held in sticks split in two. Game birds were thrown whole, unplucked and ungutted, on the glowing embers. As soon as the feathers had been consumed by the fire—or rather when the feathers had melted to form a thin sort of burnt crust—everyone would take whichever piece he liked, rub it quickly in his hands, blow on it, break off pieces and so eat it. Large game birds, like Canada geese, mergansers, oldsquaws, eiders, other kinds of ducks, brant-geese, cormorants, eagles, gulls, etc., were only plucked of their long feathers and had their tripes removed. Then we would throw them on the burning embers from which we snatched them very soon after, cooked or not, and ate them hungrily. I must point out that, both at these improvised feasts and at all other times, we never left our food bones on the ground, nor did we give them to our dogs.

Arguimaut [L'kimu] to the Abbé Maillard, Prince Edward Island, *ca* 1740. See "Lettre à Madame de Drucourt," n.d. In *Les Soirées Canadiennes*, by Pierre Antoine Simon Maillard. 1863:303-304. Translated for this publication by Margaret Anne Hamelin.

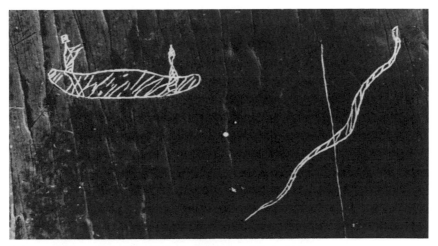

Micmac rock art, Fairy Bay, Kejimkujik National Park, N.S.

ca 1575-1580
Messamouet, Chief at La Hève, on the south shore of Nova Scotia, visited France in the late sixteenth century, where he resided at the house of Philibert de Grandmont (1552-1580), governor of Bayonne.
Marc Lescarbot. *History of New France.* 1968, Vol. II:324.
[This is the second Micmac name on record, from historical documents of 1604 and 1607. The first recorded name appears in 1597 (see entry for 1597).]

Shortly after the country was discovered by the French, an Indian named Silmoodawa [Silmutewey] was taken to Planchean (France) as a curiosity. Among other curious adventures, he was prevailed upon to exhibit the Indian mode of killing and curing game. A fat ox or deer was brought out of a beautiful park and handed over to the Indian; he was provided with all the necessary implements, and placed within an enclosure of ropes, through which no person was allowed to pass, but around which multitudes were gathered to witness the butchering operations of the savage. He shot the animal with a bow, bled him, skinned and dressed him, sliced up the meat, and spread it out on flakes to dry; he then cooked a portion and ate it, and in order to exhibit the whole process, and then take a mischievous revenge upon them for making an exhibition of him, he went into a corner of the yard and eased himself before them all.
Anonymous Micmac to Silas Rand, May 1870. In *Legends of the Micmacs,* by Silas Rand. 1894:279.

1583

The Relation of master Stephen Bellenger dwelling in Roan [Rouen] in the street called Rue des augustines at the syne of the golden tyle in frenche thuille deor of his late voiadge of discoverie of two hundreth leagues of coast from Cape Brittone nere Newfound Land West south-west at the charges of the Cardinall of Borbon this last yere 1583. With mention of some of the comodities fownde in those Cuntries and brought home into Fraunce by hym.... In many places he had traffique with the people which are of verie good disposition and stature of Bodie. They weare their hayre hanging downe long before and behynde as lowe as their browes. They go all naked saving their privities which they cover with an Apron of some Beastes skynn, and tye it unto them with a long buff gerdle that comes three times about them beeing made fast behynde and at boath the endes it is cutt into little thynn thonges, which thonges they tye rownde about them with slender quills of birdes feathers [dyed porcupine quills] whereof some are as red as if they had byn dyed in cuchanillo. Their girdells have also before a little Cod or Pursse of Buff wherein they putt divers thinges but especiallie their tinder to keepe fire in, which is of a dry roote and somewhat like a hard sponge and will quicklie take fyer and is hardlie put out. Their weapons whereof he brought hoame store to the Cardinall are Bowes of two yardes long and arrowes of one yarde hedded with indented bones three or fower ynches long, and are tyed into a nocke at the ende with a thong of Lether. In divers places they are gentle and tractable. But those about Cape Briton and threescore or fowerscore leagues Westward are more cruell and subtill of nature than the rest. And you are not to trust them but to stand upon your gard For among them he lost two of his men and his small Pinesse [ship's boat] which happened through their owne follye in trusting the salvadges to farr. Commodities brought home. He had traffique with them in divers places and for trifles, as knyves, belles, glasses, and suche like small merchaundize which cost hym but Fortie lievers which amount but to fower Poundes Englishe he had by waie of traffique comodities that he soulde in Roan at his retourne. for Fower hundreth and Fortie Crownes. Theis were some of the Comodities which he brought hoame from thence & showed them at his howsse. 1. Buff hides reddie dressed upon both sides bigger than an Oxe. 2. Deere skynnes dressed well on the inner side, with the hayre on the outside. 3. Seale skynns exceding great dressed on the ynnerside 4. Marterns enclyning unto Sables 5. Bevers skynnes verie fayre as many as made 600 bever hattes 6. Otters skynnes verie faire and large 7. A kynde of liquide muske or sivet taken out of the Bevers stones 8. The fleshe of Deere dried in the sunne in peeces a foote long 9. Divers excellent Cullors, as scarlet, vermillion, redd, tawny, yellowe, gray and watchett [blue].

D.B. Quinn. "The Voyage of Etienne Bellenger to the Maritimes in 1583: A New Document." In *Canadian Historical Review XLIII,* 1962:339-340.

It was a religious act among our people to gather up all bones very carefully, and either to throw them in the fire (when we had one), or into a river where beaver lived. I cannot tell you the reason for this, Father, for I do not know it. I only know that our ancestors used to tell us that we must throw all the bones of the beaver we ate into rivers where we could see beaver lodges, so that the lodges would always be there. All the bones of game we got from the sea had to be thrown in the sea, so that the species would always exist. They also told us that our domestic animals must never gnaw the bones because this would not fail to diminish the species of the animal which had fed us. None of the shamans [*puoinaq*], not even I, the foremost one (since I held the office before I was bathed in holy water) could give any reasons for these practices to our young people, who sometimes asked us questions on this subject.

Arguimaut [L'kimu] to the Abbé Maillard, Prince Edward Island, *ca* 1740. See "Lettre à Madame de Drucourt," n.d. In *Les Soirées Canadiennes,* by Pierre Antoine Simon Maillard. 1863:304-305. Translated for this publication by Margaret Anne Hamelin.

1593

We beat about a very long time, and yet missed it [Newfoundland], and at length overshot it, and fell in with Cape Briton.... Heere divers of our men went on land upon the very cape, where, at their arrivall they found the spittes of oke of the Savages which had roasted meate a little before. And as they viewed the countrey they saw divers beastes and foules, as blacke foxes, deeres, otters, great foules with redde legges, penguins [great auks], and certaine others. And, haveing found no people here at this our first landing, wee went againe on shipboorde, and sayled farther foure leagues to the west of Cape Briton, where wee saw many seales. And here, haveing neede of fresh water, we went againe on shore, and, passing somewhat more into the lande, wee founde certain round pondes artificially made by the Savages to keepe fish in, with certaine weares in them to take fish. To these pondes wee repayred to fill our caske with water. Wee had not bene long here, but there came one Savage with blacke long hayre hanging about his shoulders, who called unto us, weaving his hands downwardes towards his bellie, using these words, "*Calitogh, calitogh*"; as wee drew towardes him one of our mens muskets unawares shot off; whereupon hee fell downe, and rising up suddenly againe hee cryed thrise with a loude voyce, "*Chiogh, chiogh, chiogh*"; Thereupon nine or tenne of his fellowes running right up over the bushes with great agilitie and swiftnesse came towardes us with white staves in their handles like half pikes, and their dogges of colour blacke, not so bigge as a greyhounde, followed them at the heeles; but wee retired unto our boate without any hurt at all received. Howbeit one of them brake a hogshead which wee had filled with fresh water, with a great branche of a tree which lay on the ground. Upon which occasion wee bestowed halfe a dozen muskets shotte upon them, which they avoyded by falling flatte to the earth, and afterwarde retired themselves to the woodes. One of the Savages, which seemed to be their captaine, wore a long mantle of beastes skinnes hanging on one of his shoulders. The rest were all naked except their privities, which were covered with a skinne tyed behinde. After they had escaped our shotte they made a great fire on the shore, belike to give their fellowes warning of us....

Richard Strong (Master of the *Marigold*, out of Falmouth). In *History of the Island of Cape Breton*, by Richard Brown. 1869:40-41.

[Thanks to Brian Dalzell for identifying the penguins.]

1597

This day, about twelve of the clocke, we took a savage boate which our men pursued; but all the Savages ran away into the woods, and our men brought their boat on boord. The same day, in the afternoon, we brought our ship to an anker in the harborow: and the same we tooke three hogsheads and an halfe of traine [oil], and some 300 of green fish. Also in the evening three of the Savages, whose boat we had, came unto us for their boat; to whom we gave coats and knives, and restored them their boat againe. The next day, being the first of July, the rest of the Savages came unto us, among whom was their king, whose name is Itary, and their queene, to whom also we gave coats and knives and other trifles. These Savages called the harborow Cibo [*Sipu*, 'river'; present-day Sydney, N.S.].

Charles Leigh (Captain of the *Hopewell* [or the *Speedwell*, according to Hakluyt], out of London). In *History of the Island of Cape Breton*, by Richard Brown. 1869:44.

["Itary" is the first record of an individual Micmac name.]

THE SEVENTEENTH CENTURY

1600 TO 1699 A.D.

WITH THE SEVENTEENTH CENTURY, THERE IS A flowering of entertaining and informative French writing about life in the land the authors came to know as Acadie. Many of them had friends who were Micmac, some had children who married Micmac, some were themselves adopted by the Micmac. Thus, these French traders and missionaries and tourists, such as Marc Lescarbot—who apparently came to the New World solely out of curiosity—often had occasion to record the actual words and thoughts of the People whom they knew. Their writings have preserved for us—as much as this is possible—both the feelings of the newcomers to this land, and those of its original inhabitants, in a way that is positively lavish compared with the scarcity of information from the preceding centuries.

> *When the French came*
> *They asked for land*
> *We gave it freely*
> *They taught us new arts*
> *That was good*

ca 1600

It is well to observe that the Indians of the coast use canoes only for the rivers, and all have boats for the sea. These they sometimes buy from the Captains who are about to leave after having completed their fishery; but the greater part they take from the places in which the Captains have had them hidden on the coast or in the ponds, in order to make use of them on another voyage. But when the proprietors ... recognise them, they make no more ceremony of taking them back than the Indians do in making use of them.

Nicolas Denys. *The Description and Natural History of the Coasts of North America (Acadia)*. 1908:196-197.

We have had our canoes, Father, from time immemorial, and they have always been the same as you see now. In olden times, instead of the birchbark we use now, our ancestors used moose skins, from which they had plucked the hair, and which they had scraped and rubbed so thoroughly that they were like your finest skins. They soaked them several times in oil and then they placed them on the canoe frame, just as we do with birchbark today, fitted them, stretched them and fixed them by sewing them, sometimes with animal tendons, sometimes with spruce roots, and thus they sailed from the coast to a nearby island without ever going too far away from the shore.... never further than seven or eight leagues.... These are long journeys for us. We much prefer to make them in calm or good weather, since the Bad Fish which often infest these seas do not allow us to sail without worry and fear. All too often, these malicious beings [killer whales] attack the sterns of our canoes so suddenly and without warning that they sink the boat and all who are in it. Some escape by swimming, but there are always some who fall prey to these voracious flesh-eating fish. When we see them bearing down on us, we stop paddling immediately, and, taking a pole tipped with a very hard pointed bone, we try to harpoon the fish if we can. As soon as it feels the wound the creature draws off for a time. We take advantage of the short respite to paddle as fast as we can; and if it returns to the attack we repeat our actions until we see land. There is almost no way to escape if two animals attack the canoe at the same time. If we are caught without our spears, with fear and trembling we throw overboard any pieces of meat or fish we may have, one by one, to distract the fish behind us while the one in front paddles gently on without stopping. If we have nothing else to throw we take off our furs and throw them overboard. We have often thrown even our game-bird headdresses to the creatures. At last, when there is nothing left to throw, we take the longest and sharpest of the bones we always have in our canoes and tie them as best we can to the ends of our paddles. Or else we tie several arrows together, binding the points as tightly as we can, and tie the bundle to the end of a paddle or an oar with a belt. Then we lie in wait to harpoon the creature. Of course, it is not as easy to harpoon the animal with this weapon as with the spear, because the paddle is never long enough. However, this makeshift weapon has often served us well. Finally, when we have to make a journey (which we do rarely because of these fearsome animals), we take several very leafy branches and put them at the stern of our canoe, where they stick up about two feet above the rim. We know by experience that when these fish see and catch the scent of the branches, they draw away and do not come near us. Apparently they think it is a piece of land where they could become stranded.

Arguimaut [L'kimu] to the Abbé Maillard, Prince Edward Island, *ca* 1740. See "Lettre à Madame de Drucourt," n.d. In *Les Soirées Canadiennes,* by Pierre Antoine Simon Maillard. 1863:308-309. Translated for this publication by Margaret Anne Hamelin. [By the middle of the sixteenth century, the Micmac had acquired wooden sailing ships—shallops, pinnaces, etc.—from the seasonal fishermen who had begun frequenting the coasts in the summer months. These same fishermen began recording their encounters with Micmac sailing the seas from the Maritimes to Maine, Québec, Labrador and Newfoundland.]

1602

Came towards us [off the coast of Maine] a Biscay shallop, with sail and oars, having eight [Micmac] persons in it whom we supposed at first to be Christians distressed. But approaching us nearer, we perceived them to be savages. These coming within call, hailed us, and we answered. Then after signs of peace, and a long speech by one of them made, they came boldly aboard us, being all naked, saving about their shoulders certain loose deer skins, and near their wastes seal skins tied fast like to Irish dimmie trowsers. One that seemed to be their commander wore a waistcoat of black work, a pair of breeches, cloth stockings, shoes, hat and band, one or two more had also a few things made by some Christians; these with a piece of chalk described the coast there abouts, and could name Placentia of the Newfoundland; they spoke divers Christian words, and seemed to understand much more than we, for want of language, could comprehend. These people are in colour swart, their hair long, uptied with a knot in the part behind the head. They paint their bodies, which are strong and well proportioned. These much desired our longer stay, but finding ourselves short of our purposed place, we set sail....

Gabriel Archer. "The Relation of Captain Gosnold's Voyage to the North Part of Virginia, 1602." In *Collections of the Massachusetts Historical Society*, Vol. III, Third Series. 1843:73.

[See Brereton, next entry, for a second account of this meeting.]

1602

And standing faire alongst by the shore, about twelve of the clocke the same day [Friday May 14] we came to an anker wher six [Micmac] Indians, in a Baske-shallop with mast and saile, an iron grapple, and a kettle of copper, came boldly aboard us, one of them apparelled with a waistcoat and breeches of blacke serdge, made after our sea-fashion, hose and shoes on his feet; all the rest (saving one that had a paire of breeches of blue cloth) were all naked. These people are of tall stature, broad and grim visage, of a blacke swart complexion, their eiebrowes painted white; their weapons are bowes and arrowes....

John Brereton. "A Brief and True Relation of the Discovery of the North Part of Virginia, 1602." In *Early English and French Voyages*, edited by H.S. Burrage. 1906:330.

1604

Several days later the Sieur de Monts [Pierre du Gua de Monts] decided to find out where the mine of pure copper lay for which we had made such diligent search. To this end he sent me with an Indian named Messamouet, who said he knew the site well. I set out in a small pinnace of five or six tons' burden, having with me nine sailors. Some eight leagues from the island [the first French settlement at Ste Croix, now Dochet's Island, Maine], toward the river St John, we found a mine of copper which was not pure; nevertheless it was good, according to the miner's report, who said that it would yield eighteen per cent.... When we reached the spot where we hoped was the mine we were seeking, the Indian could not find it, so that we had to return, leaving this search for another occasion.

Samuel de Champlain (exploring and mapping Acadie, 1604-1607). *The Works of Samuel de Champlain*. 1971, I:278-279.
[Messamouet was a Micmac chief at what is now LaHave, N.S., called La Hève by the French; he was an accomplished shallop sailor and was apparently visiting the French settlement at Ste Croix. He had spent time in France prior to 1580.]

1604

Before we set out from Tadoussac to return to France, one of the Sagamores of the Montagnais, named Bechourat, gave to the Sieur du Pont [François Gravé du Pont] his son to take with him to France, being well recommended to him by the great Sagamore Anadabijou, who prayed him to use him well, and to let him see what the other two savages had seen whom we had brought back. We asked them for an Iroquois woman, whom they were intending to eat; and they gave her to us, and we brought her also home with the aforesaid savage. The Sieur de Prévert in like manner brought along four savages, a [Micmac] man from the coast of Acadia, a woman and two children from the Canadians.
Samuel de Champlain. *The Works of Samuel de Champlain*. 1971, I:188.

1605

On the eighteenth of June, 1605, the Sieur de Monts set out from Ste. Croix island, accompanied by some gentlemen, twenty sailors, and an Indian named Panounias [Panoniac], with his wife, whom the Indian was unwilling to leave behind. We took along these Indians to serve as guides in the country of the Almouchiquois ['dog people'; certainly not their name for themselves, this term apparently derives from the Micmac, used derogatorily; they were probably ancestral to the present Passamaquoddy/Penobscot of Maine] … as she was a native thereof.…
Farther on we met with two canoes which had come to hunt birds, the majority of which are moulting at this time and cannot fly. We accosted these Indians through our own, who went towards them with his wife, and she explained to them the reason of our coming.
Samuel de Champlain. *The Works of Samuel de Champlain*. 1971, I:311, 314, 320, 325.
[Here a mystery begins concerning Panoniac's wife. De Monts' party takes on two Indians of the region as guides, but at some point "… our {new} Indians went hunting but did not return." Panoniac's wife, who in all probability was a captured bride, apparently disappears as well about this time. Champlain's editor suggests that she has died; several days later, when canoe-loads of Almouchiquois arrive, among them their chief Honemechin (Olmechin), Panoniac is trying to interpret alone: "Our Indian could

understand only certain words, inasmuch as the language of the Almouchiquois, for so that nation is called, differs entirely from that of the Souriquois and Etechemins." Micmac anthropologist Harold McGee theorizes that Panoniac's wife has escaped and gone back to her people (personal communication 1978). Perhaps it was fear of her escaping in his absence which made Panoniac unwilling to leave her behind at Ste Croix. See subsequent entries for further escapes and failed escapes of captured Almouchiquois. These people in turn took Micmac slaves, some of whom were given up to de Monts on a later voyage.]

1606

And yet I would not so greatly depreciate the condition of the tribes whom we are to describe as not to avow that there is much good in them. For, to put it briefly, they have courage, fidelity, generosity, and human-ity, and their hospitality is so innate and praiseworthy that they receive among them every man who is not an enemy. They are not simpletons like many people over here; they speak with much judgment and good sense; and if they intend entering upon any important undertaking, their chief is listened to with attention, while he speaks for one, two, or three hours, and reply is made on each several point as the subject requires. So that if we commonly call them Savages, the word is abusive and unmerited, for they are anything but that, as will be proved in the course of this history.

Marc Lescarbot (living in Acadie, 1606-1607). *History of New France*. 1968, I:32-33.

1606

On Saturday, Whitsun Eve, being the 13th of May, we weighed anchor and put out to sea. Little by little the great towers of the town of La Rochelle faded from our view, then the Isles of Ré and of Oleron, and we bade farewell to France.... At last, on Saturday, July 15th, about two o'clock in the afternoon, the sky began to salute us with repeated cannonades, weeping, as though repentant to have kept us so long in trouble. So much so indeed that when the sun shone out, we saw coming straight towards us, we being then four leagues off shore [of North America], two long-boats with all sails set, though the sea was still running high. This gave us great content; and while we held on our course, lo! there came to us from the land odours of unrivalled sweetness, brought so abundantly by a warm breeze.... We held out our hands, as though to gather them in.... Meanwhile the two long-boats came up, one manned with savages, who had a moose painted on their sail, the other by Frenchmen from St Malo who were fishing off Canso harbour; the savages showed the greater diligence, for they arrived first. They were the first I had ever seen, and I admired their fine shape and well-formed faces. One of them made his excuses that on account of the inclemency of the weather he had not brought his beautiful beaver robe. He wore only a piece of coarse red frieze, with Matachiaz [porcupine-quill ornaments] around his neck and wrists, above his elbows, and at his waist. We gave them food and drink, and while taking this they told us all that had happened in the past year at Port Royal, which was our destination. Meanwhile the Malouins arrived and gave us the same information as the savages, adding that on the Wednesday, on which we escaped the breakers, they had seen us, and would have come out to us with the said savages, but on seeing us put out to sea had given up the attempt.... They also told us that they had been informed some days before by other savages that a ship had been sighted off Cape Breton. These Frenchmen from St Malo were in the service of the partners of M. de Monts, and complained that the Basques, contrary to the king's prohibition, had bartered with the savages and carried off more than six thousand beaver pelts.... As for the savages, before leaving us they asked for bread to take to their wives, which was given them; and they well deserved it for coming with such good courage to tell us where we were, for thereafter we sailed with constant assurance.

Marc Lescarbot. *History of New France.* 1968, II:29, 309-310.

1606

On Tuesday, the 25th, we were off Cape Sable in fine weather, and made a good run that day, for toward evening we came in sight of Long Island and St Mary's Bay, but because it was night we stood back towards the sea. The next day we cast anchor at the entrance of Port Royal, whence we could not enter by reason of the ebb; but two cannon were fired from our ship to salute the said port and to inform the French who were there. On Thursday, July 27, we entered with the flood tide, though not without much difficulty; for the wind was contrary, and gusts blew from the mountains which were like to carry us on the rocks. Amid all this our ship sailed stern-first, and more than once turned round, without it being possible to prevent it. But when at last within the harbour it was a wondrous sight for us to see its fair extent and the mountains and hills which shut it in, and I wondered that so fair a spot remained desert, and all wooded, seeing that so many folk are ill-off in this world.... Little by little we approached the island opposite the fort wherein we have since dwelt.... While we were drifting in the middle of the harbour, Membertou, chief Sagamos [*saqmaw*, 'elder'] of the Souriquois [band of Micmac], the name of the tribe in that neighborhood, rushed up to the French fort, to the solitary two who had remained, and cried out like a madman, saying in his own language: "Wake up, there. You are dawdling over your dinner (for it was about twelve o'clock), and do not see a great ship which is arriving, and we know not who they are!" At once these two men ran to the wall, and hastily loaded the cannon with good store of bullets and priming. Membertou without delay came out to meet us in his bark canoe, with one of his daughters, and finding nothing but friendship, and perceiving that we were French, he gave no alarm.... Soon we landed, visited the house, and passed the day in returning thanks to God, in inspecting the wigwams of the savages, and in wandering through the meadows.

Marc Lescarbot. *History of New France*. 1968, II:311-313.

["Membertou" is the third Micmac name to be recorded in history.]

1606

But one day going for a walk in our meadows along the river, I drew near to Membertou's cabin, and wrote in my tables [tablet-book] part of what I heard, which is written there yet, in these terms: *Haloet ho ho hé hé ha ha haloet ho ho hé*, which they repeated divers times. The tune is also in my said tables in these notes: *re fa sol sol re sol sol fa fa re re sol sol fa fa*. One song being ended, they all made a great exclamation, saying *Hé-é-é-é!* Then they began another song, saying, *egrigna hau egrigna hé hé hu hu ho ho egrigna hau hau hau*. The tune of this was: *fa fa fa sol sol fa fa re re sol sol fa fa re fa fa sol sol fa*. Having made the usual exclamation, they began yet another in these words: *Tameja alleluyah tameja dou veni hau hau hé hé*. The tune whereof was: *sol sol sol fa fa re re re fa fa sol fa sol fa fa re re*. I listened closely to this word *alleluyah* repeated many times, and could make nothing else of it....

Marc Lescarbot. *History of New France*. 1968, III:106.

[Obviously, if Lescarbot heard correctly, Membertou was incorporating what he perceived as "words of power" from the Catholic Mass into his chants: *tu veni*, as well as *alleluiah*. The word *egrigna*, its Micmac meaning now lost, was still being used in Micmac chants into the twentieth century.]

1606

This Sagamos [Membertou] is already a man of great age, and saw Captain Jacques Cartier in that country, being already at that time a married man and the father of a family, though even now he does not look more than fifty years old. He has been a very great and cruel warrior in his youth and during his life. Therefore rumour runs that he has many enemies, and is well content to keep close to the French, in order to live in safety.... This Membertou told us at our first coming thither that he wished to make a present to the King of his copper mine, since he saw that we held metals in high regards, and since Sagamores must be honourable and liberal one toward the other. For being himself a Sagamos, he considers himself the equal of the King and of all his lieutenants, and often said to M. de Poutrincourt that he was his great friend, brother, companion, and equal, showing this equality by joining together the fingers of each hand which we call the index or pointing finger.

Marc Lescarbot. *History of New France*. 1968, II:354-355.

1606

Two hours later two Indians arrived [at what is now Saco, Maine], the one an Etechemin [Maliseet], named Chkoudun, the chief of the river St John, which is called by the Indians Oigoudi; the other a Souriquois, named Messamoet, chief or Sagamos in the river of Port de Lahave.... They had much merchandise, gained by barter with the French, which they came thither to sell—to wit, kettles, large, medium, and small, hatchets, knives, dresses, capes, red jackets, peas, beans, biscuits, and other such things.... Messamouet began a harangue before the Indians, pointing out "how of past time they had often had friendly intercourse together, and that they could easily overcome their enemies if they would come to terms, and make use of the friendship of the French, whom they saw there present exploring their country, in order in future to bring merchandise to them and to aid them with their resources, whereof he knew and could the better tell them, because he, the orator, had once upon a time visited France, and had resided there in the house of M. de Grandmont, governor of Bayonne." In sum, his speech occupied about an hour, and was delivered with much vehemence and earnestness and with such gestures of body and of arm as befit a good orator. And in conclusion he flung into the canoe of Olmechin all his merchandise, which in those parts was worth more than three hundred crowns in cash, as though making him present thereof in sign of the friendship which he wished to show to him.

Marc Lescarbot. *History of New France*. 1968, II:323-324.

1607

Hear as we Cam in towards the Land from this bancke [Sable Island] we still found deepe wattr. The deepest within the bancke ys 160 fethams and in 100 fetham you shall See the Land yf ytt be Clear weather after you passe the bancke the ground ys still black oze untill yo Com near the shore. This daye wee stood in for the Land but Could nott recover ytt beffor the night tooke us so we stood a Lyttell from ytt and thear strok a hull untill the next daye beinge the Laste of July. Hear Lyeinge at hull we tooke great stor of cod fyshes the bigeste and largest that I ever Saw or any man in our ship. This daye beinge the Last of July about 3 of the Clok in the after noon we recovered the shor and cam to an anker under an Illand for all this Cost ys full of Illands and broken Land but very Sound and good for shipinge to go by them the wattr deepe. 18 and 20 fetham hard abord them.

This Illand standeth in the lattitud of 44d and 1/2 and hear we had nott ben att an anker past to howers beffore we espyed a bisken shallop Cominge towards us havinge in her eyght Sallvages and a Lyttell salvage boye they cam near unto us and spoke unto us in thear Language. And we makinge Seignes to them that they should com abord of us showinge unto them knyves glasses beads and throwinge into thear bott Som bisket but for all this they wold not com abord of us but makinge show to go from us, we suffered them. So when they wear a Lyttell from us and Seeinge we proffered them no wronge of thear owne accord retorned and cam abord of us and three of them stayed all that nyght wth us the rest depted in the shallope to the shore makinge Seignes unto us that they wold retorn unto us aggain the next daye.

The next daye the Sam Salvage wth three Salvage wemen beinge the fryst daye of Auguste retorned unto us bringinge wth them Som feow skines of bever in an other bisken shallop and propheringe thear skines to trook wth us but they demanded over muche for them and we Seemed to make Lyght of them So then the other three wch had styed wth us all nyght went into the shallop and So they depted. Ytt Seemth that the french hath trad wth them for they used many french words. The Cheef Comander of these pts ys called Messamott [Messamouet, Chief at La Hève] and the ryver or harbor ys called emannett. We take these peopell to be the tarentyns and these peopell as we have Learned sence do make wars wth Sasanoa the Cheeffe Comander to the westward whear ... we have planted and this Somer they kild his Sonne. So the Salvages depted from us and cam no mor unto us. After they wear depted from us we

hoyssed out our bot whearin my Selffe was wth 12 others and rowed to
the shore and landed on this Illand that we rod under the wch we found
to be a gallant Illand full of heigh and myghty trees of Sundry Sorts. Hear
we allso found aboundance of gusberyes, strawberyes, rasberyes and
whorts. so we retorned and Cam abord.

Anonymous English colonist, on his way to Maine. "Relation of a Voyage to Sagadahoc,
1607-1608." In *Early English and French Voyages,* edited by H.S. Burrage. 1906:81-83.

1607

At the beginning of June, the savages to the number of about four
hundred, set out from the lodge which their Sagamos Membertou had
fashioned anew in form of a town surrounded with high palisades, to go
on the war-path against the Armouchiquois, at Chouakoet, about eighty
leagues from Port Royal, whence they returned victorious by the strata-
gems which I shall relate in the description which I have given of this war
in French verse. The savages took nearly two months to assemble there.
Membertou, the great Sagamos, had had them warned during and before
the winter, sending, as special messengers to them to give them the
rendezvous, his two sons Actaudin and Actaudinech.

Marc Lescarbot. *History of New France.* 1968, II:353-354.

1607

I sing of *Membertou* and the happy victory
Which acquired for him a short time ago an immortal glory.
When he littered with dead the fields of the *Armouchiquois*
To avenge the *Souriquois* people....
To say what moved *Membertou* and his followers
To undertake such a bloody pursuit for his death
He was *Panoniac* (for such was his name)
Once a savage of great renown among his people....
Because this *Panoniac* ten months ago
Having gone to see them (for the last time)
Carrying in his boats some merchandise....
Without mercy they slaughter their neighbor,
Pillage what he had and divide it.
The companions of the dead man escape by swimming away and
Hide themselves for a time in the shadow of a rock....
[The body is retrieved, embalmed, and brought back to Port Royal.]
And to the body present there, Prince *Souriquois*

Starts to cry out in a frightful voice:
What then, *Membertou*, (he said in his language)
Will he leave unpunished such a vicious outrage?
What then, *Membertou* will not have satisfaction
For the excesses against his own and even his house?…
We have close to us the support of the French
To whom these dogs have done a similar wrong.
It is resolved, it is necessary that the countryside
Soon be bathed in the blood of these murderers.
Actaudin my dear son, and your youngest brother
Who have never once abandoned your father,
It is now necessary to arm yourselves with force and courage
Now then, go quickly one following the shore,
From here to Cap Breton, the other through the woods
Towards the *Canadians* and the *Gaspeiquois*,
And the *Etechemins* to announce this insult,
And say to our friends that I beseech them all
To carry in their souls a spirited resentment,
With the result that they arm themselves promptly
And come to find me near this river,
Where they know I have planted my banner.

Marc Lescarbot. "The Defeat of the Armouchiquois Savages by Chief Membertou and his Savage Allies, in New France, in the Month of July, 1607." Translated by Thomas H. Goetz. In "Membertou's Raid on the Chouacoet 'Almouchiquois'—The Micmac Sack of Saco in 1607," by Alvin H. Morrison. National Museum of Man Ethnology Service. Mercury Series Paper No. 23. Sixth Algonquian Conference. 1974:159-162. [One cannot help but wonder if Panoniac had made this trading voyage to the Armouchiquois in an effort to repossess his Armouchiquois wife.]

1606

As soon as the body [of Panoniac] was brought on shore, the relatives and friends began to make outcries beside it, their faces being painted all over with black, which is their manner of mourning. After a great deal of weeping, they took a quantity of tobacco and two or three dogs and other things belonging to the deceased, and burnt them upon the shore some thousand paces from our settlement. Their cries continued until they had returned to their wigwams.

The next day they took the body and wrapped it in a red coverlet which Membertou, the chief of these parts, had much importuned me to give him, inasmuch as it was handsome and large. This he presented to the relatives of the dead man, who thanked me very much for it. Then after having bound up the body, they decorated it with many kinds of ornaments, such as beads and bracelets of several colours; painted his face, and upon his head stuck many feathers and other objects the fairest they had. Then they placed the body on its knees between two stakes, with another supporting it under the arms; and about the body were his mother, his wife, and other relatives and friends, both women and girls, who howled like dogs.

Samuel de Champlain. *The Works of Samuel de Champlain*. 1971, I:443-444.

1606-1607

This [body of] Panoniac, of whom we have spoken, was kept in the cabin of Niguiroet, his father, and of Neguiadodetch, his mother, until the spring-time, when the muster of the savages was held to go to revenge his death; in which assembly he was yet again bewailed, and before they went on the warpath they made an end of his funeral, and carried him (according to their custom) to a desolate island, towards Cape Sable, some five and twenty or thirty leagues distant from Port Royal. Those isles which serve them for graveyards are secret amongst them, for fear some enemy should seek to disturb the bones of their dead.

Marc Lescarbot. *History of New France*. 1968, III:283.

1607

To return to our Indians. One day there was an Armouchiquois woman, a prisoner, who had aided a fellow-prisoner from her country to escape, and to aid him on his way had stolen from Membertou's cabin a tinder-box (for without that they do nothing) and a hatchet. When this came to the knowledge of the savages, they would not proceed to execute justice on her near us, but went off to encamp some four or five leagues from Port Royal, where she was killed. And because she was a woman the wives and daughters of our savages executed her. Kinibech-coech, a young maid of eighteen years of age, plump and fair, gave her the first stroke in the throat, which was with a knife. Another maid of the same age, handsome enough, called Metembroech, followed on, and the daughter of Membertou, whom we called Membertouech-coech, made an end of her.... This is their form of justice.

Marc Lescarbot. *History of New France*. 1968, III:216.

1607

Finally, we arrived within four leagues of Canso, at a harbour where a fine old sailor from St Jean de Luz, named Captain Savalet, was fishing.... This worthy man told us that that voyage was his forty-second to these parts, and one must remember that these Newfoundlanders [Basque fishermen coming to the New World] make but one a year. He was wondrous content with his fishing, and told us that his voyage was worth to him ten thousand francs.... He was at times troubled by the savages encamped there, who too boldly and impudently went on board his ship, and carried off what they listed. To stop this he threatened them that we should come and put them, one and all, to the sword if they did him injury. This frightened them, and they did not do him so much harm as they would otherwise have done. However, every time that the fishers arrived with their boats laden with fish, these Indians chose whatever they thought good, not bothering themselves with the cod, but taking whiting, bass and halibut....

Marc Lescarbot. *History of New France.* 1968, III:362-363.

1608

As for bestowal of names, they give them by tradition, that is to say, they have great quantity of names, which they choose and bestow upon their children; but the eldest son commonly bears his father's name, adding at the end some diminutive; thus the eldest son of Membertou will be called Membertouchis, as it were the little or the young Membertou; a younger son does not bear his father's name, but they give him such a name as they list; and his younger brother bears his name, with a syllable added; thus the second son of Membertou is called Actaudin, and the third son Actaudinech. So Memembourré had a son named Semcoud, whose younger brother was called Semcoudech. Yet to add this termination *ech* [*jiʾj*] is not an invariable rule, for the younger son [brother?] of Panoniac, of whom mention is made in Membertou's war against the Armouchiq-uois ... was called Panoniagués; so that this termination changes in accordance with the name which precedes it. But they have a custom that when this elder brother, or father, is dead, they change names, in order to avoid the sorrow that the remembrance of the deceased might bring unto them. This is the reason why after the death of Memembourré and Semcoud, who died this last winter of 1607, Semcoudech dropped his brother's name, and has not taken his father's, but has styled himself Paris, because he has lived in Paris. And after Panoniac's death, Panoniagués forsook his name, and was by one of our men called Roland; which I find wrongly and indiscreetly done, thus to profane the names of Christians, and to impose them upon infidels, as I remember another that was called Martin.

Marc Lescarbot. *History of New France.* 1968, III:81-82.

1610

The day of Saint John Baptist, June 24, 1610. MEMBERTOU, a great Sagamore, over one hundred years old, has been baptized by Messire Jesse Fleché, a priest; and named HENRY, by Monsieur de Poutrincourt [Jean de Biencourt et de St-Just], after the late king.

Extract from the Register of Baptisms in the Church of Port Royal, New France. In *Jesuit Relations and Allied Documents,* edited by R.G. Thwaites. 1896, I:109-111.

1610

Other Micmac baptised at this time included Membertou's wife, given the name Marie, and his daughter, named Marguerite; his son Membertouji'j, previously called "Judas" in jest by the French, was baptised Louis Membertou. Henri Membertou's second son Actaudin does not appear to have been present. His third son Actaudinji'j received the name Paul Membertou. One of Louis Membertou's wives was christened after Madame de Sigogne, and the other after Madame de Dampierre. Louis' oldest son was named Jehan, and his daughters Christine, Elizabeth, Claude, Catherine, Jeanne and Charlotte. Paul Membertou's wife became Renée. One of Henri Membertou's cousins, Arnest, was given the name Robert. Another cousin, Agoudegouen, was christened Nicolas; his wife, Phillipe; his elder daughter, Louise; and his younger daughter, Anne. Henri Membertou's niece was also called Anne.

See *Jesuit Relations and Allied Documents,* edited by R.G. Thwaites. 1896, I:109-111.

1610

One day when M. de Poutrincourt had gone to the breaking up of a stag killed by Louis the son of Henry Membertou, on his return, as each one was drifting about in the harbour of Port Royal, it befell that the wife of the said Louis brought forth a child, and the savages seeing that the child had but a moment to live, cried out "*Tagaria, tagaria*—Come here, come here." They went, and the child was baptized.... I shall add here an instance of the simplicity of a neophyte named Martin of Port La Have, who when ill of the disease whereof he died, on being told of the celestial paradise, asked if he should eat pasties there as good as those which had been given him to eat [by the French].

Marc Lescarbot. *History of New France.* 1968, III:43-44.

1610

Towards the end of the spring in the year 1610 the sons of Membertou tarried so long at the hunting that it came about that the said Membertou was wrung with hunger. In this want he remembered that he had formerly heard our men say that God who nourishes the fowls of the air and the beasts of the fields never abandons those who trust in Him. Thereupon he set himself to pray to Him, and sent his daughter to the mill-stream. He had been but a short time at this duty when up she came running and crying in a loud voice, "*Nouchich, beggin pechkmok, beggin pechkmok*—Father, the herring has come, the herring has come," and there was abundance of provision.

Marc Lescarbot. *History of New France.* 1968, III:45.

1611

Their food is whatever they can get from the chase and from fishing; for they do not till the soil at all; but the paternal providence of our good God, which does not forsake even the sparrow, has not left these poor creatures, worthy of his care, without proper provision, which is to them like fixed rations assigned to every moon; for they count by Moons, and put thirteen of them in a year. Now for example, in January they have the seal hunting; for this animal, although it is aquatic, nevertheless spawns upon certain Islands about this time. Its flesh is as good as veal; and furthermore they make of its fat an oil, which serves them as sauce throughout the year; they fill several moose-bladders with it, which are two or three times as large and strong as our pig-bladders; and in these you see their reserve casks. Likewise in the month of February and until the middle of March, is the great hunt for Beavers, otters, moose, bears (which are very good), and for the caribou, an animal half ass and half deer. If the weather then is favourable, they live in great abundance, and are as haughty as Princes and Kings; but if it is against them, they are greatly to be pitied, and often die of starvation. The weather is against them if it rains a great deal, and does not freeze; for then they can hunt neither deer nor beavers. Also, when it snows a great deal, and does not freeze over, for then they cannot put their dogs upon the chase, because they sink down; the savages themselves do not do this, for they wear

Father LeClercq's or Father Jumeau's ink drawing (1675-1683) of Micmac hunting moose. The Micmac costumes, the weapons, and the moose are all delightfully inaccurate.

snowshoes on their feet which help them to stay on top; yet they cannot run as fast as would be necessary, the snow being too soft. They have other misfortunes of this kind which it would be tedious to relate.

In the middle of March, fish begin to spawn, and to come up from the sea into certain streams, often so abundantly that everything swarms with them. Any one who has not seen it could scarcely believe it. You cannot put your hand into the water, without encountering them. Among these fish the smelt is the first; this smelt is two and three times as large as that in our rivers; after the smelt comes the herring at the end of April; and at the same time bustards, which are large ducks, double the size of ours, come from the South and eagerly make their nests upon the Islands. Two bustard eggs are fully equal to five hen's eggs. At the same time come the sturgeon, and salmon, and the great search through the Islets for eggs, as the waterfowl, which are there in great numbers, lay their eggs then, and often cover the Islets with their nests. From the month of May up to the middle of September, they are free from all anxiety about their food; for the cod are upon the coast, and all kinds of fish and shellfish; and the French ships with which they traffic, and you may be sure they understand how to make themselves courted....

Water game abounds there, but not forest game, except at certain times birds of passage, like bustards and gray and white geese. There are to be found there gray partridges, which have beautiful long tails and are twice as large as ours; there are a great many wild pigeons, which come to eat raspberries in the month of July, also several birds of prey and some rabbits and hares.

Now our savages in the middle of September withdraw from the sea, beyond the reach of the tide, to the little rivers, where the eels spawn, of which they lay in a supply; they are good and fat. In October and November comes the second hunt for elks and beavers; and then in December (wonderful providence of God) comes a fish called by them *ponamo*, which spawns under the ice. Also then the turtles bear little ones, etc. These then, but in a still greater number, are the revenues and incomes of our Savages; such, their table and living, all prepared and assigned, everything to its proper place and quarter.

Père Biard (a Jesuit living in Acadie, 1611-1613). In *Jesuit Relations and Allied Documents*, edited by R.G. Thwaites. 1896, Vol. III:77-83.

Ginap said, "I can drive to this place any kind of animal I want; I always have plenty of meat. When poor people come, I give them skins for clothing, and meat to eat." The wife said to her father, "Come outside.

There are three moose and a fat bear near here. He killed them with his tomahawk." There was plenty of meat for everyone.

Peter Ginnish (born *ca* 1850, Burnt Church, N.B.). In *The Micmac Indians of Eastern Canada*, by Wilson D. and Ruth Sawtell Wallis. 1955:381-382.

1611

They are in no wise ungrateful to each other, and share everything. No one would dare to refuse the request of another, nor to eat without giving him a part of what he has. Once when we had gone a long way off to a fishing place, there passed by five or six women or girls, heavily burdened and weary; our people through courtesy gave them some of our fish, which they immediately put to cook in a kettle, that we loaned them. Scarcely had the kettle begun to boil when a noise was heard, and other Savages could be seen coming; then our poor women fled quickly into the woods, with their kettle only half boiled, for they were hungry. The reason of their flight was that, if they had been seen, they would have been obliged by a rule of politeness to share with the newcomers their food, which was not too abundant. We had a good laugh then; and were still more amused when they, after having eaten, seeing the said Savages around our fire, acted as if they had never been near there and were about to pass us all by as if they had not seen us before, telling our people in a whisper where they had left the kettle; and they, like good fellows, comprehending the situation, knew enough to look unconscious, and to better carry out the joke, urged them to stop and taste a little fish; but they did not wish to do anything of the kind, they were in such a hurry, saying *coupouba, coupouba,* 'many thanks, many thanks.' Our people answered, "now may God be with you since you are in such a hurry."

Père Biard. In *Jesuit Relations and Allied Documents*, edited by R.G. Thwaites. 1896, Vol. III:95-97.

"But did you cook your food in containers of any kind [before the arrival of Europeans]?"

"We did have some sorts of pots, or cauldrons, made of very soft sandstone which we hollowed out with moose or beaver bones of various sizes. The best kind [of tool] was beaver bone, one end of which we had made almost as sharp a cutting edge as one of your chisels. It was not easy to prepare them for our purpose: they had to be rubbed for a very long time against or on a specially chosen hard stone. We made small, large and medium-sized cutting tools, for cutting the wood for the frames of our canoes and for making arrows of all sizes, at the end of which we would attach small pieces of very hard bone, which we shaped very much like the iron tips you put on your own arrows. We made our bows less by cutting than by scraping away against the grain at pieces of wood we judged apt for the purpose, using strips of the biggest bones we had, which we had allowed to dry out completely in the sun and then split for the purpose; that is, we split them lengthwise and not across. To return to those stones which we had hollowed out and rid of everything that made them rough, irregular and too heavy, we would throw our fresh and bloody meat in them without further ado, and, when they were put on a blazing fire, before long the heat released all the juice of the meat, which we drank. We also ate this meat, but when it was too dry we gave it to our dogs, except for the bones. Though I must say, Father, that when we were hungry we ate that meat too. Sometimes, when our pots were made of stones which crack and burn when exposed to heat, we would pour in water and then throw in the meat. Then we would draw out big stones from the fire, which we put there to get red hot, and placed these stones on top of the meat in the water. These red-hot stones boiled the water, cooked most of the rawness from the meat, and so made it edible, which was enough for us."

Arguimaut [L'kimu] to the Abbé Maillard, Prince Edward Island, *ca* 1740. See "Lettre à Madame de Drucourt," n.d. In *Les Soirées Canadiennes,* by Pierre Antoine Simon Maillard. 1863:306. Translated for this publication by Margaret Anne Hamelin.

1611

In order to enjoy thoroughly this, their lot, our foresters start off to their different places with as much pleasure as if they were going on a stroll or an excursion; they do this easily enough through the skillful use and great convenience of canoes, which are little skiffs made of birch-bark, narrow and closed at both end, like the crest of a morion; the body is like a large hollow cradle; they are eight or ten feet long; moreover so capacious that a single one of them will hold an entire household of five or six persons, with all their dogs, sacks, skins, kettles, and other heavy baggage.

Père Biard. In *Jesuit Relations and Allied Documents,* edited by R.G. Thwaites. 1896, Vol. III:83.

1611

They have no beards, the men no more than the women, except some of the more robust and virile. They have often told me that at first we seemed to them very ugly with hair both upon our mouths and heads; but gradually they have become accustomed to it, and now we are beginning to look less deformed.

Père Biard. In *Jesuit Relations and Allied Documents,* edited by R.G. Thwaites. 1896, Vol. III:73.

1612

They are astonished and often complain that since the French mingle with and carry on trade with them, they are dying fast and the population is thinning out.... One by one the different coasts according as they have begun to traffic with us, have been more reduced by disease....

Père Biard. In *Jesuit Relations and Allied Documents,* edited by R.G. Thwaites. 1896, Vol. III:105.

1612

During this year alone sixty have died at Cape de la Hève, which is the greater part of those who lived there....

Père Biard. In *Jesuit Relations and Allied Documents,* edited by R.G. Thwaites. 1896, Vol. I:77.

[Chief Messamouet may have died in this epidemic, as his name never recurs in the historical record after this.]

1612

After the return from this voyage there died, on September 18th, 1612, Membertou, the great Sagamos of the savages. He received the last sacrament and gave noble exhortations to his children on the concord which they should maintain among themselves and the love which they should bear to M. de Poutrincourt, whom he called his brother, and [to] his friends. And above all he charged them to love God and to remain firm in the faith which they had received, and thereupon he gave them his benediction. When he had passed from this life his body was carried to the grave in arms, with beat of drum, and he was buried with the Christians.

Marc Lescarbot. *History of New France.* 1968, III:56.

1612

[Membertou] had come from the Baye sainte Marie to have himself treated for a disease which had overtaken him. Father Enemond Massé had put him in his little Cabin, even in Father Biard's bed, and was there taking care of him like a father and servant. Father Biard, finding the patient in his bed, was very glad of this opportunity for charity.... One of their greatest hardships was to cut and carry all the wood that was needed day and night: for the nights began to be quite chilly, and there always had to be a good fire on account of the bad odor, for the disease was dysentery. At the end of five or six days of such service, the wife and daughter of Membertou came to stay with him, and so Father Biard begged sieur de Biencourt to have the invalid moved to some of the other cabins of the settlement, since there were two or three of them empty; for it was neither good nor quite seemly that there should be women in their cabin day and night; and still less that they should not be there, being the wife and daughter of the sick man. On the other hand, the cabin was so small, that when four persons were in it, they could not turn around.... [Biencourt] had one put up outside, where the invalid was taken. This change did not do him any good, for he became evidently worse from that time on, and died four or five days later.... This good Savage, having confessed and received extreme unction, told sieur de Biencourt that he wished to be buried with his fathers and ancestors. Father Biard was very much opposed to this proposition ... it was not lawful for him, a Christian, to wish to be buried with Heathen whose souls were to be lost.... Sieur de Biencourt replied for Membertou that they would have the burial place blessed, and that such a promise had been made to Membertou. Father Biard answered that that would not do; for, in order to bless the said place, they would have to disinter the Pagans who were buried there, which would cause them to be abominated by all the Savages.... The next morning the Savage, of his own free will, changed his mind, and said that he wanted to be buried in the common burying ground of the Christians, to prove his faith to all.... [The Jesuits] loved him, and were loved by him in return. He often said to them, "Learn our language quickly, for when you have learned it, you will teach me; and when I am taught I will become a preacher like you, and we will convert the whole county." The Savages have no recollection of ever having had a greater or more powerful Sagamore. He was bearded like a Frenchman; and would to God that all Frenchmen were as circumspect and prudent as he was.

Père Biard. In *Jesuit Relations and Allied Documents*, edited by R.G. Thwaites. 1896, Vol. III:201-207.

1629

On the twenty-fifth of April Desdames arrived [at Québec] with the shallop from Gaspé, and reported that neither he nor the savages had seen

Father LeClercq's or Father Jumeau's ink drawing (1675-1683) of a
Micmac conclave, with snowshoes in the foreground. The man in the
centre wears a headdress of bird wings and tail.

any ships, nor heard of any, except that some persons who came from the direction of Acadia had said that there were eight English vessels, some of them scouring the coast and others engaged in fishing. He stated that Juan Chou [possibly *Wanju*, from French 'Anjou,' and the Micmac 'w' prefix; a nickname meaning loosely 'The Frenchman'], an Indian Chief, and his Canadians, had done their best to welcome the French, promising that if the Sieur du Pont wanted to go to their country, in case our vessels [with supplies] did not arrive, he should want nothing that their chase could provide....

Samuel de Champlain. *The Works of Samuel de Champlain.* 1971, VI:26.

1629

With the [English] fleet that sailed from Port Royal in the autumn of 1629 there travelled to Britain an Indian chief, the Sagamore Segipt, his wife, and his sons. The ostensible object of the chief's journey was to do homage to the King of Britain and invoke his protection against the French. Landing at Plymouth, the Indian party broke their journey to the capital by a short stay in Somersetshire. There they were hospitably entertained. "The savages took all in good part, but for thanks or acknowledgment made no sign or expression at all."

Thomas Birch. *Court and Times of Charles I,* edited by R.F. Williams. 1848, II:60. In *Scottish Colonial Schemes 1620-1686,* by G.P. Insh. 1922:80.

1630

Those savages arrived at Plymouth were awhile entertained at my Lord Poulet's in Somersetshire, much made of, especially my lady of the savage queen: she came with her to the coach, when they were to come to London, put a chain about her neck with a diamond valued by some at near £20. The savages took all in good part, but for thanks or acknowledgment, made no sign or expression at all.

Rev. Joseph Mead to Sir Martin Stuteville, Christ College, 12 February 1630. In Thomas Birch. *Court and Times of Charles I,* edited by R.F. Williams. 1848, II:60. [John Poulet was made Baron Poulet at Henton St George, Somerset, 23 July 1627. There is no mention in Birch of the "savage's" name, or the fact that the family was Micmac, or that they came from Port Royal. One can only deduce that Insh (see above) got his information elsewhere, and did not reference it.]

1631

[The ship] commanded by Captain Daniel, sailed on the twenty-sixth of April [from Dieppe] ... and it was the sixteenth of June before they arrived at the edge of the Grand Bank, where they saw great quantities of ice. On the eighteenth they sighted land at Cape Ray; and shortly afterwards they perceived a vessel, which they took for a Turkish one, coming down upon them with the wind. This made them get under way and prepare for defense; but the Turk, perceiving a considerable number of men on the deck, drew off and bore down on a Basque vessel at which it fired some cannon-shots and then drew alongside. The grappling was not well done, however, and the vessels separated; and, as they separated, a Basque sailor who was in the stern of his vessel grasped the flag that was in the stern of the Turk and pulled it to himself. At once the Basque vessel began to make off, but in doing so it managed to fire shot after shot from the cannon that were in its stern, so that it escaped and carried off the said flag, on which were depicted three crescents....

Meantime it was necessary for Captain Daniel to establish order.... He sent his ship to Miscou to fish and trade, and placed it in charge of Michel Gallois of Dieppe; and at the same time he dispatched a pinnace of about twenty tons, the command of which he entrusted to one Sainte-Croix, sending him to Tadoussac to trade with the savages. Arriving at Miscou, the said Gallois found there two Basque vessels ... also a barque [whose captain went with Gallois to demand of the Basque vessels their licenses from the King of France, which the first ship produced]....

After this they went to the other vessel, on which they only found the Captain (named Joannis Arnandel, of St Jean de Luz) and a small boy, his men at the time being all ashore and occupied with their fishing. They asked to see his licence, but he did not try to produce it, because he had none [Gallois and his side-kick, du May, proceed to take Arnandel hostage, seizing his arms and munitions and removing all to their ship]....

This having been done, du May and Gallois returned to the vessel of the said Arnandel with some of their own people. And when they had gone on board they called all the men of Arnandel's crew who were ashore and informed them of the agreement and understanding come to between their captain and themselves. To which one of these Basques made reply, that the capture and detention of their captain were not of much consequence, since they could make another captain of a small boy on their vessel. Whereupon du May, wishing to reprove the man for such a remark ... the Basque and all his companions became enraged, and, being very impetuous by nature, they made their way to the lower part of the vessel, and seized some pikes and muskets still remaining, which du May and Gallois had not found. And with these they both defended themselves and attacked du May and his men so courageously that they forced him to retire from the ship with some of his men who were wounded, and whom he quickly caused to embark with him in his boat.

And as these people were now in a state of great excitement, not satisfied with what they had done, they continued to pursue du May until, having retreated to his own vessel, he was obliged to get Captain Arnandel to come up on deck, so that the latter might order his men to cease their violence. But the Captain, finding himself free, promptly threw himself into the water, and clothed as he was, swam to a boat in which were some of his people, thus escaping from his enemies, of whom he soon after got the better; for, having returned to his own ship, he began to speak as Captain and not as a prisoner. Then by the favour and assistance of another Basque vessel, to which he had sent to borrow powder and arms, he came swooping down upon du May, and fired two or three cannon-shots at him, commanding him not only to send back all the arms and munitions he had taken, but also to deliver up all belonging to his own vessel and that of Gallois as well; otherwise he would sink them both. Seeing how matters stood, they were forced to comply, not having sufficient strength to make resistance; so that they found themselves captured by the men whom they had captured shortly before.

While these things were taking place, there arrived from Tadoussac the pinnace commanded by Sainte-Croix, which had fallen in with some of the English, who had taken all the furs it carried.... Arriving, as mentioned, at Miscou on the same day on which the trouble occurred between the Basque and Captain du May, he found himself in turn taken by the Basque vessel....

This misfortune was followed by still another caused by the malice of these same Basques, who persuaded the savages that the French meant to poison them by means of the brandy they gave them to drink. And, as these people are very credulous, on meeting a boat with Frenchmen in it, which had approached the land in order to trade with them, these quarrelsome and barbarous people, flinging themselves on the boat, ravaged it, and plundered it of all that it contained. When the sailors resisted, one of them was killed by an arrow, and two savages were in like manner killed by the sword of a Frenchman belonging to the boat. Thus were the French maltreated by the English, the Basques, and even by the savages, and all forced to return with the vessel of Captain Gallois to the fort and habitation of Ste. Anne [on Cape Breton Island], with the very small amount of fishing and trading that they had done.

Samuel de Champlain. *The Works of Samuel de Champlain.* 1971, VI:200-211.

ca 1634

Setting out from La Haive, and having rounded Cape Doré about a league, one enters the Bay of Mirligaiche [Mahone Bay, N.S.] which is about three leagues in depth, and filled by numerous islands. Amongst others there is one of a quarter of a league in circuit; it is only a rock covered with little trees like heathers. I was in this bay with Monsieur de Razilly and some Indians who were guiding us; an interpreter told us, as we were passing near this island, that the Indians never landed upon it. When we asked him the reason, he made answer that when a man set foot upon this island instantly a fire would seize upon his privy parts, and they would burn up, so the Indians said. This afforded us matter for laughter, and especially when the Commandeur de Razilly told a Capuchin priest aged sixty years and more to go there in order to disabuse these people of their errors, and he refused and was not willing to do anything of the kind, no matter what Monsieur de Razilly could say to him.

Nicolas Denys (living in Acadie, 1633-1681). *The Description and Natural History of the Coasts of North America (Acadia).* 1908: 153-154.

[De Razilly died in 1635, so this episode occurred between 1633 and 1635.]

In the pitch of the fall [of the Saint John River] is a great hollow, of about three or four hundred feet around; this is made by the rush of the water as it passes between two rocks which form a narrow place in the river.... In this hollow is a great upright tree which floats, but no matter how the water runs it never gets out; it only makes its appearance from time to time, and sometimes is not seen for eight, ten or fifteen days. The end which appears above the water is a little larger around than a hogshead, and when it appears it is sometimes on one side and sometimes on the other. All of the Indians who passed by there in former times, and they are in great number in these parts, rendered it homage.... They called this tree the Manitou [Micmac *mn'tu'*, 'power,' 'spirit'].... The homage ... consisted of one or two beaver skins, or other peltry, which they attached to the top of the tree with an arrow head made of a moose bone sharpened with stones. When they passed this spot and their Manitou did not appear, they took it for a bad omen, saying that he was angry with them. Since the French have come to these parts, and they have been given arrowheads of iron, they no longer use any others, and the poor Manitou has his head so covered with them that scarcely could one stick a pin therein. I have seen it, and some of the men of Monsieur de la Tour [Charles Saint-Etienne de la Tour] ... have assured me that he once had ropes attached to the head of this tree, and that boats with ten oarsmen, rowing with all their strength and aided by the current, were never able to pull it out of the hollow.

Nicolas Denys. *The Description and Natural History of the Coasts of North America (Acadia)*. 1908:117-118.

ca 1634

Continuing our route we coasted along to the place where my men worked timber for carpentry and planking, with which Monsieur de Razilly was charmed, seeing so great a quantity of timber, and in such fine condition. He said a thousand good things about the excellence of the land, about the great numbers of people who suffer in France but could live in comfort in this country. He said much more about it when I had him enter a hall which I had built, covered with branches, where he found a table very well furnished, with pigeon soup, with Wild Geese and Brant.... To this course there followed another of Brant and of Teal, and to that a third of large and small Snipe, and Plover in pyramids. It was a delight to all the men to see so much game at once, but all of it did not cost more than two days' work of my hunters. Raspberries and Strawberries in abundance served for dessert, these having been brought for me by the children of the Indians whom I had employed in order not to divert my men from their work.

Nicolas Denys. *The Description and Natural History of the Coasts of North America (Acadia)*. 1908:154.

1639

In 1639, the Mohawks of Canada were at war with the Micmacs of Acadia, and a bloody battle is said to have been fought between them near the mouth of the Restigouche. The former were victorious, and the warlike character of the tribe was such that the war-whoop of the Mohawk was to their enemies the signal for flight. Even at the present day, the Indians of New Brunswick have a superstitious dread of the spirit that led the "hungry wolves of Canada" to battle.

Abraham Gesner. *New Brunswick with Notes for Emigrants*. 1847:113.

[There are many Micmac stories of their wars with the people to whom they refer as the Kwetejk (singular, Kwetej). It is not certain whether this term refers to the St Lawrence Iroquois (the people Cartier found on the Gaspé in 1534) or the Mohawk; or whether it is a term which came to include both enemy groups. In early incidents of these wars, bows are in use; later, the Micmac have muskets, obtained from Europeans.]

A Short Unwritten Indian History about Spies: Awiskookak—The Mohawk Indians. The People of Nova Scotia by reading Parkman's and Murdock's History of Canada cannot escape from knowing great deal about the life and Customs of Indians of long ago. Especially they like best to read about their old time National sports. of Tomahawking. and scalping. The latter, as some believe, originated from French Idea. Far from it. That Game is as old as the Indian Race Itself. More scalps more Honor. No scalps. No good. a squaw man.

But. The Practice of spying among Mohawk and Micmac Indians began about two hundred years before Mr. White man unfortunately drifted across the Atlantic to this Country.

The Grand Chief James Paul's unwritten Indian History. says. That Nova Scotia was inhabited and owned by Mohawk Indians probably Thousand years before Micmac Indians of Now United States took notion to drive them away or out of it. And they did drive them away. But History do not say. How long the Battle lasted to do it.

To prove that Nova Scotia was once inhabited by Mohawk Indians Paul says, we have no written proof. But we have their old Stone Relics. He says More than one half of Stone Relics found in Nova Scotia are Mohawk made. Mohawks were better and neater workers than Micmacs. And are so to this very day. Hence, every Neatly made Stone Pipe, paring knife, Tomahawk, Stone Sling, &c. May safely be attributed or taken as Mohawk Manufacture. But one certain fact, he says, That stone slings were never used by Micmac Indians. Micmac Indians were spear-men. And an expert in Archery. Hence. Their easy victory. and expulsion of their inveterate enemies. The Mohawks. from this Country. Paul says. The Micmacs found and chased Mohawks up the River St Lawrence as far as Caugnawaga. Where they are to this day....

Joseph C. Cope to Harry Piers, 21 January 1924. Nova Scotia Museum Printed Matter File.

During those wars a celebrated chief arose among the Micmacs, whose name was Ulgimoo [L'kimu, 'He Sends'], of whom many strange things were related. He drove the Kwedeches out of the region on the south side of the Bay of Fundy, they having been compelled to cross the bay in their flight from the enemy; and he urged them on farther and farther towards the north, finally driving them up to Montreal.... The Kwedeches having retired to Fort Cumberland, and thence on to

Tantama [Tantramar], before their enemies, and thence on beyond Petcootkweak [Petitcodiac], Ulgimoo built a mound and fortification at the place now called Salisbury, where the mound still remains.

This war lasted for many years, since, when many of the men had been killed off, time was required to raise another race of warriors, who were carefully educated to keep alive the spirit of retaliation. This brought Ulgimoo into the field after he had become very old.... Being a magician [*puoin*, 'shaman'], he could hear and see what was going on very far off.... Thus, when he was about one hundred and three years old, he learned by means of his mysterious art that a war-party [of the Kwetejk] was on the move to attack his village. [L'kimu sent his warriors away, and let the Kwetejk capture him].... the old man was tied, bound to a tree, a quantity of dried wood piled round him, and the torch applied. As soon as the fire began to blaze, he made one spring, and was clear of all cords and green withes, tall, straight, young, and active, and ready for fight.

"There!" said [the Kwetej shaman], "didn't I tell you it was Ulgimoo? Will you not believe me now? In a moment your heads will be off." It was even so. One blow despatched him, and similar blows fell upon the rest; and only three of the whole army of several hundred men escaped. Ulgimoo did not receive a scratch. The three that were not killed he took prisoners; he cut their ears, slit their noses, and their cheeks, then bade them go home and carry the joyful tidings of their defeat, and be sure to tell that they were all slain by one Micmac, one hundred and three years old.

Thomas Boonis to Silas Rand. In *Legends of the Micmacs*, by Silas Rand. 1894:295-296.

1650

Mons. Daunay, a French captain, with a servant, being overset in a canoe, within sight of some savages, they threw themselves into the water to save them, and the servant was actually saved. But the savage, who had pitched upon Mons. Daunay, seeing who it was, and remembering some blows with a cane he had a few days before received from him, took care to souse him so often in the water, that he drowned him before he got ashore.

M. de la Varenne, "To His Friend at La Rochelle," Louisbourg, Cape Breton Island, 8 May 1756. In *An Account of the Customs and Manners of the Mikmakis and Maricheets, Savage Nations, Now Dependant on the Government at Cape Breton*, by Pierre Antoine Simon Maillard. 1758:82.

[This is probably Charles Menou d'Aulnay, drowned from a canoe in which he was sailing with a servant on the Annapolis River, 28 May 1650; the servant was saved.]

L'kimu had a younger brother. His name was Mejilapeka'tasiek, Tied-In-A-Hard-Knot. He was living at Miramichi. This man was a *puoin*, a war-shaman, and a great fighter. He could see what is to be. So one day he is sitting silent; he is in a bad temper, and he is thinking for a long time; everybody leaves him alone.

Suddenly he jumps up, calling to his brother-in-law, who is one of his captains. "Put on your armor," he bellows, "and come with me! Do it quickly!" And he rushes out of the wigwam and down to the shore. His captain comes behind him, and sees that he has already launched the boat. He leaps into it, and off they go, fast across the cove to a high sand-bank between the cove and the sea beyond.

Mejilapeka'tasiek is paddling in the bow, his captain is steering. When they get to the other side, the canoe is beached. "Wait here," says Mejilapeka'tasiek. "Keep down. I am going to see."

He crawls up the sand dunes like he is hunting ducks. And what is on the other side, floating in the water? Fifty Kwetejk, silently paddling along in their canoes. The *puoin* Wohooweh was leading them. He has his canoe lashed to another, with a deck laid over the two, and he is standing on that deck, holding a flag, looking all around him, scouting for the enemy, using his Power.

Mejilapeka'tasiek calls up his own Power, and conceals himself in plain sight, waiting for the enemy to reach him. Old Wohooweh never spotted him. He never saw him until Mejilapeka'tasiek speaks: "My brother! Where are you going, and for what do you look?"

Wohooweh jumps. He is startled. He feels ashamed that he did not see a man standing there. So he brings his two canoes in to land, and greets him in a friendly way. "Do you know the great chief Mejilapeka'tasiek? I am looking for him."

"No. But I have heard of him; he lives far down this point of land."

"Well, I am searching for him," says Wohooweh. "And I intend to pick very thoroughly this whole bone." This means he wants to kill. He wants to kill every man and woman, every child in the whole region.

Mejilapeka'tasiek smiles. "Well," he says. "You are here. And this is my home. I have a few men with me who would be glad to meet with you." And those two chiefs call up their men to battle.

Mejilapeka'tasiek and Wohooweh will fight. They will use their tomahawks. They will use their knives. And so it begins. So rapidly do they move, to attack and to defend, that sometimes they can scarcely be seen. But it is told that Mejilapeka'tasiek did grab Wohooweh. He got him by the scalp lock, and he dragged him to a big stone, and with one blow he crushed his skull on the stone. The blow is like a clap of thunder. It is as loud as a cannon. It is heard in the village, and an old shaman hears it and laughs. "There went the head of a mighty *puoin*," he says.

Mejilapeka'tasiek is exhausted. He goes to cool himself and his wounds off in the water.

The Kwetej war captain calls a halt. "*Ta beâk!*" he shouts. "It is enough. This was Wohooweh's fight. It was his business. Not ours. Let us quit, and make peace."

Retold by R.H. Whitehead. Whitehead MS, "The Kwetejk Wars." Nova Scotia Museum Printed Matter File. Based on *Legends of the Micmacs,* by Silas Rand. 1894:212-214. "I cannot learn how long the Mohawk war lasted. I have already obtained several of the intervening incidents. The winding up of the war ... was related to me today by my friend Louis Benjamin Brooks [grandson of Chief Louis-Benjamin Peminuit Paul], Sept. 3, 1869." (Silas Rand, 1894: 212)

The Grand Chief James Paul's [Jacques-Pierre Peminuit Paul's] un-written Indian History says ... The last two surviving Chiefs of that greatest of all Indian wars killed one another somewhere near Quebec. Mijilapegatasijk [Mejilapeka'tasiek], Chief of the Micmac, killed Wasoow-ow the Mohawk Chief in Tomahawk fight in the Morning. But he also died the following day.

Joseph C. Cope to Harry Piers, 21 January 1924. Nova Scotia Museum Printed Matter File.

Tabasintak [Tabusintac] is the place pointed out on the map by Ben Brooks as the identical spot [where Mejilapeka'tasiek killed Wohooweh]. He has been there, and seen the rock on which tradition says the Kwedech's head was smashed; it lies about in the centre of the sand-bar that stretches along in front of the mouth of the river, outside of the lagoon....

The stone ... is of a singular form—hollow on the top, like a dish; and from this stone, and the circumstance related, the place has ever since borne the name Batkwedagunuchk, which no one English word

can easily translate. It indicates very poetically that on this rock a fellow's head was split; an *anvil* comes nearest to it. My informant has not seen the rock since he was a small boy; but the form, and the associations connected with it are indelibly fixed upon his memory.
Silas Rand. *Legends of the Micmacs.* 1894: 212, 215.

1657

While in the year 1657 some fishermen were lying [offshore] here, a sad thing occurred, of which I must here give an account. The Indians are in the habit of betaking themselves to the vicinity of places whither they know the fishermen will come to stand with their ships.... Now, there had been on these ships some Indians who had sold a number of skins to the fishermen, for which they had received a great quantity of brandy. In the evening, when they had come to land, they all together began to drink, next to brag and bluster, and finally to fight, inasmuch as their quarrels mostly spring from their condition, the ones desiring to be more than the others bragging of their bravery. One of the two that first had got to quarreling took up a bottle by the neck and hit his opponent with such force on the head that he fell to the earth stunned, whereupon, with the knife that he had hanging down from his neck, he stuck four deep wounds into his body, so that the blood rushed out in a stream. A brother of this wounded Indian at once flew up, and finding a gun, he meant to shoot the other one through. This one knocked the muzzle aside, so that the ball went obliquely through the neck of some one else who was entirely without blame in the matter. Thereupon the quarrel became general, and all that they could lay their hands on served as weapons. To be brief, they found next day five dead on the field of battle, and of the nine persons which there had been all told, those left over were altogether more or less wounded. Such deadly consequences does brandy some-times work among these folk, and it would have been much better if the fishermen had never done any trading with them than that they should send them the means to deprive each other of life.
Nicolas Denys. *The Description and Natural History of the Coasts of North America (Acadia).* 1908:82-83.

ca 1657

And the Indians whom the fishermen have taken to France have contributed still more to [the increasing habit of obtaining alcohol by force from European ships], through consorting [in France] with blasphemers, in pot-houses and vile places, to which they have been taken. Then [there are] the wars which the French have made among themselves to dispossess one another, through their ambition and desire to possess everything; these things the Indians know well, and, when one represents to them that they ought not to rob and to pillage vessels, they say in prompt answer that we do the same thing among ourselves. "Do not take your establishments one from another," they say to us, "and do not kill one another for that purpose; have we not seen you do it, and why are you not willing that we should do it? If one is not willing to give it to us, we will take it."

Nicolas Denys. *The Description and Natural History of the Coasts of North America (Acadia)*. 1908:451.

1671

The Chief at Richibouctou, named Denis, is a conceited and vicious Indian. All the others of the Great Bay fear him. He has upon the border of the basin of this river a rather large fort of stakes, with two kinds of bastions; inside is his wigwam, and the other Indians are encamped around him. He has had a great piece of wood placed upright to the top of a tree, with large pegs which pass through it in the manner of an estrapade and serve as steps for ascending to the top. There from time to time he sends an Indian to see if he can perceive anything along the coasts. From this place one can see far out to sea. If any vessels or canoes are seen, he has his entire force brought under arms with their bows and arrows and their muskets, and places a sentinel on the approach to ask what persons they are, and then according to his whim he makes them wait, or has them come immediately. Before entering it is required that they make a discharge of their guns, as a salute, and sometimes two. Then the leader enters, and his suite after him. He never goes out from his wigwam to receive those who come to visit him.... They all wish for his death; he is not liked by a single one.

Nicolas Denys. *The Description and Natural History of the Coasts of North America (Acadia)*. 1908:195-196.

1672

This island [Cape Breton] has also been esteemed for the hunting of Moose. They were found formerly in great numbers, but at present there are no more. The Indians have destroyed everything, and have abandoned the island, finding there no longer the wherewithal for living. It

A European artist's version of the events recorded by Nicolas Denys in 1657.

is not that the chase of small game is not good and abundant there, but this does not suffice for their support, besides which it costs them too much in powder and ball. For with one shot of a gun, with which they kill a Moose, they will kill only one Wild Goose or two, sometimes three, and this does not suffice to support them and their families as a big animal does.

Nicolas Denys. *The Description and Natural History of the Coasts of North America (Acadia)*. 1908:186-187.

1676

Our Lord inspired me with the idea of [creating ideograms] the second year of my mission, when, being much embarrassed as to the method by which I should teach the Indians to pray to God, I noticed that some children were making marks with charcoal upon birch-bark, and were counting these with the finger very accurately at each word of prayers which they pronounced. This made me believe that by giving them some formulary, which would aid their memory by definite characters, I should advance much more quickly than by teaching them through the method of making them repeat a number of times that which I said to them. I was charmed to find that I was not mistaken, and that these characters which I had formed upon paper produced all the effect that I could wish, so that in a few days they learned without difficulty all of their prayers.

Chrestien LeClercq (Récollet missionary to the Micmac on the Gaspé, 1675-1683). *New Relation of Gaspesia*. 1968:131.

ca 1677

[The Micmac] find the use of our handkerchiefs ridiculous; they mock at us and say that it is placing excrements in our pockets.

Chrestien LeClercq. *New Relation of Gaspesia*. 1968:253.

Thou reproachest us, very inappropriately, that our country is a little hell in contrast with France, which thou comparest to a terrestrial paradise, inasmuch as it yields thee, so thou sayest, every kind of provision in abundance. Thou sayest of us also that we are the most miserable and unhappy of all men, living without religion, without manners, without honour, without social order, and, in a word, without any rules, like the beasts in our woods and our forests, lacking bread, wine, and a thousand other comforts which thou hast in superfluity in Europe. Well, my brother, if thou dost not yet know the real feelings which our Indians have towards thy country and towards all thy nation, it is proper that I inform thee at once. I beg thee now to believe that, all miserable as we seem in thine eyes, we consider ourselves nevertheless much happier than thou in this, that we are very content with the little that we have; and believe also once for all, I pray, that thou deceivest thyself greatly if thou thinkest to persuade us that thy country is better than ours.... As to us, we find all our riches and all our conveniences among ourselves, without trouble and without exposing our lives to the dangers in which you find yourselves constantly through your long voyages. And, whilst feeling compassion for you in the sweetness of our repose, we wonder at the anxieties and cares which you give yourselves night and day in order to load your ship. We see also that all your people live, as a rule, only upon cod which you catch among us. It is everlastingly nothing but cod—cod in the morning, cod at midday, cod at evening, and always cod, until things come to such a pass that if you wish some good morsels, it is at our expense; and you are obliged to have recourse to the Indians, whom you despise so much, and to beg them to go a-hunting that you may be regaled.

Micmac elder of the Miramichi band, speaking to a group of Frenchmen, with Chrestien LeClercq interpreting. In *New Relation of Gaspesia*, by Chrestien LeClercq. 1968:104-106.

ca 1677

Consequently our Indians, who some time ago came to France, have not been able to hear without breaking into laughter, the raillery of certain ladies who took them for masqueraders, because they made appearance at Court painted in the Indian fashion. "They have no sense," said these Indians to their interpreter, "and their reproach is unjust, because they themselves have their own faces all mottled with black, like our Indians, from which it appears that they are always in mourning, judging by their manner of painting themselves."

Chrestien LeClercq. *New Relation of Gaspesia.* 1968:97-98.

I am greatly astonished that the French have so little cleverness, as they seem to exhibit in the matter of which thou hast just told me on their behalf, in the effort to persuade us to convert our poles, our barks, and our wigwams into those houses of stone and of wood which are tall and lofty, according to their account, as these trees. Very well! But why now

... do men of five to six feet in height need houses which are sixty to eighty? For in fact, as thou knowest very well thyself, Patriarch—do we not find in our own all the conveniences and the advantages that you have with yours, such as reposing, drinking, sleeping, eating, and amusing ourselves with our friends when we wish?

Micmac elder to Chrestien LeClercq. In *New Relation of Gaspesia*, by Chrestien LeClercq. 1968:103.

ca 1677

The names that our Gaspesians give to one another, or that father and mother apply to their children, are all very full of significance.... Those of our Indians express and indicate either the fine deeds, or the natural and predominant characteristics, of those who receive them.... Thus our Indians, if they are good hunters, are called *Smagnis* [*makwis*, 'fish-hawk'] or *Koucdedaoui* [*kwetatawey*, 'pigeon-hawk'], which is equivalent to saying "Hawk," and so on for the others.

Chrestien LeClercq. *New Relation of Gaspesia.* 1968:142.

1677

[LeClercq sets out to snowshoe from Nipisiquid to Miramichi, with a Micmac hunter named Koucdedaoui (Kwetatawey) and his wife, Marie, their baby, and Phillipe Enault le Sieur de Barbaucannes, a French physician born in 1651 at Saumur.]

We took each one his pack upon his shoulders, and set out upon our way, with snowshoes on our feet. After four to five leagues of advance, the approach of evening obliged us to make a camp in which to pass the night. It was necessary, in order to make this camp as comfortable as the country would permit, to dig a hollow four or five feet deep in the snow, which we had to throw out with our snowshoes until we reached the ground; and this our Indian woman covered with branches of fir, all fresh and green, on which we lay.... We passed the first night, like all the others of our voyage, at the Sign of the Moon and of the Beautiful Star....

The next morning ... we continued our voyage, always ascending and following the shores of the River Nipisiquit.... The extreme desire I had to go without delay ... to commence the mission, made me decide so much the more easily to take the route by the burnt woods.... In order that you may understand what these burnt woods are, I will tell you that the heavens, being one day all on fire, full of tempest and thunder ... a thunderbolt fell at a time when the dryness was extraordinary, and not merely set in flames all the woods and forest which lay between Mizamichis [Miramichi] and Nipisiquit, but also burnt and consumed more than two hundred and fifty leagues of country in such a manner that nothing was to be seen except very tall and quite blackened trunks of trees, which showed in their frightful barrenness the evidence of a conflagration widespread and altogether astonishing.... A matter which gives more trouble to the voyagers who traverse these burnt woods is that they cannot find places to camp under shelter from the wind, nor wood suitable for warming themselves. It was, nevertheless, in these sad solitudes, and in these wastes ... that we lost our way....

This march, extraordinarily painful and fatiguing, added to the dearth of provisions, there being no more than a small morsel of bread to eat each day, reduced us to extreme misery. Our Indian became tired out, and his wife with her little child aroused my compassion; and I tell you frankly, for my part, that I was completely done out.... I came near being swallowed up in a deep gulch which was covered with snow.... Scarcely was I a gun-shot from this precipice, when, wishing to cross a little river, one of my snowshoes broke, and I fell into the water up to my waist.... [But finally] Monsieur Henaut and the Indian, who preceded us, gave a cry of joy and of cheer for the happy discovery they had made of the very fresh track of an Indian who had passed that morning on his way a-hunting.... You can judge of the joy that I felt at seeing this charitable Gaspesian [named Ejougouloumouet] who was coming towards me, and who would show us our road....

Chrestien LeClercq *New Relation of Gaspesia.* 1968:164-173.

1677

The Indian [Ejougouloumouet], who was acting as guide, becoming impatient because I remained so long a time kneeling in a place removed from the bustle of the camp, approached me, and, believing that I had some revelation, or had received the gift of prophecy, begged me in all seriousness to predict to him that which would happen to us during the day. "Thou speakest to God," said he to me, "thou teachest the way of the sun, thou art a Patriarch, thou art clever, and it must be believed that he who has made everything will have granted thy prayer. Tell me then, whether today we shall kill many moose and beavers with which to feast thee after the many fatigues and miseries which thou hast suffered up to this time." [He] was not yet baptised although he was fifty to sixty years old....

Chrestien LeClercq. *New Relation of Gaspesia.* 1968:173-174.

1677-1680

You will take notice that each juggler [shaman] has his own particular bag in which are all the articles that he uses in his jugglery.... One of these bags has come into my hands, having been given me by a juggler for the purpose of testifying to me that he wished to pray to God and to be instructed. I received him with so much the more joy, in that I had been hoping for a long time to gain this soul to God by making him leave his errors in order to follow the truths of Christianity. He delivered the bag into my hands with the intention of becoming a Christian, giving me notice that if I preserved it to send to France, and to make it go out of the country, I should not live more than four or five days, and that if I threw it into the fire, I ought to be apprehensive lest the house be reduced at once to ashes, because of the extraordinary effects which his *Ouahich* would cause when it found itself in the flames. It is well to treat the Indians with consideration, and sometimes to delay instructing them until they have removed the obstacle which is opposed to their conversion. This gives them more esteem and veneration for Christianity, which they then believe is not compatible with their errors. This person had several times testified to me that he wished to be baptized in order to enter with the others into the "Wigwam of JESUS", that he might pray to the God of the Sun. I knew, however, that he was one of the most famous jugglers of all this nation, a fact which obliged me to treat him with some indifference every time that he spoke to me of instructing him. He understood very well that all his advances would be useless if he did not change his conduct, and if he did not renounce his *Ouahich* for ever. I told him that all the promises he had made me up to that time had been without result, and that if his heart would speak wholly good he must give me more sincere indications of it than he had in the past. "Ah," said he to me, "Thou believest then that I wish always to deceive thee, as I have done up to the present! Thou deceivest thyself, and in order to convince thee effectively that I have a genuine disposition to abandon my errors, and to come to prayer, take," said he to me, "my jugglery-bag which I place in thy hands in order never more to make use of it...."

Our Indian juggler was, however, much troubled as to what had become of his bag, and as to the use I had made of it. Five to six weeks after he had given it to me, he wished to inform himself on this point, and came for the purpose to the wigwam where I was. I told him that he had no further need to be concerned about his bag, which had deserved to be thrown into the fire, since it was the property of the Devil who had dwelt therein so long a time, and that no ill had befallen either me or the house, although in giving it to me he had threatened me with some misfortune. Being convinced straightway that I had burnt it, he said, "Alas! I have indeed discovered as much during the voyages I have made since I have given it to thee, for I have been hungry and I have been weary, something which never happened to me when I had my bag. I used to take my Devil in my hands and press it strongly against my stomach. 'Hey, how is this?,' I used to say to him, 'wilt thou permit that I be overwhelmed by hunger and fatigue, thou who hast never abandoned me? Grant, for mercy's sake, that I get something to eat; give me some comfort in me.' He would hear my prayer and promptly grant my vows." I made him admit, however, in showing him his *Ouahich*, that this was another relic of his fancy and of his foolish imaginings, indicating to him several incidents in which he had suffered much without having received any aid from his Devil, whose virtue was so feeble that it had not the power to aid or comfort itself in the excess of its sufferings.

Chrestien LeClercq. *New Relation of Gaspesia.* 1968:220-221.

When the priests first came 'most all the Indians were witches [shamans]. Some were willing to be christened, some were unwilling. They asked the priest: "What is christening for?"—"If you are not christened, you are lost for good."—"Lost, in the woods?"—"No, in hell."—"Where is hell?"—"Black place, fire there burns the soul."—"How do you go there, by road?"—"No, your soul goes there."—"Where is my soul?"—"You might sicken and die. After you die, you might see your soul."—"How can a soul go out from the birchbark cover around the dead body, tightly bound?"—"You should dig a hole and put the dead in it."—"That would be even harder to get out of, couldn't go anywhere then."—"Yes, you could go to Heaven."—"Heaven? What is Heaven?"—"If you do not fight, do not talk bad, you can go there. If you murder, steal, you will go to Hell, for your sin."—"Sin? What is sin?" They knew *nothing*. Finally, very few refused to be christened, and afterwards, as the priest wanted, to come to confession. But three men would not go to be christened, among them the biggest witch of them all. He was very much against the priests. He said, "No Heaven, no Hell. When you die, you gone, can't speak." He was the worst fellow of all. He was about forty-five. Old lady [his wife] coaxed him, "Better go, get christen', like the rest." At last he went. "What name do you like?" they asked him. "Best name, the Lord." The priest said, "Nobody can have that name, only one Lord. What other name?"—"I'll be named the Devil."—"No. You can't have that name."—"Well, I'll be named Swallow (*tum'hatolnes*)."—"No. You can't have that name. That's a bird's name."—"I have proposed three names. You refuse them all. I am going home."—"No, you can't go." Then the friend he went hunting with said he would give him a name— Gabrio (Gabriel). "All right," he agreed to that, "That's a nice Indian name." He was a heavy witch, he had a bag of little bone animals. If he wanted anybody to be sick he sent an animal to him, if he wanted you well, he sent an animal to you. They wanted to take away his bag (*bu'owino'di* [*puoinoti*], the whole outfit). "All right," he said, "since I am going to be christened you can take my *bu'owino'di* to the priest." The priest told some men, "Tie this bag with rope, put hooks on it and great big stones. Put it in a canoe, go to the deepest water and sink the bag, so it never comes back to him." Two men did this, they sank the bag in deep water, deeper than their long poles. The man was lonesome after he lost his bag. He took his pipe and smoked. He thought, "Sometimes my bag did me good. When I asked him to send me moose down here, moose came."—The old woman said, "No, God Almighty did not want that." He took a big smoke. In the morning the bag was under his head, it had come back. The old lady went to tell the priest, "That bag you fixed, he's got it under his head this morning."—"Well, well, well. Very queer that bag came back. The Devil himself brought it back," said the priest. "Tell the man to bring it to me himself." She told her husband. "What does he want it for? The bag is all right. It was christened as well as myself. It won't hurt anybody any more."—"It will," said the old lady. Well, at last he carried the bag to the priest. The priest said, "Come, kiss this Bible, promise to give up the bag for good."—"Didn't you christen it yesterday? I will take it to Heaven with me."—"No, you must give up that bag for good."—"What will you give me for that?"—"Nothing, but I will send you to Heaven, if you're a good old man and don't hurt anybody. But that bag you've got to give up." He took off his cap, got down on his knees. The priest closed the Bible with a slam and said, "You've got to give up the bag for good."— "All right."—"Have you got the canoe ready?"—"Yes."—"Well, I am going along this time. Tie up the bag, fasten *three* stones to it this time." So in the deepest water they could find they sank 'um. Last end. That bag never came back to him. Ever since then folks have been christened, praying, paying Indian taxes.

Isabelle Googoo Morris to Elsie Clews Parsons, 1923. "Micmac Folklore," by Elsie
Clews Parsons. In *Journal of American Folklore.* 1925, Vol. 38:91-92.

1675-1683

Our poor Indian women have so much affection for their children that
they do not rate the quality of nurse any lower than that of mother. They
even suckle the children up to the age of four or five years, and, when these
begin to eat, the mothers chew the meat in order to induce the children
to swallow it. One cannot express the tenderness and affection which the
fathers and mothers have for their children. I have seen considerable
presents offered to the parents in order that these might give the children
to certain Frenchmen who would have taken them to France. But this
would have torn their hearts, and millions would not induce them to
abandon their children for a moment.

Chrestien LeClercq. *New Relation of Gaspesia.* 1968:91-92.

**An Indian woman, when in a canoe one day, feeling herself pressed by
the pains of childbirth, asked those of her company to put her on shore,
and to wait for her a moment. She entered alone into the woods, where
she was delivered of a boy; she brought him to the canoe, which she
helped to paddle all the rest of the journey.**

Chrestien LeClercq. *New Relation of Gaspesia.* 1968:89.

1677

Our Indian woman, wife of Koucedadoui [Kwetatawey], with whom we
had come from Nipisiquit, was encamped, in the absence of her husband,
quite close to the fort of Monsieur de Fronsac [Richard Denys de
Fronsac, son of Nicolas Denys] with an Indian woman of her acquain-
tance, who had an infant at the breast. Through lack of birch bark they
covered their camp with branches of fir, and they found it convenient to
make use of straw to rest upon during the night. The cold was extreme,
and its rigour was increased by a wind from the north-west which blew
with all its force, so that these women were compelled to make a much
larger fire than usual. They went quietly to sleep without any presenti-
ment of the evil which was coming upon them; but scarcely had these two
unfortunate Indian women closed their eyes when the fire caught in the
straw, and, making its way to the branches of fir, it consumed and
reduced to ashes the entire wigwam.

I leave it to be imagined to what extremity these poor women were reduced when they saw themselves completely shut in and surrounded by flames. They uttered at once cries so piercing that these reached our ears almost as soon as they left their mouths. It is safe to say that they would never have escaped from this terrible conflagration if one of these two Indian women, preserving throughout a presence of mind admirable in so pressing a danger, had not made an opening in the wigwam, through which, all naked as she was, she threw herself, with her infant, into the midst of the snow.

Her companion was not so prudent nor so fortunate. Almost immediately she lost her presence of mind, as well as her hope of saving herself, and, giving herself no further concern for her own life except for the sake of saving that of her dear infant which she held in her arms, she would not abandon it until her sight was obscured by a great burst of fire and flame, and she was compelled to let the child fall into the midst of the fire. It was a great piece of good fortune for her that she found herself, although by chance, at the place through which her companion had saved herself with her little infant. A flickering light which appeared at first before our eyes, together with the wailing and the groaning of these poor unfortunate wretches, made us understand and comprehend, almost at the same moment, the sorrowful accident which had happened. One was lying in the snow with her infant, the other was still at the door of the wigwam without power to come out therefrom, and she suffered a grief so keen that she did not heed the sparks and coals falling continually upon her flesh.

Everybody knows that the fir is a tree full of resin, which some call turpentine; and since, through the violence of fire, this gum fell all in flame upon the body of this Indian woman, it is probable that she would have expired along with her son in this horrible torment, if Monsieur Henaut had not, by strength of arm, rescued her from this sinister conflagration. I entered the wigwam, which was still all on fire, in order to try to save her child; but it was too late, for this little innocent was smothered in the flames and half roasted. He died, in fact, a moment later in my arms, leaving me no other comfort, among so many matters for grief, than that of having baptized him [Pierre] before my departure from Nipisiquit.

One cannot express the acute sorrow of this afflicted mother when she reflected upon the loss and the manner of death of an only son whom she dearly loved. Overwhelmed by grief and bitterness for the death of this dear child, she closed her ears to everything that could be said to give her consolation in her misfortunes. The Sieur Henaut, with his usual charity, took the care of dressing her wounds, and he would have cured them entirely if the ointments had not been lacking. She had been baptized and named Marie by one of our missionaries. I had prepared her for confession, so that having always performed the duties of a good Christian, especially towards the end of her illness, she made a general confession of her sins the morning of Ash Wednesday, and died at evening, leaving me great hopes of her salvation.

Chrestien LeClercq. *New Relation of Gaspesia.* 1968:180-184.

1677

The body remained all night in the wigwam…. Two Frenchmen and two Indians were assigned to remain near the deceased during the night. Ejougouloumouet was one of the number. He, imagining that the blessed taper was composed of moose's grease, ate it all up.

Chrestien LeClercq. *New Relation of Gaspesia.* 1968:184.

Her husband, however, who knew nothing of all that had happened in his absence, returned from hunting two hours after we had buried this Indian woman. He lamented bitterly the death of his wife, and since he had tenderly loved his child…. he often visited their tomb, and there one day, when on his knees, with hands and eyes raised towards heaven, and his heart all rent with grief, he was heard to pronounce these words in the form of a prayer: "O great God, who governs the sun and the moon, who has created the moose, the otters, and the beavers, be appeased: be no more angry against me; and be satisfied with the misfortunes which overwhelm me. I had a wife; Thou hast taken her from me. I had a child that I loved even as myself; but I have none any more, because Thou hast willed it. Is that not enough? Grant me then for the future as much of good as now I endure of ill. Or, if Thou art not yet satisfied with that which I suffer in my heart, make me die as soon as possible, for it is impossible for me to live thus any longer."

Koucdedaoui [Kwetatawey]. In *New Relation of Gaspesia*, by Chrestien LeClercq. 1968:185-186.

1677

I was a good deal surprised to see a fine cross, embellished with beads, in the place of honour, and in the most important part of the camp, between the two wives which our Ejougouloumouet possessed, one as his legiti-

mate wife, and the other as his concubine, who had, said he, come miraculously from heaven to his aid at a time when he was abandoned by all the Indians, and cruelly afflicted with illness in the depths of the woods, he, his wife and his children, without any hope of human aid.
Chrestien LeClercq. *New Relation of Gaspesia.* 1968:176.

Here, however ... are some of the chief reasons which have compelled me to believe that the Cross had been held in veneration among these barbarians before the first arrival of the French in their country. For, wishing one day to make these pagans admit that the missionaries who had preceded me had taught them the manner in which they ought to worship the Cross, the leading person said to me, "Well, now, thou art a Patriarch. Thou wishest that we believe everything that thou tellest us, but thou art not willing to believe that which we tell thee. Thou art not yet forty years old, and for only two hast thou dwelt with the Indians; and yet thou pretendest to know our maxims, our traditions, and our customs better than our ancestors who have taught them to us. Dost thou not still see every day the old man Quioudo, who is more than a hundred and twenty years old? He saw the first ship which landed in our country. He has repeated to thee often that the Indians of Mizamichis have not received from strangers the use of the Cross, and that his own knowledge of it has been derived through tradition from his fathers, who lived for at least as long a time as he. Accordingly, thou canst judge whether we received it before the French came to our coasts.... Thou knowest that ... the Indians of Ristigouche are our brothers and our compatriots, who speak the same language as ourselves.... tell us why the Patriarchs should have given the usage of the Cross to us in preference to our brothers of Ristigouche, whom they have baptized but who nevertheless have not had the symbol of the Christian in veneration always, as have our ancestors who have never received Baptism?"
Chrestien LeClercq. *New Relation of Gaspesia.* 1968:191-192.

1677

It is a fact that the Indians of Ristigouche are baptised, and that nevertheless they do not wear the Cross, but the figure of a salmon, which in old times they hung from the neck as the mark of honour of their country. For it is to be noted that it has always been the custom of all our Gaspesians to wear some particular figures, which are somewhat like

Chrestien LeClercq teaching his parishioners to say their catechism, using ideograms. Ink drawing (1675-1683) by LeClercq or Father Jumeau.

coats of arms, to distinguish them from the other Indians, in accordance
with the different places where they ordinarily live.

Chrestien LeClercq. *New Relation of Gaspesia.* 1968:192-193.

1680

As I was wholly convinced of the sincere affection which the Gaspesians
had for me, and as they supposed I was once more to spend the winter
with them in the woods, I believed that I ought to entrust the secret, and
to make the announcement of my intention to return to France, to that
one of the Indians who called himself my father, and of whom I called
myself the son, since the time when he had "given me birth" in the midst
of the usual feasts of the Gaspesian nation with the corresponding
ceremony. It would be really difficult for me to express to you the
consternation which the news caused in the mind of this [man], who, by
the change in his colour, and by the grief and sadness which appeared all
at once in his countenance, soon made me know that he was keenly
touched by the resolution in which I appeared to him to be, of embarking
in the first ships of our fishermen. He left me gruffly, contrary to his habit,
and entered into the woods, perhaps to conceal the tears which commenced to flow from his eyes. He came out thence some time after, and
thought well to send one of his children, with two or three young Indians,
to carry the news of my departure to the Gaspesians who were at the
salmon fishery, and to invite them all to assemble at once with him in
order to bid me adieu. He ordered these deputies not to approach their
wigwams except with the same ceremonies which they invariably observe
when they go to announce the death of some one of their prominent
persons, because they considered that I was going to die, so far as they
were concerned, and they would never see me again.

Chrestien LeClercq. *New Relation of Gaspesia.* 1968:306.

If someone among them laments, grieves, or is angry, this is the only
reasoning with which they console him. "Tell me, my brother, wilt
thou always weep? Wilt thou always be angry? Wilt thou come
nevermore to the dances and the feasts of the Gaspesians? Wilt thou die,
indeed, in weeping and in the anger in which thou art at present?" If
he who laments and grieves answers him no, and says that after some
days he will recover his good humour and his usual amiability—"Well,
my brother," will be said to him, "Thou hast no sense; since thou hast
no intention to weep nor to be angry always, why dost thou not

commence immediately to banish all bitterness from thy heart, and rejoice thyself with thy fellow-countrymen?" This is enough to restore his usual repose and tranquillity.... In a word, they rely upon liking nothing, and upon not becoming attached to the goods of the earth, in order not to be grieved or sad when they lose them....

Chrestien LeClercq. *New Relation of Gaspesia.* 1968:243.

The Chief of our Gaspesians [then] parted the crowd, approached me, and appeared in the midst of the assembly with a face all dismayed with grief and sadness.... He took me by the hand, and regarding me fixedly with eyes ready to burst into tears, he addressed me in these very words—"Well then, my son, the resolution has been taken; thou wishest to abandon us and return to France. For there lies the great wooden canoe" (pointing out to me the ship in which I was to embark) "which is going to steal thee from the Gaspesians in order to take thee to thine own land, to thy relatives and thy friends...."

"I say, what now, my son?" added he, "Is it possible that thou hast lost so soon the recollection of the feast which thou gavest us once at Gaspé, the first time that thou camest to live in our wigwams, when, having formed, with flour kneaded in the fat and marrow of moose, as many hearts of paste as we were of Gaspesians, thou arrangedst them in the same bark plate, desiring to persuade us that the largest of these hearts, which covered and concealed all the others, was the representation of thine own, whose zeal and charity enclosed within itself all the hearts of the Indians, neither more nor less than mothers enclose their children in their wombs.... Tell me then now, is this heart no more the same to-day as of yore? Has it then become wholly French, and is it more at all Gaspesian? Or indeed, does it wish to throw forth the Indians for ever, after having welcomed and tenderly loved them?... dost thou not know, my son, that I am thy father, and the Chief of the Gaspesian nation? And as I am thy father, thou canst not be ignorant thus far of the sincerity of my friendship. I assure thee that I will even love thee always as tenderly as one of my own children.... Alas my son," added this Indian, with tears in his eyes, "if some one of us comes to die in the woods, who will take care to show us the road to Heaven, and to aid us to die aright? Was it then needful to take so much trouble to instruct us, as thou hast done up to the present, only to leave us in an evident peril of dying without the sacraments which thou hast administered to my brother, my uncle, and several of our dying old men? If thy remains still insensible to everything I have said, learn, my son, that mine sheds and weeps tears of blood in abundance so great that it chokes my utterance."

Chrestien LeClercq. *New Relation of Gaspesia.* 1968:311-313.

"If it is thus," answered in the same instant a certain Nemidouades, "it is necessary that I go to France with the Patriarch [LeClercq]...." He was going to say something else when the captain notified us that it was time to start.

Chrestien LeClercq. *New Relation of Gaspesia.* 1968:315.

[This is 1680. By October 1681, LeClercq had returned to New France and was on his way home to the Gaspé Micmac who had adopted him.]

The Beaver is of the bigness of a water-spaniel. Its fur is ... very soft and suitable for the making of hats. It is the great trade of New France. The Gaspesians say that the Beaver is the beloved of the French and of the other Europeans, who seek it greedily; and I have been unable to keep from laughing on overhearing an Indian, who said to me in banter, "*Tahoé messet koguar pajo ne daoui doguoil mkobit:* In truth, my brother, the Beaver does everything to perfection. He makes for us kettles, axes, swords, knives, and gives us drink and food without the trouble of cultivating the ground."

Chrestien LeClercq. *New Relation of Gaspesia.* 1968:277.

1686
An account of the trip which I made in Acadie at the King's command, beginning October 11, 1686....

On the 15th [of November] I embarked in my two canoes, accompanied by a third, in which were the two Indians and a Frenchman who was to act as interpreter.... After having suffered for six or seven days near a river called Chediae [Shediac], I met with a north-west wind which greatly helped me on my way, for, although it was very strong, it was a following wind and I could not resist profiting by it to use my sails. This wind lasted for a day and a half and enabled us to cover nearly fifteen leagues. During that time I believe we ran as great risks as when we were shipwrecked: my three canoes were sometimes a league and a half from the shore, and, although we were always fairly close to one another, the waves were so high that most of the time each canoe thought that the

Father Jumeau presenting crosses to the Micmac at Miramichi, 1675-1683. Ink drawing by Jumeau or LeClercq.

other two were lost, for most often one could see neither yards nor sails. This was especially true the second day, for the wind blew only in gusts, and my mast came loose at three o'clock in the afternoon, and I found myself a distance from shore and in grave danger. However, the Indian who was managing my canoe was so skilful that he got me out of the difficulty. He wished to land, but, seeing that if he did the canoe would inevitably fill with water, he very cleverly put out to sea long enough to give himself time to mend the sail and the mast.

Jacques Demeulle. In *Acadiensia Nova*, by William Inglis Morse. 1935, I:91, 101-102.

1691

On the second spring of my captivity, my [Maliseet] Indian master and his squaw went to Canada, but sent me down the [Saint John] river with several Indians to the fort to plant corn.... Early the next morning we came to the village.... I had no sooner landed, but three or four Indians dragged me to the great wigwam.... This was occasioned by two families of Cape Sable [Micmac] Indians, who, having lost some friends by a number of English fishermen, came some hundreds of miles to revenge themselves on poor captives. They soon came to me and tossed me about till I was almost breathless, and then threw me into the ring to my fellow captive, and taking him out repeated their barbarities on him....

Then those Cape Sable Indians came to me again like bears bereaved of their whelps, saying, "Shall we who have lost relations by the English, suffer an English voice to be heard among us?" &c. Then they beat me again with the axe....

The priest of this river was of the order of Saint Francis, a gentleman of a humane and generous disposition. In his sermons he most severely reprehended the Indians for their barbarities to captives. He would often tell them that, excepting their errors in religion, the English were a better people than themselves, and that God would remarkably punish such cruel wretches, and had begun to execute his vengeance upon such already. He gave an account of the retaliations of Providence upon those murderous Cape Sable Indians above mentioned, one of whom got a splinter into his foot, which festered and rotted his flesh till it killed him. Another run a fish bone into her hand or arm, and she rotted to death, notwithstanding all means that were used to prevent it. In some such manner they all died, so that not one of those two [Micmac] families lived to return home.

John Gyles. *Memoires of Odd Adventures, Strange Deliverances, etc.* 1869:22-23, 32-33.

[Gyles was an English boy captured by the Maliseet at Pemmaquid, Maine, 2 August 1689; he was later sold to a Frenchman and then released in June 1698.]

1692

Last year [M. Baudoin, priest at Beaubassin] beat one of them, and left him for dead, and I cannot refrain from giving the reason. This Indian had married in the native manner at Chedabucto; his squaw left him for another man some months later, which, among them, is regarded as a dissolution of marriage. Her husband took her back in response to the pleadings of her parents, but it was not long before she again went off with another, and by him had a child. The first husband, therefore, had no further desire to see her and took a second squaw with as little ceremony as he had the first. M. Baudoin, not being aware of this, had promised another Indian that he should have this woman when they returned from hunting. The first Indian and his second squaw went to Beaubassin, and M. Baudoin told him that he must leave her and take back the first. He protested, saying that she had abandoned him and had borne a child to another man; he was ready, he said, to marry this squaw in the church. When M. Baudoin found that neither he nor his concubine would exchange mates he threw himself on the Indian, and, having kicked him in the stomach and given him as many blows with a stick as he pleased, left him covered with blood and returned to the village to boast of his martial exploit. I trust that what I have related will be credited, because it is the plain truth.

Joseph Robinau de Villebon to Count Ponchartrain, 1693. In *Acadia at the End of the Seventeenth Century*, by John Clarence Webster. 1934:50-51.

1694

Memorandum of presents to the value of 3640 livres, accorded by His Majesty to the Indians of Acadia, for their warfare against the English. 2000 lbs of powder. 40 kegs of bullets. 10 kegs of swan shot. 400 lbs of Brazilian tobacco. 200 tomahawks, for which M. de Bonaventure will provide a model. 60 selected muskets like those sent this year. 200 Mulaix shirts, averaging 30 sous each. 8 lbs of fine vermillion. 200 tufts of white feathers to be given to the Indians as a distinguishing mark in case of a night attack, which should not cost more than 6 to 7s a piece; to be selected in Paris by M. de Bonaventure. These presents will be distributed among the Indians when they are assembled at the appointed rendezvous.

Joseph Robinau de Villebon to Count Ponchartrain, 1694. In *Acadia at the End of the Seventeenth Century*, by John Clarence Webster. 1934:71.

1695

I then pointed out the obligation they were under to the King, because of the presents which, as they were aware, he sent them every year, and which, he had intimated to me, he would continue to send, providing they carried on the war against the English vigorously, and abstained from all negotiations with them, for as I had already told them, the English had only encouraged them in order to strike a blow at some of their kinsmen.

Joseph Robinau de Villebon to Count Ponchartrain, 1695. In *Acadia at the End of the Seventeenth Century,* by John Clarence Webster. 1934:79.

ca 1696

The gentleman with whom I lived [as an English boy captured by the Indians and then traded to the French] had a fine field of wheat, in which great numbers of blackbirds continually collected and made great havoc in it. The French said a Jesuit would come and banish them. He did at length come and having all things prepared he took a basin of holy water, a staff with a little brush, and having on his white robe, went into the field of wheat.... Then the Jesuit, dipping his brush into the holy water, sprinkled the field on each side of him, a little bell jingling at the same time, and all singing the words, *Ora pro nobis.* At the end of the field they wheeled to the left about, and returned. Thus they passed and repassed the field of wheat, the blackbirds all the while rising before them only to light behind.... [The Jesuit] told the lad that the sins of the people were so great he could not prevail against those birds. The same friar as vainly attemped to banish the musketoes from Signecto [the Chignecto Isthmus between Nova Scotia and New Brunswick], but the sins of the people there were also too great for him to prevail, but, on the other hand, it seemed that more [mosquitos] came, which caused the people to suspect that some had come for the sins of the Jesuit also.

John Gyles. *Memoires of Odd Adventures, Strange Deliverances, etc.* 1869:54-55.

1699

After having described the various movements of the Waves & the Winds, & everything that befell me on the Crossing from la Rochelle to Port royal in Acadia, I must now give an Account of all I observed in that Land.... History of the Indians: I shall begin with their Hunting Exploits with a feat which surprised me greatly, one which, perhaps, may be no less amazing to others who learn of it.

An Indian, with his musket armed, set out
With Comrades on a Hunt, and as he crossed
A vast Lake on a sheet of ice, formed by
The Winter over it, he there stopped short,
And through his nostrils drew the frosty air
Which wrapped him round, and to the band he led,
He said, I smell a Bear, it is on those high Hills.
Then were his Comrades utterly amazed
Because he pointed to a spot, more than
A quarter of a league away. He led
Them on into the wind, so straight that they
At length came to the place, and found
The Creature hibernating there. When she
Perceived herself surrounded, she by flight
Tried to preserve her life, but soon
Her course was checked by murderous lead,
And her career cut short; thus died this Bear
Which should have lived there half the year.

Le Sieur de Dièreville (living in Acadie, 1699). *Relation of the Voyage to Port Royal in Acadia.* 1968:127-128.

[Dièreville originally set out to write about his travels entirely in poetry, but eventually only portions, such as this, remained in verse form.]

1699

The Indians have not such cruel hearts; our Sailors, going to the Spring for water one evening, met two of these People who appeared very gentle; they were, however, armed with Musket & Hatchet. I had doubtless alarmed them, & they feared that they might be taken by surprise & were therefore on the defensive; who would not have done the same under the circumstance? They maintained a kind & resolute attitude in the presence of our Men, who had no sooner made themselves known as French, than the Indians lowered their arms.... Early the following morning, three of their Chiefs came in a little bark Canoe, to pay us a visit.... In order to offer them more adequate entertainment, which was perhaps that for which they had come, I gave them a good breakfast of Meat & Fish & they munched Biscuit with the best appetite in the world, & drank Brandy with relish & less moderation than we do.... on sitting down to table, they said their Prayer devoutly & made the Sign of the

Cross, &, when they had finished, they gave thanks with the same piety.... I had given them ammunition in order that they might bring me some Game, & they doubtless would have done so, but the wind on the following night become favourable for leaving this Haven ... so we hoisted sail at dawn....

Le Sieur de Dièreville. *Relation of the Voyage to Port Royal in Acadia.* 1968:76-77.

1699

I saw one of these Indian Chiefs, called Sagamores, come to the fort on the St. John River to receive the presents which France sends to them.... [He] was the grandson of an Indian who had been ennobled by Henry IV for having driven the English Indians from his Domain. [Since Henri IV died in 1610, the chief mentioned may be Membertou, "ennobled" for his raid on the Armouchiquois of Maine in 1607; *his* son Louis Membertou sometimes lived on the Saint John River.] Nothing distinguished him from those in his Party, neither his appearance, nor his clothing; he was of medium height, & all his qualities must have been of the heart or the head. When he had entered the Fort, after certain compliments addressed to the Officers, which I did not understand, I observed that though he maintained a dignified bearing, he seated himself without much ceremony, while the rest of his Party, some twenty or thirty in number, remained standing around the Room in which they were being received; it was the first mark of deference which I saw paid to him.

A diverting scene was provided for the Spectators at the Fort by one of these Indians who detached himself from the rest, & came to bow himself down very profoundly before me, repeating twenty times, as his only greeting, the word: Brother. I did not consider him as such, except in Jesus Christ, & I merely answered by bows proportionate to his own, but I recognized him as one of those who had been entertained by me at Chiboueto [Chebucto], & to whom I had given powder & shot.... the wife of one of the chief Officers, high-spirited, & a very pretty woman, went up to him, laughing heartily over the incident, & asked him in the Indian language, which she spoke as well as she did French, where he had seen me. In reply he told her that which I have just mentioned, & said that he had taken every kind of Game to Chibouetou for me, in return for all the benefits I had conferred upon him, but to his sorrow he had been unable to find me....

Le Sieur de Dièreville. *Relation of the Voyage to Port Royal in Acadia.* 1968:150-151.

These wretched People are very liable to be drowned; it happens only too frequently, because their bark Canoes capsize at the slightest provocation. Those who are fortunate enough to escape from the wreck make haste to rescue those who remain in the water. They then fill with Tobacco smoke the bladder of some animals, or a long section of large bowel, commonly used as receptacles for the preservation of their Fish & Seal oil, & having tied one end securely, they fasten a piece of Pipe or Calumet into the other, to serve as an injection Tube; this is introduced into the backside of the Men who have been drowned, &, by compressing it with their hands, they force into them the smoke contained in the bowel; they are afterwards tied by the feet to the nearest tree which can be found, & kept under observation; almost always follows the satisfaction of seeing that the smoke Douch forces them to disgorge all the water they had swallowed. Life is restored to their bodies, and before long this astonishing & beneficent result is made manifest by the twitching movements of the suspended Men.

Le Sieur de Dièreville. *Relation of the Voyage to Port Royal in Acadia.* 1968:180.

THE
EIGHTEENTH
CENTURY
1700 TO 1799 A.D.

THE ORAL AND WRITTEN HISTORIES WHICH HAVE
survived from the eighteenth century are almost universally
about violence: the continual jockeying for power over Acadie
between the French, the Micmac and the English. The latter
acquired Port Royal from the French in 1710, settled Halifax
in 1749, deported the French Acadians in 1755, and ultimately destroyed French power in the area with the taking of
the Fortress of Louisbourg. The Micmac were caught in the
middle, suffering both the indifference and political machina-
tions of their French co-religionists and the campaigns of the
English, who loosed their Mohawk allies against them and
commanded that they be exterminated. There was no one
who did not lie down to sleep in fear.

By 1761, "tired of a war that destroyed many of our
people," the Micmac negotiated a truce with the English. But
the great numbers of Loyalist settlers, fleeing the American
Revolution, made vast inroads on traditional Micmac lands.
Game was no longer plentiful; salmon rivers were blocked by
dams and choked with sawdust. The fur-trade was in decline,
and smallpox epidemics swept the Maritimes. The Micmac,
their seventeenth-century population already reduced by
approximately 90 percent, were particularly hard-hit. This
period was the seal of despair on traditional Micmac life, a
change which had begun in 1500. The eighteenth century
stamped the Micmac forever into a different shape.

How great art thou, through thy great, great, great grandfather, whose memory is still recent, by tradition, amongst us, for the plentiful hunting he used to make. There was something of the miraculous about him, when he assisted at the beating of the woods for elks, or other beasts of the fur. His dexterity at catching this game was not superior to ours; but there was some unaccountable secret he particularly possessed in his manner of seizing those creatures, by springing upon them, laying hold of their heads, and transfixing them at the same time with his hunting-spear, though thrice as strong and as nimble again as he was, and much more capable with their legs only, than we with our rackets [snowshoes], to make their way over mountains of snow: he would nevertheless follow them, dart them out with his chace [*sic*], bring them down, and mortally wound them. Then he would regale us with their blood, skin them, and deliver up the carcass to us to cut to pieces.

Anonymous Micmac orator at a feast, *ca* 1740. In *An Account of the Customs and Manners of the Mikmakis and Maricheets, Savage Nations, Now Dependant on the Government at Cape Breton*, by Pierre Antoine Simon Maillard. 1758:8-9.

1708 Census Excerpts
Micmac at Port Royal

Paul Cop, 45 [Coppe, Copee, Cope, Emcap, Copk; possibly deriving from *kopit* (archaic *mkobit*), 'beaver']
Cecille, 35
Jean-Baptiste, 10
Thereze, 8
Marie, 5
Margueritte, 1

Grand Claude, 68
Marie, 55
Claude, 21
Joseph, 17
Martin, 15
François, 5
Marie Catherine, 19
René, son of Grand Claude, 23
Marie, 17
Cecille, 1

Jacques Nemecharet, 25 [Amecouret, Amquaret, Anecouaret, Annqualet, Memcharet, Momquaret]
Elisabet, 16

Ambroise Canibechiche, 23 [*kanipekji'j*, 'little Caniba/Kennebec'?; Kinibechcoech]
Catherine, 17
Claude, 1

Estienne Janneperis, 68 [Jeanperis, Jean de Perisse. It may be remotely possible that this name derives from 'Paris'; a Port Royal Micmac, Semcoudech, *ca* 1607, called himself Paris after a visit to that city.]
Anne, his wife, 50
Jean-Baptiste, his son, 23
Guillaume, 19
François, 3
Anne, 35
Margueritte, 16
Marie, 13

François Jeanperis, 27 [Janneperis, Jean de Perisse; this may be the "Francis Jean de Perisse" of Cape Sable, mentioned in the entry for 16 November 1752]
Agnès, his wife, 23
Agnès, his daughter, 5
Marie, 1

Excerpted from "General Census Made in the Month of November 1708, of the Indians of Acadia who reside on the East Coast...," by Père LaChasse. Edward E. Ayer Collection, Ayer MS 751, Newberry Library, Chicago. Translated for this publication by R.H. Whitehead and Bernie Francis.

[This census is one of the few lists of Micmac names ever made, and many of those who appear in these census excerpts will reappear as major figures throughout the rest of this century's documentation. Two years after the census was taken, Port Royal was in the hands of the English. Francis Nicholson, the first British governor of Nova Scotia, led a British expedition against Port Royal (now Annapolis Royal); Subercase, the French commander, surrendered to him on 2 October 1710.]

But if thy great, great, great grandfather made such a figure in the chace [*sic*], what has not thy great, great grandfather done with respect to the beavers, those animals almost men? whose industry he surpassed by his

frequent watchings round their cabbins, by the repeated alarms he would give them several times in one evening, and oblige them thereby to return home, so that he might be sure of the number of those animals he had seen dispersed during the day, having a particular foresight of the spot to which they would come to load their tails with earth, cut down with their teeth such and such trees for the construction of their huts. He had a particular gift of knowing the favorite places of those animals for building them.

Anonymous Micmac orator at a feast, *ca* 1740. In *An Account of the Customs and Manners of the Mikmakis and Maricheets, Savage Nations, Now Dependant on the Government at Cape Breton*, by Pierre Antoine Simon Maillard. 1758:9-10.

1708 Census Excerpts
Micmac at Cape Sable

Paul Tecouenemac, 45 [de Conoumak; possible translation: 'who stays with us']
Marie Agathe, 50
Guillaume, his son, 17
Anthoine, 14
Philipe, 6
Marie, his daughter, 12
Cecille, 1

Mathieu Emieusse, 26 [possibly Mius, a descendant of Philipe Mius d'Entremont, living at Pubnico 1651, married to a Micmac woman]
Madelaine, 20
Joachin, 1

Louis Talgoumatique, 45 [Telgumart, Telgumast, Tideumart, Tudeumart]
Marie Agathe, 30
Michel, his son, 6
Anne, his daughter, 13
Marie Madelaine, 10
Anne, 2

Excerpted from "General Census Made in the Month of November 1708, of the Indians of Acadia who reside on the East Coast…," by Père LaChasse. Edward E. Ayer Collection, Ayer MS 751, Newberry Library, Chicago. Translated for this publication by R.H. Whitehead and Bernie Francis.

But now let us rather speak of your great grandfather, who was so expert at making of snares for moose-deer, martens, and elks. He had particular secrets, absolutely unknown to any but himself, to compel these sorts of creatures to run sooner into his snares than those of any others; and he was accordingly always so well provided with furs, that he was never at a loss to oblige his friends.... Now let us come to your grandfather, who has a thousand and a thousand times regaled the youth of his time with seals. How often in our young days have we greased our hair in his cabbin? How often have we been invited, and even compelled by his friendly violence, to go home with him, whenever we returned with our canoes empty, to be treated with seal, to drink the oil, and anoint ourselves with it? He even pushed his generosity so far, as to give us of the oil to take home with us.

Anonymous Micmac orator at a feast, ca 1740. In *An Account of the Customs and Manners of the Mikmakis and Maricheets, Savage Nations, Now Dependant on the Government at Cape Breton,* by Pierre Antoine Simon Maillard. 1758:10-11.

1708 Census Excerpts
Micmac at La Have and the surrounding area

Leading Family:
Pierre Eptemek, 65
Madelaine, his wife, 66
Anne, his daughter, 17
Catherine, his daughter, 12

Anthoine Ziziquesche, 50 [Iguesche, Ziziguesch, Eziquesich, Gisigash]
Barbe, his wife, 40
François, his son, 22
Claude, 12
Guillaume, 1
Margueritte, 15
Marie, 9
Cecille, 6

Philipe Mieusse, 48 [a descendant of Philipe Mius d'Entremont]
Marie, his wife, 38
Jacques, his son, 20
Pierre, his son, 17
François, his son, 8

Philipe, his son, 5
Françoise, his daughter, 11
Anne, his daughter, 3

Excerpted from "General Census Made in the Month of November 1708, of the Indians of Acadia who reside on the East Coast...," by Père LaChasse. Edward E. Ayer Collection, Ayer MS 751, Newberry Library, Chicago. Translated for this publication by R.H. Whitehead and Bernie Francis.

As to the origin of the name Bemenuit [Peminuit], it is stated it arose in this way. In the early wars of the Micmacs, on one occasion the women of the tribe went away in a canoe, while the men stood to give battle. While the women were thus on their way to the head stream of the Shubenacadie River, one of the Indian women while in the canoe gave birth to a boy child. This child and his descendants were called Bemenuit, which means, in Micmac, 'Born on the way'. They were called Pauls by the English.

Jeremiah Bartlett Alexis [alias Jerry Lonecloud] to Harry Piers, 17 September 1917. Nova Scotia Museum Printed Matter File.

[Jeremiah Bartlett Alexis, who was illiterate, gave himself the name Jerry Lonecloud. Sometimes he and Nova Scotia Museum curator Harry Piers spelled "Lonecloud" as one word, sometimes as two. I have chosen to spell it as one.]

1708 Census Excerpts
Micmac at Minas

Leading Family:
Charles Peminouite, 54 [*pem-*, 'in the process'; *peminuit,* 'born on the way'; Beminuit, Pemminurch, Pemmeenauweet, Pemmenwick, Pominout]
Marie, his wife, 54
René, his son, 15
Madeleine, his daughter, 20
Agnès, his daughter, 18

Anthoine Anecouaret, 30 [Amecouret, Amquaret, Annqualet, Memcharet, Momquaret, Nemecharet]
Catherine, his wife, 22
Jeanbaptiste, his son, 1

Jacques Naucoute, 45 [Necoot, Nicoute, Nocket, Nockwed, Nocout, Nogood, Nokut, Noocot, Nuffcoat, Knockwood]

Marie, his wife, 40
Claude, his son, 13
René, his son, 9
Jacques, his son, 6
Marie, his daughter, 18
Louise, 16
Jeanne, 2

Excerpted from "General Census Made in the Month of November 1708, of the Indians of Acadia who reside on the East Coast...," by Père LaChasse. Edward E. Ayer Collection, Ayer MS 751, Newberry Library, Chicago. Translated for this publication by R.H. Whitehead and Bernie Francis.

But now we are come to your father: there was a man for you. He used to signalize himself in every branch of chace; but especially in the art of shooting the game whether flying or sitting. He never missed his aim. He was particularly admirable for decoying of bustards by his artificial imitations. We are all of us tolerably expert at counterfeiting the cry of those birds; but as to him, he surpassed us in certain inflexions of his voice, that made it impossible to distinguish his cry from that of the birds themselves. He had, besides, a particular way of motion with his body, that at a distance might be taken for the clapping of their wings, insomuch that he has often deceived ourselves, and put us to confusion, as he started out of his hiding-place. As for thyself, I say nothing, I am too full of the good things thou hast feasted me with, to treat on that subject; but I thank thee, and take thee by the hand.... All the praises my tongue is about to utter, have thee for their object. All the steps I am going to take, as I dance lengthwise and breadthwise in thy cabbin, are to prove to thee the gaiety of my heart, and my gratitude.

Anonymous Micmac orator at a feast, *ca* 1740. In *An Account of the Customs and Manners of the Mikmakis and Maricheets, Savage Nations, Now Dependant on the Government at Cape Breton*, by Pierre Antoine Simon Maillard. 1758:11-12.

1708 Census Excerpts
Micmac at Musquodoboit

Leading Family:
Laurent Medagonuitte, 53
Brigide, 39
René, 12
Michael, 1

Jeanne, 16
Marie, 14
Jeanne, 11
Catherine, 9
Therese, 4

Claude petit pas, 45 [a Frenchman]
Marie Thereze, 40
Berthelemy, 21
Paul, 13
Joseph, 9
Isidor, 5
Judie, 15
Marie Louise, 7
Françoise, 2

Orphans:
Jacques, *fils dekacouas* [de Kacouas?], 20

Anthoine arguimeau, 6 [L'kimu, 'he sends'; Alagomartin, Alegemoure, Algamud, Algimault, Algomatin, Alguimou, Alkmou, Argimooch, Argoumatine, Arguimaut, Arguimeau, Argunault, Elgomarddinip, Ulgimoo, etc.]
Michel, his brother, 4

Excerpted from "General Census Made in the Month of November 1708, of the Indians of Acadia who reside on the East Coast...," by Père LaChasse. Edward E. Ayer Collection, Ayer MS 751, Newberry Library, Chicago. Translated for this publication by R.H. Whitehead and Bernie Francis.

Ulgimoo [L'kimu, 'he sends'] was a great magician, and one of his principal sources of magic was the pipe. His store of tobacco would sometimes become exhausted; but his *teomul* ['spirit-helper'], which was in his case Keoonik [Kiunik, the Otter], would go a long distance and bring him any amount he desired. Being a magician, he could hear and see what was going on very far off....

Ulgimoo lived to be an hundred and three years old; he died twice, having come to life after he had been dead all winter; so says the tradition.... It was in the beginning of winter when he died; he had directed his people not to bury him, but to build a high flake and lay him on it. This they did, and all left the place. He had told them to come back the following spring. They did so, and to their astonishment they found him walking about—exhibiting, however, proofs that his death was real, and not a sham. A hungry marten had found the corpse, and had gnawed an ugly-looking hole through one of the old man's cheeks; he still exhibited the gaping wound.

Thomas Boonis to Silas Rand. In *Legends of the Micmacs*, by Silas Rand. 1894:294-297. [The name L'kimu appears in a number of historical documents, spelled variously Alguimou, Arguimeau, Arguimaut, Algamud, Alegemoure, Argimooch, Argoumatine, Ulgimoo, etc.]

1708 Census Excerpts
Micmac at Chignecto

Leading Family:
Françoise arguimeau, 40 [L'kimu, 'he sends'; Alagomartin, Alegemoure, Algamud, Algimault, Algomatin, Alguimou, Alkmou, Argimooch, Argoumatine, Arguimaut, Arguimeau, Argunault, Elgomarddinip, Ulgimoo, etc.]
Catherine, his wife, 35
Jeanne, his daughter, 11

Anthoine arguimeau, 35
Margueritte, 34
Louis, 13
Jean, 9
Jean-Baptiste, 6

Philipe arguimeau, 38
Anne, his wife, 30
Charles, his son, 13
Joseph, 10
Guillaume, 7
Michel, 4
Joseph, 1
Jeanne, his daughter, 5
Françoise, 2

Pierre arguimeau, 90 [born 1618]

Excerpted from "General Census Made in the Month of November 1708, of the Indians of Acadia who reside on the East Coast...," by Père LaChasse. Edward E. Ayer Collection, Ayer MS 751, Newberry Library, Chicago. Translated for this publication by R.H. Whitehead and Bernie Francis.

The day before [L'kimu's second] death, he informed his friends that he would die on the morrow, and that they must bury him; but after one night they must open the grave, and he would come out, and remain with them forever. He gave them a sign by which they would know when to open the grave. The day would be clear, and there would be not even a single cloud to be seen; but from the clear, open sky there would come a peal of thunder just at the time when the spirit would reanimate his clay. But he did not rise; his friends and his tribe preferred to let him remain in his resting-place. They not only did not dig him up, but took special care that he should not be able to get out of his grave, even should he come to life. Hence they dug his grave deep, and piled stones upon him to keep him down. The plan succeeded; he has never risen from the dead.

Thomas Boonis to Silas Rand. In *Legends of the Micmacs,* by Silas Rand. 1894:295-297.

1708 Census Excerpts
Micmac at Cape Breton

Isidore, 52 [Isidorus, Jeddore; We'jitu, 'I found it']
Madelaine, 45
Claude, 19
Philipe, 17
Paul, 1
Louise, 12
Marie, 6

Joseph piguidaouaret, 28 [*pekitaulet,* possible translation 'he carries (something) on his back for a long time'; Piguidaouaret, Pequidalouet, Beguiddavalouet, Peguidalouet, Piquadauduet, Piquid Oulat]
Therese, his wife, 26
Jean, his son, 3
Charles, his son, 1

Jacques Pirouynou [French, Perroneau?], 24
Jeanne, his wife, 19
Hélaine, his daughter, 1

Jean quespougouyden, 56 [*kespukwitn,* literally 'end of the flowing water,' but used to indicate the southern part of Nova Scotia, where this man was apparently from.]
Louise, his wife, 45

Jacques, his son, 9
Marianne, 15
Marie, 6
Françoise Lesprague, 80

Widows:
Marie Cobeguiat, 55 [Cobeguiades]
Genevieve Robert, 47
Louise Despourdre, 55
Agnès Bellille, 23 [Belle Isle]
Magdelaine Robert, 70
Marie, widow of lesprade, 25 [see Lesprague above]
Perinne [?], *veuve du Malouin*, 24

Excerpted from "General Census Made in the Month of November 1708, of the Indians of Acadia who reside on the East Coast ...," by Père LaChasse. Edward E. Ayer Collection, Ayer MS 751, Newberry Library, Chicago. Translated for this publication by R.H. Whitehead and Bernie Francis.

[Seven of these eight women, including Françoise Lesprague, appear to have been the widows, or perhaps the grass-widows, of Frenchmen.]

Wedge-it-doo [We'jitu, Isidore] was a great Indian who died, it is said, at age of 113 years. In his young days he saw a vision, and afterwards became the most powerful person in the tribe [a *kinap*, with great physical strength]. Made the men of his tribe great in athletic sports, so that they won from men of other tribes, in competitions. His camping ground was on eastern side of First Dartmouth Lake, about halfway or so up the lake. [The] name Wedge-it-doo apparently related to Isidore, and the Indians Jeddore were descendants of his. Noel Jeddore of Halifax was his grandson. Joe Cope's father, Peter Cope (born about 1816, died in 1913, aged 97 years), had seen Wedge-it-doo.

Joseph C. Cope to Harry Piers, 14 January 1914. Nova Scotia Museum Printed Matter File.

[If Noel Jeddore was his grandson, his son must have been Ned Jeddore, also called Ned Isidore. The Micmac word *we'jitu* means 'I found it,' which may relate to his vision.]

1716

The Island of Cape Breton, now called Isle Royale, has a circumference of eighty-three leagues. It is inhabited by a tribe of Indians ... under a chief called Isidorus. This man, who is very simply dressed, has the impudence to assert that he and the King of France are comrades and that he suffers the presence of the French on the island only because of the annual gifts he receives.

Chancels de Lagrange. "Voyage Made to Isle Royale or Cape Breton Island in Canada in 1716 Aboard the Frigate *Atalante* Commanded by M. de Courbon St. Leger." In *Revue d'Histoire de l'Amérique Française*. Vol. XIII, No. 3. 1959:424.

There had existed for some time a state of hostility between the Kenebeks and the Micmacs. Two parties of the former, led by two brothers, had come down to Pictou, and had fortified themselves in two blockhouses a little below the mouth of the Pictou River. These blockhouses were constructed of logs, raised up around a vault first dug in the ground. The buildings were covered over, had each a heavy door, and were quite safe fortifications in Indian warfare. About seven miles to the eastward, at Merrigomish, the Micmacs were entrenched in a similar manner. It was some time before there was any fighting; the parties kept a careful eye upon each other, but there was neither friendly intercourse nor actual conflict between them.

Peter Toney [Antoine] to Silas Rand. In *Legends of the Micmacs,* by Silas Rand. 1894:179. ["Kenebek," "Canibat" or "Canniba" was a name given to a band or tribe originally living in the Kennebec River area of Maine. Nominally allied with the French, their war parties apparently sometimes travelled to Louisbourg on Cape Breton Island or to Île St-Jean (Prince Edward Island) to receive annual presents from the French. Opinions are divided about their relationship to modern tribes.]

1716

Apart from the three main fortified posts there are several villages on the island [of Cape Breton], the French population numbering almost three thousand, not counting those who come every day from Acadia, which was ceded to the English in the last peace treaty. Acadia is full of French influences and its new masters fear—with good reason—the close relationship that exists between the indigenous people and the French. The Acadian Indians recently seized a 60-ton barque from them and give no quarter to any English they capture, even though the French have forbidden this since peace was declared: they say the King of France has no business giving them orders.

Chancels de Lagrange. "Voyage Made to Isle Royale or Cape Breton Island in Canada in 1716 Aboard the Frigate *Atalante* Commanded by M. de Courbon St. Leger." In *Revue d'Histoire de l'Amérique Française*. Vol. XIII, No. 3. 1959:427.

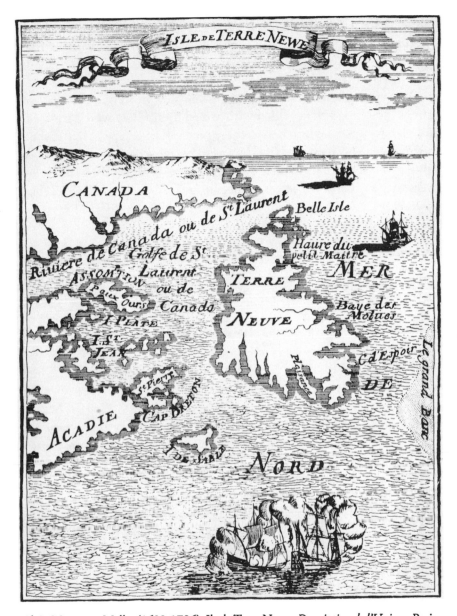

Alain Manesson Mallet (1603-1706). Ile de Terre Newe. *Description de l'Univers*, Paris, 1683.

One night a party of Micmacs went out torching—catching fish by torchlight. They were watched by the Kenebeks, who ascertained that they did not return to their forts after they came back to the shore, but lay down on the bank about midway between the fortifications of the hostile parties. This was too strong a temptation to be resisted; two canoes came upon them, filled with armed men. They were surprised, and all but two were butchered; these made their escape. They rushed to the water and swam for life, but were hotly pursued. They came to a place where a tree had fallen over into the water from the bank; it lay there with a quantity of eelgrass piled up and lodged upon it; there they took refuge, hiding under the eelgrass and under the tree, so that their pursuers missed them in the darkness.

Peter Toney [Antoine] to Silas Rand. In *Legends of the Micmacs*, by Silas Rand. 1894:179.

1716

The Fathers of Charity have established a hospital in each of the three main forts on the island. On the 1st of October we agreed on the date of our departure for Sainte Anne [Port Dauphin], and three Christian savages dressed in bear skins came on board to deliver letters from the Paymaster. They liked the bread, wine and meat we gave them. They were tall, well-proportioned and very thin, with blue streaks on their faces. The next day five more fur-clad savages came to dine on board. They spoke a little French. We gave them brandy and gunpowder....

Chancels de Lagrange. "Voyage Made to Isle Royale or Cape Breton Island in Canada in 1716 Aboard the Frigate *Atalante* Commanded by M. de Courbon St. Leger." In *Revue d'Histoire de l'Amérique Française.* Vol. XIII, No. 3. 1959:429.

After the search had been abandoned, the canoes returned, and the two men came from their hiding-place and hastened home to spread the alarm. Their dead companions had been scalped, and their bodies consumed by fire; the news roused all the warriors, and they resolved to attack the party that had committed the outrage, and avenge it. They had a small vessel lying inside the long bar that makes out at Merrigomish; this was immediately emptied of its ballast, drawn across into the sea, filled with men, arms and ammunition (for it was since the advent of the French), and immediately moved up to the Kenebek ports, where it was run ashore. The party was led by a *kenap* [*kinap*], whose name was Kaktoogo [Kaqtukwaq, 'Thunder']—or, as this name, first rendered into French and then transferred back into Indian, has come down, Toonale (Tonnerre). They ran the vessel ashore, and in his eagerness for the encounter he leaped into the sea, swam ashore, and rushed upon the fort without waiting for his men. Being a mighty *powwow* [*puoin*, 'shaman'], as well as a warrior, he could render himself invisible and invulnerable; and they fell before him....

Having despatched them all, he piled their bodies into the building and set fire to it, thus serving them as they had served his friends. When all was accomplished, his wrath was appeased. He then, at the head of his men, walked up towards the other fort without any hostile display; the Kenebek chief directed his men to open the door and admit them in a peaceable manner. This chief had taken no part in the fray; he had disapproved of the attack upon the torching-party, and had tried to dissuade the others from it. So, when Toonale entered the fort, there was no display of hostility. After their mutual salutations, Toonale dryly remarked, "Our boys have been at play over yonder." "Serves them right!" answered the chief; "I told them not to do as they did, for it would be the death of us all."

Peter Toney [Antoine] to Silas Rand. In *Legends of the Micmacs,* by Silas Rand. 1894:179-182.

1716

On the 17th [of October] I was present at the great banquet given in honour of our allies the savages who had come to receive the usual gift (valued at 4,000 francs) which the King's ship brings over from France every year. They camped near the government administration centre in those big cabins which they put up in a matter of hours: about 300 souls, including women and children. They were regaled with meats, wine, brandy and bread In the open air where they danced and sang the King's praises. Then they were presented with the gift, to wit: four pounds of powder and eight of lead to each man and, to be distributed among them, 25 rifles, 40 white woolen blankets, flannel and lengths of cloth for their women, cauldrons, pots and other cooking utensils. They refused these gifts (which had been reduced to one third) saying they were to be sent back to the King, whom they thanked for having set them on the path to salvation, for having supplied them with missionaries and for having honoured them with his protection. They declared they would repair to the English to buy what they lacked. This was a tacit threat that they could cease their alliance with us and form one with the English. The Governor and principal officers were thus constrained to supplement the gifts to satisfy the discontented chiefs who had been waiting two months for them. One band of savages had travelled eighty leagues from Baie des Chaleurs, which lies in the direction of the Saint Lawrence River, led by Father Michel, a Recollet missionary priest, who has lived among them these last twenty years, eating raw meat like the savages, sleeping in the cold and even fasting when food was scarce. He told me he had not eaten bread in six years. He can scarcely speak French now without intermingling it with Indian words. The savages give him the honour and respect due to a father. At the end of one month he returned to Baie des Chaleurs with his band.

Chancels de Lagrange. "Voyage Made to Isle Royale or Cape Breton Island in Canada in 1716 Aboard the Frigate *Atalante* Commanded by M. de Courbon St. Leger." In *Revue d'Histoire de l'Amérique Française.* Vol. XIII, No. 3. 1959:431.

It is now proposed that they make peace, and live in amity for the future; a feast is made accordingly, and they celebrate it together. After the eating come the games.... In all these games the Micmacs get the victory.... After the games were ended, the Kenebek chief gives the word: "*noogoo elnumook!*" (Now pay the stakes!) A large blanket is spread out to receive them, and the Kenebeks strip themselves of their ornaments and cast them in; the following articles were enumerated by the historian: '*mchoowale* (epaulets), *pugulak* (breastplates), *niskumunul* (brooches), *nasaboodakun* (nose-rings), *nasogwadukunul* (finger-rings), *nasunigunul* (a sort of large collar loaded with ornaments, more like a jacket than a collar), *epelakunul* (hair-binders), *egatepesoon* (garters, sometimes made of silver, as in the present case), *ahgwesunabel* (hat-bands). These articles were piled in, and the blanket filled so full that they could scarcely tie it; then another was put down, and filled as full. After this the Kenebeks returned to their own country; a lasting peace had been concluded, which has never been violated, and probably never will be.

Peter Toney [Antoine] to Silas Rand. In *Legends of the Micmacs,* by Silas Rand. 1894:182.

1716

M. Gaulin, the Saint Sulpice priest, is the Indians' second patriarch, for so the savages style the missionaries among them. He has embraced all their customs, officiates at their weddings, baptisms and burials, celebrates the Mass for them and conducts their prayers every day. He often eats meat and fish without bread, sleeps on the snow, suffers the extreme cold and has also adopted the savages' footwear, which is made from seal skins. He too left with the band to make his way to St. Pierre de Canso.

Chancels de Lagrange. "Voyage Made to Isle Royale or Cape Breton Island in Canada in 1716 Aboard the Frigate *Atalante* Commanded by M. de Courbon St. Leger." In *Revue d'Histoire de l'Amérique Française.* Vol. XIII, No. 3. 1959:429, 431-432.

1716

Among the savages living on the island and nearby there are about 400 men who can bear arms. They are excellent gun handlers. They are a tall olive-skinned people with long black hair. Their women are tall and fat. Their cabins are covered with oil-treated birchbark which they roll up and carry with them in their boats. The fireplace is in the centre and the family sits round it…. The same Isidore is one of their leaders; he speaks French and is a most wily man. His daughters are quite handsome even though they wear the savage dress: that is, their bodies are covered but their arms, legs and thighs are naked.

Miguel is another of their leaders. They are all baptised Christians and use all familiarly—even the Governor, whom they call Father. They are subtile and very adroit to achieve their desire. I myself have met some who show great common sense and argue most soundly.

Chancels de Lagrange. "Voyage Made to Isle Royale or Cape Breton Island in Canada in 1716 Aboard the Frigate *Atalante* Commanded by M. de Courbon St. Leger." In *Revue d'Histoire de l'Amérique Française.* Vol. XIII, No. 3. 1959:432.

1720

Annapolis Royal, May 26

The Chief of this River Indians, who are but few and inconsiderable, among the rest has been with me accompanyed with half a score of others, and desir'd me to resolve him, if the French were to leave this Country, whether the Two Crowns were in alliance, whether I intended to debar them of their religion or disturb them in their traffick; to all which Querys I answer'd to satisfaction, and sent them away in good humour, promising they would be very peaceable while the Union lasted between the Two Crownes.

Governor Richard Phillips to Secretary Craggs, 26 May 1720. In *Selections from the Public Documents of the Province of Nova Scotia,* edited by Thomas Akins. 1869:32-33.

1720

Prudent Robicheau, Junr. aged Twenty four yeares a French Inhabitant of Annapolis Royal being examined upon Oath before His Excellency Richard Phillips Esqr. Captain General &c; & his Majesty's Council at

His Garrison of Annapolis Royal aforesd., the 24th August 1720.

Declares: That this sumer being at St. Peters on Cape Breton, he heard several times among the french there, that the Indians intended some time this summer to fall upon Cansoe and Plunder it.... That this Depon't. sett out from St. Peters on the 9th Instant in a Shallop haveing Michael richards, Father Vincent a Popish Priest of Shignecto & several French passengers on board bound there, the next day being off the gutt of Cansoe. Several Indian Squawes came on board & informed them that the Indians had taken Cansoe, at the same time they heard several gunns which they Judged to be there. Sometime after on the same day being in the gutt aforesaid they saw a Shallop following them; which in a little time came up haveing about fourteen or fifteen Indians on board more or less who informed them that they with fifty five or sixty five Indians had taken Cansoe and plunder'd it and forc't all the English People to retire on board their Vessels, that several of the Indians were for burning two ships rideing there but that the chief of the Indians from Cape Breton were against it. That they had killed one English man & wounded four. This Depon't. saith he was on board the Indian Shallop & knew several of the Indians on board, who belonged to Menis the other to Cape Breton & thereabouts.... This Depon't. saith the two shallops kept compa[ny] about two houres then parted the Indians for Cobequet & so for Menis while they made the best of their way for Chignecto.

Gustave Lanctot. *Documents Relating to Currency, Exchange and Finance in Nova Scotia ... 1675-1758*. 1933:132-133.

ca 1710-1730

Official correspondence of Louisbourg, that mighty fortress which the French built on Micmac lands, refers to at least eighty fishing and trading vessels captured by the Indians during the period 1713-1760, and this is by no means complete. Antoine Gaulin, a Canadian-born missionary who was with the Micmac during this period, claimed with pride in 1718 that his Indians in their little canoes had taken more than 20 English coastal vessels. In 1727 about 30 Indians took a 70-ton schooner at Port aux Basques, Newfoundland, and sailed it to Mirliquèche on Bras d'Or Lake in Cape Breton.... The Micmac liked to cruise in their captured ships before abandoning or ransoming them, sometimes forcing their prisoners to serve as crew....

Most of this sea activity by the Micmac against the English seems to have occurred between 1710 and 1730, followed by a comparative calm for two decades, with another period of activity of lesser proportions in the fifties. A peak was reached in 1722, when French officials reported Indians taking 20 to 25 vessels in the Bay of Fundy and off the coast of Acadia.

The English response to this was to formally declare war on the Micmac, a war which lasted from 1722 until 1726. When the New Englanders sent out two sloops each armed with 60 men, the Micmac responded by sending out a vessel carrying 15 Indians to attack one of them. The battle lasted for two hours, with the Micmac finally saving themselves by swimming ashore, leaving five dead behind them. The English put the heads of the dead men up on pickets at Canso.

Olive Dickason. "Sea Raiders of Acadia." In *Tawow, Canadian Indian Cultural Magazine*, Vol. 5, No. 2. 1976:11.

1723

In 1723 there was a very general war commenced by all the tribes in this quarter, the Richibucto [band of Micmac, or perhaps the Maliseet are meant], the Micmacs, and Penobscots. In the latter part of July they surprised Canso and other harbours near to it, and took 16 or 17 sail of fishing vessels, all belonging to Massachusetts. Governor Philips happened to be at Canso, and caused two sloops to be manned, partly with volunteer sailors from merchants' vessels, which were loading with fish, and sent them, under the command [of] John Elliot of Boston, and John Robinson of Cape Ann, in quest of the enemy. Eliot [*sic*], as he was ranging the coast, espied seven vessels in a harbour, called Winnepaug, and concealed all his men, except four or five, until he came near to one of the vessels which had about 40 Indians aboard, who were in expectation of another prize falling into their hands. As soon as he was within hearing, they hoisted their pennants, and called out, "Strike, English dogs, and come aboard, for you are all prisoners." Elliot answered, that he would make all the haste he could. Finding he made no attempt to escape, they began to fear they had caught a Tartar, and cut their cable, with intent to run ashore, but he was too quick for them, and immediately boarded them. For about half an hour, they made a brave resistance, but at length, some of them jumping into the hold, Eliot [*sic*] threw his hand grenadoes after them, which made such havock, that all which remained alive took to the water, where they were a fair mark for the English shot. From this or a like action, probably took rise, a common

95

expression among English soldiers, and sometimes English hunters, who, when they had killed an Indian, made their boast of having killed a black duck. Five only reached the shore.

Anonymous. *A General Description of Nova Scotia.* 1825:46-47.

1731

4 P.M. Friday [18 June]: An Indian on shore seeing us pass by—He came off in his Canoe to us, with his Squaw, 2 Papouses & Dogg, as he was wretchedly poor, we gave him 3 or 4 Biskets, a little Tobacco & pipes.

Robert Hale. "Journal of an Expedition to Nova Scotia, 1731." In *Report of the Board of Trustees of the Public Archives of Nova Scotia for the Year 1968.* Appendix B:20.

A ship taken by Micmacs off Indian Point, head of St. Margaret's Bay. Micmac Indian, a famous one, called El-go-mard-dinip [L'kimu, Alagomartine, Algomatin] (whom Lone Cloud thinks was Andrew Hadley Martin, a chief of Annapolis district), was once with Indians camped at Indian Point, near French Village, head of St. Margaret's Bay. A Spanish ship came in and anchored, and the crew all went ashore. The Indians under the above-named chief (El-go-mard-dinip) fell on the crew and killed every one of them. Then they took gold out of the vessel, and set it on fire in the Bay, & it drifted out in flames. The gold the Indians buried in a hollow or cleft in a barren granite island close to Indian Point (but not the island at the Point, and not the lighthouse island, Cr[oucher's?]}. It is said from Ingrahamport, a cleft can be seen in the granite rock of one of the islands off there.

Jeremiah Bartlett Alexis [alias Jerry Lonecloud] to Harry Piers, 24 July 1916. Nova Scotia Museum Printed Matter File. "This was told to Lone Cloud years ago in United States by an old woman who was a descendant of one of the Indians concerned in this affair. He was afterwards also told the same tale by an old Indian man in Nova Scotia." (Harry Piers)

1732

25th of July: On Thursday evening the 13th instant there came into René LeBlanc's House, at Menis [Minas], three Indians vizt. Jacques son to Winaguadishnick named Jacques, Antoin, his brother, and Andress their cousin, all living upon Piziquit River [Avon River], who in a most villanous manner, and approbrious language, insulted the said René LeBlanc and Peter his brother, saying that all the LeBlancs were dogs, and villains, except François, and that as for René, he had a dagger (putting his hand at the same time under his coat where tis supposed the dagger hung) for him, for that he was going to build a Fort for the English (Mr. Cottnam and myself present) when I assured them, there was no such thing or order given at present, but supposed the King of Great Britain thought it convenient to build a fort there, who had any thing to say against it; one of them answered that he would not suffer it, for that he was King of that Country, for that King George had conquered Annapolis, but not Menis; and in a most insolent manner ordered Mr. Cottnam and me to be gone....

Henry Cope, deposition to Major Paul Mascarene and Council at Annapolis Royal. In *Selections from the Public Documents of the Province of Nova Scotia,* edited by Thomas Akins. 1869:97-98.

1736

Sorry to have an unpleasant reason for writing. Is informed that the Brigt. "Baltimore", Andrew Buckler, merchant, being owner, and Richard White master, sailed from Dublin on Oct. 7th, 1735, with 18 persons on board for Annapolis, Maryland. Driven out of her course, she fell in with "the Tusketts" (near to Pobomcoup by Cape Sables) they got all safe through meer providence into a Harbour Called Tibogue the 5th day of December last where they all Died, Except two Sailors & a Woman who remained on Board till the 4th of April last; The day whereon Anthony Telgumart [Talgoumatique], a Cape Sable Indian, with his Wife, His Brother Anastase & two Children went on Board & Carryed the unfortunate Gentlewoman along with them after having Robbed her, as she Saith....

Governor Lawrence Armstrong to the Governor of Cape Breton, Annapolis Royal, 17 May 1736. In *A Calendar of Two Letter-Books and One Commission-Book in the Possession of the Government of Nova Scotia, 1713-1741,* edited by Archibald MacMechan. [1900]:99. [The above is partly in the Governor's words, and partly MacMechan's paraphrase; MacMechan does not distinguish between the two. The woman was later discovered to be one of a shipload of convicts who apparently murdered the ship's crew, beached the ship, and vanished; her account of robbery and kidnapping by the Indians was nothing but a fabrication. "The story told by the woman was confused and contradictory, and little doubt was entertained that she had been deeply involved in the guilt; but it was satisfactorily proved by Mr. Dontremont {d'Entremont} that neither the French nor the Indians had been concerned in it." (Thomas Chandler Haliburton. *An Historical and Statistical Account of Nova Scotia.* 1829:106)]

1737

At a Council held by order of the Honble Lieut Governor Lawrence Armstrong at his own house in His Majesty's Garrison of Annapolis Royal on Friday the 10th June 1737. A letter from Stephen Jones, master of the sloop *Friend's Adventure*, dated from Menis the 4 June 1737, setting forth his having been robbed and plundered by some Indians of that place while he was peacefully trading in Piziquite River [Avon River] that they boarded his vessel on the first instant about midnight and forced him to come to sail and carry his vessel down that river and that on their arrival at Cape Tendue in the way to Coboquite they robbed him of all his English goods, silver money &c to the value of £800—Threatening his life by cocking and presenting their fire arms to his breast—that the names of the said Indians were Thorna [Thomas] their chief, Claude Nicoute [Naucout, Nocoot, Knockwood, etc.], François Nicoute, Biscaroon [Biskerone] and his son Paule, Bartlemy the Chief's wife's Son, Jacques Ashe [Sake'j, Jacquesh, Jaque Hishe, Jack Cash] and his son with several others, who divided with them as upon file.... Gregorie Biscaroon's Son and Honik [this must be a misspelling] the Chief was not on Board but the said Jones was Informed it was done by his Order & also that he assisted in dividing the Plunder. Signed Stephen Jones, Nova Scotia, June 8, 1737. Sworn the 18th June 1737, before the Honble the Lieut Gov, & Council, Otho Hamilton, Secty.

C. Bruce Fergusson, ed. *Minutes of His Majesty's Council at Annapolis Royal, 1736-1749.* 1967:14-17.

This nation counts its years by the winters. When they ask a man how old he is, they say, "How many winters have gone over thy head?" Their months are lunar, and they calculate their time by them. When we would say, "I shall be six weeks on my journey"; they express it by, "I shall be a moon and a half on it." Before *we* knew them, it was common to see amongst them, persons of both sexes of a hundred and forty, or a hundred and fifty years of age. But these examples of longevity are grown much more rare.

Pierre Antoine Simon Maillard. *An Account of the Customs and Manners of the Mikmakis and Maricheets, Savage Nations, Now Dependant on the Government at Cape Breton.* 1758:48-49.

ca 1740-1745

Fifteen years ago I was on the Isle St. Jean [Prince Edward Island], about sixty leagues from Isle Royale, to instruct the savages who had gathered there in great numbers. I met a certain Arguimaut [L'kimu], an old Micmac shaman who was there with his whole family as well as several other old men who had recently been baptised but who had not yet made their first communion.... Arguimaut the old shaman [spoke], helped by the other old men who had come to his wigwam on purpose to see me, because I was a stranger—new to them, and to answer my questions, because they love being asked questions.

He began thus: "Father, what does the Prayer of your King, which is your own Prayer, and which is now ours, too, require of us? Does your Prayer really come from on high? I think that our Father, the King, is not a man, but more than a man, that he is much above you and us. We are led to think this by the way in which all the people who come here on His behalf speak of Him."

I stopped him there and said, "Listen, my son, it is late. The sun has set. I shall wait till tomorrow to answer your questions. Gather as many of the old men as you know; have them meet here before midday immediately after Mass and then we can all talk together. But before our discussion it is fitting that we should all eat together. That is why I told the interpreter Barthelémi Petit [Petit pas, son of Claude Petit pas] here, to tell the young men of your village this evening to go and bring back from Port La Joie three minots of corn, a quintal of flour, forty pounds of pork, and ten jars of molasses."

"You do things very well, Father," he said, interrupting me. "But add the crowning touch by giving at least all the men one or two little drinks of brandy. You have no idea how grateful we would be."

I replied that they would get no brandy, but that I would be delighted to give each of them one generous drink of wine, but no more.

Pierre Antoine Simon Maillard. "Lettre à Madame de Drucourt," n.d. Translated for this publication by Margaret Anne Hamelin. In *Les Soirées Canadiennes*. 1863:299, 310. [Abbé Pierre Antoine Simon Maillard was sent to Cape Breton in 1735 by the Society of Foreign Missions in Paris; he learnt the Micmac language and was much loved by his Micmac and French parishioners. He died in Halifax, a pensioner of the British government, in 1762.]

He praises the master of the feast, who has so well regaled him and all the company. He compares him to a tree, whose large and strong roots afford nourishment to a number of small shrubs; or to a salutary medicinal herb, found accidentally by such as frequent the lakes in their canoes. Some I have heard, who, in their winter-feasts, compared him to the turpentine-tree, that never fails of yielding its sap and gummy distillation in all seasons: others to those temperate and mild days, which are sometimes seen in the midst of the severest winter.

Pierre Antoine Simon Maillard. *An Account of the Customs and Manners of the Mikmakis and Maricheets, Savage Nations, Now Dependant on the Government at Cape Breton.* 1758:7-8.

[Maillard is speaking of a Micmac orator.]

1742

At a Council Held by order of the Honble Paul Mascarene Esq President of His Majestys Council for Nova Scotia and Commander in Chief of His Majestys said Province for the time being On Friday The 9th April 1742 at ten o'clock A.M. His Honr acquainted the Board that as Mr. Trefry Master of a Trading Vessell was Returned hither from the Grand Pré at Mines [Minas] and Reporting that he had been Robbed by a number of Indians and Otherwise very Ill Used by the said Indians who surprised his Sloop and Cut her Cables; and as he had no Anchors Desired the Loan of the Anchors that Belong'd to the Brigt *Baltimore* that was Some time ago Brought hither from Tibogue and had Lain so long under the fort for Want of a Claimer.... Then his Honor the President Acquainted the Board that he had Received Some Letters from Mines vizt from Messrs Bourg and Mangeant and two of the chief Captains of the Indians Informing him that the Inhabitants of that Place as well as the said two Indians Missing Trefrys Sloop but finding her Anchors & Cables were thereupon much surprised & suspecting that he had been Taken by some Indians They Thereupon Agreed to Send Out some Canoes in Search of them But not finding them Mr. Bourg fitted out a small Vessell, and being accompanied with Mr. Mangeant, The Deputies of the Grand Pre Bujeau & Bourg Together with about Sixteen more men They had the Good fortune to meet with and had Taken from them Part of the Goods They had Robb'd Whereupon it was Judged Necessary to signify to Mr. Bourg That his Honour and the Gentlemen of The Council are Well Satisfied with the Behaviour of The Inhabitants and also With the Good Intention of these Honest and Well minded Indians.... the Master resolving to return to Mines It was Agreed That his Honour the President should Write to the Deputys—The Indian Missionary and also to the two Indian Captains, vizt Jaques Momquaret [Jacques Nemecharet, Amquaret] and Thomas Wuito [Ouytau].... Signed P. Mascarene.

C. Bruce Fergusson, ed. *Minutes of His Majesty's Council at Annapolis Royal, 1736-1749.* 1967:37-39.

ca 1740-1750

By all accounts, too, their populousness is greatly decreased. Some imagine this is owing to that inveterate animosity, with which these so many petty nations were continually laboring one another's destruction and extirpation. Others impute it to the introduction by the Europeans, of the vice of drunkeness, and.... not improbably too, numbers impatient of the encroachments of the Europeans on their country, and dreading the consequences of them to their liberty, for which they have a passionate attachment, and incapable of reconciling or assimilating their customs and manners to ours, have chosen, to withdraw further into the western recesses of the continent, at a distance impenetrable to our approach.

But which ever of these conjectures is the truest, or whether or not all of these causes have respectively concurred, in a lesser or greater degree, the fact is certain, that all these northern countries are considerably thinned of their natives, since the first discovery of them by the Europeans.

Pierre Antoine Simon Maillard. *An Account of the Customs and Manners of the Mikmakis and Maricheets, Savage Nations, Now Dependant on the Government at Cape Breton.* 1758:49-50.

[Diseases introduced by Europeans, to which the indigenous peoples had no immunity, were among the greatest factors contributing to Micmac deaths. Epidemics of typhus and smallpox and the continued ravages of tuberculosis took an enormous toll.]

1744

Fryday the 4th of May 1744, at Ten O'Clock A.M.

Being Mett according to Adjournment the Same Members Present. His Honour the President Acquainted the Board That he had Receiv'd Two Letters by one Antoine Gilbert alias "Clearemont" To witt one from Mr. Alexr Bourg and one from the Indians at Mines Representing Their Great Concern for the murder of an English Crew on the Eastern Coast Committed by Six of the Chickinakady [Shubenacadie] Indians and Referring his Honour to said Clearemont for a more Particular Account.... Antoine Gilbert alias Clearemont, from Louisbourg Winter'd last fall at the Grand Pre of Mines from whence he Return'd to the Eastern coast about Easter to see in what Condition The Effects he had Left There were in, That at Theodore [Jeddore] he mett with six Indians Belonging to Chickabenakady Tribe, of whome the Chief Called Renne Madogonouit [René Medagonuitte] was one and Told him, The said Clearemont, That they had Taken an English Vessell, whereof the

101

Masters Name was Rich or Ridge "Belonging to one Tasker", And that They had killed the whole Equipage Except a Boy, the Number killed being five and that the said Chief Told that he Took out his Commission and said to the Rest That were with him, That his Commission Order'd him to kill the Englishmen. Whereupon They Immediately fell upon Them and put Them to Death that the Boy who speaks french Told him to the Same purpose what the Chief and the other Savages had Done, And That he had Engrav'd upon a stone an account of what had Pass'd and Befallen him and the Vessell, that such English as might Come There might know their fate which the Indians suspecting They Broke the Stone in Pieces and Threw it into the sea or River That being Thus Inform'd he made what Dispatch he could to Inform the Government here and Says That if the Government will Instruct and Employ him he Doubts not of Recovering the Boy, and with the Assistance of the other Indians, who are much Enraged with the aforesaid Actors and to Whom he is Very well known Haveing Traded Amongst them for several years he will Bring the said Chief and these Others That were with him, Either to This place or to Canso as he may be Order'd and Directed, And he further Declares That the six Indians which committed the murder were the above Named, Renne Madogonouit and his son in Law Bernard Bernard and LaMartier, and his Two sons Which being "Again" interpreted to him in french he sign'd the Same....

C. Bruce Fergusson, ed. *Minutes of His Majesty's Council at Annapolis Royal, 1736-1749.* 1967:44-46.

1744

In 1744, towards the end of October, Mr. Gorrhon [John Gorham], commanding a detachment of the English troops, sent to observe the retreat the French and savages were making from before Port Royal (Annapolis) in Acadia (Nova Scotia): this detachment having found two huts of the Mickmaki-savages, in a remote corner, in which there were five women and three children, (two of the women were big with child), ransacked, pillaged, and burnt the two huts, and massacred the five women and three children. It is to be observed, that the two pregnant women were found with their bellies ripped open. An action which these savages cannot forget, especially as at that time they made fair war with the English. They have always looked on this deed as a singular mark of the most unheard-of cruelty.

Anonymous [possibly Thomas Pichon]. In *An Account of the Customs and Manners of the*

Mikmakis and Maricheets, Savage Nations, Now Dependant on the Government at Cape Breton, by Pierre Antoine Simon Maillard. 1758:62-63.

1744

... an arm'd Brigantine and a Sloop bringing fifty Indians or Rangers of woods arriv'd from Boston.... a wild Indian come with the Rangers and left behind [while out gathering firewood], straggled out too farr, was seiz'd [by the Micmac] and carried off by the Ennemy....

The Company of [Mohawk] Indians or wood Rangers come last from Boston have prov'd of great service to this Place, they fell soon after their arrival on a family of Indians, kill'd some and scatter'd the rest and by their excursions they have kept off the Indian Ennemy who in small partys rov'd continually about us, which hindred the Inhabitants from supplying of us with fire wood, materials and other necessarys we wanted. As our regular Troops are not us'd to that way of annoying the Enemy, it would be a great advantage to this Place if such a Company could be establish'd here in time of Warr....

Governor Paul Mascarene to Governor Shirley of Massachusetts, Annapolis Royal, December 1744. In *Selections from the Public Documents of the Province of Nova Scotia,* edited by Thomas Akins. 1869:146,149.

1744-1745

Five months before this action [see previous entry], one named Danas, or David [David Donahoe], an English privateer, having treacherously hoisted French colors in the Streights of Fronsac, by means of a French deserter he had with him, decoyed on board his vessel the chief of the savages of Cape-Breton, called James Padanuque [Jacques Padanuques, Padanke], with his whole family, whom he carried to Boston, where he was clapped into a dungeon the instant he was landed; from which he was only taken out to stifle him on board of a vessel, in which they pretended to return him safe to Cape Breton. His son, at that time a boy of eight years of age, they will absolutely not release; though, since their detention of that young savage, they have frequently had prisoners sent back to them, without ransom, on condition of restoring the young man to his country: but though they accepted the condition, they never complied with it.

In the month of July 1745, the same Danas, with the same success, employed the same decoy on a savage-family, which could not get out of their hands, but by escaping one night from their prisons.

About the same time one named Bartholomew Petitpas, an appointed savage-linguist, was carried away prisoner to Boston. The savages have several times demanded him in exchange for English prisoners they then had in their hands, of whom two were officers, to whom they gave their liberty, on condition of the Bostoners returning of Petitpas; whom, however, they not only kept prisoner, but afterwards put to death.

Anonymous [possibly Thomas Pichon]. In *An Account of the Customs and Manners of the Mikmakis and Maricheets, Savage Nations, Now Dependant on the Government at Cape Breton,* by Pierre Antoine Simon Maillard. 1758:63-65.

[See B.L. Balcombe, "Micmacs at Louisbourg: A Training Manual for Animators." (unpublished MS, Canadian Parks Service, 1979:35) Balcombe has identified Danas with the privateer David Donahoe, and written about Jacques Padanuques, who appears in a French census of the period as Jacques Padanke.]

1745

Another letter from the inhabitants of Grand Prée, river Canard and Pizziquid [Avon River], in conjunction, assuring him of their intention to continue faithful subjects ... they have a favor to ask, having learnt by indirect means that several armed vessels were arrived from New England, and that they had pressed by violence several inhabitants of Annapolis Royal to go against the Indians and serve them as pilots, and hearing they were coming up the Bay to do the same, and to destroy all the inhabitants that had any Indian blood in them, and scalp them, that as there was a great number of Mulattoes amongst them, who had taken the Oath, and who were allied to the greatest families, it had caused a terrible alarm, which made many put themselves on their guard, being very much frightened, for which reason all the inhabitants being assembled of each district, had sent to him, to submit themselves to his mercy, and to represent that in case they were obliged to make any Sorties or go against the Indians, that barbarous and inhuman nation would assassinate them every day, while they were at their work and separated from one another without being able to have any succour from the Government as it was so remote, which they had well foreseen when they reserved in taking the Oath of fidelity a dispensation from every thing that related to war; the favor therefore that they demand is to know whether the people of Boston have a right to force them, and expose them to such danger.

Governor Paul Mascarene, "at a Council held by order of the Honble. Paul Mascarene, Esq., President and Commander in Chief &c., at his own house in the fort of Annapolis

Royal on Friday the 4th of January 1745." In *Selections from the Public Documents of the Province of Nova Scotia*, edited by Thomas Akins. 1869:153-154.

Another of my tasks is to encourage them to hunt well during the season so that they can pay off their debts, clothe their women and children and, finally, gain some credit. It is enough among their people to be a good hunter and to pay off one's debts well to merit the name of *virtuosus*.... It is just that, to their way of thinking, to be a good hunter and to be meticulous in paying one's debts is the greatest, finest and highest ideal. I have often said, in conversation and in my sermons, "Do you really think that all merit should be subject to that criterion? Do you truly believe that all virtues are inferior to that which you recognize in the good hunter and debt-payer?" "Yes," they reply. "He represents what is best among our people. He represents, among us on earth, what a savage must of necessity be. What is he without it? Unworthy of the name, unworthy to be who he is, and more contemptible than the least of our women. If we were all like our ancestors in this respect, why, Father, you would see how happy and peaceful the life of all savages would be. We would never lack for food and clothing. And we would have enough furs to pay for all the supplies, materials, etc., we borrow every autumn. We would be better able to help those among us who can no longer range the forests or manage a canoe, either because of their old age or because of some other impediment. You must understand, Father, that he who truly contributes to our well-being here on earth is the man who above all deserves our highest respect. We agree with you that all the virtues that flow from prayer are most commendable in themselves, and that they should be preferred above the other. But you will note that they are the main adornment of the soul of the one praying, and that they serve to enhance his well-being in the other life. These virtues are of a different order altogether; let us not compare them to the other."

Pierre Antoine Simon Maillard. "Lettre à Madame de Drucourt," n.d. In *Les Soirées Canadiennes*. 1863:297-298. Translated for this publication by Margaret Anne Hamelin.

1745

The same year, 1745, several bodies of the savages, deceased, and buried at Port Tholouze, were dug up again by the Bostoners, and thrown into the fire. The burying-place of the savages was demolished, and all the crosses, planted on the graves, broke into a thousand pieces.

Anonymous [possibly Thomas Pichon]. In *An Account of the Customs and Manners of the Mikmakis and Maricheets, Savage Nations, Now Dependant on the Government at Cape Breton,* by Pierre Antoine Simon Maillard. 1758:66.

1746

Extract of a letter, Cape Breton [*sic*], October 3:

"I am sorry I lost the first opportunity of writing from this place, which is called St. John's [New Brunswick]. Capt. Scott brought us hither, and immediately upon landing our men we met with a terrible misfortune, for whilst they were mowing grass to make hay for a few cattle we had procured, a party of Indians came out of the woods, destroyed and took all our men except three, who saved themselves by swimming, and one woman, who was murdered in the sight of her husband. These wild people are encouraged by the French to these desperate undertakings, by a reward for what they call scalping the English. (Scalping is cutting the skin from the eyebrows round the head and peeling it off, and the French give them a reward of three pounds sterling for each scalp.) We lost sixty head of oxen and milch cows, thirty calves, two hundred sheep, fifty horses, ninety pigs, seven swivel guns mounted on timber, two hundred cartridges of grape shot, thirty stand of small arms, and ammunition in proportion, twenty-seven soldiers, and seven sailors. When the Indians made their first appearance, Capt. Scott was that moment going on shore, but was prevented by their fire, by which he and some ... of us escaped being massacred. A flag of truce was sent by the French to Governor Knowles, that he might redeem such as were wounded and taken prisoners; upon which Capt. Scott was sent on a second command, but is not yet returned."

Anonymous settler. In *Documents Relating to Currency, Exchange and Finance in Nova Scotia ... 1675-1758,* by Gustave Lanctot. 1933:248.

1746

Here is the story of a partly forgotten naval disaster suffered by a powerful French Armada on the high seas, and in the unfortified harbor of Halifax three years before its settlement when it was still known as "Chebucto." An immense fleet under the command of Admiral Jean-Baptiste d'Anville [Jean-Baptiste Louis Frédéric Roye de la Rochefoucauld d'Anville et de Roncy] set sail from France in the summer of 1746 with the intention of re-taking Louisbourg from an amateur New England garrison, and then of proceeding towards Boston to consign it to flames in retaliation for the capture of strategic Louisbourg during the preceeding year.

The whole undertaking was a calamitous failure, because in addition to storms dispersing the ill-starred squadron, a fatal disease infested the men, causing an alarming number of them to die at sea and also on shore in this harbor of Chebucto....

The weather during that fateful autumn of 1746 was very cold and rainy in this neighborhood. Records of those in charge show that the numbers of sick and dying in the tents at French Landing and on the ships continued to increase daily.... All the while the epidemic continued to spread in the camp. The Micmac Indians, who traditionally were settled in the shelter of Birch Cove stream, mingled with the sick and wore the clothes of the victims. As a consequence they also became so infected with the malady that about one-third of their tribe is said to have perished.

John Patrick Martin. *Our Storied Harbour, the Haven of Halifax.* 1948:1,18.

Al-e-soo-a-way-ga-deek, which means 'At the place of measles,' is the Micmac Indian name for the place near the old tannery, Fairview, where the Indians who were camped there took "measles" (or some fatal disease) from the French; and then the Indians died like flies, and were buried on the right hand side of the brook (going up the brook) a little below a small pond or stream back of the site of Forrest's Tannery at Fairview, Bedford Basin, near Halifax. Mounds could be seen years ago where the Indians were buried. They did not camp there again. Said to have been about a couple of hundred years ago. It was "not the place where the French were buried."

This name, and account [came] from a very old Indian, now about 89 years of age, now of Springhill, N.S., who was familiar with the spot & said he could find it. He told it to Jerry Lonecloud who told it to H. Piers, 15 March 1922. This must have referred to the time when d'Anville's men had fever there in 1746 and the Indians died from it.

Harry Piers. Unpublished notes, 15 March 1922. Nova Scotia Museum Printed Matter File.

The Indians were attacked by [the same] disease which affected d'Anville's men in 1746, while the Indians were encamped on a stream which flowed to Forrest's Tannery, to the westward of Fairview, near Halifax, N.S. Lonecloud says the Indians called the disease Hol-lo-sool, 'Black Measles' (Rand [in his *Micmac-English Dictionary*] gives Aloosool as Micmac for measles). And the place was afterwards known as Hol-lo-sool ou-way-ga-deek, 'at the place where black measles were,' or 'the place where black measles occurred.' He says it was a very deadly disease. They died so rapidly the French & Indians put dead bodies in a little pond on the stream. The Indians were infected from the French who landed [with] this disease, he says. There was a second smaller burying-ground about 150 yards north of the larger one.

Jeremiah Bartlett Alexis [alias Jerry Lonecloud] to Harry Piers, 16 September 1929. Nova Scotia Museum Printed Matter File.

[Lonecloud had got this information from a "very old Indian."]

1746

No time was fixed for their departure, for the mortality among the people still continued, and they had buried 1130 since the formation of the encampment. The Indians, who flocked thither in great numbers for supplies of arms, ammunition and clothing, took the infection, which spread with such rapidity, that it destroyed more than one third of the whole tribe of Micmacs.

Thomas Chandler Haliburton. *An Historical and Statistical Account of Nova Scotia.* 1829, I:129.

Peter Al-a-go-martin [L'kimu, Algomartin, Elgomardinip, Elgomartin], a chief from Milton; he was at French Landing to meet the French fleet in 1746. He went back [to Milton] and told about the fever. He was killed (it is not known whether by whites or Indians) and thrown into Milton Pond, for fear he would get the disease and spread it.

Jeremiah Bartlett Alexis [alias Jerry Lonecloud] to Harry Piers, 2 October 1929. Nova Scotia Museum Printed Matter File.

1746

In 1746, some stuffs that the savages had bought of the English, who then traded in the bay of Megagouetch at Beau-bassin, there being at that time a great scarcity of goods over all the country, were found to be *poisoned,* so that more than two hundred savages of both sexes perished thereby.

Anonymous [possibly Thomas Pichon]. In *An Account of the Customs and Manners of the Mikmakis and Maricheets, Savage Nations, Now Dependant on the Government at Cape Breton,* by Pierre Antoine Simon Maillard. 1758:66-67.

Duc [was] a dog owned by Joe Copee [Cope], a Micmac Indian who lived at Indian Orchard at the head of the tide on or near the farm now owned by John Devenny of Windsor Forks. The Indian had rescued the dog from the ill-fated French fleet of the Duc d'Anville which was forced into Chebucto Harbour (Halifax) in the fall of 1746. The dog was appropriately named Duc and taken back to the Indian camp at the Pisiguit River. Near Joe Copee's camp at the fording place in the river there was a family named Labrador and Duc soon became fast friends with the three children in the family.

The Labrador family lived on a point of land which was almost surrounded by the river. One winter's day the tide rose to an unusual height and the water and ice completely surrounded the Labrador farm. It was soon realized that the point of land was in danger of breaking from the shore and drifting out on the turn of the tide. The inhabitants of the area collected nearby but no one wished to risk taking a canoe into the dangerous tidal waters.

At length, Joe Copee instructed Duc to swim across the icy water to the stranded family. The dog soon returned with the youngest child tied to his back. Duc returned twice more and the two other children were carried across the channel in the same manner. Joe Copee then dispatched Duc with one end of a rope and when the dog arrived on the opposite shore, Paul Labrador tied the rope to a toboggan and his wife was pulled across to safety. In a similar manner Paul Labrador was brought ashore. The news of the rescue of the Labrador family by Joe Copee's dog, Duc, became well known throughout the Acadian country and the legend has been told and retold many times.

Rev. W.B. Bezanson. *Stories of Acadia*. 1933:16-24.

1749

The necessity of a permanent British settlement and Military Station on the Atlantic Coast of the Peninsula, had long been considered the only effectual means of preserving British authority, as well as for the protection of the coast fishing, which, at this time, was deemed of paramount importance to British interests. But lately the continual breaches of neutrality on the part of the French, together with the loss of Louisburg, under the Treaty of Aix-la-Chapelle, in October, 1748, rendered such an establishment indispensibly necessary to the support of the British Crown in Nova Scotia. Advertisement soon appeared under the sanction of His Majesty's authority, "holding out proper encouragement to officers and private men lately discharged from the Army and Navy, to settle in Nova Scotia...." The encouragements appeared so inviting, that in a short time 1176 settlers, with their families, were found to volunteer....

Thomas Akins. *History of Halifax City*. 1973:4, 7.

[When the Micmac men are drinking] some of this elite group who can still speak (there are always some orators among them, particularly on these occasions) stand in front of the Priest and speak thus to him: "You, you are from heaven and we, we are from the earth. You are an angel and we are but men. You are our Priest, made to instruct us, and we are made to listen to you. You are from heaven, but you are nevertheless a man like us, we know. But you are from heaven because He Who made you a Priest truly is from heaven. Heaven is His home and the earth is our home. But you, too, are on earth, and you will leave it just as we will leave it, by dying. And yet you are from heaven, we can see it in the horror and disgust you feel for our amusements. In a word, you are not made to act and think like us. Does one live in heaven as one lives down here? No. You are an angel; how could you possibly adjust to our way of life? How could you consort with women? How would you set about reproducing yourself by them so as to leave behind you a living breathing image of yourself? But where is your power for doing this? Have you not told us that angels do not have bodies? Have you not told us that among these angel people there is no male and no female? They are therefore unable to reproduce themselves, but on the other hand, they do not know death. What need, then, do they have for generating organs?

"Ah, God is wise! We men down here die without dying through living beings who come out of us, and in whom we live, after having seemed to disappear. Now, you are an angel; you don't have a body. You are not arranged in the same way as we men are so that you could play your part with whichever slave woman from among the ones you see here who pleased you most. You are the Priest. You baptize, you say Mass, you can cleanse whomever confesses to you that he is sunk in the mire of sin: what great power you have! You know what has been, what is and what will be. Thousands of writings tell you that you are unlike us! Ah, why take the trouble to imagine you are more than a man? You are made to instruct us, and indeed you do: you preach to us, you reproach our faults, you show us how we should behave here below to be one day worthy of seeing what is invisible. But you are not carrying out this task now, and it is not appropriate to do so now: you are too wise not to be able to distinguish the times when you should open your mouth to instruct us, and especially when to reprimand us for any faults you see in us.

"But what do you see in us now that is reprehensible? Is it because we are drinking brandy? It has the same effect on us as on all other men. Who brings us brandy? Are they not men of your country? You have often told us that brandy is bad for our souls, but we are not convinced of this. Is it bad for the souls of your countrymen? Do you think that, if brandy were as harmful to us as you say, your compatriots, the French, would give it to us? They are too much our friends to wish to do us harm in this way. Besides, where do you see that we drink to excess? Look Father: we only drink one draught at a time, and we often find a single draught is enough, unlike you people who, not content with one draught, drink ten, twenty, thirty more after the first."

The Indian orator has a nearby woman bring him a wooden bowl or a bark container big enough to hold at least a pint and a half of liquid. He has it filled with brandy and presents it to the Priest, saying, "Would you like to do as I do, Father? This one draught is for you; I will take another. You will see that I shall only drink this one draught and that I shall be content not to drink any more." He lifts the bowl to his lips and swallows the contents at almost one gulp. Then he tries to continue the tenor of his remarks, but soon he does not know what he wants to say, and he blushes, becomes pale, dribbles and froths at the mouth, rises to sing and dance in his fashion, draws his dagger and brandishes it like a man ready to disembowel the first man he sees. He fulminates against an unseen enemy, most often mentioning the English, whose heart he wants to eat and whose blood he wants to drink. The others, drunk like himself, applaud him, rise like him, and brandish their knives. Their fierceness towards each other is enough to chill the blood of any onlooker.

Pierre Antoine Simon Maillard. "Lettre à Madame de Drucourt," n.d. In *Les Soirées Canadiennes*. 1863:311-314. Translated for this publication by Margaret Anne Hamelin.

1749

Governor Cornwallis' first dispatch to England, after arriving at Chebucto, bears the date 22nd June, the day after his arrival.... "The coasts are as rich as ever they have been represented; we caught fish every day since we came within 50 leagues of the coast. The harbour itself is full of fish of all kinds. All the officers agree the harbour is the finest they have ever seen. The country is one continued wood; no clear spot is to be seen or heard of. I have been on shore in several places. The underwood is only young trees, so that with difficulty one is able to make his way anywhere."

[An anonymous settler wrote on 25 June:] "We have already cleared about 20 acres, and every one has a hut by his tent.... As the Governor is preparing to lay out the lots of land, we shall soon have a very convenient and pleasant town built, which is to be called Halifax. There are already several wharves built, and one gentleman is erecting a saw mill; public store houses are also building, and grain of various sorts have been sown. We have received constant supplies of plank and timber for building and fresh stock and rum in great quantities, 20 schooners frequently coming in in one day.... The French Deputies who came to make submission have promised to send us 50 men for the purpose [of cutting a road], and to assist us as far as they are able; we have received the like promise, and friendship and assistance from the Indians, the chief having been with the Governor for that purpose."

Thomas Akins. *History of Halifax City*. 1973:12-13.

Netnan elnoüi chagmak deloüikemoüâtigel kchibouktouk edli gou-velnéüleouilich.

Chagmau:

Oülà éimen, oulà edli oüîkademenkik, oulà edli élidoûn oüaga-loujan, oulà paoüè demen néguèch. Ktélikichkatpâchin, oulà néguèch kedoüi mechtayaljou demen magamiguéou, nân nai, nân anuchema edli ougichkaliei, nân nîl elnoüi telei, nân n'magamiguem; kedèlba nân kijoûlk ignemouich n'oüèmtaguin yapchiou.

Tokshkemtouk k'télimoulintan dèlkoüitk n'kamélamoun-kîlktiniunkèl. Ludenân égélèg mou n'témelchiktagoun kchibouktouk néguèch edlidoûnel. N'téléguèm ak kilktéléguèm kickatkenachîtich-enel magamigal; nân tchelkichkouk oüègiylagoudigik. Chkadounîl luba égéliak n'tilagoudinen, kiznè n'daunkoüanen kilou. Teguendo nîlelnoüi bîgidech? èchâin kil; tamidô paoüèdemen n'téliéligagin? kichchoüelmeher mech tâtoûn oula magamiguéou, tan tédougi m'chéguik, namcher nil echkoüi nemep kchibouktouk, Ndoko kîl apch nân kechkèl temoüin, tchelpaoüè. demen k'outchaîn; netnam oüègi k'chijoûlek k'taginen moun'pouni n'doubélik tatinen, ak amlteau n'tilagoudinen, oüègi medechkin k'pigoüelnau. nîl téguéli elnoüi mokoüèch tami oüègi melguidèlchiou, pachik kijoûlkiktouk; Ludenân nègueum kégidok toudélèg, jougichich talâlougel mèch nedauoin'chkouat. nîl elnoüi égélèg mou tchel kichkatch n'pégilidèlmoukchin jougîchich. abîch tok ouschiech n'piptaganeman kédoüi écoüimkel.

Mokoüèch élidèdemou Teophchkik k'téli optakademen, kichogoch châkmou nân oüègi dèlmoulou, chkadou néguèch naoüiak mou

J.F.W. DesBarres, *The Harbour of Halifax*, 1777. Engraved, from *Atlantic Neptune*.

n'kelougiu déli éouchami kemoudeminel. oüigoupchik pèl najamoul-
tech, tchiptouk kédèl oulchedemoüidex kedoüi d'limoulan'l. oulche-
doüin ak oulabougoüen, ak elp menakachkichkagidè dèdemenktéli
oulikichkajâtoun deli oulabougamen. nân ouschi *k'chijouliech* pa chik
oulôdi k'paoüè demen. Koulaman kédèl *mehei* yliédal kokoüèl. net
dègimouk ak nougouch mou apch kadoui chechpemoulou.

oüèch kakelmoul, chagmau.
Pol toulouze edloüikagik nân ougnâg echkou menakchen Michel
Pechkeoüimouk.

The place where you are, where you are building dwellings, where you
are now building a fort, where you want, as it were, to enthrone
yourself, this land of which you wish to make yourself now absolute
master, this land belongs to me. I have come from it as certainly as the
grass, it is the very place of my birth and of my dwelling, this land
belongs to me, the Indian [literally, 'to me, the human person'] yes I
swear, it is God who has given it to me to be my country for ever....
Show me where I the Indian will lodge? you drive me out; where do you
want me to take refuge? you have taken almost all this land in all its
extent. Nothing remains to me except Kchibouktouk. You envy me
even this morsel....

Your residence at Port Royal does not cause me great anger because
you see that I have left you there at peace for a long time, but now you
force me to speak out by the great theft you have perpetrated against
me.

I salute you, my Lord.
Written at Port Toulouse, five days before St. Michael's Day.
The Micmac elders and chiefs to the Governor at Halifax. Quoted by the Abbé Maillard,
in a letter to the Abbé du Fau, 18 October 1749, Archives du Séminaire de Québec,
Québec. In *Le Canada Français*. 1888, I:17-19. English translation in *Micmacs and
Colonists*, by L.F.S. Upton. 1979:201-202.

1749
Tradition says that on clearing the ground for settlement [of Halifax] a
number of dead bodies were discovered among the trees, partly covered
by the underwood, supposed to have been soldiers of the Duke D'Anville's
expedition which put into Chebucto Harbor in 1746, but the Governor
in his letter does not mention the fact.
Thomas Akins. *History of Halifax City*. 1973:11.

Then if they have any English prisoners—men, women, girls or boys of any size—they bring them out with their hands tied in front of their chests. Then they will suddenly split their heads in two with an axe, or disembowel them with their daggers to tie them to trees to serve as targets for their young boys. If the missionary is wise he will be very careful to say not one word then against these horrors, because not only will he speak in vain, but he will also be in grave danger of suffering the same fate, or at the very least of being severely maltreated.... During the last twenty years the Indians have staged fewer of these scenes than before. However, three have occurred during my time here [beginning in 1738], once on the Isle of St-Jean eighteen years ago, once at a place they call Maligaouèche, a little peninsula on Isle Royal about twenty-two leagues east of Louisbourg. There, eleven years ago, the Indians of my mission allowed their young men to kill five English children who had been their prisoners for some time and whom I had hoped eventually to convert to Catholicism. That is what the brandy [which] Frenchmen wintering nearby traded for pelts made them do.

Pierre Antoine Simon Maillard. "Lettre à Madame de Drucourt," n.d. In *Les Soirées Canadiennes*. 1863:311-312. Translated for this publication by Margaret Anne Hamelin.

1749

Premium for Dead Indians; Supplies to be Purchased.

At a Council held on Board the *Beauport* on Sunday the 1st Octobr. 1749. Present: His Excellency the Governor, John Horseman, John Gorham, Charles Lawrence, Ben. Green, Edward How, John Salusbury, Hugh Davidson, esqrs. That a Premium be promised of Ten Guineas for every Indian Killed or Taken Prisoner. That Mr. William Clapham be directed to raise a Company of Volunteers in this Settlement who may scour the country round the Bay, who shall have the same pay and provisions as the Troops here & reward of Ten Guineas for every Indian they shall take or destroy.

Gustave Lanctot. *Documents Relating to Currency, Exchange and Finance in Nova Scotia ... 1675-1758*. 1933:281-282.

The same thing [killing captives] happened a third time ten years ago at the Miré portage, eleven leagues from Louisbourg. A resident of Louisbourg, whose name I will not mention, had gone out there partridge shooting and, in exchange for some furs, gave them a small brandy cask, the equivalent of four or five jars. They became drunk and then mercilessly tortured a poor young Englishman, who was eighteen at most, whom they had captured three days before. Unfortunately for him I was not at Miré at the time; had I been there I would undoubtedly have saved his life, as I have been able to save the lives of many people in similar circumstances. The women were the most savage and cruelest of all towards the young man, because on that occasion most of the women, too, were as drunk as the men. An Indian servant of mine, who had stayed because he had to guard our little birchbark chapel and our wigwam nearby, told me how he had been able to make the youth understand that as soon as his arms were untied he should cross himself, calling out the holy names of Jesus, Mary and Joseph, and also that he should shout repeatedly for Father Maillard, as if he were trying to make the Indians understand that he knew me and wanted to see me. In this way, he understood, he might be able to escape what seemed certain death, and at least his death would be delayed. The youth followed my servant's instructions almost exactly. However, one thing the Indian omitted to do was to tell the young man to cross himself with his right hand and not his left; and this was his undoing. As soon as his hands were free he crossed himself, using his left hand.... The Indians, drunk as they were and just about to cleave his head, could not help noticing these signs of Christianity and even Catholicism. They stayed their hand and looked at each other in perplexity; they knew not what to do, for they thought he must be a Christian.

Then one of their old women, [named] Canidies, seeing them transfixed, cried out, "Who has persuaded you to spare this slave? What a small thing it takes to change your mind! If you thought about it for a moment, you would see that instead of being moved to spare his life you would be better to take it immediately, because he is deceiving you. He is not a Catholic! Have him make the sign of the cross a second time. If I can convince you he is deceiving you, hand him over to me and I shall know very well what to do with him!"

"Agreed, grandmother," they replied. The old witch then approached the young man and said, "Hey! Idiot! *Tchiktoui, n'touèm.* Make the sign of the cross again, *apch k'louchioktogi.*" My man succeeded in interpreting this for the youth, still, however, forgetting to tell him to use his right and not his left hand. So the Englishman crossed himself with his left hand, and thinking he was acting correctly, repeated the action a dozen times.

The old Indian woman turned to the others who were looking on in amazement, and said, "Did you all see which hand he used to cross himself? Our Priest has told you and me that we must always use the right hand, and not the left to cross ourselves. And what hand did he use, I ask you? You have all been witnesses. He is therefore not a Catholic, but an Englishman, *aglachièw wlà.*" They replied, "What you say is true: we had not noticed. Take him, grandmother, he is yours."

So the wretch was handed over at once to the women who, like so many Furies, seized him and tied him to a tree trunk with his legs bound together.

They built a very hot fire in front of and very near him and, seizing blazing branches, they applied them to the soles of his feet, which they had stretched out to the fire. Then you would have seen [them] screeching insults at the pitiful screams of this poor wretch, taking live coals and putting them on the most sensitive parts of his body, leaping and dancing around him ... using their knives to cut him deeply and painfully about the back and shoulders, taking him away from the fire when they saw his heart failing, bringing him back to it once he had regained consciousness, plunging his charred feet and legs into a cauldron of boiling water, and then scalping him.... They were unable to make him suffer more, because he died after the last torture. But they did cut out his tongue, even though he was dead, planning to force another English prisoner, an old man, who was destined for the same fate, to eat it.

Pierre Antoine Simon Maillard. "Lettre à Madame de Drucourt," n.d. In *Les Soirées Canadiennes.* 1863:319-320. Translated for this publication by Margaret Anne Hamelin.

1749

For these causes we, by and with the advice and consent of His Majesty's Council, do hereby authorize and command all Officers Civil and Military, and all His Majesty's Subjects or others, to annoy, distress, take or destroy the savages commonly called Mic-macks wherever they are found, and all such as are aiding and assisting them; and we further by and with the consent and advice of His Majesty's Council do promise a reward of Ten Guineas for every Indian, Mic-mack, taken or killed to be paid upon producing such savage taken or his scalp (as is the custom of America) if killed, to the Officers commanding at Halifax, Annapolis Royal or Minas. Given at Halifax, the second day of October, one thousand seven hundred and forty nine and in the twenty third year of His Majesty's Reign.

Thomas Akins, ed. *Selections from the Public Documents of the Province of Nova Scotia.* 1869:582.

I returned from my journey the next day. As soon as I had heard the whole story I demanded to know if there was any brandy left, and if anyone was still drunk. My man and several other Indians, both men and women, whom I trusted, told me that all was peaceful, but that I should wait till the next day to say what I wanted, so that my remarks would bear fruit.... I had the chapel flag hoisted as a signal for a meeting at the wigwam of the chief's deputy.... All the men hastened there, and I did too. "Doubtless, Father," they said to me, "you have some important news for us, or some weighty advice to give us, since you have yourself gone to the trouble of summoning us to a meeting so early in the morning."

"It is indeed one or the other, my children," I replied. One by one, each man took his place and fell silent. As we were on the eve of losing Louisbourg at that time, I refrained from saying all I would have said under different circumstances. I very much wanted them to go to the town under cover of some dark night there, to join a detachment of French which awaited them in the Miré woods under the command of M. Beaubassin de La Vallière. So all I did at first was to propose a reading of the regulations drawn up at Port Toulouse five years before by their own leaders and the other elders in the presence of M. de Bourville, the King's Lieutenant, and acting commandant during the absence of M. de Saint-Ovide de Brouillan....

I spoke to them thus: "My children, we find ourselves today in circumstances which are sadder and more trying than I can say. If Louisbourg is captured, then be sure that all Isle Royale will revert to the English. It seems very probable that Louisbourg will fall into their power: if they do not win it by force of arms, they will capture it by starvation. This is not to say that all the officers, all the soldiers and all the other Frenchmen are not making enormous efforts to repulse the English and that they are not doing everything in their power night and day to raze the outlying buildings to prevent the enemy creeping too near the walls and launching a surprise attack. You have just heard how five hundred English soldiers, led by Brastrie, surprised the garrison at Islot one very dark night, under cover of a thick fog, and put them all to the sword. You have just heard, I say, how that garrison was treated: a great many of the troop died miserably. This is the way to get rid of an enemy. The French have used fire and sword against them, and wrought ceaseless carnage among them, except when they have begged for quarter. Then the French have given quarter to those who were seen to lay down their arms. They made prisoners of them and kept them for exchange. My children, this is how war is waged, legitimately, reasonably and nobly.... If circumstances arise when it becomes absolutely necessary to kill a prisoner whose life we have spared.... we look on him as a troublesome piece of booty which we can neither keep nor carry with us without obvious risk to his life. We therefore get rid of him, because we must, as simply and quickly and also gently as we can. It is thus that all countries act towards each other in all wars, disputes and differences that may arise between them.... Take note of what I say now: a man, be he a Catholic or not, is still a man. It is his misfortune if he does not follow the True Way, and his good fortune if he does. Any man, Christian or not, is still a man; that is, he is a living being, very different from a dog, from a fox, from a beaver, from a moose, and from all other living things on this earth. Remember what differentiates him, as a man, from all other creatures.... If I must once more explain this difference to you today, I cannot begin without a feeling of deep sorrow as a result of the events that recently took place here, because I shall be completely unable to avoid making you feel you are far less perfect than you should be."

Pierre Antoine Simon Maillard. "Lettre à Madame de Drucourt," n.d. In *Les Soirées Canadiennes*. 1863:320-325. Translated for this publication by Margaret Anne Hamelin. [As he says later, "In truth, I may venture to say, without presumption, that I talk the Micmaki language as fluently, and as elegantly, as the best of their women, who most excell in this point" (1758:3). He is indeed quite eloquent on the evils of torture, but his political motivations, and the context of his times, also stand out quite clearly. This piece of Maillard's oratory is included for balance, to show the level of violence acceptable — even to the Church—in the seventeenth century, whether promulgated by "civilized" English and French, or "savage" Micmac and Maliseet.]

ca 1750

In the mean time, the abundance of words in [the Micmac] language surprized, and continues to surprize me every day the deeper I get into it. Everything is proper in it; nothing borrowed, as amongst us. Here are no auxiliary verbs. The prepositions are in great number. This it is that gives great ease, fluency, and richness to the expression of whatever you require, when you are once master enough to join them to the verbs. In all their absolute verbs they have a dual number. What we call the imperfect, perfect, and preter-perfect tenses of the indicative mood, admits, as with us, of varied inflexions of the terminations to distinguish the person; but the difference of the three tenses is expressed, for the preter-perfect by the preposition *Keetch;* for the preter-pluperfect by

Keetch Keeweeh; the imperfect is again distinguished from them by having no preposition at all.... their prose itself naturally runs into poetry, from the frequency of their tropes and metaphors; and into rhime, from their nouns being susceptible of the same termination.... All their conjugations are regular and distinct.

Pierre Antoine Simon Maillard. *An Account of the Customs and Manners of the Mikmakis and Maricheets, Savage Nations, Now Dependant on the Government at Cape Breton.* 1758:33-36.

My great-grandmother was a Thomas. Well, the original Thomas was a deserter from Cornwallis's outfit, when they first came to—I guess when Halifax was founded, round about 1749—and there were a lot of Indians, quite a settlement up on—now they call 'em Dartmouth Lakes, different names. But the Indian name was *Panu'k.* This was where all the Indians lived, because this was the main highway to Shubenacadie. And this Navy lad—he was one of the Navy lads—his name was Thomas, got goin' with an Indian girl, deserted the Navy, and went to live among the Indians. And they were livin' at one of these lakes, and I guess he was not the only one, when the Shore Patrol came looking for the deserters. Thomas was dressed like an Indian, and when they knew the S.P.s were coming, his future brother-in-law said, "We'll make believe we're about to launch the canoe." So they put the canoe over their heads and headed for the shore. And the S.P. just looked under; they were dressed in buckskins, and the S.P. didn't realize that one of them was a sailor, this Thomas, so they kept agoin'. They kept goin' until they got to Shubenacadie. And his girl came after.... They think they'll go far enough out of the way of the S.P.s they'll have to go to Shubenacadie. Well, at that time there were Indians living in Grand Lake; well, I guess all along, but the big settlement was in Shubenacadie. They had quite a church there and the Indians protected the priest [the Abbé LeLoutre] from Cornwallis.... His son Louis Thomas married a Maurice woman. [He had another son named] Absalom Thomas. And there was Clara Thomas ... one of the original daughters [of this deserter]....

Max Basque to R.H. Whitehead, taped interview, March 1984.

ca 1750

About 1750 an American fishing schooner was cast away at Port Joli and the crew were taken prisoners by the Indians. The "Pigtow" [Pictou] family of Indians were numerous at that place at that time. The prisoners were tortured in a most cruel manner. A large rock known as "Durham Rock" which lies on the western side of the entrance into St. Catherine's River was heated by a large fire being built upon it. Upon this these unfortunate men were forced, there either to roast or to jump into the sea and perish which they did. In 1754 a similar occurrence took place. While an American fishing craft was lying in Port Joli, at anchor, the crew being below taking their rest, it being about midnight, one of them awakening from his sleep heard a noise under the stern of the vessel. He went on deck and found a canoe full of Indians under the stern trying to destroy the rudder so as to render the vessel unmanageable. They destroyed the canoe by dropping stones into her, and all the Indians were drowned except a squaw named Molly Pigtow [Marie Pictou], who was rescued and carried to the States. Her family had previously been engaged or implicated in the affair at St. Catherine's River some few years before.

James F. More. *The History of Queens County, N.S.* 1873:121.

You men! who look on me as of an infirm and weak sex, and consequently of all necessity subordinate to you, know that in what I am, the Creator has given to my share talents and properties at least of as much worth as yours. I have had the faculty of bringing into the world warriors, great hunters, and admirable managers of canoes. This hand, withered as you see it now, whose veins represent the root of a tree, has more than once struck a knife into the hearts of prisoners, who were given up to me for my sport. Let the river-sides, I say, for I call them to witness for me, as well as the woods of such a country, attest their having seen me....

Micmac woman at a feast. In *An Account of the Customs and Manners of the Mikmakis and Maricheets, Savage Nations, Now Dependant on the Government at Cape Breton,* by Pierre Antoine Simon Maillard. 1758:15-16.

1751

Governor Cornwallis in a letter to the Lords of Trade, dated 24th June, 1751, says: "A large party of Indians came down to a small village opposite Halifax where I was obliged to put some settlers that arrived last year, in the night attacked it and did some mischief by killing of the inhabitants, I think four, and took six soldiers who were not upon guard that night. Our people killed six of the Indians, and had they done their duty well, must have killed many more."

Mrs William Lawson. *History of the Townships of Dartmouth, Preston and Lawrencetown.* 1893:14.

How great, O moon! is thy goodness, in actually, for our benefit, supplying the place of the father of the day, as, next to him, thou hast concurred to make us spring out of that earth we have inhabited from the first ages of the world, and takest particular care of us, that the malignant air of the night, should not kill the principle and bud of life within us.... Thou guidest us in our nocturnal journies. By the favor of thy light it is, that we have often struck great strokes in war; and more than once have our enemies had cause to repent their being off their guard in thy clear winter-nights. Thy pale rays have often sufficiently lighted us, for our marching in a body without mistaking our way; and have enabled us not only to discover the ambushes of the enemy, but often to surprize him asleep.

Micmac orator. In *An Account of the Customs and Manners of the Mikmakis and Maricheets, Savage Nations, Now Dependant on the Government at Cape Breton,* by Pierre Antoine Simon Maillard. 1758:47-48.

1751

Private letters from Halifax state that there had been skirmishes with the Indians, in which several of the English had been killed and scalped. "Some days ago," says the writer of one of these letters, "about sixty Indians attacked the town of Dartmouth, whose fence is only a small brushwood, and killed about eight of the inhabitants, and after that exercised their cruelties by pulling down some houses and destroying all they found, not sparing women and children. A sergeant who was in his bed, went to the assistance of the inhabitants. They pursued and killed him, and not being contented with his life, cut his left arm off and afterwards scalped him. In returning from the town, they carried off about fourteen prisoners in triumph. The company of Rangers posted there gave no assistance. But one Indian scalp had been brought in under the offer of fifty pounds reward made some four months ago. This is attributed to the care of the Indians for their dead, as they always carry their fallen comrades with them when retiring from a scene of slaughter."

Another letter from Halifax, dated 30 June, 1751, says that "a few days since the Indians in the French interest perpetrated a most horrible massacre in Dartmouth, where they killed, scalped, and frightfully mangled several of the soldiery and inhabitants. They spared not even women and children. A little baby was found lying by its father and mother, all three scalped. The whole town was a scene of butchery, some having their hands cut off, some their bellies ripped open, and others with their brains dashed out."

By these extracts it will be seen that the accounts of the massacre vary considerably.

Mrs William Lawson. *History of the Townships of Dartmouth, Preston and Lawrencetown.* 1893:15-16.

They have also a kind of feasts, which may be termed war-feasts, since they are never held but in time of war, declared, commenced, or resolved. The forms of these are far different from those of pacific and friendly entertainments. There is a mixture of devotion and ferocity in them, which at the same time that it surprises, proves that they consider war in a very solemn light, and as not to be begun without the greatest reason and justice; which motives, once established, or, which is the same thing, appearing to them established, there is nothing they do not think themselves permitted against their enemy, from whom they, on the other hand, expect no better quarter than they themselves give.

Pierre Antoine Simon Maillard. *An Account of the Customs and Manners of the Mikmakis and Maricheets, Savage Nations, Now Dependant on the Government at Cape Breton.* 1758:18-19.

1752

At a Council holdon at the Governour's House, On Thursday, Sept. 14th, 1752.... His Excellency the Governour acquainted the Council that one of the Mickmak Indians, who calld himself one of their Chiefs, was come in, with proposals of renewing a peace &c., who was sent for before the Council, and being told he was welcome was desired to sit— Then the Governour desired he would acquaint the Council what proposals he had to make, who replyed that he was come in upon the Encouragement given him in a letter from Govr. Cornwallis, and that his proposals were—That the Indians should be paid for the land the English had settled upon in this Country. He was asked if he was one of the Chiefs, who replyd, That he was chief of that part of the Nation that lived in these parts of the province and had about forty men under him. He was then askd, why no more of them came in with him? who replyd That they had empowerd him to treat in behalf of them all.

He was also asked, How he proposed to bring the other tribes of the Mickmack Nation to a Conference here—who replyd That he would return to his own people and inform them what he had done here, and then would go to the other Chiefs, and propose to them to renew the peace, and that he thought he should be able to perform it in a month, and would bring some of them with him if he could, and if not would bring their answer.

Then his Excellency informed him that he should have an answer tomorrow, and ordered proper refreshments for him. P.T. Hopson.

P.T. Hopson. In *Selections from the Public Documents of the Province of Nova Scotia*, edited by Thomas Akins. 1869:671.

1752

At a Council Sept. 15, 1852 [*sic;* 1752]:

The answer prepared for the Indian Chief was read to him, and being approved of by him as satisfactory, It was ordered that the same should be fairly drawn on parchment, in French and English in order to be ratified & exchanged on the morrow. P.T. Hopson.

P.T. Hopson. In *Selections from the Public Documents of the Province of Nova Scotia*, edited by Thomas Akins. 1869:672.

1752

At a Council holden at the Governour's House at Halifax, on Saturday, Sept. 16th, 1752:

The following answer to the proposal of the Indian Chief was interchangeably signed & seald; after which he took his Leave, and embarkd on board the vessel that brought him, and saild the same day.

The answer of his Excellency Peregrine Thomas Hopson, Esq., Capt General and Governour in Chief in and over his Majesty's province of Nova Scotia or Accadie, Vice Admiral of the same, and Col. of one of his Majesty's Regiments of Foot, &c., and his Majesty's Council, for the sd. province. To the proposals of peace and friendship made by Jean-Baptiste Cope Major, for himself & his Tribe and to his offers and Engagements to endeavor to bring here the other Micmack Tribes to renew ye peace.

Friend,

It is with pleasure that We see thee here to commune with us touching the burying of the Hatchet between the British Children of his puissant Majesty King George and his Children the Mickmaks of this Country. We do assure you that he has declared unto us, that you are his Children. and that you have acknowledg'd him for your great Chief and Father. He has ordered us to treat you as dear Brethren, and We did not commence any new Dispute with you upon our arrival here—but what is passed shall be buried in Oblivion, and for the time to come we shall be pleasd & charmd to live together as Friends.

We will not suffer that you be hindered from Hunting or Fishing in this Country as you have been used to do, and if you shall think fit to settle your Wives & Children upon the River Shibenaccadie, no person shall hinder it, nor shall meddle with the lands where you are, and the Governour will put up a Truck House of Merchandize there, where you may have everything you stand in need of at a reasonable price, and where shall be given unto you to the full value for the peltries, feathers, or other things which you shall have to sell.

We approve of your Engagement to go and inform your people of this our answer.... When you return here as a mark of our good Will we will give you handsome presents of such Things, whereof you have the most need: and each one of us will put our Names to the Agreement that shall be made between us. And we hope to brighten the Chain in our Hearts and to confirm our Friendship every year; and for this purpose we shall expect to see here some of your Chiefs to receive annual presents whilst you behave yourselves as good and as faithful children to our great King—and you shall be furnished with provisions for you and your Families every year. We wish you an happy Return to your Friends and that the Sun and the Moon shall never see an End of our Friendship— And for a more particular mark of our Sincerity, we have given you a golden Belt, a laced Hat for your self, and another for your Son.

Given under our Hand and Seal at the Council Chamber at Halifax, this 16th Sept. 1752, in ye 26th year of his Majesty's Reign....

**The mark of Jean-Baptiste Major Cope/P.T. Hopson

In *Selections from the Public Documents of the Province of Nova Scotia*, edited by Thomas Akins. 1869:672-674.

[See also Public Archives of Nova Scotia, Halifax, CO 217, Vol. 40, p. 371-377.]

1752

My Lord: I have the Honour to acquaint your Lordship that I arrived here the 26th July landed the 27th and took on the Government the 3rd of August.... I send your Lordship enclosed copy of an agreement I have made with Council with Chief of the Mickmack Indians who came here as he said for that purpose and called himself Baptiste Jean Major Cope. These tribes are so treacherous that there is very little dependence to be had on them, but I hope this will have a good effect, & my duty to try anything that was most likely to promote what would be of so much advantage to the Province and would tend to lessen the Expense....

P.T. Hopson to the Right Honourable the Earl of Holdernesse, 10 October 1752. Public Archives of Nova Scotia, Halifax. CO 217, Vol. 40, p. 371.

1752

His Excellency Peregrine Thomas Hopson, Esquire, Captain, General and Governor in Chief in and over His Majesty's Province of Nova Scotia or Accadie, Vice Admiral of the same & Colonel of one of His Majesty's Regiments of Foot, and His Majesty's Council on Behalf of His Majesty, and Major Jean-Baptiste Cope, chief Sachem of the Tribe of Mick Mack Indians Inhabiting the Eastern Coast of the said Province, and Andrew Hadley Martin [André, Micmac *Antle*, was often written in English as a double name, Andrew Hadley], Gabriel Martin & Francis Jeremiah, Members and Delegates of the said Tribe, for themselves and their said Tribe their Heirs, and the Heirs of their Heirs forever, Begun, made and Concluded in the manner, for and Tenor following....

It is agreed that the said Tribe of Indians shall not be hindered from, but have free liberty of Hunting & Fishing as usual: and that if they shall think a Truckhouse needfull at the River Chibenaccadie [Shubenacadie] or another place of their resort, they shall have the same built and proper Merchandize lodged therein, to be Exchanged for what the Indians shall have to dispose of, and that in the mean time the said Indians shall have free liberty to bring for Sale to Halifax or any other Settlement within this Province, Skins, feathers, fowl, fish or any other thing they shall have to sell, where they shall have liberty to dispose thereof to the best Advantage.... That a Quantity of Bread, Flour & such other Provisions as can be procured, necessary for the Familys, and proportionable to the number of the said Indians, shall be given them half yearly for the time to come....

P.T. Hopson. In *Selections from the Public Documents of the Province of Nova Scotia*, edited by Thomas Akins. 1869:683-685.

1752

In September, 1752, John Baptist Cope, commonly called Major Cope, a Mic-Mac chief, head of the Shubenacadie Indians, came in with terms of peace, which were agreed to. This bears the date the 15th September, in that year. Immediately after this document was signed, Cope left town in a vessel, having requested Capt. W. Piggot should be sent to Indian Harbour, to meet the Indians there, to ratify the Treaty. Mr. Piggot was accordingly dispatched, and brought up with him two or three Indians, who appeared before the Council, after which they were sent back to Beaver Harbour, under the conduct of Mr. Piggot, with blankets, provisions, etc. The terms of the Treaty were agreed to and confirmed in Council, and the whole was engrossed on parchment and ratified on 22nd November, 1752.... Mr. Saul received directions to issue provisions, according to the allowance of the troops for six months, for 90 Indians, that being the number of the tribe under Cope, occupying the eastern part of the province.

Thomas Akins. *History of Halifax City.* 1973:33-34.

Old Franklin Brooks, Indian, oar-maker, of Tufts Cove, Dartmouth, N.S., now about 90 years of age, told "Dr." Jerry Lone Cloud, Indian, in July 1916, that his (Brooks') father had often told him about the Treaty made by John Baptiste Cope, Indian Chief, with the English at what is now Richmond at northern end of Halifax. This Cope was a chief, living at Halifax in summer, and at Stewiacke in winter, and going and coming by way of the Dartmouth Lakes and Shubenacadie River. Chief Cope was then camped at Richmond, near the shore, and the treaty, the tradition says, was signed on the hill which is now Fort Needham, above Richmond. Tradition says the treaty was made with an English admiral, or some such official. Halifax was nothing but woods, and the English ships were anchored at head of the Harbour, off Richmond, and the officials landed there. He said it was there the first treaty was signed. Must have been about 150 years ago. The Chiefs from Bear River, Partridge Island, Pictou, etc., also assembled here for the Treaty. Just after the treaty was signed, an English sentry stationed in the vicinity used to call out in a loud voice, when in the course of his beat he came close to Cope's camp at Richmond, which disturbed Cope's sleep and angered him, & he swore to shoot the sentry. One night, when there was a heavy land fog, Cope came out of his camp, after being thus disturbed, and in the obscurity went close to the sentry and fired at him and killed him. Cope himself was therefore the first one to break the treaty he had just signed. Owing to the darkness and fog it was not known who had fired the shot and the Indians kept the matter quiet, and so Cope was never punished for it. Some French people were living in Bedford Basin, near what is now Fairview (French Landing), and their Priest used to minister to the Indians at Richmond. The Priest learnt from Cope, doubtless in confession, that he had shot the sentry, and the Priest told him and the Tribe not to do such a thing again.

Jeremiah Bartlett Alexis [alias Jerry Lonecloud] to Harry Piers, 17 July 1916. Unpublished notes, Nova Scotia Museum Printed Matter File.

[Micmac Joseph How was told this by his mother. He told it to Jerry Lonecloud. Old Maggie Paul confirmed this to Lonecloud in 1922; she was about 75 years old then; her father lived at Ponhook Lake.]

1752 [When this treaty was signed] ... the hatchet and a sword were buried close to a willow on the brook which came down at Richmond (Mulgrave Park).

Maggie Paul to Jeremiah Bartlett Alexis [alias Jerry Lonecloud], 1922; Lonecloud to Harry Piers. Nova Scotia Museum Printed Matter File.

1752

Whereas the Treaty or Articles of Peace and Friendship hath been Renewed on the 22nd Inst. between this Government and Major Jean-Baptiste Cope, Chief Sachem of the Chibenaccadie Tribe of Mick Mack Indians, Inhabiting the Eastern Coast of this Province, and the Delegates of the said Tribe fully empowered for that purpose.... I have therefore thought fit ... strictly to Charge and Command all His Majesty's Officers, and all others His Subjects whatsoever that they do forebear all Acts of Hostility against the aforesaid Major Jean-Baptiste Cope, or His Tribe of Chibenaccadie Mick Mack Indians from and after the day of the date of these presents, as they shall answer the contrary at their Peril. Done in the Council Chamber at Halifax this 24th day of Novr. 1752, and In the 26th Year of His Majesty's Reign. P.T. Hopson.

P.T. Hopson. In *Selections from the Public Documents of the Province of Nova Scotia*, edited by Thomas Akins. 1869:685-686.

1752

On the 16th November, two Indians appeared before the Council, who had been sent from Lunenburg by Col. S. Sutherland. They stated that they were of the tribe of Cape Sable Indians, which consisted of about 60 people with two chiefs; that Baptiste Thomas, one of their priests, was one of their chiefs, and the other Francis Jean de Perisse [François Jeanperis, Janneperis] was not a chief, but deputed by the other chief.

They stated that they had never joined with the other Indians to molest the English; that on the contrary they had always exhibited a friendly spirit, in consequence of which they had never received any assistance from the French. The Council gave them 200 pounds of bread, 3 barrels of pork, 20 blankets, 30 pounds of powder, some shot, tobacco and other articles, also gold-laced hats for their chiefs, and one silver-laced for the deputy.

Thomas Akins. *History of Halifax City*. 1973:41.

1753

On the 12th of April, 1753, Glaude Gisigash [possibly the "Claude Ziziquesche" who appears, aged 12, on the 1708 Census for LaHave; descendants may have taken the name Claude or Glode], an Indian who styled himself Governor of LaHave, appeared before the Council, and having declared his intention of making peace, terms of amity were drawn up and signed by the governor and the Indian Chief, on the part of himself and his people. The terms were the same as those made with Major Cope, and it was arranged that some of his tribe should come up and ratify the treaty.

Thomas Akins. *History of Halifax City*. 1973:40.

1753

John Connor and James Grace, who arrived yesterday [April 15] in the harbour, in an Indian canoe, and brought with them 6 Indian scalps, appeared before the council, and gave the following account ... they, the said Connor and Grace, with Michael Haggerty and John Poor, sailed on the 6th February from this port, in the schooner *Dunk*, bound alongshore to the eastwards, and on the 21st of the month arrived at a place between Country Harbor and Torbay. That next morning, a canoe with four Indians came off and hailed them—that they answered them, and the Indians then fired several balls at them—that being near the coast, and the wind southerly, the vessel could not get off, but run ashore, and two canoes with six Indians came on board—that they the said Connors and his companions, submitted themselves, and that there was another canoe with three Indians ashore—that they gave the Indians victuals and drink—that they ordered them to hoist the sails, and the Indians steered and run the vessel into a creek, where they all came ashore—that the Indians then sent them into the forest to cut wood, and upon their return, they sent two of them in company with three Indians towards the water—that the said Connor and Grace saw the Indians knock Michael Haggerty and John Poor on the head with their axes, and kill and scalp them—that the next morning they carried the said Connor and Grace ten miles into the country, where they continued prisoners until the 8th day of this month—that about the 6th day of the month, some of the Indians separated from the rest, and left Connor and Grace with four Indians, a woman and a boy—that on the 8th day of this month, being Sunday, they came down to the shore, where the vessel lay off upon an island about a mile distant—that the four Indians went to the vessel for a keg of beer—that two of the Indians told them the others designed to kill them, and being almost famished for want of provisions, and in danger of starving, they took the opportunity to destroy the Indians, and make their escape; that, accordingly, they first killed the woman and boy, and then secured their arms and ammunition, and waited for the return of the Indians, when they rushed upon them and killed them, with their guns and axes; and having taken one of their canoes, arrived at Halifax yesterday.

Records of the Council Chamber, 16 April 1753. In *An Historical and Statistical Account of Nova Scotia*, by Thomas Chandler Haliburton. 1829:154.

1753

16 April 1753: Yesterday (the 15th of April) arrived from the Eastward two men, in an Indian Canoe, who have brought six scalps of Indians. The account they gave of the affair, upon their examination was, that James Grace, John Connor (a one-eyed man, formerly one of your bargemen) with two others, sailed from this port about the middle of Febry last in a small Schooner, and on the 21st were attacked in a little harbour to the Westward of Torbay, by nine Indians, to whom they submitted, and that the same day on which they landed the Indians killed their two companions in cold blood; that Grace and Connor continued with them till the 8th of this month, when some of the Indians separating they remained with four Indian men, a squaw, & a child: that the four Indians left them one day in their Wigwam with their arms & ammunition, upon which, hoping to recover their liberty, they killed the woman and child, and at the return of the men killed them also, and then taking the canoe made the best of their way to this place. This is the substance of their story; but as the Indians complained, a little after the sailing of this Schooner, that one exactly answering her description put into Jedore where they had their Stores, and robbed them of forty barrels of provision

given them by the Govr, 'tis supposed that these men might afterwards have been apprehended by some of this tribe whom they killed as they describe.

The Surveyor Morris to Lord Cornwallis. Prefixed to Anthony Casteel's Journal. British Museum, Brown MSS, Add. 19073, f.ll, No. 23. Copy in Public Archives of Nova Scotia, Halifax; RG1, #23.

They are no longer, as to us, under a favourable aspect. They shall dearly pay for the wrong they have done us. They have not, it is true, deprived us of the means of hunting for our maintenance and cloathing; they have not cut off the free passage of our canoes, on the lakes and rivers of this country; but they have done worse; they have supposed in us a tameness of sentiments, which does not, nor cannot, exist in us.

Micmac declaration of war, made to the Sun. In *An Account of the Customs and Manners of the Mikmakis and Maricheets, Savage Nations, Now Dependant on the Government at Cape Breton*, by Pierre Antoine Simon Maillard. 1758:25-26.

1753

But the fact was still blacker than he [Morris] suspected. After having robbed the Indian store houses, the Crew of this unfortunate schooner was obliged to encounter the fury of the deep. They suffered shipwreck; were found by the Indians drenched with water, and destitute of every thing; were taken home cherished, and kindly entertained. Yet watched their opportunity, and to procure the price of scalps murdered their benefactors, and came to Halifax to claim the Wages of the atrocious deed. The Indians, as may well be supposed, were exasperated beyond measure at this act of ingratitude & murder. (Revenge boils keenly in their bosoms, and their teeth were set on edge.) To procure immediate retaliation they sent some of their Warriors to Halifax, to complain of the difficulty they found to keep their provisions safe during the fishing season, and to request that the Govr would send a small Vessel to bring their families and their stores to Halifax. In compliance with this desire, the Vessel and Crew mentioned in the Journal were engaged....

Prefixed to Anthony Casteel's Journal. British Museum, Brown MSS, Add. 19073, f.ll, No. 23. Copy in Public Archives of Nova Scotia, Halifax; RG1, #23.

Sun! be thou favorable to us in this point, as thou art in that of our hunting, when we beseech thee to guide us in quest of our daily support. Be propitious to us, that we may not fail of discovering the ambushes

that may be laid for us; that we may not be surprized unawares in our cabbins, or elsewhere; and, finally, that we may not fall into the hands of our enemies. Grant them no chance with us, for they deserve none. Behold the skins of their beasts now a burnt-offering to thee! Accept it, as if the fire-brand I hold in my hands, and now set into the pile, was lighted immediately by thy rays, instead of our domestic fire.

Micmac declaration of war, made to the Sun. In *An Account of the Customs and Manners of the Mikmakis and Maricheets, Savage Nations, Now Dependant on the Government at Cape Breton,* by Pierre Antoine Simon Maillard. 1758:26-27.

1753

On the 16th day of May 1753, I sailed from this port (Halifax) at 8 o'clock in the evening in company with Capt. Bannerman, Mr. Samuel Cleaveland, and four bargemen to convey these Indians to Jedore, and there transact certain business by order of his Excellency.... The same evening we came to an anchor in Rouse's Cove, where we spent the night. The Indians being desirous to go on shore, Mr. Cleaveland accompanied them. They returned early the next morning.

On the 17th we set sail at 4 o'clock in the morning, and as we passed by Musquadoboit, two of the Indians being urgent to go ashore (*Joseph Cope & Barnard*) their Canoe was launched out, & they immediately put to land. We kept our course to Jedore, and after we came too, which was near 12 o'clock, *Francis Jeremy* was desirous of going ashore likewise. Accordingly our boat was manned with two hands and he put ashore at the eastern side of the harbour. At about 4 o'clock in the afternoon an Indian came down to the waterside and hailed the sloop: Upon which I informed Capt. Bannerman that it was major Cope. He replied then you must go ashore and speak to him. Accordingly two hands stepped into the boat with me, and as we were going over the side I told them by no means to step ashore, but to put off the boat and return on board as soon as I was landed; which they did. At meeting major Cope embraced me in the manner he used to do, & called me his son, and after common compliments passed, he asked me what we were come for; In reply I said, have you not seen any of your people; He answered me no; then I informed him that we were come to fetch the provisions they had. He desired that after we had the provisions we would not go immediately away, for he wanted to write to his Brother the Govr; that he was in very great danger, for the Indians threatened to kill him wherever they found him, and that if he thought the Govr would provide a Priest for him he would come to Halifax with his family; and after he had done with the Priest, made confession and received the Sacram[en]t, He would not care if the Indians did kill him; than [*sic*] he should be prepared.

During this discourse I observed that he often looked towards a point up the Bay, where I apprehended I saw somebody move, and asked him whether any person was there. He said yes, there were his daughters Margaret and Anne, who were afraid because it was a Vessel they had not seen before. I desired him to call them, he did, and they came. I *saluted* them, and conversed with them, for some time, upon *indifferent* subjects. We then parted, major Cope promising to come the next day to have his letter wrote. They having got some distance from me, I hailed the boat, and was put on board.

On the 18th, about 11 o'clock, there came four Indian men and one woman to the water side, who hailed the vessel and desired to be put on board.... they asked if we would go and take the provisions. Upon which Capt. Bannerman called me aside, & asked how far up the harbour their provisions were: I informed him of the place: He replied, the boat could not fetch the provisions in a day or two, and concluded as we had the Indians aboard to go up to it with the Vessel. Accordingly we went that day, and upon our arrival, I with two of our men and two Indians went on shore.

As soon as I landed I went up to the store house, and at first found nothing but pease. I coopered the Cask as well as I could. I sent 15 barrels and a half one in three boat loads together with a barrel of flour that I found After the pease were out, we returned on board the sloop, the two Indians being with us with the last load. After we got on board I asked the Indians whether they had seen Major Cope, they said they had, but that he was ill and could not come that day. The Indians then left us in a friendly manner. When they were gone, Mr. Bannerman asked me if there were any more pease ashore; I told him there was but not fit to bring away; He replied it was a pity that those pease should be lost when he had a pig starving at home. I told him we had gone beyond our orders in coming up there....

On the 19th some of the people took the boat and put a little off from the sloop, where they killed some flat fish, which we dressed and breakfasted upon. Afterwards Capt. Bannerman said he would go ashore: accordingly he emptied our meat and bread bag, and went in the boat with four hands to get the pease that were left; whether armed or not I cannot say. Mr. Cleaveland went to work below to ease the sliding door of the forecastle, while I was lying in the Cabin having watched the night before. As near as I can guess, in an hour after they were gone I heard a very extraordinary noise, notwithstanding the noise Mr. Cleaveland made of sawing and hammering in the hold of the Vessel. I jumped immediately on deck, and saw several canoes coming towards us. I called to Mr. Cleaveland, and told him I believed our people were taken, for there were a parcel of Canoes coming on board. Before I had done speaking they began to fire at me both from the Canoes & shore; I whipped up an ax & cut the Cable, & jumped into the hold immediately; where I had not been long before the Indians boarded on each side of the Vessel. They called us to come up & promised to give us good quarter.... The Indians had now hoisted the sail of the Sloop and stood up the harbour: While we were taken on shore on the western side of the Harbour, where were some huts, and where the Indians had a *strong* consultation with many high words. I addressed myself to my Comrades, and told them that I believed we were not long for this world, and that we had best recommend our Souls to God.... Immediately they all fell upon their knees, except Capt. Bannerman, who lay flat on his face on the ground. He lifted up his hands, turning his face towards me, & said, "this is no more than I expected."

After the consultation which lasted about half an hour, one of the Chiefs got up, and asked what country I was of. I told him I was a Frenchman and desired him to ask those people who had been so often at Chebucto, whom I had told I was a Frenchman when in no danger. He asked them, and they confirmed the truth. With that he pulled a cross from his bosom, & told me by virtue of that cross I should not die by their hands, and bade me kiss it, which I did. I had scarcely kissed it before Capt. Bannerman's head was split in two, and the rest slain before my eyes. Then Majr Cope was ordered to take me away. We walked together upon the beach about 500 yards, when he ordered me to give him my watch, with my boots, cap and great coat, and likewise to give him what money I had. I pulled out 6 Dollars & 5 half pence: he returned me the 5 half pence again. Then he travelled me as nearly as I could guess 3 miles thro' the wood over to Musquedocket, where we came to his canoe, & where some of his Indians joined us. He put me in the *bow* of the canoe, and put from the shore standing for an Island in the middle of the harbour, but before we reached it one of the Indians made 7 screeches, the last different from the rest. Upon going ashore, we went to Majr Cope's Wigwam, where he gave me a pair of Bearskin Mockasens, and where I tarried till it was quite dark. Then three Indians took me into the woods with them, where they lighted a fire & tarried half the night. To save me from the others, who had got rum from on board, they made an alarm, and said that the English were a coming. The three Indians hauled me violently thro' the woods to a Canoe belonging to one of the Chiefs. I embarked with Anthony Batard and his Brother. We went up into the Bay into a river called Musquadocket, where we went ashore, lighted a fire & tarried the remaining part of the night.

Sunday 20th. In the morning they trimmed the scalps, and fixed them into little round hoops, and, after drying them with hot stones, painted them red. Here Major cope put his hands a kimbow & said to the Indians, "You say I am not a good soldier; I took Pickets [Piggot's?] vessel and went to Chebucto; & I was the occasion of taking this." Then we embarked, and I was put with two strangers. We continued in that river two days, and on Tuesday morning, the 22nd, we got into a Lake which led us into Shubbenaccadie river, in which we continued all that day, and at night we arrived at a place called Shubbenaccadie. Upon our landing, there came down an Indian Squaw, to whom I pulled off my hat. She spake to the Indians, naming [me?] La Glasiere [possibly asking if he is English: *aglachièw'* is the term used by Maillard]; the moment she was answered she took me by the hair of the head, and hauled me up part of the hill. An Indian ran after her, cleared me from her hands, and gave her two scalps which were hanging to his middle. With which she and Majr Cope's daughter danced till the foam came out of their mouths, as big as my fist, which occasioned tears to gush out of mine eyes. The Indian men perceiving it, sent me with a little boy to the houses where the rest of the Indians were: that night they made me fry them some pancakes....

Friday 25th. We crossed a Bay and marched to a place called Remsheag; and when we came in sight of an Indian Camp that was there, one of the Indians in company repeated the screeches of death and fired two guns. A canoe then came across the harbour to convey us over to the other side where was my Master's wife and family. When we arrived I was ordered into his Wigwam, where I found an old lame man who was father in law to my master. He told me I was very lucky in being a Frenchman, for if I had not I would have been killed with the rest. He further said, "that he was surprized the English began first: That they had done no manner of harm for a long time and that the English had been killing their people: That they had taken up two men that had been cast away, who were but just alive and whom they were sorry for, and nourished, and told that as soon as they had an opportunity they would send them home: but the season having come on to go into the woods they left these two miserable men (who had two of their Companions drowned) with two Indian men, three women and two children (one of which was an infant at the breast) who were all slain; the Englishmen taking an opportunity in the night when the Indians were asleep, whom afterwards they sunk in a canoe, a thing they would never forgive nor forget; For were they to get as many scalps as there were hairs on their heads for those people killed they would not be satisfied; for they had always spared as many women as ever they could when they took them; and that now they would not spare even the child in the mother's womb." The manner of the above mentioned Indians being killed Joseph Morrice declares is as above related, and, if desired, is willing to come to Halifax, and give evidence of what he knows of that affair.

Anthony Casteel's Journal. British Museum, Brown MSS, Add. 19073, f.ll, No. 23. Copy in Public Archives of Nova Scotia, Halifax; RG1, #23.

1753
Louisbourg, 12th May
My lord:
Rumour had it last March that the Indians had made peace with the English. In fact at the start of the navigation season I learnt that the man called Coppe, a bad Micmac whose conduct has always been regarded as uncertain and suspect by both nations, had made several journeys to the English settlements in Acadia, after what happened last year among his brethren at Canso and at Port Toulouse, and that in the end he had signed some kind of treaty at Halifax, which has been ratified by only ninety to a hundred Indians, men, women and children, all bad subjects.

The English wanted to make use of this treaty to attract other Indians. They proclaimed and displayed it in all their posts in Acadia, where they flattered and showered with gifts all those who presented themselves. The results, however, have not met the expectations of the English authorities.... I have not as yet had any news about Saint John river. It appears that neither the Micmac nor the Maliseet have made any move, since Father Germain, who is in charge of that mission, has sent no news by the Canada messengers who passed by his dwelling twice during the winter.

I only know that, after a journey M. Manach, the missionary at Cobequid, made to restrain any Indians who might have wished to join Coppe's children [followers?], who had arrived laden with gifts from the English, two Maliseet warriors went to the fort, became drunk with the soldiers, and, before returning to us, took two scalps. This action doubtless incensed the English. It also serves to restrain our Indians, who fear their rancour and dare no longer visit them as heretofore.

The Indians of this Island and of Nartigouneche [Antigonish] went as far as Martingo [?] on the coast of Acadia to the southwest of the Canso Islands. They espied a small English schooner making its way along the coast and pursued her to the port of Mocodome, where she ran aground and was lost. She was carrying nothing but apples and onions [the goods robbed from the Indian storehouse at Jeddore?]. According to the Indians, some of her crew drowned. I do not believe this, since the Indians seized four men, who would certainly have been enough to man such a vessel. They claim that two of these Englishmen fell ill and died. Others say they killed them. I have not been able to verify this, but they did keep two, who contrived, April the 15th, to surprise the Indians asleep in their wigwam, to murder them all, men, women and children, and to elude those who were not present at the time.

The two bands, prompted by a spirit of vengeance, saw their opportunity on the night of the 21st to the 22nd of last month. Between Ouatique Island and Isle Madame they captured an English schooner sailing from Port Royal to Louisbourg. They found ten men, nine Englishmen and an Acadian, who had signed on as pilot. The Englishmen were all killed and the Acadian set ashore at Port Toulouse, where they sank the schooner after having entirely looted her....

Prevost to the Minister. Louisbourg, 12 May 1753. National Archives of Canada, MG 1, Archives des Colonies, Série C 11 B, Correspondance général, Vol. 33:159 ff. Translated for this publication by Margaret Anne Hamelin.

1753
Isle Royale, the 17th of June
My Lord,
My letter of May the 12th contains all the details of what the Indians have done in the King's dominions and on the frontiers. Since then I have heard of no incidents at Beauséjour or on Isle St. Jean [Prince Edward Island]. Numbers are down on the Isle at present because the elder warriors, along with the younger men, are ranging up and down the

eastern coast of Acadia looking for a chance to avenge the death of their brethren. In fact I have just heard that they came upon an Indian from Cape Sable, one Joseph, who had been hacked almost into separate pieces and then tossed into the bottom of a little river on the English coast. They only recognized him by his dagger and tobacco pouch. His woman, who was pregnant, had suffered the same fate: they found her body beside his, also hacked to pieces. They are convinced it was done by the English. However, the ones who are most loyal to the King had the wit to tell the others that the murder would never have happened if they had avoided contact with the English. Still possessed by the spirit of vengeance, they made their way to the bands near Halifax which had attached themselves to Cope and, after having seen him, they brought him back to Ramchic [Remsheg], from whence they claim he is to be taken to Canada along with some Englishmen and an officer whom they had captured. Then they persuaded some of the Indians who had signed or agreed to Cope's treaty to go to the Governor at Halifax and demand the gifts and provisions they had been promised as well as transport to a certain river some leagues away from Chibouctou Bay [Halifax Harbour]. The Indians were well received and sent speedily on their way aboard a well-laden schooner manned by a crew of ten. After the unloading was done, however, the Indians set fire to the ship and killed all the crew. They then fled, scattering to various parts of Acadia to continue, they say, to smite their enemies. I do not know, my Lord, what effect this may have had on the English authorities. No word has yet reached me, and everything is quiet at Halifax....

Prevost to the Minister. Louisbourg, 17 June 1753. National Archives of Canada, MG 1, Archives des Colonies, Série C 11 B, Correspondance général, Vol. 33. Translated for this publication by Margaret Anne Hamelin.

[This and the previous letter seem to be a third-hand report of the Anthony Casteel voyage, and of the Grace and Connor murders, with various errors. The taking of the ship and killing of the crew occurred *after* the ship's captain attempted to steal supplies of peas from the Indian storehouse; this French report, however, implies that the summoning of the ship may all along have been for the purposes of revenge. If Cope had been constrained by his associates, and taken to Remsheg to answer to judgment, it may explain his conversation with Casteel before the incident. His later boasting of the ship's capture to the other Micmac can be seen as an attempt to reinstate himself.]

1754

During the winter of 1753-1754, there had been no disturbance from the Indians, and the Government availed themselves of the opportunity of sending out proper persons to make a survey of the country around. The winter was mild and the frost not so severe as usual or of so long continuance. The valley of the Shubenacadie had been examined, but it was not found available for settlement, being the principal resort of the Indians under Cope.

Thomas Akins. *History of Halifax City.* 1973:42-43.

1754

Journal of the March by the River Shebenaccadia.

August. Tuesday 6th: We Marched quite round the Cove [Shubenacadie Grand Lake], and fell in with the River again about half after Eleven; this is properly the Source; the Stream is gentle & Shallow, little more than Knee Deep, the Water very clear and the Bottom a fine Reddish colour'd Sand. The Land on the Banks is flatt & Fertlle, the Woods tall & open, and consists chiefly of Oak, Ash & Maple; as we Discovered by the Tracks the Moose are plenty, & many Wigwams on each side of the River shews it to be a Place of important resort. We encamped about five Miles down the River.

August. Thursday 8th: About eight in the Morn, We came opposite to the Mouth of the Oustinoogan or Sheedewer River [Gay's River?]; the junction of this Stream with Chebenaccadie makes a sudden change both in breadth and depth. Half after Twelve we came to the Masshouse, which I think is the neatest in the Country, tis Adorned with a Fine lofty Steeple and a Weather Cock. The Parsonage House is the only Habitation here, the Land is good & seems to be more so on the opposite side.

Matthew Floyer. *Captain Matthew Floyer's Survey Report: Journal of the March by the River Shebenaccadia.* 1958:17.

1754

Captain [Major Jean-] Baptiste Cope arrived from Cobequid; he had gone to Bay Verte, and had informed the village of savages in that place that a hundred of the English had left Halifax and crossed the woods as far as Chigabenakady [Shubenacadie], the place of my mission.... I confess, Sir, that the savages are much surprised at this step, and that it should be taken at a time when it is proposed on both sides to treat of a durable peace.... this Baptiste Cope, another mikmak who speaks French, and Toubick, Chiefs of the Medoctek [Meductic] savages of the river St. John, undertook on Sunday last, after high mass, to inform all these [Acadian French] refugees, that, if any of them should be bold enough to return to the habitations which are now under English rule, they, the savages, speaking in the name of the whole nation would look upon them as enemies, and would treat them as such.

LeLoutre, ptre. g.v., Beausejour, august 27th, 1754. To Mr. Lawrence, Commander in chief at Halifax.

LeLoutre to Lawrence, 27 August 1754. In *Selections from the Public Documents of the Province of Nova Scotia*, edited by Thomas Akins. 1869:216-218.

Major Jean-Baptiste Cope was killed (shot) at Point Pleasant, Halifax, and buried there.

Joseph How to Jeremiah Bartlett Alexis [alias Jerry Lonecloud], to Harry Piers, 11 August 1922. Nova Scotia Museum Printed Matter File.

Chief J.B. Cope was a bad Indian and tricky, and Lone Cloud thinks he also heard of his having killed a man about Memramcook, N.B. The Indians do not know just how he died or where he was buried, but they have a tradition that he was shot at Pt. Pleasant and no doubt buried there. [They] think he was murdered by Francis Paul (Beminuit) [Peminuit Paul].

Maggie Paul (born *ca* 1850, Ponhook Lake, N.S.) to Jeremiah Bartlett Alexis [alias Jerry Lonecloud], to Harry Piers, 5 April 1927. Nova Scotia Museum Printed Matter File. [A later note adds "buried by the Martello Tower."]

1754

The more familiar I become with this project the more inclined I am to think that our Abenakis, Malachites [Maliseets] and Micmacks should never be permitted to conclude peace with the English. I consider that these Indians are the mainstay of the colony and in order to maintain this spirit of hatred and vengeance, they must be deprived of every opportunity to yield to corruption. The present position of Canada requires that those nations which are strongly allied should strike without delay, provided it does not appear that it was I who gave the order, for I have definite instructions to remain on the defensive.

Ange de Menneville, Marquis de Duquesne, to the Abbé Jean-Louis LeLoutre, Micmac missionary, 15 October 1754. In *Thomas Pichon, the Spy of Beausejour*, by John Clarence Webster. 1937a:56.

This old Cope family has died out now, and no male descendants are now left, most of them having no sons. The present Cope family is

descended from Cope women, sisters or perhaps daughters of John Baptiste Cope, with Irishmen as fathers, Murphys and Knowlens, such as those about Fish Lake [the Fish River] and Murphyville, near Little River, Musquodoboit, the children taking the Indian mothers' name, and so being called Cope.

Jeremiah Bartlett Alexis [alias Jerry Lonecloud] to Harry Piers, 17 July 1916. Nova Scotia Museum Printed Matter File.

1755

During my visit to Gaspereau, I secured, by means of a few presents, conversation with an Indian from Cape Sable, Jean-Baptiste Phillipe de Conoumak [Tecouenemac], by name, and Madelaine le Songeur, his wife, who speaks French very well. I learned that, at the village of Tattemlgougouche [Tatamagouche], there are 20 Indians fit to bear arms; at Pektou [Pictou], 50; at Chediak [Shediac], 20; at Richibouktou [Richibucto], 17; at Miramichi, 150; at Baye des Chaleurs, 120; at Remickik [Remsheg], near Baye des Chaleurs, 120; at Gaspereau, 57; in all 449 men or youths, not counting women and children. The two chiefs of Gaspereau village are called Arguimaut [L'kimu] and François. There is another named Antoine Mius, son of Jacques, also a chief, but no one knows where he comes from.

Thomas Pichon to T. Hussey[?], 13 January 1755. In *Thomas Pichon, the Spy of Beausejour*, by John Clarence Webster. 1937a:82.

Sir: After the writing, which you gave me to show my people, had been read, they decided to go to Halifax. We are therefore making ready and shall set out in two days. We are sending Francis Arsenau to get from you the letter which you promised us, which should be your assurance that the Government will grant us a domain for hunting and fishing, that neither fort nor fortress shall be built upon it, that we shall be free to come and go wherever we please. Moreover, you know what we told you, we have said the same thing in the Council; and it would be vexatious for us to undertake this journey, if you do not give us some reason to hope.

We await this letter, which you are not to seal. When we return, we shall see you. ALKMOU CHIEF. Gasparau, 19 January 1755.

Chief L'kimu to T. Hussey. In *Thomas Pichon, the Spy of Beausejour*, by John Clarence Webster. 1937a:84.

1755

An attempt was made this year to involve the Government in a dispute with the Indian tribes. Paul Laurant, an Indian Chief of the Mic-Mac tribe, appeared before the Council on 12th February, 1755, and informed them that he and another Indian Chief named Algamud [L'kimu], had set out from Beausejour for Halifax in order to treat of peace, but that the Chief had fallen sick at Cobequid and had intrusted him with the proposals. They demanded the whole eastern section of the Province, from Cobequid to Canso, to be set apart for them as feeding and hunting grounds. Being asked what security he could give that the Indians would keep the peace, he said he could say nothing to that, being only desired to bring in the terms.

Thomas Akins. *History of Halifax City.* 1973:46-47.

1755

Moses [the Abbé LeLoutre] went to Baye Verte yesterday to bury an Indian. He has returned. Four Indians brought him a letter from Manach, from whom they parted at Tatemigouche; he will not return from his missions before mid-Lent. These Indians announce war between England and France. They say this news comes from Halifax.

Thomas Pichon to T. Hussey [?], 3 February 1755. In *Thomas Pichon, the Spy of Beausejour,* by John Clarence Webster. 1937a:89.

1755

June ye 7 AD 1755. Plesant Day we Pitched our Tents all in a Regular Form on ye affore:mentioned Hill the French & Indians Fire on us Every Night & yet Briskly So yt the whole Camp is Disturbed by them.

June ye 16 AD 1755. thare was a Senasation of arms was agreed on to Continue until Two of the Clock In which Time a party of Indians Fired on our Centrys the whole Campe ware Emediatly put under arms we Fired on them. Killed one of thare Principle officers & Brought him into Camp but ye woods being very thick the Rest of them made thare Escape the Terms ware agreed on about 6 of ye Clock P:m: & about 7 our Troops Entered the Foart & Called it Foart Cumberland the Conditions of Agreement ware yt the Enemy should Diliver up the Foart & Kings Stores but Should be Transported to Lewisburge with all thare Private Effects at the Expense of his majesty King George. this Fortress was Called by the French Fort Beausejure & Commanded by monsieur Villea.

John Thomas. "Diary of John Thomas." In *Journals of Beausejour*, edited by John Clarence Webster. 1937b:15-17.

There is but little known of the Chegoggin settlement [of Acadians]....
It was from this settlement that a girl having strayed to gather berries,
found on her return that all her family had been carried away. She fled
to the Indians for safety; and, in after years, when her family returned,
she could not persuade herself to leave the people with whom she had
cast in her lot. A very few still living recollect having seen her, as an old
woman coming to town with the Indians.
J.R. Campbell. *A History of Yarmouth, Nova Scotia.* 1876:21-22.

1755

August ye 25: 40 men Returned upon Party that have bin out with Capt willard to Cobigate [Cobequid] &c thay Brought in Serveral Prisoners Burnt Several Fine Viliges.

August ye 28: major Frye with a Party of 200 men Imbarked on Board Capt. Cobb & Newel & adams to Go to Sheperday [Shepody] & take what French thay Could & burn thare Viliges
John Thomas. "Diary of John Thomas." In *Journals of Beausejour*, edited by John Clarence Webster. 1937b:23.

1755

It was at the time of the expulsion of the Acadians. Acadians who were settled in the vicinity of Paradise and Belleisle had had no intimation of the fate that had overtaken their fellow Acadians at Grand Pre. The terrible tidings that their compatriots were held prisoners in the church at Grand Pre by the English and that ships lay waiting to convey them and their families to distant and unknown lands was brought to them by Indians. Their dusky friends of the forests had stolen ahead to warn them that a similar fate was about to overtake them.

What to do? That was the question.... About sixty determined on flight. Heavily loaded with all they could carry, they took a sad farewell of their companions who had resolved to remain behind.... Near what is now Kingston, they halted and encamped, their Indian friends acting as pickets and spies.... The provisions they had brought with them soon became exhausted. It was late autumn and the weather was cold. In hastily-dug graves the survivors laid their loved ones and left them there in the Aylesford sands. They, themselves, though ill and broken-hearted, pressed on. Over the mountain, across the Bay of Fundy, and on to Quebec was their destination.

But the icy hand of winter had locked the waters of the Bay of Fundy.... Here at Morden they were compelled to tarry, and here they erected rude huts to shelter them.... They heard from the Indians that all the Acadian homes in the Valley had been burned to the ground.... Through it all the faithful Indians had shared with them their trophies of the chase, but as the winter dragged on, the Acadians relied mainly on the supply of mussels they found clinging to the rocks.... Spring came at last and old Pierre Melanson of Belleisle with an Indian boy crossed the bay for help. On their return, as the canoe grounded on the Morden shore, the aged Frenchman was discovered dead in the bow.

Clara Dennis. *Down in Nova Scotia.* 1934:111-112.

1755

Sept ye 2: Plesent Day major Frye Sent Leiut Jno. Indicut on Shore with men to Burn a Vilige at a Place Called Petcojack after thay had Burnt Several Houses & Barns thay ware about to Burn a New masshouse a Large Number of French & Indians Ran upon them out of the Wood and Fired on them So yt thay ware obliged to Retreat Doc march who had Just Joyned him with 10 men from Capt. Speakmans Party who Came on Shore the other Side of ye Vilige was killed on the Spot 22 more Killed & taken Seven wound Badly

John Thomas. "Diary of Beausejour." In *Journals of Beausejour,* edited by John Clarence Webster. 1937b:23.

1755

September 5th saw here a tragic sight. It stands out darkly in our history. The Masstown beach was thronged with weeping women and children.... The men were herded onto the [English] ship. Later in the day the women and children, all except two women who had escaped, were placed on a separate ship.... One of the women who had been left behind returned that night to her home, which was still standing. In her arms she carried her babe.

"My husband's mother, who died aged 102, remembered that baby well," said a woman of Masstown to me, "although the baby was an old, old woman when mother knew her. The baby who had been brought back to Masstown, grew up and married. She and her husband were the first settlers on Folly Mountain. She died in 1844."

I learned the story of that baby's mother. After the vessels had sailed away that night, she fell unconscious and remained so until morning. On regaining her senses, she was too weak to stand. She crawled to the door.... the church was a heap of blackened ruins. Her cow came to the door lowing to be milked. She forced herself to milk the cow and to drink some of the milk. The milk revived her and she set out to see if she could find anyone in the village. But there was not a solitary soul to be seen.

Cattle had broken into the fields and were gorging themselves on the wheat; horses were running in droves; pigs that were fastened in the pen were squealing with hunger, while those which had managed to get out were uprooting the gardens; oxen, waiting in vain to be freed from the yoke (they had been used in moving the goods to the vessels) were bellowing with hunger. They hooked and fought with each other, running through the marsh, upsetting the carts or tumbling into the ditches, till death ended their sufferings.

In the evening the cows and goats came to their accustomed milking places. The lonely woman sank down on a doorstep and mournfully gazed on the scene, seeing it, but with unseeing eyes.

Presently an Indian came to her. He bade her come with him. She enquired as to the fate of her people. "Gone!" he said, "All gone! People everywhere prisoner. See smoke rise! They burn all here tonight." The Indian spoke only too truly, for blazing fires in the distance attested the truth of his words. He helped the woman to gather some of the most valuable things that were left, then piloted her to his wigwam.

Here she found about a dozen of her people—all who were left.... The party waited more than a month to see if any others would be found. Then they set forth for Miramichi.

Clara Dennis. *More about Nova Scotia*. n.d.:51-52.

[Dennis got her material from Elizabeth Frame's *Descriptive Sketches of Nova Scotia* (Halifax, A & W MacKinlay, 1864:235-237).]

1756

But what has, at least, an equal share in attaching the savages to our party, is the connivence, or rather encouragement the French government has given to the natives of France, to fall into the savage-way of life, to spread themselves through the savage nations, where they adopt their manner, range the woods with them, and become as keen hunters as themselves.... We employ besides a much more effectual method of uniting them to us, and that is, by the intermarriages of our people with the savage-women.... But it is not only men that have taken this passion for a savage-life; there have been, though much rarer, examples of our women going into it. It is not many years since a very pretty French girl ran away into the woods with a handsome young savage, who married her after his country fashion. Her friends found out the village, or rather ambulatory tribe into which she had got; but no persuasions, or instances, could prevail on her to return and leave her savage, nor on him to consent to it; so that the government not caring to employ force, for fear of disobliging the nation of them, even acquiesced in her continuance amongst them, where she remains to this day....

M. de la Varenne. In *An Account of the Customs and Manners of the Mikmakis and Maricheets, Savage Nations, Now Dependant on the Government at Cape Breton,* by Pierre Antoine Simon Maillard. 1758:89, 94-95.

[An English deserter surnamed Thomas married a Micmac woman and had several children.] His son married a Morris woman.... Louis Thomas was his name. He had another son named Absalom [Anselm]. Absalom Thomas. And there was a Clara Thomas, one of the original daughters of this deserter was named Clara [Claire]. She was held as hostage, as a prisoner in Halifax for a long time. I don't know where in the world I heard that story.... She was held hostage for quite a while, I don't know why, I suppose when they had the bounty on Indians.... I suppose they collected it in Fort Edward, near Windsor?... Some of the Chiefs were ambushed down Ponhook Lake. Grandfather Sack used to tell us all them stories.

Max Basque to R.H. Whitehead, personal communication, 1977; taped interview, 1984.

[Max Basque is descended from Louis Thomas.]

1757

[October] The old garrison embarked to-day for Halifax, and with them two Indian captives, a brother and sister, who passed by the names of Clare and Anselm Thomas; they are of the Mic-mac nation; she is comely and not disagreeable; her complexion was not so fair as the British, nor yet so dark as the French in general are; her features were large, with sprightly black eyes, hair of the same colour, thin lips and a well-shaped nose; I believe she may be about twenty-three or four years of age, not taller than five feet five inches; somewhat Dutch-built, but was very sprightly, and had much of the French in her manner and behaviour....

Their family have been converted to (what is commonly called) Christianity, as may partly appear by their names; but I have a stronger reason for this suggestion, by their having crucifixes; Clare had one of silver, that hung down from a large bunch of beads, which she wore about her neck; Anselm's was made of wood, and hung by a leathern string from a button-hole of his coat; their cloathing they got from the Officers of the garrison, except a turban the female had on her head, and a pair of paltry pendants from her ears: these, I am told, were her own. When I first went into the room where they were confined, the sister rose up from her seat, approached me eagerly, and saluted me after the French manner. Her brother, who was neither so fair nor so tall, came toward me in a fearful skulking manner, grasped one of my hands, and shook it with great emotion, accompanied with an unintelligible jargon: he was a mean-looking fellow, not so sprightly as the other; yet he was well proportioned, and seemed to be active, but he had not the engaging openness of countenance of Clare, nor could I discern the smallest resemblance between them. These Indians were not very talkative; I spoke to them in French, and they answered me, but what they said was so low and thick, that I could not understand them; I am told their language was a mixture of their own mother-tongue and of French; in a second visit, which my curiosity led me to make them, Clare made a sign to me for pen, ink, and paper, these I accordingly procured for her, and she instantly filled one side of it with a writing, or characters, which are to me unintelligible; I have it now before me, and, though there are some letters in it apparently similar to part of our alphabet, yet it is utterly impossible to make any discovery from it. Some months ago this man and woman, with two other brothers, came to Mayass Hill, within a mile of the garrison, under the flag of truce: an Officer with an interpreter were immediately sent out, to inquire their errand, and to invite them in, which they accordingly accepted of. They said—"they belonged to a settlement at Pan-nook [*panu'k*, 'it opens out'], in the county of Lunenburg (which lies to the eastward of us, about three or four and twenty leagues) and that they were sent by their father to treat in behalf of their family and the rest of the tribe; that they were desirous of burying the hatchet, and becoming true friends to the English, with whom they now hoped to put a final period to all animosities; and, if we did not choose to trust and employ them as allies, prayed that they may be reputed and treated hereafter at least as neutrals." So eager were they to be confided in, that Anselm and Clare voluntarily proposed to continue here as hostages, while the other brothers should go to Pan-nook, for their father, and one or two other Chiefs of their nation, the better to convince the English of their sincerity. Having got a favourable answer and reception, the two brothers accordingly departed from the fort with some trifling presents, and directed their course towards Lunenburg, in order to procure, through the channel of some acquaintances they had there, a British escort to conduct them, either back to their garrison, or to Halifax: in their journey they called at Pan-nook, and, upon their favourable report to their father, he, and two other Chiefs, accompanied them towards the German settlement before-mentioned; but unluckily, in their march thither, they were way-laid by an accidental party of our people, who knew nothing about them, nor their errand they were going upon; in this affair the father of Anselm fell; the rest betook themselves to flight, and the party not pursuing immediately, as they did not yet know the number of the Indians, gave the old Chief time to recollect himself and escape also. This had such an effect on the Sachems and their companions, who concluded it to be the result of treachery, that they thought it in vain to renew their sollicitations, and (no doubt vowed revenge at a proper season) per-suaded that the English were a faithless people; they resolved to return to their habitations, and remain quiet, until they should hear the fate of Clare and Anselm; these circumstances being yet unknown to the Commanding Officer here, except an imperfect account brought, within this fortnight, by a sloop from fort Edward in this province, *viz.* that a scouting party of the enemy had been way-laid near Lunenburg; that one old man was killed (this was supposed to be the father of these captives) whom the rest carried off before our people could venture upon a pursuit, &c. and, the two brothers not returning pursuant to their promise, it was concluded they must have been the suspected enemy, and therefore it was resolved that Anselm and Clare should be detained, and brought to Halifax, there to be disposed of as the Governor should think proper: as I was very particular in my description of these savages; I thought it necessary to account for the manner in which they fell into our hands.

John Knox. *The Journal of Captain John Knox: An Historical Journal of the Campaigns in North America,* edited by A.G. Doughty. 1914, I:89-90.

["Mayass Hill" is a corruption of Maillard's Hill, named for Joseph Doucet, surnamed Maillard, and "is now known as Gates Hill." (A.G. Doughty, Vol. I:91)]

I have often brought about alliances, which there was no room to think could ever be made; and I have been so fortunate, that all the couples

whose marriages I have procured, have been prolific, and furnished our nation with supports, defenders, and subjects, to eternize our race, and to protect us from the insults of our enemies.

Micmac woman, speaking at a feast. In *An Account of the Customs and Manners of the Mikmakis and Maricheets, Savage Nations, Now Dependant on the Government at Cape Breton*, by Pierre Antoine Simon Maillard. 1758: 17.

1758

April 1st. The weather is exceeding cold, with flying showers sleet and snow; this morning two shots were discharged on Mayass-Hill, and a flag of truce was hoisted.... the enemy did not seem so shy as they were on the 20th ult. We demanded of them their errand, and they answered, *They came to know whether we would exchange prisoners with them?* They offered four men for the two Indians, viz. Clare and Anselm Thomas, (as mentioned under the 17th of October last); the persons who appeared to us were the father and another brother of the two captives, with a Frenchman; but we could discern there were others in the skirts of the woods, at a distance behind them: the old Sachem was told, that we had heard he was dead, being shot by an accidental party of our people, who were ignorant of the particulars of his own and his family's case and resolutions, &c. to which he replied, there was sufficient cause for such a rumour, but that he himself was most culpable. Upon this we interrogated him, and related to him what we had heard of the matter; to which he answered—"It was not so, for he was actually, at that time, with an English party; that he grew diffident of their sincerity, and, being suddenly seized with a panic, he slipped behind them, with an intent to make his escape; that the English turned about and fired at him, which he avoided by falling prostrate on the ground, and from thence he supposed our people might have thought he had been killed."—This Chief appeared to be an honest, chearful, well-looking old man much resembling his daughter, though of a swarthier complexion: he was meanly dressed, and not at all like an Indian; his son, who had also a good open countenance, was habited quite in character, with a turban on his head, adorned with an extravagant number of beads and feathers of various colours, which these creatures much affect, and are very fond of: they were told, that Clare and Anselm were both well at Halifax; upon this they took their leave of us, retired to the woods, and made fires for themselves; our party returned to the fort....

We have been since informed, that the Squaw and her brother died at

Halifax of the small-pox, a disorder very fatal to the Indians, who have so great a dread of it, as to be intirely disheartened upon the first symptoms, and cannot be prevailed on to use any means for their recovery. We had no knowledge of their deaths on the first of April.

John Knox. *The Journal of Captain John Knox: An Historical Journal of the Campaigns in North America,* edited by A.G. Doughty. 1914, II:145-146.

ca 1758

And as there was a bounty on Indian Scalps (a Blot on Britain's Escutcheon), the Soldiers soon made the supplicating Signal, the Officers turn'd their Backs and the French were instantly shot and scalp'd. A Similar Instance happened about the same time. A Party of the Rangers brought in one day 25 Scalps pretending that they were Indian. And the Commanding Officer at the Fort then Col. Wilmot, afterwards Gov. [Thomas] Wilmot (a poor Tool), gave Orders that the Bounty should be paid them. Capt. Huston who had at that time the Charge of the Military Chest objected such Proceedings both in the Letter & Spirit of them. The Col. told him, "That According to Law the French were all out of the French [*sic*], that the Bounty on Indian scalps was according to Law, and that tho' the Law might in some Instances be strain'd a little yet there was a Necessity for winking at such things." Upon which Huston in Obedience to Orders paid down £250, telling them that the Curse of God should ever attend such guilty Deeds.

John Knox. *The Journal of Captain John Knox: An Historical Journal of the Campaigns in North America,* edited by A.G. Doughty. 1914, II:197. "This document is found in the Nova Scotia Papers, Canadian Archives, M651A [Brown Collection in British Museum Add. MSS 19071], and is printed exactly as found. The MSS agrees with the printed version in N.S. Historical Papers, 1879." (A.G. Doughty)

1758

About six miles from fort Edward, in our way to Halifax, we saw a great smoke in the woods, about two hundred yards from the road; why we paid no regard to it, I will not pretend to say; going a little farther, our guide, who was at some small distance before our advanced-guard, saw twelve or fourteen of the enemy sitting together at their dinner; they immediately bounced up and ran off towards the woods: on their flight our guide fired at them and wounded one of them, having tracked his blood afterwards on the snow; our party by this time came up and pursued them, upon which the enemy drew up behind their usual fences (the trees) fired at our people and then ran off. Our whole loss amounts to two men killed on the spot, one of whom was our guide: we had none wounded; what execution we did among them, I will not pretend to say; but our advanced-guard gave them very brisk firing, until they were ordered to desist: the Commanding Officer, not having any instructions how to act in a case of this kind, did not think it proper to pursue the enemy any farther; we therefore went back to the place where they had been first alarmed, and got three camp-kettles, a sealskin gun-case, several haversacks of the same skin, with many little odd things in them, particularly a lock of a fire-lock belonging to the 43rd regiment, and a pair of large silver buckles, which they got some time before from a Serjeant of rangers who fell into their hands. After we had collected our plunder, we proceeded on our march to Halifax, and never halted until we reached fort Sackville, where we arrived at eight o'clock in the morning, and the other twelve miles we came at our leisure; I must observe to you, that I saw among the enemy a well-looking man with white cloaths, and his hat and waistcoat were laced; which makes us imagine he is a French regular Officer, &c. &c.

Officer of the 43rd Regiment to John Knox, 6 April 1758. In *The Journal of Captain John Knox: An Historical Journal of the Campaigns in North America*, by John Knox, edited by A.G. Doughty. 1914, II:169-170.

1759

21 January. The whole company of rangers went out this morning to scour the country towards Bay Verde; they returned in the afternoon, and brought with them a sleigh which our unhappy sufferers had taken out with them, and on it were laid the bodies of four of our men, and one ranger, who were killed and scalped; the rest are still missing; at the place where these people were waylaid, there was a regular ambush, and designed probably against the rangers.... The ranger was stripped naked, as he came into the world; the soldiers were not, except two, who had their new cloathing on them; these (that is the coats only) were taken; I am told this is a distinction always made between regulars and others.... the ranger's body was all marked with a stick, and some blood in hieroglyphic characters....

John Knox. *The Journal of Captain John Knox: An Historical Journal of the Campaigns in North America*, edited by A.G. Doughty. 1914, II:289-290.

1759

The Indians ... often harassed the English settlements in various parts of the Province. Consequently, the Government raised Volunteers to hunt down the Aborigines, offering a premium of twenty-five Pounds for any male Indian prisoner above sixteen years old; twenty Pounds for each female prisoner; the same price for a man's scalp; and ten Pounds for every child prisoner. These Volunteer Companies were placed under the command of Colonel Scott and Major Samuel Rogers, afterwards Representative of Sackville in the House of Assembly. He was assigned the Western Section [of the province], including Digby. The following graphic acount of an engagement near the latter town, was related to the Author in 1873 by an old resident, since deceased, who received it from Mr. Richard Robert Annabury, one of the pursuing party who subsequently lived and died much respected at Trout Cove, near Centreville:

Intelligence having reached Annapolis in the Autumn of 1759, that a hostile Micmac Village existed at Green, now Crowley's, Point, on the north side of the Racket, Major Rogers, who had just arrived thither from Canada, at once advanced with his celebrated Rangers in pursuit. Marching overland with a scanty supply of provisions, they reached Bear River.... Then crossing to Baxter's Point, at the south of Digby Town, they espied the object of their search through a spy glass. Here they encamped for the night.... Rogers went next morning before daybreak to reconnoitre the Village by moonlight, arriving near the property of late Sheriff Taylor. He surveyed the Indian Settlement and its rude inhabitants, whom he found engaged in festive Entertainment, wholly unaware of the presence, almost in their midst, of a British Soldier, preparing for a battle, which, ere another sun should set, would finally destroy the collection of wigwams dotting the forest ground, with their happy inmates, in retribution for former acts of violence committed by their race on the English Settlers in the Colony. After a thorough examination, Rogers rejoined his Company, and reported: "I see the Indians are in a great frolic; they will retire at day break. Now, my boys, be prepared to meet them in the morning before they awake." Those brave defenders of English liberty marched boldly after daybreak, attacked the Indians asleep in their camps, killing their Chief on the spot. The savages thus surprised, being destitute of any effective weapons of defense, fled in disorder before the disciplined pursuers, who followed the skulking tribe along the shore to Rogers' Point, so called in consequence, near the Light House. Here most of them were slain; some being shot on the bank, while others plunged into the water and were drowned. A miserable remnant escaped to the woods.

Abraham Gesner. *New Brunswick with Notes for Emigrants.* 1847a:25-26.

After all the flesh and bones were burned white, so that, when touched, they would fall apart, the deceased's wife came and uncovered the end of his toe, which was very hot. Two men who were standing there, watching, stirred up the flames, and remained by the body until it was merely ashes. The old man's wife held a piece of his bone on her knee. The men who were watching asked what she intended to do with it. "I want to keep it. I shall wrap it in a rag, put it in a box, and think of him when I see it." "I suppose you will eat it." "No, I shall not eat it. He treated me well; I liked him; he will never come back, and I want to have this much of him." "No, you may not keep it. All must be burned." When she saw the man stirring the ashes, she cried.

Peter Ginnish [?], Burnt Church, N.B. In *The Micmac Indians of Eastern Canada*, by Wilson D. Wallis and Ruth Sawtell Wallis. 1955:408.

> *Then your Fathers spoke to us*
> *They said, put up the axe*
> *We will protect you*
> *We will become your Fathers*

1761

During the sitting of the Council on the 13th [of February], Roger Morris [Maurice], one of the Mic-Mac Indians, appeared and brought with him three Frenchmen who were lately arrived from Pictou, and another Indian called Claude Renie [René], who said he was Chief of the Tribe of Cheboudie [?] Indians. He states that he had left 70 of his people at Jeddore; the men were out killing moose and their families were in want of provisions. It was arranged that provisions should be sent to them and that the men should forthwith come up and conclude a peace. Treaties of peace were afterwards concluded on 10th March following with three Mic-Mac Chiefs, viz., Paul Laurent, chief of the tribe of LaHave, Michael Augustine, chief of the tribe of Richibucto, and the before-mentioned Claude Renie, chief of the Cheboudie and Musquodoboit Indians; the treaty was signed in Council on that day, and they received the annual presents. Another treaty of peace was signed in Council on 15th October, 1761, with Jannesvil Peitougawash [Janvier Piktukewa'j, 'person from Pictou'], Chief of the Indians of the Tribe of Picktock [Pictou] and Malagomish [Merigomish].... The following summer Joseph Argunault [L'kimu], Chief of the Mongwash [Pugwash?] Indians, with a number of followers, appeared before the Council and executed a final Treaty of peace.... The Abbé Mallaird [Maillard] being introduced, interpreted the treaty to the Chief.... The Chief then laid the hatchet on the earth, and the same being buried the Indians went through the ceremony of washing the paint from their bodies, in token of hostilities being ended, and then partook of a repast set out for them on the ground, and the whole ceremony was concluded by all present drinking the King's health and their Haggas [Sachems?]. This ceremony is said to have been performed in the Governor's garden, westward of the old English burial ground, where the Court House now stands [Spring Garden Road, Halifax].

Thomas Akins. *History of Halifax City.* 1973:64-66.

1761

During the winter, eight more Indian chiefs surrendered themselves; and the whole Micmac tribe, which then amounted to 6,000 souls, abandoned the cause of France, and became dependant upon the English. The following are the names of the Chiefs that signed the obligation of allegiance, and their places of abode: Louis Francis [François], Chief of Miramichi; Dennis Winemowet, of Tabogunkik; Etienne Abchabo [Aikon Aushabuc], of Pohoomoosh; Claude Atanage, of Gediaak [Shediac]; Paul Lawrence [Laurent], of LaHave; Joseph Alegemoure [L'kimu], of Chignecto, or Cumberland; John Newit [Noel], of Pictou; Baptiste Lamourne, of St. John's Island [Prince Edward Island]; René Lamourne, of Nalkitgoniash [Antigonish]; Jeannot Piquadaduet [Pekitaulit], of Minas; Augustin Michael, of Richibucto; Bartlemy Annqualet [Amquaret], of Kishpugowitk. The above Chiefs were sent to Halifax, and on the lst of July, 1761, Joseph Algimault [L'kimu] (or, as he was called by the Indians, Argimooch), held a *great* talk with Governor Lawrence. The hatchet was formally buried, the calumet was smoked ... the several bands played the national anthem; the garrison and men-of-war fired royal salutes....

Abraham Gesner. *New Brunswick with Notes for Emigrants.* 1847a:46-47.

1761

And, it is no unauthenticated tradition, that during that terrible first winter [at the new settlement of Yarmouth], the Indians supplied the new comers with eels and the flesh of the moose, to the extent of saving their lives.... That the Indians were in the habit of supplying the settlers in very early times with Moose meat, and that at rates that raise a sigh for "the good old times" in that respect at least, the following curious examples will show: "Paid Indon Peter for 16 lbs. Mos Met, @1 1/2 d. Called also Cap. Peter, and again Old Peter...."

£0 2s. 0d. For 14 1/2 lbs. mos @ 1 1/2d

1s. 9d. For 19 lbs of mosmet

2s. 4 1/2d. For 7 1/2 lbs. of mos meet @ 3 cop[p]ers per lb.

J.R. Campbell. *A History of Yarmouth, Nova Scotia.* 1876:19-22.

1761

Treaty of Peace and Friendship concluded by the Honorable JONATHAN BELCHER Esquire President of His Majesty's Council and Commander in Chief in and over His Majesty's Province of Nova Scotia or Acadia &c &c with JOSEPH SHABECHOLOUEST of the Merimichi Tribe of [Micmac] Indians at Halifax in the Province of Nova Scotia or Acadia:

I, Joseph Sabecholouect [Shabecholouest], for myself and the Tribe of Merimichi Indians of which I am Chief Do acknowledge the Jurisdiction and Dominion of His Majesty King George the third over the Territories of Nova Scotia or Acadia, and we do make Submission to His Majesty in the most perfect ample and solemn manner....

And for the more effectual Security of the due performance of this Treaty and every part therof, I do promise and engage that a certain number of persons of my Tribe which shall not be less in number than Two persons shall on or before the Twenty first day of September next reside as Hostages at Fort Cumberland or at [whatever] place or places in this Province of Nova Scotia or Acadia shall be appointed for that purpose by His Majesty's Governor of said Province, which Hostages shall be exchanged for a like number of my Tribe when requested....

I do promise for myself and in behalf of my Tribe, that we will most strictly keep and observe in the most solemn manner. In Witness whereof I have hereunto put my Mark and Seal at Halifax in Nova Scotia this Twenty-fifth day of June One thousand Seven hundred and Sixty one and in the First year of His Majesty's Reign.

JOSEPH SABECHLOUCT [*sic*] His Max [mark].

Joseph Shabecholouest to Jonathan Belcher. In *Selections from the Public Documents of the Province of Nova Scotia*, edited by Thomas Akins. 1869:699-700.

1761

The ceremony observed upon this occasion was conducted in the following manner. The Honorable Mr. President Belcher assisted by His Majesty's Council, Major General Bastide, the Right Honorable the Lord Colvill and Colonel Forster, Commanding Officer of His Majesty's

Forces and the other Officers and principal Inhabitants of Halifax, proceeded to the governor's Farm where proper Tents were erected and the Chiefs of the Indians being called upon, His Honor Spoke to them as follows, the Same being interpreted by Mr. Maillard.

"Brothers. I receive you with the hand of Friendship and Protection in the Name of the great and Mighty Monarch King George the third Supreme Lord and proprietor of North America. I assure myself that you submit yourselves to his allegiance with hearts of Duty and Gratitude as to your merciful Conqueror, and with Faith never to be Shaken and deceived again by Delusions and boastings of our Enemies, over the power of the mighty Fleets and Armies of the August King of Great Britain."

"You see that this triumphant and Sacred King can chastise the Insolence of the Invader of the Rights of his crown and Subjects, and can drive back all his Arrows, and trample the power of His Enemies under the footstool of his Sublime and lofty Throne. As this Mighty King can chastise and Punish, so he has Power to protect you, and all his Subjects against the Rage and Cruelties of the Oppressor."

"Protection and Allegiance are fastened together by Links; if a Link is broken the Chain will be loose. You must preserve this Chain entire on your part by fidelity and Obedience to the Great King George the Third and then you will have the Security of his Royal Arm to defend you."

Then the Chiefs were conducted to a pillar where the Treaties with each Tribe were to be Signed, and there the Commander in Chief went on with his Speech.

"I meet you now as His Majesty's graciously honored Servant in government, and in his Royal Name to receive at this Pillar, your publick Vows of obedience—to build a Covenant of peace with you, as upon the immovable Rock of Sincerity and Truth—to free you from the Chains of bondage—and to place you in the wide and fruitful Field of English Liberty."

"In this Field you will reap Support for yourselves and your Children, all brotherly affection and Kindness as fellow Subjects, and the Fruits of your Industry free from the baneful weeds of Fraud and Subtility. Your Traffick will be weighed and Settled in the Scale of Honesty, and Secured by Severe punishment against any attempts to change the Just Ballance of that Scale."

"Your religion will not be rooted out of this Field—your patriarch will still feed and nourish you in this Soil as his Spiritual Children."

"The Laws will be like a great Hedge about your Rights and Properties—if any break this Hedge to hurt and injure you, the heavy weight of the Laws will fall upon them and punish their Disobedience."

"In behalf of us, now your Fellow Subjects, I must demand, that you Build a wall to secure our Rights from being broken down by the feet of your people—that no provocation tempt the hand of Justice against you and that the great Lenity of His Majesty in receiving you under the Cover of his Royal Wings in this desertion of you by your leader to the Field of Battle, against the Rights of his Crown, when he stipulated for himself and his people without any regard to you, may not be abused by new injuries."

"You see the Christian Spirit, of the King's Government, not only in burying the memory of broken Treaties by some of your People, but in Stretching out the Hand of Love and Assistance to you. Lenity despised may not be found any more by your Submission, and like Razors set in Oil will cut with the keener Edge."

At this period the Presents were delivered to each of the Chiefs, and then the Commander in Chief proceeded.

"In token of our sincerity with you, I give you these pledges of brotherly affection and Love—That you may cloath yourselves with Truth towards us, as you do with these Garments, That you may exercise the Instruments of War to defend us your Brethren against the Insults of any Injurious Oppressor, That your cause of War and Peace may be the Same as ours—under one mighty Chief and King, under the same Laws and for the same Rights and Liberties."

The Indians were then carried to the place prepared for burying the Hatchet where he concluded his Speech.

"While you Blunt the Edge of these Arms and bury them in Symbol, that they shall never be used against us your fellow Subjects, you will resolve and promise to take them up, sharpen and point them against our Common Enemies."

"In this Faith I again greet you with this hand of Friendship, as a sign of putting you in full possession of English protection and Liberty, and now proceed to conclude this Memorial by these solemn Instruments to be preserved and transmitted by you with Charges to Your Children's Children, never to break the Seals or Terms of this Convenant."

The Commander in Chief, having finished his Speech, proceeded with the Chiefs to the pillar where the Treaties were subscribed and sealed, and upon their being delivered and the Hatchets buried, the Chief of the Cape Breton Indians in the name of the rest addressing himself to his Britannick Majesty Spoke as follows, which was likewise interpreted by Mr. Maillard:

"My Lord and Father! We come here to assure you in the name of all those of whom we are Chiefs, that the propositions which you have been pleased to cause to be sent to us in writing have been very acceptable to me and my Brethren, And that our Intentions were to yield ourselves up to you without requiring any Terms on our part."

"Our not doubting your Sincerity has chiefly been owing to your Charitable, mercifull and bountifull behaviour to the poor French wandering up and down the Sea Coasts and Woods without any of the necessaries of Life; certain it is that they, as well as we, must have wretchedly perished unless relieved by your humanity, for we were reduced to extremities more intollerable than Death itself."

"You are now master here; such has been the will of God; He has given you the Dominion of those vast Countries, always crowning your Enterprises with Success—You were, before these Acquisitions, a very great People, but we now acknowledge you to be much more powerfull; tho less great in the extensiveness of your possessions than in the uprightness of your Heart whereof you have given us undoubted and repeated proofs, since the Reduction of Canada—you may be confident that the moderation and Lenity wherewith we have been treated has deeply imprinted in our Hearts a becoming Sense of gratitude—Those good and noble Sentiments of yours towards us in our distressed and piteous Circumstances have emboldened us to come out of the woods, our natural Shelter, from whence we had previously resolved not to stir, till the Establishment of Peace between both Crowns, whatever Hardships we might have suffered."

"Your generous manner, your good heart, your propensity to Clemency, make us hope that no mention will ever be made of any Hostilities that have been committed by us against you and yours. The Succours so seasonably given us in our greatest wants and necessities have been so often the Subject of our Thoughts that they have inspired us with the highest Sentiments of gratitude and Affection."

"We felt ourselves in consequence Forcibly drawn to Halifax to acquaint the Representative of the King, not only with the resolutions we had taken in his favour, arising from his kindness to us, but also to let him understand, that the many proofs he has given us of the goodness of his Heart at a time and in a Conjuncture in which we could not hope for such favourable Treatment, have so intirely captivated Us, that we have no longer a will of our own: His will is ours."

"You now, Sire, see us actually in your presence; dispose of us as you please. We account it our greatest misfortune that we should so long have neglected to embrace the opportunity of knowing you so well as we now do—You may depend we do not flatter. We speak to you at this time according to the dictates of our Hearts. Since you are so good as to forget what is past, we are happy in its being buried in Oblivion. Receive us into your Arms; into them we cast ourselves as into a safe and Secure Asylum from whence we are resolved never to withdraw or depart."

"I swear, for myself, Brethren and People, by the Almighty God who sees all things, Hears all things, and who has in his power All things visible and invisible, that I sincerely comply with all and each of the Articles that you have proposed to be kept inviolably on both Sides."

"As long as the Sun and Moon shall endure; as long as the Earth on which I dwell shall exist in the same State you this day see it, so long will I be your friend and ally, Submitting myself to the Laws of your Government; faithful and obedient to the Crown, Whether things in these Countries be restored to their former state or not; I again Swear by the Supreme commander of Heaven and Earth, by the Sovereign disposer of all things that have life on Earth or in Heaven, that I will for ever continue in the same Disposition of mind I at present am in."

"There is one thing that binds one more strongly and firmly to you than I can possibly express, and that is your indulging me in the free Exercise of the Religion in which I have been Instructed from my Cradle. You confess and believe as well as I, in Jesus Christ the eternal Word of Almighty God. I own I long doubted whether you was of this Faith. I declare moreover that I did not believe you was baptised; I therefore am overwhelmed with great Sorrow and repentance that I have too long given a deaf ear to my Spiritual Director touching that Matter, for often has he told me to forbear imbruing my hands in the Blood of a people who were Christians as well as myself. But at present I know you much better than I did formerly; I therefore renounce all the ill Opinions that have been insinuated to me and my Brethren in times past against the Subjects of Great Britain."

"To conclude in the presence of him to whom the most hidden thoughts of Men's Hearts are laid open; in your presence, governor, (For I conceive that I see in your person him who you represent and from whom you derive your Authority as the Moon borrows her light from the Rays of the Sun); and before all this noble Train who are round about you, I bury this Hatchet as a Dead Body that is only fit to become rotten, looking upon it as unlawful and impossible for me to make use hereafter of this Instrument of my Hostilities against you."

"Let Him be happy and blessed for ever, the august person for the sake of whom I make to Day this funeral! Great God, let him be happy, and blessed during his whole reign over his Subjects. May he never have occasion to scruple calling us his Children, and may we always deserve at his hands the treatment of a Father. Sir, we pray you most humbly, as you are intrusted by George the Third our King, that you will be pleased to inform his Majesty, as soon as possible, of what you have this Day seen and heard from our people, whose Sentiments have now been declared unto the King by my mouth."

The Ceremony concluded with Dancing and Singing, after their manner upon Joyful occasions, and Drinking His Majesty's Health under three Vollies of Small Arms.

"Ceremonials at Concluding a Peace with the several Districts of the General Mickmack Nation of Indians in His Majesty's Province of Nova Scotia and a Copy of the Treaty. 25 June 1761." Public Archives of Nova Scotia, Halifax. RG1, Vol. 37, #14.

1761

Thursday [30 July]—Set Sail from Boston between 11 & 12 Clock A.M.

Tuesday [4 August]: a Fine morning. we Saw divers Islands—Cathartic. —at 10 clock A.M. arrived at Chester [Nova Scotia] and weighd Anchor in a most beautifull Harbour; a hot day—many guns fir'd at our arrival; went on shore and refresh'd our Selves at Mr. Bridge's. Took a view of the Saw mill—very hot. at night an Indian Dance.

Fryday [7 August]: a little rain in ye morning. Two Indian Squaws brought in a Birch Conoe 5 Salmon & 80 Salmon Trout. one of the Salmon weigh'd 22 pound. one dozen of the Trouts weigh'd 14 pounds.

[17 August]: Fair warm day. Din'd on Fresh Cod fish fry'd, & Cucumbers—P.M. went with Cap. Houghton and Others to Gold River, & viewed Mr. Abr: Whitney's Lot, Aaron Mason's &c. Saw several Indian Wigg-wams. Drank fresh Lemon Punch by the Sea-Shore, or rather by the River side.

[29 August]: Fair weather. Settling the affairs of the Town, as drawing, & laying out Lotts. din'd on Bacon Pork & Cabbage. Wine &c.—The Proprietors at Mr. Bridges till between ten & Eleven at night. 2 Indian Squaws brought seil skin & Eels to sell....

Wednesday [16 September]: Cloudy cold. Wind East. Paul Labadore [Labrador] an Indian brought 5 Partridges to Mr. Bridges, who lately killed four Moose, and two Bears. bro't also Dry'd Moose & Tallow. din'd on Salt Fish, Cariots, Eggs & Spanish Potatoes. Indian Squaws brot mink Skins. & a large Bear Skin, sold for a quart of Wine. Some rain.

Wednesday [23 September]: Foggy morning. Fishing at Mill Pond. caught 2 doz. Trout. 1 Pout. 3 Doz. Pond Pearch—Din'd at the Mill-House—Roasted fish &c. Indians brot 2 Salmon: & 30 Dozen great Trouts.

Satterday [17 October]: Fair warm day & calm. Cap. Houghton and Some Others went in the Whale Boat to view some Lots up middle &

Returning to camp with a fish and a duck. Detail from a watercolour by Hibbert Newton Binney, *ca* 1791.

Gold River. see Ab: Whitney's, Mrs. White's, &c. Saw two Wiggwams, & Indians, & Apple trees,—&c. &c. Pork and Cabbage for Supper.

[18 October]: Lords day. Rose early, and Set Sail for Halifax at 8 ho in Floyds Sloop. but the wind proving contrary, we came back abt half after 3 P.M. din'd on board on boild Pork & Cabbage—A very pleasant morning—but began to rain abt 4 P.M. Saw a Shark after mackerel &c & a Turd-eater—supped on Roasted Coots, Indians at Mr. Bridges. &c Cap. Smith & company sang Psalms in the Evning. &c. Thunder'd & Lightned & rained. a warm time.

[20 October]: Got up at l ho. to go to Halifax—Set Sail abt 3 ho. at Night. wind chiefly at north east. we caught 9 Mackerell & 6 Cod fish at Prospect Island. Killd a Pinguin—Struck another with the Boat hook. &c. Two Indians came to ye side of ye vessel, with Ducks & Pinguins on board. we dined on Chowder. The Sea *very calm* all ye passage. vomited at 10 oclock A.M. & again at 5 P.M. The Indians begg'd Tobbacco of us. &c.

Satterday [21 November]: Fair, cool—Pork & Cabbage Turnep &c for dinner—P.M. went with Mr. Bridges to ye Mill, & to view a Lot. Supped on Moose Stakes, dry'd meat. Indians brought in wild Fowl. Bever &c.

[22 November]: Lords day. a very warm pleasant day like May. Preach'd A.M. from Exod. 20:7, P.M. from Ps. 26:9. Indians brot in a Moose (kill'd this morning) and abundance of Ducks, Coots, &c &c. &c. Dined on Broil'd Salmon, some Moose Stakes &c. Supped on fresh Moose Stakes. Very good.

Rev. John Seccombe. "The Diary of Rev. John Seccombe." In *Report of the Board of Trustees of the Public Archives of Nova Scotia for the Year 1959.* Appendix B:20-37.

These old firs, these ancient spruce-trees, full of knots from the top to the root, whose bark is falling off with age, and who yet preserve their gum and powers of life, do not amiss resemble me. I am no longer what I was; all my skin is wrinkled and furrowed, my bones are almost everywhere starting through it. As to my outward form, I may well be reckoned amongst the things, fit for nothing but to be totally neglected and thrown aside; but I have still within me wherewithal to attract the attention of those who know me.

Micmac woman, speaking at a feast. In *An Account of the Customs and Manners of the Mikmakis and Maricheets, Savage Nations, Now Dependant on the Government at Cape Breton,* by Pierre Antoine Simon Maillard. 1758:17-18.

1761

FRIDAY, November 6. PUT myself into the hands of the Indians. There was an old Indian Squaw, with one eye, and her two great sons: they were of the Pookmoosh tribe of Mickmacks—We embarked in a canoe—set our blanket-sail about eleven o'clock—reached Chipagon [Shippegan, N.B.] in the afternoon—this is three leagues from Caraquet—staid here all night.

SUNDAY, November 8. ONE of the Indians carried the bark canoe, the other carried the blankets, guns, and paddles, while the squaw carried the kettle to cook in, with birch bark, and other small things. After we had walked a league further, we pitched our tent for all night.

MONDAY, November 9. ALL this part of the country very low marshy land, full of inlets, where are salt marshes, and abundance of lakes, with vast quantities of wild fowl. Our Indians did not stop to kill any. About noon, arrived at Pookmoosh—here are five or six large cabins of Indians—Their chief called a council upon my coming amongst them— they had just signed a treaty with the English, which I knew; but they said the English had deceived them, by telling them it was peace, whereas the French tell them it is war still.... In answer to what they said, I told them it was war still with the French but peace with the Indians; that the people I had been trading with, had made their submission, and were English subjects. I made the squaw of the chief a present of some trifles such as ribbons, &c. I lodged in a wigwham—ten or a dozen men, women and children all together round a fire—lay upon branches of spruce [fir], and covered with blankets—the fire in the middle of the wigwham—There is a hole at top which lets out the smoak—this is a very large cabin—it would hold twenty people—it was hung round with fish, cut into shreds—they preserve their fish, their geese, and their game, in that manner without salt—they take the bones out, and cut the flesh very thin; then dry it in the smoak for their winter's provision—The name of the chief is Aikon Aushabuc [Etienne Abchabo].

As I did not understand Indian they appointed an Interpreter, who spoke broken French; besides, a person in such a situation as I was then in, is very quick of apprehension; a look or a gesture is often sufficient intimation of their signs. When they wanted to inform me that the French and them were in one interest, they said they were so, (pointing the same way with the forefingers of their right and left hands, and holding them parallel); and when, that the English and Indians were in opposite interests, this they described by crossing their forefingers. Their chief made almost a circle with his forefinger and thumb, and pointing at the end of his forefinger, said there was Quebec, the middle joint of his finger was Montreal, the joint next the hand was New-York, the joint of the thumb next the hand was Boston, the middle joint of the thumb was Halifax, the interval betwixt his finger and thumb was Pookmoosh, so that the Indians would soon be surrounded, which he signified by closing his finger and thumb.

TUESDAY, November 10. ABOUT noon my guides came fresh painted, and we parted from Pookmoosh; and glad I was to get rid of a people who had such absolute power in their own hands, and bore such an enmity to the English.

TUESDAY, November 17. THE storm still continues—have not seen sun, moon, or stars, this seven days—Took a resolution all of us to remove to an Indian camp, about six miles from hence, up the country; but such a road sure never was travelled before—mid-leg deep in water—sometimes crossed brooks up to the middle; some fallen trees and thick underwood made it as bad as possible. I was prodigiously fatigued, as were two of the Indians—we were four hours in getting there. Upon our arrival we found the Indians had deserted their wigwhams; but there was a good covered cabin. In another hut we found some fish and dried geese: I took two of the geese, and paid five shillings sterling to one of the savages, who said he entertained a good opinion of their new allies the English. The savages took fish without ceremony, as their custom is to go into huts, and help themselves to any thing they can find—to eat and drink, without saying one word—Made a large fire, and expect to lie dry to-night, which I have not done these eight nights past.

WEDNESDAY, November 18. LAST night proved a cold dry night—the weather moderate—went back the way we came to our canoe, where we had left our baggage—arrived there about twelve o'clock; and wet as I was, immediately embarked, and with a fair wind reached Merrimichi about six o'clock. I was obliged to be carried out of the canoe into a hut, to warm and dry myself; for I had almost lost the use of my limbs with sitting steady in a bark canoe six hours, wet up to the middle.

FRIDAY, November 20. The chief of the Indians [Louis François, Miramichi] came to me—shewed his treaty with the Governor of Halifax, and said he would conduct me to Fort Cumberland.

SATURDAY, November 21. The Indians here are about fifty fighting men—they are the Merrimichi tribe of Mickmacs.

SATURDAY, December 5. Left our canoe, and went up the creek about a mile; crossed a small river upon the ice, to a deserted house of the French—we found the Indians had been here, but they were gone up the river a hunting—We found the head of a dog smoaked whole, the hair singed off, but the teeth and tongue standing—The Indians, when they make a great feast, kill two or three dogs, which they hold as a high treat— at such times they have a grand dance.

Gamaliel Smethurst. *A Narrative of an Extraordinary Escape out of the Hands of the Indians in the Gulph of St. Lawrence.* 1774:12-14, 16, 18-19.

[This preparation of a dog's head, smoked with the teeth and tongue exposed, was also done when contemplating war. The war chief placed it upon a staff, and passed it to his choice of second in command, who then accepted the honor or declined and passed it to another. Further in his narrative, Smethurst tells us that there had been some talk of war; it had obviously come to nothing.]

1762

… You'll be pleased Sir to excuse my mentioning a Circumstance or two relating to the late Revd. Monsieur Maillard a French Priest [of] the title of Vicar General of Quebec who has resided here some [years] as a Missionary to the French & Indians who stood in so m[uch need] that it was judged necessary to allow him a salary from our Government; He died here the 12th of August last, on the day before his Death at his own Request, I performed the Office for the Visitation of the Sick according to our Form in the French Language to him in the Presence of all the French whom he ordered to attend for that purpose: Our Lt. Governor ordered him to be Buried in our Churchyard, & his Pall was supported by the President of the Council, the Speaker of the House of Assembly & four other Gentlemen, and I performed the Office of Burial according to our form in French in presence of almost all the Gentlemen of Halifax & a very numerous Assembly of French & Indians; most of the Indians here understand French & some few of them English. I was frequently with Mr. Maillard at his Request for several Weeks before he Died; and this visible Respect he shew'd me before the French & Indians may be a Means of my Reasoning with some Success with them to throw aside the Superstitions of Popery, and Embrace & Practice our Pure Religion, which I shall Use my Endeavors at Least to Excite them to, on all Occasions…. Be pleased to Pay my Dutiful Respects to the Venerable

Society, & Permit me to Subscribe myself, Reverend Sir, Your most Obedient & most hble Servt, Thos. Wood. Halifax in Nova Scotia, 27th Oct.:1762. To the Revd. Dr. Burton.

Handwritten copy by Harry Piers: "Rev. Thomas Wood to Rev. Dr. Burton of the Society for the Propagation of the Gospel in Foreign Parts. The Society for the Propagation of the Gospel in Foreign Parts, Lambeth, Letter B.25; Nova Scotia 1760 to 1786." Nova Scotia Museum Printed Matter File.

1763

Indian Tribe of Amquaret [Amecouaret, Anecouret, Annqualet, Momquaret, Nemecharet, Memcharet], now hunting between Cornwallis and the River between the two plains on the Annapolis Road—Summer Residence on the River Pizequid [Avon River] and Gaspero:

Captain Joseph Bernard, 1 boy, 1 girl
Pierre Bernard
Barth[olom]y Amquaret, 2 boys
Bartholomy Amquaret, Jr.
Pierre Amquaret
Paul Amquaret
Phillipe Amquaret, 2 boys, 1 girl
Joseph Dugas [Acadian surname]
François Michel, 1 girl
[Simon?] Amquaret
Blaize Amquaret
Jean Argoumatine [L'kimu, Arguimeau, Alagomartin, etc.], 1 boy, 2 girls
Joseph Argoumatine
Joseph Denis "Jos"
14 men
6 married women
2 aged women
8 boys, 6 girls

Tribe of Nocout [Naucoute, Nicoute, Nocket, Nockwed, Nuffcoat, Nogood, Knockwood], now hunting on Kenecoot [Kennetcook] River in the Township of Newport, Summer residence there also.
Captain Joseph Nocout, 1 boy, 1 girl
Bartholomew Nocout (Joseph Lewis), 2 boys, 3 girls
Thomas Nocout, 1 boy
Paul Segoua [Segueroa], 2 boys, 1 girl
Paul Biskerone [Biscaroon], 1 boy, 2 girls

François Segoua [Segueroa]
Janiver [Janvier] Nocout
14 men
9 married women
3 aged women
9 boys
7 girls

Ft. Edward December 20th, 1763

François Nocout, 1 boy, 2 girls
Claude Nocout
Charles Nocout
René Nocout
Jacques Nocout
Lewis Nocout
Cha[rle]s Segoua
Michel Thoma[s]
Joseph Thoma[s]
Phillipe Nocout
Louis Michel
18 men
19 women
41 children, among which are several orphans
Isaac Deschamps. Public Archives of Nova Scotia, Halifax, MG1, Vol 258, Item 8:8, 20-21.

1764
Jinot Picquid Oulat [Jeannot Pekitaulit] and Bernard, Chiefs of the Mickmack Indians of Cape Breton, being on board his Majesty's Ship *Lark* under my command (when off the Island of Codroy [Newfoundland] in September last) to renew a Treaty of Peace with his Majesty (a copy whereof I have already sent you)....
Captain Samuel Thompson, HMS *Lark*, to Philip Stevens, Secretary to the Lords of the Admiralty, 16 April 1764. Admiralty Records, London, 1/2590, #4. Courtesy Jerry Wetzel, Conne River Band Council, Nfld.

1764
Jenot Piquid Oulat [Jeannot Pekitaulit] and Bernard, two Micmac chiefs, went aboard a warship and informed the captain that they were there to renew the treaty. Then they asked for goods: cloth, gunpowder,

shot, kettles, muskets, hatchets, shirts, twelve cod lines, a salmon net, a compass for a shallop, canvas, and twine. Somewhat taken aback, the captain agreed to bring them what they had requested. He informed the Lords of the Admiralty, and they wrote the Lords of Trade, who replied that it would be highly improper for a ship of the Royal Navy to deliver Indian presents. The Admiralty then informed Governor Wilmot of the situation and stated that if the Indians concerned were of "sufficient rank and consideration," he might meet their demands. By that time Oulat [Pekitaulit] and Bernard were long forgotten.

L.F.S. Upton. *Micmacs and Colonists.* 1979:63-64. See Captain Samuel Thompson, HMS *Lark,* to Philip Stevens, Secretary to the Lords of the Admiralty, 16 April 1764. Admiralty Records, London, 1/2590, #4.

1765

Sometime before there had been a French smuggling vessel upon the coast, on board of which was an artful priest, who had told the Indians, that the Pope had received a letter from Jesus Christ; copies of which his Holiness had been so good as to send to them by him, for which they must pay him thirty pounds of beaver (worth about seven pounds sterling) for each copy; and if they would follow the orders in that letter, a French fleet would come at such a time, and drive the English from their country; in expectation of meeting this fleet the Indians were collected.... that the Indians should refrain, such a limited time, from drinking rum or cyder (the strong liquors the English could furnish them with); they had liberty to drink claret or brandy (what the smuggler was loaded with); and that they should not let the English read one of these letters. I saw one of them hanging to a ribbon, round the neck of a chief, guarded with eight or ten folds of bark—the Indian would have parted with his life as soon as with this paper.

Gamaliel Smethurst. *A Narrative of an Extraordinary Escape out of the Hands of the Indians in the Gulph of St. Lawrence.* 1774:47.

1765

I have sent to the Indians to get a New Sett of Snow Shoes and Dog Slay's made for the whole party, and to get some of them to serve me as Guides to which they will be very Ready, on giving them the Least hopes, of Having a Priest, they have Behaved very well to us but are all praying for that favour. It would be Dangerous for us to tell them to the Contrary. They sent Last Summer one of their Chiefs with a formal Deputation here to Lieut. Colo. Pringle, to beg his Assistance, and to Promise to be as Trusty to King George as they were to King Louis/if they had a Father to Keep them in the Right way (as they Call it).... as they have the King of France's Bust on a Silver Medal which they hang on their Necks it would not be Amiss to Change them for our own Kings. Colonel Pringle made the Chief a Present of a Gorget, and British Collours, with which he was much Pleased.

Samuel Holland. "Letter from Samuel Holland Esqr. surveyor Genl. of the northern district of America, to the Secry., dated Novr. 24, 1765." In *Holland's Description of Cape Breton Island and Other Documents*. Public Archives of Nova Scotia Publication No. 2, 1935:40.

1766

The Salmon come down the Lake in the Fall of the Year; at which Time the Indians take great Quantities. To these parts also great Numbers of Moose Deer & Bears resort. The Entrance of this Bay [Collard's Bay, Cape Breton Island] is very open, & the Bottom shoaly, which renders it unsafe for any Kind of Vessels. There are but four or five Indian Families of the Mickmach Tribe who reside constantly on this Island; they build their Huts on the North West point of this Bay, during the Summers, & in the Winter they move all round the Lake for the Conveniency of Hunting. The whole Tribe have crossed over from the Continent these last two Summers, two Parties of which, came in during the Time the Lake was surveying, one of them was of sixty, the other of one hundred & twenty; & the Summer before there were upwards of three hundred Families.

They behaved very peaceably, but seemed disatisfied at the Lake being surveyed, saying we had discovered now all their private Haunts, which the French never attempted to do. The Reason these People assigned for their rendezvousing here; was to see an old Indian who is upwards of one hundred & twenty years old, quite decriped with Age & Disease who resides constantly on the Island, this Man they say, is the Eldest of their Tribe; & upon his Counsel & Advice they set great Value; but it appears to me that their Chief Motive for assembling here is as they are mostly bigotted Papists, to deliberate upon what Steps they shall take to get a Priest amonst them, for which they are very anxious & frequently spoke to our surveying party in the Lake about it, & also mentioned they would be glad to have a Tract of Land along St. Patrick's Lake & Channel, granted them by His Majesty for the Conveniency of Hunting, & in which they might not be molested by any European Settlers: But as Jannot [Jeannot Pekitaulit] their Chief in this Island, was not yet returned from Newfoundland, to which Place he went last Fall; they could not fix upon the Extent they would have, untill they saw him.

Samuel Holland. "Letter from Samuel Holland Esqr. surveyor Genl. of the northern district of America, to the Secry., dated Novr. 24, 1765." In *Holland's Description of Cape Breton Island and Other Documents*. Public Archives of Nova Scotia Publication No. 2, 1935:67-68.

Long ago [in Newfoundland] there were men hunting moose [caribou; there were no moose in Newfoundland at this time], living far out in the woods, not near the shore at all, living at ponds in the woods. Those were red folks [the Beothuk Indians; the last Beothuk died in captivity in 1823]. [Micmac] men hunting moose came to the pond, and could not go around it. They saw one wigwam. They saw one Red fellow come out with his wife and baby. The Red people had canoes of moose hide with double paddle. The Red man went towards his canoe, to cross to where the hunters were hiding. One hunter said, "What will we do to them now?—I am going to shoot into the air to scare them." The others said, "You better not, those people are witches, *buowina* [*puoinaq*], they might do something to us."—"I don't care," said the man, "I'm going to shoot into the air."—As soon as the Red fellow put down his bow, he shot into the air. The Red man and woman were so frightened they dropped down into the deep moss. After they felt a little better, they sat up and felt themselves all over. The man threw the little baby over his back and jumped, jumped like deer, not like us. He and the woman went jumping away off.

The fellows in hiding came out to look at the leather canoe. They looked into it and saw a leather bag. They opened it. It was full of little bone animals, deer, moose, fox, wild-cat, every animal that goes in the woods. One man said, "You better leave that bag alone." They looked at the wigwam. It was round, set up with sticks, very close with no birch bark cover. There were no boughs on the ground, only little holes to lie in, three holes there, for man, woman and baby. There were plenty of hides. (There was nothing to sit on, no chair, no log, they must have been like monkeys, wasn't that funny?) One man said, "I'm going to take this bag."—"No, don't take it. Dear knows what it will do to you." He took it and they all left, they went along quickly, perhaps there were more of these Red people. They went sneaking along. About five miles away they found another camp.

Butchering a moose before the family wigwam. Detail from a watercolour by Hibbert Newton Binney, *ca* 1791.

They sneaked up to the door, they opened the door and said, "Gweh!" [Micmac greeting, *kwe*]. In there were a girl and a middle-aged woman. They grabbed them and took them away with them to their homes. The woman's breasts were full of milk. (Must have been another wigwam there, where her baby was.) She was crying, crying every day. The people used them well. They could not understand one word they said. One day the two women went up the brook and found some soft red stones. In the evening the older woman mixed the red stones (*wioj*) [*wiukuj*, 'red ochre'], with grease (beaver castor, *kobit wigau*) and put the red paint on her face and hands and all over her body. They combed their hair with stone combs, and made two braids hanging in front.... After three moons [their captors] said, "Now we'll put questions to the women. Wonder what their names?" One fellow coaxed them, he asked, "What your name?"—"Simum (Wild goose)," one said. The other said, "Blauwich [*plawej*] (Partridge)." The girl became sick, she was so lonesome. The boys who stole them found everything running short, they were in hard lines. The Red folks had bewitched them for stealing the two women. One old man told them, "You better take the women back." When the girl got better, they took them back.

Mary Doucet Newell [Noel] (born *ca* 1800 in Newfoundland). In "Micmac Folklore," by Elsie Clews Parsons. *Journal of American Folklore*, 1925, vol. 38:55-133.

ca 1767

James Brown, born Apl 12, 1741, came from Ipswich Mass. in 1767 to Yarmouth to settle at what is now called Chegoggin near Zachariah Chipmans, built a log house and after living there, went back to bring his wife to her new home—When they got back (they could then sail up to their home) they found the Indians had possession of the house and were just roasting a moose which they had killed in front of the fireplace. They had some difficulty in driving the Indians out and had to keep watch with their guns for the night—Mrs. Brown was quite alarmed they being the first Indians she had seen.

From an old document found in the Bethiah Brown Bain Family Bible. Courtesy Deborah Trask.

[James and Mary Potter Brown were Bethiah Bain's parents. The bible is still in the family, in the possession of Mr and Mrs Stuart Trask.]

1772

The population of Nova Scotia, in a report to the Board of Trade, is stated at 17,000, exclusive of 1300 Acadians in Nova-Scotia, 800 in Cape Breton and 20 blacks. The militia returned at 3000. The small population of Indians at 865.

Thomas Chandler Haliburton. *An Historical and Statistical Account of Nova Scotia.* 1829, II:250.

1777

[During the American Revolution] the Indians were holding a Grand Council at Bartibog Island, and had resolved upon the death of every individual belonging to the infant [New Brunswick] settlement. While the Council was sitting.... the *Viper* sloop-of-war, commanded by Captain Harvey, appeared in the Bay. She had captured the American Privateer *Lafayette*, and in order to decoy the savages, she was sent up the river under American colours. But the Indians were too chary to be deceived by this stratagem, and, by assuming the character of pirates, they resolved to make a prize of the vessel. Upwards of thirty of them were allowed to come on board. After a desperate struggle, they were overpowered; and such as were not killed in the affray were put in irons. Among these desperadoes was one named Pierre Martin, whose strength and savage courage were truly characteristic of his tribe. Two marines were unable to bind him, and he nearly strangled two others with whom he was engaged. After he had received several severe wounds, he tore a bayonet from the hands of a sailor, and missing his thrust at one of his opponents, he drove the weapon through one of the stanchions of the vessel. Covered with wounds, the savage at last fell, as was supposed to rise no more; but even in his dying moments, when his flesh was quivering under deep sabre-cuts, and his body was bathed in blood, he sprang to his feet, and fastened himself upon the throat of one of his companions, upbraiding him with cowardice. He had almost strangled the trembling Indian, when he was despatched by one of the crew. The wretches thus taken were sent to Quebec, and nine of them were afterwards put on board a vessel bound to Halifax.

On her passage the vessel engaged an American privateer. Etienna Bamaly [?], one of the prisoners, requested leave to fight for King George. Permission was given him—his irons were removed, a musket put in his hands, and he killed at two different times the helmsman of the American cruiser. The English gained the victory; and when the prize was brought to Halifax, Bamaly was liberated on account of his bravery. Of sixteen Indians carried away, only six ever returned to Miramichi....
Abraham Gesner. *New Brunswick with Notes for Emigrants.* 1847a:48-49.

1778

The concern of supplying themselves [with annual presents from the French government] while renewing their fidelity to the King of France, was not the only motivation which led the Micmac to Saint-Pierre et Miquelon. They benefitted each time from their visit to perform their devotions and receive the sacrament. We have counted 22 baptisms, 6 marriages, and 3 burials among the Micmac. A marriage bond, dated the 26th of July, 1778 [reads]: "The dispensation of three banns obtained and granted by us, by our apostolic powers, and for serious reasons, such as all dispensation of consanguinity on account of need, except notwithstanding consanguinity of the first, as well as the second degree; all dispensation by us due to our apostolic powers (such as we have explained, because we could not define anything clearly about these good people, except that it seemed to us that the spouses were never relatives, neither in the first or second degree), I, the undersigned [Abbé Paradis], apostolic prefect, having questioned, on the one part, Louis ... called Beguiddavalouet [Pekitaulit], aged about 27, therefore oldest son of Bernard ... called Beguiddavalouet, and of Marie-Anne Gougou, his wife—recently dead by an accident of a rock-slide, passing under a cape along the mainland of Newfoundland—his father and mother, baptised in Cape Breton, by the late M. Maillard, former missionary to the Indians, Bishop of Québec; and, on the other part, Jeannette Doujet [Doucet], aged about 20, younger daughter of Guillaume Dojet [*sic*], and of Marie-Magdelaine Pegilahadeschz, his wife, her father and mother, baptised on Isle St-Jean, by M. Cassiet, parish of St. Louis in the northeast, Bishop of Québec: both at present living on the islands of Berjaus [Burgeo] in Newfoundland, and now visiting the island of Miquelon; after receiving their mutual consent, I saw in the middle of the night the necessity of their sudden departure from Miquelon; solemnly joined them in marriage by words, and then gave them the wedding benediction. For witnesses, there was the whole band of Indian men and women, who had come to us for their Easter [Devotions], and who, out of friendship, wanted to have as witnesses Pépin Pichard, whom I used around them as interpreter, and Germaine Pichard, his brother, both living on this island."

Jean-Yves Ribault. *Les Iles Saint-Pierre et Miquelon.* 1968:30-31. Translated for this publication by Scott Robson.

[The name Gougou also appears as Cooko, Gogo, Gogoo, Googo, Gougon, and Gontgont—the letter *u* being read mistakenly as *n*.]

1779

Abstract of Expenses incurred by the Indians of Nova Scotia between the 10th of June 1778, and the 20th Octo. 1779, Occasioned by their Committing several Acts of Hostilitys and Outrages, and Exhibiting evident marks of their Intention to Cooperate with his Majestys Rebellious Subjects in America, and other the Kings Enemies, viz:

from March 25 to May 4

To Expences incurred by sending to Tatamagushe, Margomishe, and Pictou, to compose a quarrel that had arisen between the Indians of that Neighbourhood, and Martin Meagher Master of the Snow *Industry*, frozen up at Margomishe; whom they were preparing to destroy, together with the Settlements of Pictou, on Easter Day if no[t] redressed before;

the Quarrel happend about the 16th of February—85 pounds 8 shillings 9 1/2 pence.

Public Archives of Nova Scotia, Halifax. CO 217, Vol. 54.

[A "snow" is a type of sailing vessel.]

1782

Finally we reached the shore of Acadia and sighted the bay of Halifax with general jubilation…. We were brought to Halifax because there were already enough troubles in New York and the other provinces with the royalists, and therefore unloading could not be done safely…. The savages, as far as I could observe, always behaved properly. Supposedly this had not always been the case, and the governor is said to have had them confined militarily to stop their natural behaviour regarding sex. When they were full of rum and happy, they began to conduct a dance right down at the shore, dancing to a kind of muttering to which some of them improvised the rhythm with pebbles. On our longer excursions we came into their wigwams [erected] near rocks and brooks; most of them had withdrawn deeper [into the forest]. I never heard that they harmed any of our men; and if so it probably would have been the fault of the European. Some were on our side [during the American Revolution], some on the side of the Republicans, according to their mood and situation; it would have been hard to decide whether they were cheated more here or there.

For a long time they have been quite skilled with guns, and generally they carried old, large, long Dutch muskets, with which they could hit with exquisite accuracy from several hundred yards' distance, and they shot many a guard from the thickers, without anybody knowing from whence the bullet came.

When the French were masters of Canada, they endeavoured through their missionaries to fence the Americans into Christianity; so some of the old ones amongst them, when hearing the bells, will cross themselves and say " *au nom de Dieu, du pére, du fils, et du saint esprit.*" That seemed to be the only remnant of their knowledge of [the French] language and religion….

Those [Micmac] that I have seen were a tall, beautiful, sinewy kind of people, with longish regular features like the original Brandenburgers. I don't remember having seen anyone taller than 5'9" or shorter than 5'3"; so there was rarely anybody as small as my person, which is not regarded as dwarfish amongst us….

Normally they came [into Halifax] by sea, in their birchbark boats, which were masterfully built, and which they knew how to guide superbly with their little paddles.... They made long voyages along the coast in these boats, and go out to sea in them for extraordinary distances.
Johan Seume. *Mein Leben.* 1961:73-77. Translated for this publication by Horst Deppe.
[Seume was a corporal in the Hessian contingent of the British Army, and was stationed in Halifax between 1782 and 1784.]

1783

A License for Paul Pemmenwick [Peminuit] and the Indians in the District of Shubenaccadie, & Cobequid, To Occupy a Tract of Land Situate Laying and being on the River called Stewiake, to the Eastward and Adjoining land granted to late Erl [*sic*] of Egmont, and others extending one mile Back on each Side the said River, and Two Miles in a right line up the said River, Measuring from the Eastern Bound of said Egmon's [*sic*] land Containing Two Thousand and Five hundred and Sixty Acres, & for hunting & fishing as Customary.
Public Archives of Nova Scotia, Halifax. RG1, Vol. 430, 23.5, 17 December 1783.
[This Paul Peminuit seems to have been the ancestor of all the hereditary chiefs at Shubenacadie known to the English as Pauls. The English took the baptismal name and used it as a surname, but these descendants regarded themselves as the "Peminuit Paul" lineage, as distinct from other lines of descent having the surname Paul. On 19 December, Jacques Peminuit, written "Jack or James Pemminwicke"—possibly Paul Peminuit's brother—was also granted land at Shubenacadie. See *Our Land: The Maritimes,* edited by G.P. Gould and A.J. Semple. 1980:41.]

1782-1784

I remember an incident that much entertained us. I was on guard duty in a small outer battery [for Halifax Harbour]; I sat on a cannon and looked out to sea, which was quite rough. And I spotted something floating a great distance out; everyone was trying to guess what it might be, but nobody guessed right. When it drifted closer in, we saw that it was an Indian canoe of birchbark, which the wind was pushing ashore. We ran down and found in the bottom an old native, sleeping quietly through the storm. Beside him lay one empty and one half-empty bottle of rum, which must have contributed to his sleep. We could not wake him, and his condition could easily be guessed. We took him up to the guardhouse, laid him down in the quietest part on a camp-bed, where he continued his sleep. We pulled the boat ashore, saved the bottle; I took the purse that he carried on his belt and in which there were 40 Spanish Dollars, and locked them up in a cabinet, out of concern.

When he sobered up and woke, he looked around him most wildly and astonished to find himself in a European outpost. When we explained to him the dangerous situation in which we found him, he became cheerful and was just starting to thank us when he looked at his belt and missed his purse; his face became longer and wider and a mixture of feelings appeared to work in his soul, which said it all: "Ha, ha! That's it? You are now among the white people"; but as I gave him the purse from the cabinet and he confirmed that everything appeared to be there at first glance, and assuming that we would not have kept part if we could have kept the whole, his joy became profound. He embraced one after the other of us, and one could see that it was not the money that he cared for, but the company of honest people; and when he finally counted the sum, he insisted that the people on duty should take a handful of the money. I had good reason to reject that; but we had to take some.

Then he shoved himself back into his canoe, with good memories, and warnings against the rum bottle. He seemed very thankful. The weather had improved, and he paddled happily across the bay and out into the ocean.

Johan Seume. *Mein Leben.* 1961:88. Translated for this publication by Brigitte Beckershaus Petersmann.

1785

The three mentions of burials we have found in parish registers of the colony pose a morbid question. The 21st of April the Indians brought with them the body of a certain Jacques, who had died in Newfoundland the 15th of February previous; the 12th of September of the same year, there was buried at Saint-Pierre, the body of Marie, widow of André, who had died in Newfoundland, aged 91 years, four months earlier; and the next year, on the 6th of September, the Indians brought the body of Anne Etiennchuit, widow of André Gougou, who had also died in Newfoundland, the preceding 25th of May. How was it that the Micmac could conserve the bodies of their dead for such a long time? It is probable they used a technique similar to that of drying fish, preserving the bodies in salt.

Jean-Yves Ribault. *Les Iles Saint-Pierre et Miquelon.* 1968:31-32. Translated for this publication by Scott Robson.

1786

Having arrived at the Indian Village in company with Mons. Bourg Grand Vicar and Missionary to the Tribe of Restigouche Indians last night at 11 o'clock, we in pursuance to the important objects of Our Commission from his honor the Commander in Chief and Honorable Council of Quebec assembled Joseph Claude 1st Chief of this Tribe, Joseph Gagnon 2nd and Francis Ewit dit Condo [*kuntaw,* 'stone'] 3d and having by means of an Interpreter, (furnished us by Mons. Bourg) explained to them the following address we delivered it in writing to them, that they might have an opportunity of and consideration of its contents of presenting a Real State of their grievances and claims....

Nicholas Cox, Lt. Govr. John Collins, Dept. Survr. Genl. Restigouche New Mission, June 29th, 1786. Source unknown.

1790

The Honorable Thomas Crawley then represented to the Board that he learned from good authority that in open violation of the first Ordinance posted to prevent the destruction of Moose and Caraboo, near 9000 Moose were killed in this Island [Cape Breton] during the year 1789 merely for the sake of their skins, the meat being left to perish in the Woods and notwithstanding the late Ordinance in addition to the former, large Gangs of People are now collected in different parts of this Island chiefly consisting of persons not inhabitants thereof, with the sole intention of destroying the Moose for the sake of their skins....

Extract, Council Minutes, 9 March 1790. Public Archives of Nova Scotia, Halifax. RG1, Vol. 319:315.

The moose and caribou ... are the principal animals; the former now comparatively scarce, owing to an indiscriminate massacre which took place for the sake of the hides, soon after the English settled in the country. So murderous was the destruction of this fine animal, that hundreds of carcasses were left scattered along the shore from St. Ann's to Cape North; the stench from which was so great, as to be wafted from the shore to vessels at a considerable distance at sea.

R. Montgomery Martin. *A History of Nova Scotia and Cape Breton.* 1837:100.

1791

Walking in one of the streets I observed an Indian Canoe, which had been conveyed thither from the water; it was between 18 & 20 feet in length

and measured two feet 8 inches across in the broadest part.... The
Company which came in this boat consisted of three women, a boy about
15 years old, and an infant at the breast as I saw them in the street I desired
them to follow me home. These women were somewhat low in stature
and all of them had a yellowish or copper coloured complexion with long
straight black hair—Their dress consisted of a flowered woollen jacket
reaching to the waist and a coarse blue short petticoat, a cap mad[e] of
cloth angular to the upper and back part of the head, and ornamented
with small white beads; round their neck, they likewise wore several
strings of different coloured beads to which was affixed a silver cross. The
boy had on a coarse blue jacket and canvas trousers. What little these
Indians understood of the English language was spoken with a very
drawling accent, they appeared well acquainted with the value of each
article they had brought (viz Cranberries & wild fowl) singly, but when
they had sold several at the price they required they were entirely at a loss
in what manner to calculate the amount or sum total—In this respect,
therefore, they were wholly at the mercy of the Whites, who might readily
have cheated them with impunity and without fear of detection, seeing
that these poor Indians implicitly relied on their honesty—I am afraid
there are many in this Province who take every advantage of them. I
offered these Indians each a glass of spirits which I imagined they were
fond of, but they rejected it with marks of abhorrence, giving me to
understand that they could eat bread or biscuit. I presented them with
some of the latter, which they accepted with visible pleasure. I understood they had left their Wigwams this morning and intended returning
immediately. Their residence therefore could not be a great distance from
Halifax. After buying of them their Ducks, &c. &c.

J. Clarkson. *Clarkson's Mission to America, 1791-1792.* Public Archives of Nova Scotia,
Halifax 1971:69-70.

1791

Then setting out pretty early, we set up sails in both canoes, and
alternately sailed, poled, and paddled.... Many more streams falling into
this river below the Kain [Cain's River, N.B.] than above, heightened the
prospect all along, till we arrived at the point where the river Renow
[Renous] falls into the Merimashee [Miramichi] on the north side. Here
we saw an Indian and his Squa making some small, but very neat baskets
of Porcupine quills of various colours. Their method of dying the quills
is as follows: They pick up small pieces of cloth of every colour they can

find. These they scrape down as small as they can, and boil separately in kettles, till the dye is extracted from the wool; then put in the quills in them. This dyes them, and gives them as fine colours as can be wished; indeed I never saw any more brilliant.... Having encamped and slept all night on the banks of the [Restigouche] river, we set out pretty early next morning, and.... I observed two Wigwams; I went in to see them, and found both of them without an inhabitant. The families had been then either fishing or hunting. The furniture of these temporary habitations consisted of several dishes made of birch bark, finely ornamented, and boxes of Porcupine quills, as I supposed for sale. Besides these, I saw a root drying, which the Indians use as a cure for many complaints, and took a piece of it along with me. The name they give it, I think, is Calomet [*Acorus calamus*, sweet flag]. It has a strong spicy taste, an aromatic scent, and heats the stomach almost as much as a dram.

Patrick Campbell. *Travels in North America*. 1968:61, 76-77.

My great-great-grandfather was called Francis Basque. He was a Basque, Basque fisherman, married to an Indian in St. Peters, and went native. He lived amongst the Indians. I guess he was really a strong Catholic. Then [together] with this Pierro or Cremo, I think it was Cremo, it's not very likely he was an Indian either, well, they built the first church in Chapel Island, about 1790. This Francis Basque had quite a few sons; I often think they must have went back to sea, most of them. But he had quite a few boys, and they were cuttin' timber for the church. My father, Simon Basque, said Francis must have been a very religious man, because these fellows was cuttin' timber for the church, and they got to tellin' dirty stories. And great-great-grandfather didn't like the idea, he told them, the rest, the foreman or whoever they were, "We're cuttin' wood for Our Lord's house, and if your gang's goin' keep on tellin' dirty stories, I'll take my crew away, my sons away. I won't help yous any more." So they had to cut out the dirty yarns, or anything else, cuttin' this timber. So that's the kind of a man he was.

Max Basque to R.H. Whitehead, taped interview, March 1984.

1792

"By His Excellency William Macormick, Lieutenant Governor and Commander in Chief, in and over the Island of Cape Breton, and its Dependencies, etc. Permission is hereby granted to Francis Bask [François Basque, a Basque fisherman], Tomma Michael [Thomas Michel] and

Micmac woman making a splint basket. Detail from Hibbert Newton Binney's watercolour of a Micmac camp, *ca* 1791.

others the native Indians of the Island of Cape Breton and its Dependencies to take possession of the Island commended situate lying and being in Grenville for the purpose of erecting thereon a Chapel to be used and appropriated for performing Divine Service agreeable to the Rites and Ceremonies of the Roman Catholic Religion—to hold, use, occupy and possess the same during His Majesty's pleasure. Given under my hand and seal of Arms at Sydney in the Island of Cape Breton this [28 November 1792]. W. Macormick."

True copy, [made at] Restigouche, June 27, 1911. J. Pacifique. Original grant, all worn out, in possession of Noel Googoo of Truro.

Père J. Pacifique, Restigouche, Québec, to Harry Piers, June 1911. Nova Scotia Museum Printed Matter File.

Francis Basque was the first one to use knife and fork and spoon politely at the table. And the Indians, they had been Catholic a long while, but they still had that old habit of eatin' with their hands. And they thought it was awful: "He thinks more of the white man's tools than he does of our Good Lord's tool." Said, "His hands ain't good enough, he has to use them man-made articles to eat with," and they didn't think much of him. But when he got a saucer for his cup, that was the pay-off. They said, "Our Lord's ground, our Mother the earth, ain't good enough for him, he's got to set it on somethin'." And they began to talk about putting him to death for his blasphemy. Said a man like that should be put to death, 'cause he ain't fit to live. He had a hard time to talk them out of it. At that time I guess they spring-poled them. They'd get a long slender birch or somethin' stronger, climb up and bring it down like a spring pole, then tie the prisoner to it, and when the thing was released, it snapped their necks. They claimed that's the way they used to hang people. But great-great-grandfather managed to talk them out of it. Yes, they were going to put him to death for usin' forks; well, they didn't say too much about him usin' knife and fork, but when he used a saucer to put his cup on, they said Our Lord's ground's not good enough for him. So they said he should be put to death.

Max Basque to R.H. Whitehead, taped interview, March 1984.

THE
NINETEENTH
CENTURY
1800 TO 1899 A.D.

AT THE BEGINNING OF THE NINETEENTH CENTURY, population figures for the Micmac were so low that it was expected that they would soon follow the Beothuk Indians into extinction. Various governmental and philanthropic groups had hopes of establishing the People in the practice of agriculture, so that they might once more have a dependable food supply, settle down, and become "responsible citizens" cut to a European pattern. An auspicious start to the farming communities thus set up was doomed when in 1844 the potato blight appeared—the same blight which caused the Irish famine. For at least three years, this disease, the "poison wind," raged. In two of those years, wet weather ruined the hay and grain crops also, and this in turn affected the livestock. A wheat weevil and a drought were the last straws, and the Micmac were forced back into whatever diminished subsistence the forests could provide, and a life of roaming from place to place, selling or bartering baskets, axe handles, butter churns and other works of their hands. Borderline starvation was the rule. Tuberculosis and other diseases reaped their own harvests. Infant mortality was extraordinarily high—single families often lost 12 or more of their offspring. But the 1800s also saw—perhaps as a result of Chief Louis-Benjamin Peminuit Paul's appeal to Queen Victoria— the beginnings of some sense of compassion on the part of the colonial government. Now the setting aside of reserve lands was begun, and the creation of Indian agencies to provide financial and medical relief, and—at least in theory—legal recourse for the Micmac People.

> *Fathers, they promised to leave us*
> *Some of our land*
> *But they did not*

1800

Mr. Monk presented a Petition of David Marc Antoine, in behalf of himself and forty families of Indians belonging to the District of Antigonishe, Pomquet and Tracadie in the Gulf of St. Lawrence, addressed to his Excellency the Lieutenant Governor, and by his Excellency recommended to the Consideration of the House and the same was read, setting forth: that the Petitioners are in a starving Condition, and almost destitute of Clothing, in consequence of the Failure of Game in their Hunting Grounds; and the difficulty of catching Fish from the great thickness of the Ice, and the uncommon depth of Snow adjoining the Shores, and praying relief, and thereupon, *Ordered,* That the Petition do lie on the Table.

Legislative Assembly of Nova Scotia Journals. 2 April 1800.

Mrs. Andrew Paul, of Tufts Cove, Dartmouth, now about 84 years of age, says her grandfather Toney trapped beaver with wooden dead-falls at Black-Duck Pond (Egg Pond) on the flat part of the Commons at Halifax, and that afterwards when work was done there remains of Beaver work cuttings were found there, in her own recollection. Her father Joe Toney, who died at age of 102 years, was the last man to kill a Moose on [what is now] the Halifax Common near the Pond.

Mrs Andrew Paul to Jeremiah Bartlett Alexis [alias Jerry Lonecloud] to Harry Piers, 20 December 1915. Nova Scotia Museum Printed Matter File.

[Mrs Andrew Paul was born about 1831; her first husband's name was Glode.]

1800

Joseph Purnall [Bernard] has made several attempts to settle [in Pictou County] by planting potatoes, Indian corn, beans, &c. Indeed, the greater part of the Indians who frequent this quarter have shown a disposition to settle, by planting a little, as above, in several parts of this district. An Indian from "Mathews Vineyard" [Martha's Vineyard, Mass.], named Samuel Oakum, who has married into this tribe, is a tolerable mechanic in several branches, particularly coopering and rigging vessels, and is also a pretty good sailor.

Edward Mortimer to Judge Monk, Superintendent of Indian Affairs. In *History of the County of Pictou, Nova Scotia,* by George Patterson. 1972:193.

1800

Names of Indians Belonging to Kings County ...

Francis Nicholas, 99, Widow.

Caledonia [?], 68, widow of John Bobbei or Batiast [Baptiste]; Peter, 28, & Paul, 19, his sons.

Malaan Algomatin [Mary Anne L'kimutin], 27, wife of Peter B[obbei] or Batiast; 1 daughter, 3.

Josiah Solomon, 14.

Joseph Philip, 43; Molly Algomatin his wife, 40; Joseph, 18, Sally, 16, Hannah, 14, Peter, 4, Mal [Marie] Joseph, 2, their children.

Magdalen Algomatin, wife of Peter Algomatin who died here, 63; Samuel Algomatin, 19; Molly Algomatin,15, her children.

Bartholomew Amquaret, 64; Mally [Marie] Sally his wife, 43; Louis, 13, Andrew, 18, Susannah, 2.

Cloud Antoni [Claude Antoine], 20; Ativite [?] Antoni, 9, Mary Son [Jane] Antoni, 15.

Peter Francis, 28; Magdalen Segow, his wife, 27; 1 young child.

Magdalen Segow, 65; Molly, 17, Sally, 19.

Francis Nogood [Knockwood], 75.

John Wilmot, 45.

Daniel Toney, 40.

Joseph Penhall [Bernard].

Joseph Nogood.

Jon. Crane's Account, 1800. Public Archives of Nova Scotia, Halifax. RG1, Vol. 430, #77.

[I have included this and other census material to show, first, the pitifully few people included therein, and also because here one can see how nomenclature is changing. There are still some Micmac names used as surnames, but both they and the French baptismal names are undergoing transformations. 'Antoine' has become 'Antoni,' 'Tonny' and 'Toney'; 'Naucoute' is now 'Nogood,' but not yet 'Knockwood.']

1801

Return of Indians resident in the District of Pictou:

Luland [Laurent] Mercateaey, son of Francua [François]

Sap'r [Xavier] Mercatuwia [Mercateaey], son of Francua [the two names Mercateaey and Mercatuwia appear to derive from "*mercateria {mercatzalia}*, which is a word of reproach among them, borrowed of the Basques, signifying a cheese-parer {a stingy person}." (Lescarbot, 1963, III:213)]

Maltil Sapier [Martin Xavier], son of Sapier Mercatuwia
Newel Sapier [Noel Xavier], son of Sapier Mercatuwia
John Tonny, son of Captain Tonny [Antoine]
Chas Tonny, son of Captain Tonny
John Patlis [Patlass], son of Petitiou
Mulis Petitiou, son of Petitiou
Newell Patlis, son of John Patlis
Old Paul, son of Sallan [Jerome]
Assum [Abram?] Paul, son of Old Paul
Francis Paul, son of Old Paul
Sapier Paul, son of Old Paul
Joseph Purnal [Bernard], son of Peter Pernal
John Pernal, son of Joseph Pernal
Peter John, son of Patist [Baptiste]
Peter John Jr., son of Peter John Sr.
Francis John, son of Peter John Sr.
Silly Boy Levi ['Sylliboy' is the Micmac pronunciation of 'Levi'; the word
   here read as Levi is, however, indistinct and could be 'Luci'—the
   French name Alexis is sometimes written Luci or Luxi. However,
   people were often called by both the Micmac and English versions of
   their names, as in Andrew Hadley.]
Francis Wilmot, from A.K.W. [?]
Jne. William & 2 Brothers, Saldlnah [?]
Old Mitchell, no father's name given
Sam'l Oakum [an Indian from Martha's Vineyard, Mass., who married
   a Micmac woman]
Francis, blind man & mother
Allmis Pulpis, son of Palpis [Porpus]

Public Archives of Nova Scotia, Halifax. RG1, Vol . 430, #62. 19 March 1801. Edited
for this publication by R.H. Whitehead.

One good story of an Indian outwitting a Priest, I must tell as I found
it in my Father's Diary, who was the Chaplain of one of his Majesty
King George's frigates, on the North American Station [*ca* 1800-1810?]:
   "An Indian lost his father. The Priest, representing to him the
Torments of Purgatory, persuaded his apparently simple Votary to
purchase the parent's release by paying certain skins for the requisite
number of Masses. The Masses were said, the day of Payment arrived,
and the Indian appeared, bringing with him the skins, the ransom of
years of damnation. The Priest eyed his imagined Prize with feelings

of Exultation. The Indian enquired if the Priest had fulfilled his part of the contract, and being answered in the affirmative, he repeated the demand with increased earnestness, if [the Priest] was quite sure his Father was out of that Horrible Place? 'Quite sure,' replied the Priest. 'Damned fool him to go back again, then,' said the Indian, and shouldering his Pole of Skins, away he walked to the utter dismay of the disappointed Padre."

Campbell Hardy. "Evangeline's Land." Unpublished MS, *ca* 1910. Nova Scotia Museum Printed Matter File.

"Campbell Hardy was born at Norwich, Norfolk, England, on 10th October 1831, and was the eldest son of the Rev. Charles Hardy, M.A., of Whitewell, Hertfordshire. In the earliest years of the nineteenth century the latter had been a chaplain on one of King George's frigates on the North American Station, and had visited Nova Scotia." (Harry Piers, "Obituary, Major-General Campbell Hardy, R.A." 1919)

ca 1801
An Account of Indians that belongs to Queens County:
Joseph Groade [Claude, Glode], self, 4 children & Mother
Joseph Atley [André], dead, mother & sister, & 2 children
Peter Beatle [possibly Bateau; see 1808-1809 entry], self, wife, & 2 boys
Andrew Beatle, wife & 2 children
Paul Williams, & 3 children
John Williams, wife & 1 child
Sellon Grodd [Jerome Claude], wife & 3 children
Molti Groad [Martin Claude], & wife
Martin Groad, wife & 6 children
Pelig Gload [Peleg Claude], wife & 6 children
Joseph Groad, 2d, wife & 4 children
Andrew Groad, wife & 6 children
Joseph Groad, 3d, wife & 5 children, mother and daughter
Nicolas Groad, single man
Francis Groad, young man
Peter Groad
Newel & mother, wife, & 2 children
Joseph Pigtoe [Pictou], wife & child
Lewey Pigtoe, & Molti Pigtoe
Paul Pigtoe, mother & son
The Priest belonging to Sicabo [Sissiboo; the Abbé Jean-Mandé Sigogne]

William Barss' Account, n.d. [possibly in response to questionnaire sent out 23 January 1801]. Public Archives of Nova Scotia, Halifax. RG1, Vol. 430, #57.

1802

Return of Indian Meal, Blankets & Potatoes ... for the use of decayed &
orphan Indians residing in the Eastern District of Nova Scotia between the
1th day of January 1802 & 31th March Included:
Molly Porpus [Palpis, Pulpis], widow & several children
Fransway [François], a Lame Indian & Wife old
Captn Marble [L'Amable], wife and Children very poor
Captn Thomas, wife & family old
Old Catherina with four Grand Children
To Widows with Familys at Country Harbour
Mary Soloman, widow, & child
Widow Prosper with seven children
John Batist wife and Family a Cripple
Hannah very old Indian Woman
Mary Joseph old Indian Woman
Manach Micheal [Monique Michel?], widow & three children
Joseph Gays widow
Margeret Joseph widow
Newil Brinaugh & Family
Molly Peter & child
A Cripple Orphan girl Maintaind by Porpus
Molly Setone Orphan
Luce Marble & Two Children
Willmot & Lequire [Gregoire?] old men lives at Pomquet
Sarah Indian Woman
Phillip old Tracida [Tracadie] Indian
Mary Marble & Child
Molly Martin Widow & Family
Hanah Orphan Girl
John Batiste Junr, Squa & Several children
William Nixon's Account. Public Archives of Nova Scotia, Halifax. RG1, Vol. 430,
#109.

1808-1809

For Sundries supplied the Indians by Order of His Excellency Governor
Wentworth:
James Paul [Jacques-Pierre Peminuit Paul], Goram Paul [Gorham Paul],
Clode Paul [Claude Paul], Thomas Francis and Thomas Morris, No-
vember 21; Noel Sanpier [St Pierre], Lewis Anthony and John Anthony,
November 23; Thos Boittow [Bateau, Batteaux, Beauto, Boittow,

Boittom, Beatle, 'Beetle John'], Paul Bask [Basque], December 3; Paul Labadore [Labradore], Gabreal Barnard [Gabriel Bernard], Cheremi & Hannah Cherome [Jeremy Jerome], December 5; Jos Bask & his wife, Jacob Bask & Widowed Mother, December 7; Paul Morris and sons, December 11; Joseph Philip, December 14; John Bask & his wife, December 18; Joseph Paul, Paul Bonnis [Ibon, Bon, Bonis, Bonus, Boonis], December 22; Lewis Paul, Simon Paul and a Blind Indian, December 24; John Nocout, December 28; Joseph Paul and Thomas Bell, December 30; Captain Philip Peter, Peter Morris, Penaad Argamatin [Bernard L'kimutin], Francis Penard, John Penard, Jno. Muse, December 31, 1808.

Thos & Jos Ball [Paul], Paul Martyn, January 1; James Paul Jr., January 4; Nootus (?) Paul, January 11, 1809.

Public Archives of Nova Scotia, Halifax. RG1, Vol. 430, #146.

Paul Malti [Martin] was the Chief of the Indians, and he had his reserve up there [on Foster's Point, Queens County, N.S.]. Paul Malti was a great friend of my great-grandfather, Asa Morine. One day he came in and found Dorcas his [Asa's] wife crying. "Why you cry, Dahcus?" "Oh," she said, "Asa's gone privateering, and I haven't heard a word from him." "Eh, Dahcus? All I hear was Ase go privateerin', Ase go privateerin'. Now Ase is gone, may the Devil pity ya and the Lord Almighty dry up your tears."

Paul went down to the wharf for something, and on his way back, he went into Dorcas's; Dorcas gave him something to eat. He went out again, and he got drunk, and he fell in the brook (and that brook is still running ...). Well, Dorcas looked out the window, she says, "Oh, Paul's head is in the water, and he'll drown." And he was drunk. So she went down with a rope and she hauled him out, and hauled him back to the house. Took his blanket and dried it, and gave him somethin' 'r 'nother.... And when he got up to go, he pulled his tomahawk out; she was scared. And he said, "Dahcus, you good woman, you damn fine woman." And he carved his totem on the door. The Indians before that had walked right in, never knocked. Nobody, no Indians, ever walked into Dorcas's house after that. They seen the totem over the door, and they knew that was the chief's totem, and they respected it, and knocked.

Ella Marguerite Letson to Blake Conrad, Port Medway, N.S. Taped interview, 4 April 1983. Courtesy Blake Conrad.

[Dorcas Cahoon Morine's mother was born in Salem, Mass., and came to Port Medway,

N.S., as a small child, in the 1760s. Dorcas herself lived to be more than 100 years old; she and her daughter (who also lived to be 100) and granddaughter (Ella Letson) all lived in the house with the totem on the door. Ella Letson was 96 in 1983, but the house is gone.]

"Did Paul Malti, did he leave any family around here?"

"Oh, he had a whole slew of 'em. After that, he and Hannah Jeremy married, and Dorcas was invited to the wedding, and she was treated like a queen. Their benches was furs, and she and her cousin ... was seated on these furs and treated with everything. She said she was treated like a queen. But they left before the real ... fun began. I guess they all got drunk.... But they were at the wedding.

[Paul's people] buried their dead in Petite Rivière, and my aunt said she could remember them chanting as they rowed down the river. They went to Great Island, and there was what they call a carry-over, or a portage, and then they took and walked on the other side and then rowed to Petite Rivière, where they buried their dead.... And after that they had the Catholic cemetery (you know where that is?), and a good many of them are buried there, [to] save them goin' all the way to Petite Rivière. I don't know where Paul was buried.... And now those stories I had from my grandmother [Dorcas' daughter].

Ella Marguerite Letson to Blake Conrad, Port Medway, N.S., ca 1812. Taped interview, 4 April 1983. Courtesy Blake Conrad.

1814

To Louis Benjamin Pominout [Peminuit Paul]:

Greeting. Whereas an Address has been presented unto me by the Revd. John Mandetus Sigogne in behalf of the Indians of the Micmac Tribe stating among other things that the said Tribe have made choice of you the said Louis-Benjamin Pominout to be their Chief. Wherefore relying upon the Loyalty Zeal Sobriety and good character of you the said Louis-Benjamin Pominout I do ratify and confirm the choice which the said Tribe has made and do hereby appoint you Chief of the Micmac Tribe of Indians this in [sic] Province. You are therefore to use your utmost endeavours to keep all persons belonging to the said Tribe Loyal Industrious and Sober, and to render them good Subjects and Christians, and the said Tribe are hereby required to obey you as their Chief.

Sir John Coape Sherbrooke to Louis-Benjamin Pominout, 28 April 1814. Parchment document 31.24 in the Nova Scotia Museum Collection, Halifax.

[It seems likely that the Paul Peminuit granted land at Shubenacadie in 1783 was Louis-Benjamin Peminuit Paul's father or grandfather. These Peminuits were called Pauls by the English as they took this ancestor's first name as a surname, or as a nickname. Louis-Benjamin may have been named after Micmac-French Louis-Benjamin Petitpas, interpreter for the Abbé Maillard.]

1816

23rd November: Took a long walk today ... round by Point Pleasant and the woods, skirting the Northwest Arm. No game or living thing to be seen except 4 old Indian native women, sitting like savages round a bit of fire, pictures of misery.

George Ramsay, Ninth Earl of Dalhousie. *The Dalhousie Journals,* edited by Marjory Whitelaw. 1978, Vol. 1:22.

1816

Mr. Bourke having gone to Ireland, we were the only two priests for the town of Halifax and its suburbs, where there were many Catholics, without counting the Mic-macs, who are the Indians inhabiting Nova Scotia.... they sing mass fairly well, especially the tone Royal, and the mass for the dead.... More than a hundred times they have sung it for me.

Vincent de Paul. *Memoir of Father Vincent.* Translated by A.M. Pope. 1886:13-14.

1817

Soon I felt constrained to go further into the Province of Nova Scotia to minister to the wants of the poor, neglected inhabitants. The first place to which I went was a parish called Chezzetcook, composed of French Acadians.... When it possessed a missionary, the Indians had been accustomed to go there. They were not long in learning of my presence, and came from a circuit of fifteen or twenty leagues. I had a transparency representing the suffering souls in purgatory.... At once penetrated with compassion and charity for the suffering souls in purgatory they began to weep, and to look up the money they had with them so as to have the Holy Sacrifice offered on behalf of these suffering souls, and that without my having said anything to give them the idea.

Vincent de Paul. *Memoir of Father Vincent.* Translated by A.M. Pope. 1886:16.

1817

The feast of St. Anne is a great festival for the Indians, and I made a point of being at Chezzetcook on that day. Two hundred Indians assembled, most of them came in a spirit of devotion, but some of them had evil designs, for they meditated killing their king and all his family. I discovered this plot in time, and learnt the cause with astonishment. It was that they believed that the chief and all his family would change their religion, that they had become Protestants, or that they intended to do so. This is how it came about. Some heretics called Methodists, had done all in their power to attract the king of the Indians to their sect, going so far as to give him all sorts of provisions, and other valuables, such as cows, pigs, farming implements, &c.... In this way the report got about that their Chief, Benjamin [Louis-Benjamin Peminuit Paul] had joined the Methodists.... [I] myself knew this to be false, for Benjamin himself, whom we had warned against the dangers that threatened him, had replied, "The potatoes, cows, and the other provisions of Bromlet [Walter Bromley, who was more a philanthropist than a Methodist] are good, I have taken them and made use of them, but his religion is worthless, I will have none of it."

In consequence of this we assembled the Indians in the church of Chezzetcook, which was not large enough to hold them all, and we made the king repeat his profession of faith in their presence, so that they should no longer doubt his sincerity. He did this in a most edifying manner. His example was followed by all his officers, who also made their profession of faith. We remarked in particular one of his brothers [probably Francis Peminuit Paul, First Captain for Chief Louis-Benjamin Peminuit Paul] who was conspicuous by the touching beauty and eloquence of his speech, and by the earnestness of the gestures which he employed. Some fragments of his discourse were rendered into our language by an Acadian interpreter, who understood Micmac pretty well.

"How," said he, "could we leave our religion that will save our souls if we follow it, this religion that comes from God, whose son died on the cross for our salvation? Shall we lose our souls that have cost Him so dear, for which he suffered so much, and which he shed all his blood to purchase? No, better die than change our faith and do such a great wrong."

Vincent de Paul. *Memoir of Father Vincent*. Translated by A.M. Pope. 1886:17-19.

1817

Fifty-one Indians, men, women and children are at Miquelon, stranded with no provisions, following the loss of the rudder of their shallop. They had come from the west coast of Newfoundland on their way to Saint-Pierre to fulfill their annual observances.

Emile Sasco and Joseph Lehuenen. *Ephémérides des Iles St.-Pierre et Miquelon.* 1970:23. Translated for this publication by Margaret Anne Hamelin.

1817

On the eve of St. Anne's feast, they made a bonfire, and while the wood burned they fired off guns and danced around the fire, clapping their hands in imitation of musical instruments. This lasted for a great part of the night, however, they had previously said their evening prayers, and sung hymns and canticles.

Vincent de Paul. *Memoir of Father Vincent.* Translated by A.M. Pope. 1886:19.

1820

27th January: Old Paul, an Indian, brought me in today the head of a very large Moose. Talking with him about it, he tells me he had followed a pair of them for 8 miles & shot them both.

30th January: A party of Gentlemen lately explored the woods from Horton Corner, South to Sherbrooke settlement, with the intention to ascertain the distance & nature of the soil. They took an Indian to guide them in the path thro' the forest. They soon saw he was not leading them correctly, but rather trying to mislead & confound them. At last he stopt & said there was no more path & attempted to run away; but they persevered by compass & soon found not only a path, but a sort of bridge over a stream, made after the manner of the Indians. He then told them, that there was there the only hunting ground left them in the Province, & that he did not wish the English should find it, as they soon would go take it like other parts. I did not imagine there was any such feeling as this remaining in the mind of the miserable tribe of Micmacs yet left.

George Ramsay, Ninth Earl of Dalhousie. *The Dalhousie Journals,* edited by Marjory Whitelaw. 1978, vol. 1:182.

Chief John Noel tells me that during the winter of 1820, the squaw of Joseph Louis (lu-we) was crossing the harbour near Charlottetown, P.E.I., with her infant son (Peter Louis, who died about 1905), strapped and wrapped in an Indian cradle at her back. The mother was overcome with the intense cold and died from exposure, being found frozen stiff the next morning, but the infant on being unwrapped was apparently little, if any, affected by the cold. Chief Noel assures me positively this is correct.

John Noel to Harry Piers, n.d. Nova Scotia Museum Printed Matter File.

1821

The Indians a few days ago in their pursuit of eels happened on a congregation of them in the East River, 60 or 70 barrels have already been drawn from the quietness of their winter's repose, and the living mass is not yet exhausted.

The Colonial Patriot. Pictou, N.S., 22 February 1828.

1822

Narrative of a Journey Across the Island of Newfoundland in 1822:
To accompany me in the performance, I engaged into my service, first, a Micmack Indian, a noted hunter from the south-west coast of the Island....

September 5th: Being now removed with my Indian from all human communication and interference, we put on our knapsacks and equipments in order and left this inland part of the sea-shore in a north direction, without regard to any track, through marshes and woods towards some rising land, in order to obtain a view of the country.... At sunset we halted, and bivouacked beneath the forest. As the weather was fine, and no prospect of rain, our camp consisted merely of a fire and a bundle of spruce boughs to lie on. My Indian, Joseph Sylvester by name, at midnight rolled himself up in his blanket, and evidently slept perfectly at home.

October 12th: Soon afterwards, to my great delight, there appeared among some woody islets in front, which precluded the view of the other side of the lake, a small canoe with a man seated in the stern, paddling softly towards us, with an air of serenity and independence possessed only by the Indian. After a brotherly salutation with me, and the two Indians kissing each other, the hunter proved to be unable to speak English or French. They, however, soon understood one another, for the stranger, although a mountaineer [a Montagnais named James John] from Labrador, could speak a little of the Mickmack language, his wife being a Mickmack. The mountaineer tribe belongs to Labrador, and he told us that he had come to Newfoundland, hearing that it was a better hunting country than his own, and that he was now on his way hunting from St. George's Bay to the Bay Despair to spend the winter with the Indians there.... This was his second year in Newfoundland; he was accompanied by his wife only. My Indian told him that I had come to see the rocks, the deer, the beavers, and the Red Indians, and to tell King George what

Left to right: Joseph Howe Jeremy, Chief John Noel, Marie Antoinette Thomas Sack Noel, and Catherine Sack Maloney, St Anne's Day, Shubenacadie, N.S.

was going on in the middle of that country. He said St. George's Bay was about two weeks walk from us if we knew the best way, and invited us over with him in his canoe to rest a day at his camp, where he said he had plenty of venison, which was readily agreed to on my part.

The island on which the mountaineer's camp was, lay about three miles distant. The varying scenery as we paddled towards it, amongst innumerable islands and inlets, all of granite, and mostly covered with spruce and birch trees, was beautiful. His canoe was similar to those described to have been used by the ancient Britons.... It was made of wicker-work, covered over outside with deer [caribou] skins sewed together and stretched on it, nearly of the usual form of canoes, with a bar or beam across the middle, and one on each end to strengthen it. The skin covering, flesh side out, was fastened or laced to the gunwales, with thongs of the same material. Owing to decay and wear it requires to be renewed once in from six to twelve weeks. It is in these temporary barks that the Indians of Newfoundland of the present day navigate the lakes and rivers of the interior.... His wigwam was situated in the centre of a wooded islet at which we arrived before sunset. The approach from the landing place was by a mossy carpeted avenue, formed by the trees having been cut down in that direction for firewood. The sight of a fire, not of our own kindling, of which we were to partake, seemed hospitality. It was occupied by his [Micmac] wife, seated on a deer skin, busy sewing together skins of the same kind to renew the outside of the canoe we had just found.... A large Newfoundland dog, her only companion in her husband's absence, had welcomed us at the landing-place with signs of the greatest joy. His wigwam was of a semicircular form, covered with birch rind and dried deer skins, the fire on the fore ground outside. Abundance and neatness pervaded the encampment. On horizontal poles over the fire, hung quantities of venison stakes, being smoked dry. The hostess was cheerful, and a supper, the best the chase could furnish, was soon set before us on sheets of birch rind.... A cake of hard deer's fat with scraps of suet, toasted brown, intermixed, was eaten with the meat; soup was the drink. Our hostess after supper sang several Indian songs at my request. They were plaintive, and sung in a high key. The song of a female and her contentment in this remote and secluded spot, exhibited the strange diversity there is in human nature. My Indian entertained them incessantly until nearly daylight with stories about what he had seen in St. John's. Our toils were for the time forgotten.

William Cormack. "Narrative of a Journey Across the Island of Newfoundland in 1822." In *The Beothucks or Red Indians*, by J.P. Howley. 1915:130, 135, 148-149.

1822

October 18th: My dress, once gray, now bleached white, was seen by some of the Indians as we emerged from a spruce thicket, a great distance off. The party were encamped in one large wigwam.... We entered with little ceremony, my Indian kissing them all—male and female.... A deer skin was spread for me to sit on, in the innermost part of the dwelling. My Indian interpreted, and introduced me in the same particular terms as before. They were Mickmacks and natives of Newfoundland, and expressed themselves glad to see me in the middle of their country, as the first white man that had ever been here.... Here were three families amounting to thirteen persons in number. The men and boys wore surtouts made of deer skins, the hair outside, buttoned and belted round them, which looked neat and comfortable. Their caps were of mixed fur;

they had not procured much fur for sale, only a few dozen marten, some otter and musk rat skins; of beaver skins they had very few, as beavers are scarce in the western interior, it being too mountainous for woods, except on the sheltered borders of some of the lakes. In the woods around the margin of this lake the Indians had lines of path equal to eight or ten miles in extent, set with wooden traps, or dead falls, about one hundred yards apart, baited for martens, which they visited every second day. They had two skin canoes in which they paddled around the lake to visit their traps and bring home their game.... All the Indians in the Island, exclusive of the Red Indians, amount to nearly a hundred and thirty, dispersed in bands, commonly at the following places or district: St. George's Harbour and Great Cod Roy River on the west coast; White Bear Bay, and the Bay Despair on the south coast; Clode [Claude] Sound in Bonavista Bay on the east; Gander Bay on the north coast, and occasionally at Bonne Bay and the Bay of Islands on the north-west coast. They are composed of Mickmacks, joined by some of the mountaineer tribe from the Labrador, and a few of the Abenakies from Canada.

William Cormack. "Narrative of a Journey Across the Island of Newfoundland in 1822." In *The Beothucks or Red Indians,* by J.P. Howley. 1915:150-151.

1822

In 1822, when the first settlers at Caledonia [N.S.] were clearing their land preparatory to farming (on the 10th of March) Joseph Gload [Claude], chief of the Mic-Macs, came to the camp of Patrick Lacy and Thomas Jones, and having got his breakfast returned to the forest. By three o'clock the next day he had killed fifteen moose, though he had at no time wandered farther than thirteen miles from the camp.

James F. More. *The History of Queens County, N.S.* 1873:124.

One hundred years ago San Sosef [Jean Joseph] went with six men to Kanawagik [Caughnawaga, now Kahnawake] (at Montreal) to make peace with those witches. They were called *Gwedich* [*Kwetej*], or when they came fighting here, *Auwisku* [*Owisku'k,* 'Spies']. They made agreement. They had long beads [wampum belts], they read them, Montreal beads, Cape Breton beads.

Isabelle Googoo Morris to Elsie Clews Parsons, Chapel Island, N.S. St Anne's Day, 26 July 1923. In "Micmac Folklore," by Elsie Clews Parsons. *Journal of American Folklore.* 1925, Vol. 38: 93.

1823

So recently as the month of August, 1823, I was in a parish called Havre-à-Bouchers, when twenty-six canoes filled with Indians arrived there; they came to have their children baptised, and for confession, &c. There were eight singers among them, and during the week that they remained, they sang mass for me each day, and one might say conducted themselves like canons or like Trappists! They have clear voices.

Vincent de Paul. *Memoir of Father Vincent.* Translated by A.M. Pope. 1886:15.

1824

In the [ship] *Mars,* we are informed that the Chief Andrew Meuse, who exercises a kind of Sovereignty over the Indians in the Western extremity of this Province, went as a passenger. He is the same person who some years ago harangued so successfully at the bar of the House of Assembly against a Bill calculated to deprive the poor Micmacs of their porpoise catching; since that he has been elected a Chief and his present purpose in going to England is supposed to be to solicit Government for permanent grants of land to the Indians, in order that they may become cultivators of the soil. He is a remarkably intelligent man, sober in habits, and has saved a little money, and although ignorant of letters, his memory and understanding are uncommonly strong by nature. He is good looking, and is attired in the costume of the tribe.

The Halifax Journal. Halifax, 27 December 1824:3, col. 3.

1825

The present Indians of Nova Scotia are all one nation, known by the name of Micmacs, and were among other natives the original inhabitants of the country. They are by no means numerous, and are fast diminishing in numbers, as they wander, like those of New Brunswick, in extreme wretchedness, and detached parties, throughout the Province. Many of them are found along the Annapolis River, who encamp at the entrance of the bay, for the purpose of shooting porpoises, during the season in summer. They are very expert in killing this animal, as it rises upon the water, which is a great source of amusement as well as of profit.... I reached the camp soon after this season was over, and the Indians had returned from a successful excursion, in hunting the moose-deer in the neighbouring woods. Their chief, Adelah [André Mius] is a person of very sober habits, and naturally of a penetrating, sagacious mind. He had visited England, and expressed much regret that he did not see his great father, with the four Canadian chiefs, who were in London, and introduced to the king, in the spring of 1825.... [He] expressed a great desire to settle with his tribe, on lands for which he had often made application, as contiguous to their fishing and hunting grounds, but which he had not then obtained. His country, he said, was getting very poor, and the soil almost all taken up by people who came to it, which made him wish to raise some produce from the land, and see his Indians, with their families, in better circumstances. "I go," he remarked, "once more [he had already visited England in 1811] about the grant, may be they think I come too often, perhaps turn their back, then I turn my back, and never ask again."

John West. *A Journal of a Mission to the Indians of the British Provinces of New Brunswick and Nova Scotia, etc.* 1827:244-246.

1825

On Thursday last an inquest was held on the body of an Indian, called Joseph Morris [Maurice], found drowned in the harbour. On the night previous, just about dusk, as a boat was returning from George's Island, a canoe was seen on the water turned bottom upwards. On reaching it there was the body of an Indian attached to it by the legs, having apparently become entangled in the bars, which run across and strengthen these fragile barks. The body was brought on shore and soon recognized as the body of an Indian, who had left the Eastern Passage, where his wigwam was located. When he left the ship he was in a state of intoxication; and it is supposed he met his death by losing proper balance and overturning his canoe.

The Novascotian or Colonial Herald. Halifax, 10 August 1825:6, col. 2.

1825

This intelligent chief [André Mius] would often take me into his canoe, during my visit to his tribe, and in the course of conversation, frequently surprised me with his pertinent and striking remarks on the subject of religion. He expressed much surprise, and difficulty, at the many different denominations among Protestant Christians, which he had heard of. "There," said he, pointing to a small cove in the Bay, as he was paddling his canoe along shore one morning, "I saw five or six persons plunged for baptism, a short time ago." Then holding up the paddle, he added, as the water dripped from it, "I think the Great Spirit can as easily bless that small quantity for the purpose, as he can all the water in the basin around us."

He is a decided Roman Catholic, as are all the Indians of the Province;

and a circumstance occurred in the death of a child, while I was in the camp, which proved how strongly the Priests have entrenched them within the pale of their bigotry and dominion. I offered to bury the child, as they knew me to be a Priest, but they refused, with the remark, that it must be buried by their Priest; and the mother of the deceased child took the corpse upon her back, and carried it the distance of thirty miles to the French village of Sissaboo [Weymouth, N.S.], where the Priest [Abbé Jean-Mandé Sigogne] resided, for burial. I merely observed to Adelah [André], on this occasion, that I supposed Indians were all of the Roman Catholic religion, he said, "*yes,*" adding, "you know in England, quakers, when born, all come little quakers, so Indians, all come little Catholics."

John West. *A Journal of a Mission to the Indians of the British Provinces of New Brunswick and Nova Scotia, etc.* 1827:246-247.

Peter Cope (who married a Salome) and fought with a Bear in Sheet Harbour Woods:

This Peter Cope met a bear in Sheet Harbour Woods and fired at it, hitting it. It ran off. Then it sat up on its haunches and began to lick the wound on its foreleg. Then it lay down and Cope thought it was dead. He stood his gun against a tree and went up to the bear and kicked it. The bear sprang at him, and a fierce struggle began. Cope had only his sheath knife and could not get it. Bear tore Cope's arms and chest with its claws. It had its mouth wide open. Cope saw that his only chance for life was to use some uncommon tactics. He waited a chance when bear's mouth was very wide open, and then suddenly rammed his right hand (he was a *very* strong man) down the animal's throat, and gripped the base of the tongue till the bear was smothered. Some say he tore out the bear's tongue, but this was not so. He gripped the base of the tongue till the bear was smothered. Left bear's carcass and went home, out Sheet Harbour Road, and when he arrived there was covered with blood. His wife doctored him, and he was three months on his back as the result of this struggle for life. They used to like bear's meat, but Mrs. Cope went to where the bear's carcass was, and chopped it all up with an axe and threw the pieces about.

Joseph C. Cope to Harry Piers, 1926. Nova Scotia Museum Printed Matter File.

"This Peter Cope was grandfather of the present Joe C. Cope of Enfield, who told me this story as told to him by his father Peter Cope." (Harry Piers)

[Mrs Cope's actions would appear to be a fascinating survival of the belief that in order to persuade animal kills to reincarnate in the neighbourhood, for one's future use, one treated the remains with respect. Obviously Mrs Cope had no desire for this particular bear to reincarnate at all, anywhere.]

That we may live,
And our children also,
Where is now our land?
We have none

1826

When [the Ojibway minister Rev. Peter] Jones arrived at the palace, he was informed that an Indian chief and his son were there. The parties met in the room where the gold plate of the King was kept, and the Indians shook hands and attempted to converse in their own languages but were forced to use English, which the chief [André Mius, Chief at Bear River] spoke fluently. It developed that he was of the Micmac tribe of Nova Scotia. The Indians, after being conducted over the palace, were taken to a drawing room and received by the King and Queen [William and Adelaide] who were standing when the Indians entered. The Micmac chief was first presented to King William, while Jones was introduced to one of the lords in waiting. Their majesties returned the bows of the Indians; the King asked questions about the tribes and inquired the ages of the men.... he considered the son of the Nova Scotia chief [James Mius] a model of the American Indian.

After half an hour with the royal party the guests were conducted to a luncheon of "roasted chickens, beef, potatoes, tarts, wines &c. and they ate out of silver dishes." The Indians were notified that the King had ordered two medals to be struck for the chiefs. After dinner the party entered a long beautiful hall, to meet the ladies and children of the royal family, among whom was Prince George. They were "shown the King's private apartments ... all glittered with gold tapestry ... taken to see the horses ... most handsome creatures I ever saw...." Jones learned that the Micmac chief had gone to England to buy farming implements....

Carolyn Thomas Foreman. *Indians Abroad: 1493-1938.* 1943:154-155.

[Quotes are from the journals of Rev. Peter Jones. *Life and Journals of Kan-ke-wa-quo-na-by, Wesleyan Missionary.* Toronto, 1860.]

1826

The Indians who frequent the County of Annapolis having made known to his Majesty's Government through their leader John Meuse [André

Mius, also called Andrew Hadley Meuse and possibly James Meuse], who went to England for that purpose, their wish to fix their abode, and apply themselves to cultivation of the soil, and his Majesty's Government being anxious to encourage such inclination, instructions have been given to the Governor to facilitate their design. Accordingly His Excellency had an interview with Meuse, who explained the plan he had formed for settling and civilizing of a part of his tribe and pointed out a tract of land on Bear River, granted many years ago to C. Benson and family, as on many accounts a favourable situation for them to begin upon. His Excellency therefore considering Meuse's plan likely to succeed and as emanating from an Indian, the more deserving of encouragement, has directed the necessary steps to be taken to reinvest the right of this land in the King, in order that he may regrant a part of it for the use of these Indians....

Public Archives of Nova Scotia, Halifax. RG1, Vol. 146, 2 January 1826.

pre-1827
Among the Indians [in Pictou County] two were particularly noted, and are still remembered by the older generation, viz.: Patlass and Lulan [Laurent]. The former was particularly distinguished for his skill in draughts, so that his death was announced in a Halifax paper, as that of "the celebrated draughts player." At this game, it is a question whether he was ever beaten. When he met a stranger, he would allow him to win the first game, but then he would induce him to play for a wager, which was all he wanted to show his skill.

He was also noted for that grim humor, characteristic of the red man. On one occasion a sea captain had brought a fighting cock ashore, and set it fighting with one belonging to the town. Patlass came along, where a number of persons were standing looking on. After looking at the scene for a few minutes, he seized one of the combatants, and walked off with it. The captain called out angrily after him to come back, asking him what he was about. "Take him to jail, fightin' on the streets," was Patlass' reply....

He was drowned near Middle River Point, on the 1st September 1827.

George Patterson. *History of the County of Pictou, Nova Scotia.* 1972:188-190.

pre-1827
Lulan [Laurent, possibly Paul Laurent or a descendant] was of a milder disposition, though reputed to have been a great warrior in his youth. He

used to boast that he had scalped ninety-nine persons, though there was probably some bounce in this. He was rather below the middle height, but straight and broad-shouldered, and in his later years corpulent for an Indian. He was the means at one time of saving the life of the writer's grandfather, old John Patterson. The latter was crossing the ice, when it gave way, and he fell into the water. The Indians put out to his help, and succeeded in rescuing him, but he was insensible for a time, and when he recovered, he found himself in a large tub in Lulan's camp. Lulan was ever after freely entertained at my grandfather's house, of which he did not fail to take advantage. As an instance of the attachment induced by kindness, we may mention an incident that occurred at my grandfather's funeral. It being customary then to hand liquor round to all present, some was offered to Lulan, who replied, "Me no drinkem long time, but bleev take some to-day; me most dead grief my friend."

After my grandfather's death, however, he continued to expect from my grandmother the same attention as in his life time. "Me save your husband's life," was the appeal which he supposed would never lose its efficacy, which he rendered more impressive by adding particulars: "Walk out on thin boards; only head and arms out of water; most lose my own life save his." And after her death, their sons' store was laid under contribution on the same ground. He died about the year 1827, when he was said to have been in his 97th year, so that he must have nearly reached manhood when Halifax was founded, and been in full vigor when Louisburg and Quebec surrendered.

His son is still well remembered as Jim Lulan. He had somewhat of the dry humor of some of the race. Mr. Carmichael had built a vessel, which, in honor of the old Chief, he called the *Lulan*. Some persons, teasing his son, said to him that he ought to make her a present of a set of colours. "Ugh!" said Jim, "me build big canoe, call it Old Carmichael."

George Patterson. *History of the County of Pictou, Nova Scotia.* 1972:190-191.

pre-1827

The only instance of [Micmac revenge] of which we have heard, which threatened serious consequences, was an affair between Lulan and Rod McKay. Soon after the arrival of the latter, he had in some way seriously offended the former, who came all the way from Merigomish to the East River to shoot him. It was night when he arrived, and McKay was at work in his forge. Lulan looked in but as he saw the glare of the fire on his face, and the sparks flying from the anvil, and heard the reverberation of his

blows, he became scared, and his hands could not perform their enterprise. For long after the two were good friends, and Lulan used to tell the story, graphically describing his feelings, "Sartin, me taut you debbil."
George Patterson. *History of the County of Pictou, Nova Scotia.* 1972:185.

1827

In the summer they located round Bedford Basin, and several families were encamped at Sandy Cove. In one of those camps there was seen a very pretty little white girl. Curiosity was rife to find out where she came from and how she got there. It appeared that a man named Hickey, who had lost his wife while living at Ship Harbor, left this one child, and an old squaw took a fancy to her, and for a small equivalent took possession of her. She lived with this family of Indians—Toney Paul and his wife, who was commonly called "Silver Sal" (why she was thus designated I do not know, unless it was because she was better off in her worldly affairs than many of her neighbors). They were devotedly attached to this little girl, whom they called Madeline. She continued to live with them and grew up to womanhood, and had many admirers among the Indian boys living beside her. This family removed to Shubenacadie and settled on a small farm, on what is called the Indian Town Road, about four miles from the village of Shubenacadie, and built a small house, in which they lived and were quite comfortable, having some cattle and a horse and waggon. Madeline was the sunshine of that house, and the idol of Sally's heart. It was my good fortune to travel over the Indian Town road in 1827 in company with a friend, and coming to the Indian Settlement, we found a number of them dressed in their holiday clothes. There had been a wedding that morning—two of their tribe had been married by the Rev. Father Kennedy, and they were keeping high holiday. We came to the house occupied by Toney Paul, and curiosity led us to stop and call in. Here we found Madeline dressed in Indian costume, as much admired in that household as a queen. I had not seen her since she was a little girl in the camp at Sandy Cove, Dartmouth. We were invited to partake of their hospitalities. There was a clean white cloth spread on a small table, and such good things as they had provided for us, with a dish of strawberries picked that morning by the hand of the fair Madeline, who superintended the arrangements and presided at the table with Toney Paul and his wife and two guests. At parting we thanked our hosts for their kindness and offered them pay, but this was refused. Some time after this Madeline was discharging a gun in her own hand, or some one near her was doing so, I am not quite certain which; the gun burst, and part of the contents hit her face, and disfigured her very much. [This story is strangely close to that of Mary Anne Paul, white child adopted by Gorham Paul of Indian Town Road, who had been disfigured in the face by the kick of a horse; see the second entry for 1844.] She recovered from this, but the scars remained. She was married after this to one of the Indians, but whether living now [1883] or not I have no way of knowing, but the probability is they are all dead.

"Recollections of Halifax: Some of the Notabilities of Ye Olden Time." In *The Acadian Recorder*. Halifax, 4 August 1883:2, col. 4.

1828

Indian Gallantry: A few days ago three Indian men, namely Joseph Selby [Levi; in Micmac, Sylliboy, Silevi, Silibey] Joseph Wilmot, and Lewis Paul, went off from the encampment, in company with Mary Hadley [André], wife of Andrew Ruijo [André Rousseau?], now absent at Antigonish, and Mary Poito [Bateau, Boittow], an Indian girl; as this is looked upon as a regular elopement, the whole tribe are thrown into grief and confusion, at so gross a violation of Indian honour. We were waited upon by a few of the relatives of the females, and requested to raise a HUE AND CRY after them, as they knew not the road they had taken, but not knowing any law that would warrant their apprehension, under the circumstances of the case, we suggested to them, the propriety of sending a deputation of their own tribe, in pursuit of the delinquents, which, we are informed, they have since done.

The Colonial Patriot. Pictou, N.S., 21 May 1828.

1825-1830

I have often crossed an arm of the sea in order to visit other Micmacs who live in Cape Breton. This Cape is surrounded by little islands, and there is there a lake seven leagues in length and five or six in width, on which I was once shipwrecked. We were two priests in a bark canoe, paddled by two Indians, and were carrying the consolations of religion to many families of Indians who lived on the other side at the foot of a mountain. A storm suddenly arose, a long stick, which served as a mast and carried a sail, was broken, and during the two hours that the bad weather continued, we momentarily expected to be engulfed by the immense waves that rose like hills and fell, breaking against our feeble bark, although the pilot endeavored to avoid them as much as possible, while the other Indian tried to break their force by means of his paddle. One of these Indians, the elder of the two, and the more experienced, trembled, fearing every moment that we should be lost, and he was not so afraid for us as we were for ourselves.

Vincent de Paul. *Memoir of Father Vincent.* Translated by A.M. Pope. 1886:27-28.

1825-1830

We found a new plantation made by the Indians, that is to say, some tracts of cultivated land, some animals, and some frames of houses.... in nearing their habitations we were exposed to great danger from the horns of a bull that was ferocious and was in the habit of rushing at passers by. God delivered us from this peril also, although the animal in question was quite near to us. These Indians set before us for our supper, tea, milk, butter, potatoes and some fruit that resembled small apples.

Vincent de Paul. *Memoir of Father Vincent.* Translated by A.M. Pope. 1886:28.

1825-1830

Another time that I started on a mission to this same Cape Breton the Indians who conducted me in a canoe perceived three monstrous fish [killer whales] called *maraches,* and they were frightened, as these fish are very dangerous. Their teeth are made like gardeners' knives, for cutting and boring, or like razors slightly bent. They are extremely voracious, and often follow boats, attacking them with violence. Bark canoes cannot resist them, they rend them open with their teeth, so that they sink to the bottom, which is why the Indians have such a terror of them. Happily for us these fish did not follow us....

Vincent de Paul. *Memoir of Father Vincent.* Translated by A.M. Pope. 1886:29.

ca 1830

Tracadie was usually my starting place when I left for the Indian mission of Cape Breton. I had from eighteen to twenty leagues to journey by water.... one day to make the journey in a bark canoe, that is if the wind be not contrary. The Micmacs of the Cape (Breton) knowing that I was on the road, and would soon arrive at the mission, would all gather there to the number of five or six hundred.... Three canoes came to meet us— I was then accompanied by another missionary. This was to do honour to us, to show respect and gratitude. When we approached to the island two canoes were sent ahead to announce to the king that we would arrive immediately. The king had all his braves armed, for they all have guns, and the moment we landed he commanded them to fire, after which he formed them into lines and made them kneel to receive our benediction. They then arose and we passed among them. They accompanied us to the church where we chanted the "Te Deum," or rather it was chanted by them in thanksgiving for our arrival. This is the ordinary ceremony of honouring the arrival of a missionary.

Vincent de Paul. *Memoir of Father Vincent.* Translated by A.M. Pope. 1886:30.

An old Indian, long since dead, called "Old Joe Cope" … was for years nearly bent double by a severe beating received from the forefoot of a wounded moose which turned on him. For safety, there being no tree near, he jammed himself in between two large granite boulders which were near at hand, but the aperture did not extend far enough back to enable him to get altogether out of the reach of the infuriated bull.

Campbell Hardy. *Forest Life in Acadie.* 1869:74.

[Hardy adds that this is not the Joe Cope known to him, who died in 1869, but a much more ancient Joe Cope. One wonders whether this is what became of Jean-Baptiste Cope's son Joseph, or if he was also the Joe Copee who had a dog named Duc (see Micmac entry following 1746 entry).]

1832

I knew several Indians, while I was in Nova Scotia, who undertook a voyage by water to [Montréal] Canada in their Canoes. They crossed the Bay of Fundy, went up the river St. John. On their return they showed me several letters from the people of Caghnawaga to this tribe and what pleased me most, a draught of the River St. John, New Brunswick. The draughtsman had nothing to assist him in the operation, but a pen and pencil, an acute eye, a sound judgement. On comparing it with the best modern plan, and with the most accurate mathematical instruments, I found them to coincide exactly; every creek, cove and village, being regularly delineated.

Thomas Irwin. In *The Novascotian.* Halifax, 5 September 1832.

To the Great Councillors of Prince Edward Island.
The Speech of Oliver Thoma [Thomas], Louis Francis Alguimou [L'kimu], Piel Jaques [Pierre Jacques], and other Chiefs of This Island:
Fathers:
Before the white men crossed the great waters, our Woods offered us food and clothes in plenty—the waters gave us fish—and the woods game—our fathers were hardy, brave and free—we knew no want—we were the only owners of the Land.

Fathers:

When the French came to us they asked us for land to set up their Wigwam—we gave it freely—in return they taught us new arts—protected and cherished us—sent holy men our fathers amongst—who taught us Christianity—who made books for us—and taught us to read them—that was good—and we were grateful.

Fathers:

When your fathers came and drove away our French fathers—we were left alone—our people were sorry, but they were brave—they raised the war cry—and took up the tomahawk against your fathers.—Then your fathers spoke to us—they said, put up the axe—we will protect you—we will become your Fathers. Our fathers and your fathers had long talks around the Council fire—the hatchets were buried—and we became friends.

Fathers:

They promised to leave us some of our land—but they did not—they drove us from place to place like wild beasts—that was not just....

Fathers:

Our tribe in Nova Scotia, Canada, New Brunswick and Cape Breton, have land on which their Families are happy.—We ask of you, Fathers, to give us a part of that land once our fathers'—whereon we may raise our wigwams without disturbance—and plough and sow—that we may live, and our children also—else, Fathers, you may soon see not one drop of Indian blood in this Island, once our own—where is now our land?—we have none.

Fathers, we are poor—do not forsake us—remember the promises your fathers made to ours. Fathers, we salute you.

Louis Francis Alguimou, Piel Jacques, Oliver Thoma, Peter Tony, Michael Mitchell. In *Legislative Assembly of Prince Edward Island Journals,* 1832:11.

[The lines of unreferenced poetry interspersed throughout the text are taken from this speech.]

1832

If a highly polished language be a mark of no ordinary mental qualities, then well may the Mickmac boast of his.... If we consider the variety of their verbs—the regularity of their various shades of difference—the number of moods and tenses—the utmost infinite number of terminations—the beautiful manner of forming complex ideas by compounding different words—the melody of the language—all shew that they were minds of no common cast who framed it, or who now use it. Indeed it is not before the age of 30 or 35 that men attain a complete knowledge of it, and females seldom or never.

Thomas Irwin. In *The Novascotian*. Halifax, 5 September 1832.

[Irwin contradicts the Abbé Maillard, who said that old women spoke the best Micmac.]

Old Ben Morris, a blind Micmac [born *ca* 1818], said that on the Halifax Common, when he was young, there was a quantity of White Pine and Red Oak, and he used to shoot ducks at the Black-duck Pond (Up-kuch-coom-mouch way-gad-die).

Ben Morris to Jeremiah Bartlett Alexis [alias Jerry Lonecloud] to Harry Piers, 20 December 1915. Nova Scotia Museum Printed Matter File.

1834

DEMISE OF A NATIVE SOVEREIGN AND CONSEQUENT INTERREGNUM: Whilst in Spain the departure from this life of the "Beloved Ferdinand" has involved that kingdom in a civil war, it is gratifying to observe the comparative tranquillity which has prevailed in this quarter of the Globe, notwithstanding the late demise of the King of the Aborigines of this Island. It will be within the knowledge of many of our readers that the Sovereignty over the Indians of Cape Breton is stated to have been conferred by a former King of France upon a particular individual of the tribe of Indians here, and by whom in virtue thereof, the sceptre was borne. The last of this tribe, invested with the Kingly office here, was his late Majesty King Tomah [Thomas], who notwithstanding the adverse and conflicting claims of others, finally ascended the Throne and was fully admitted [?] to sovereign power over his tribe several years since—his authority not being merely acquiesced in by his subjects, but reported to have been acknowledged by a Right Reverend Prelate on the part of the See of Rome, and by His Excellency Sir James Kempt on behalf of the Court of St. James's. King Tomah having now quitted this transitory scene, the Throne has become temporarily vacant. The succession therein we believe was formerly rather more hereditary than elective—that is, the regal line was kept in view, provided its members were eminent warriors, the question in such case being merely which individual in that line should be elected: but of late the elective principle has been so extended as to admit others not of the regal line to the throne, to the exclusion of the whole of such line. The Royal line of Gogoo which was formerly in possession of the Throne has consequently been latterly debarred from the Crown, and which family it is reported is now in possession of one of the emblems of Royalty or symbols of authority; but which its enemies state it clandestinely obtained from a late King, in a manner somewhat similar to that by which we read in the history of England, Blund obtained the Crown from the Tower. It is said that the late King a few hours before dying, expressed a wish that his brother Christmas should be his successor and left with him the Royal Archives: others state that his son-in-law Francis Gregoire was left in charge. Further rumor exists that the Gogoo family will be Candidates for the Crown.

With respect to the extent of this Kingly power, it is very limited, though a responsible and burdensome office, and is exercised in full subordination to the British Government and to the Government of the Colony: and whatever Republicans may advance against monarchies in general, as to their profuse expenditure, and the immense cost of supporting them, these objections do not apply to the one in question; for we believe no Republic exists which is supported at less expense to its subjects or citizens, than that imposed by the King and Royal Family of the Aborigines of this island on those under its rule.

Some time will probably elapse before the vacancy to the Indian Throne will be filled, as we understand that the election of a Sovereign will not take place until July next. We know not whether a Christmas, a Gregoire, a Gogoo or who else will accept the sceptre. We trust, whoever may obtain it, that the peace of Europe will not be affected thereby. Indeed we feel confident that the Throne will be ascended by a Sovereign not likely to embroil either Europe or America in hostilities. This is a consolatory reflection in this tumultuous and eventful age.

Since preparing the above article we have been favored with a more full account than is there given of the demise of King Tomah—of his funeral obsequies—and comprehending an interesting historical narrative relative to the Indians in this Island. Should want of room compel us to omit its insertion this week, it will appear in our next number.

The Cape-Bretonian. Sydney, 25 January 1834.

1834

THE INDIANS AND THEIR KING (From *The Cape-Bretonian*):
Died—at his Palace at Escasoni, on the first instant. Thom Thoma [Thomas Thomas], the H. Chief of the Micmac tribe of this Island. He exercised his Royal Prerogatives with disinterested impartiality towards

his subjects, and died at the advanced age of 80 years. He succeeded his father of the same name who lived to complete his 102nd year, and is said to have inherited many of his virtues, but resembled him little in his warlike and manly pursuits. Thoma the I was endowed with extraordinary natural strength and courage; it is recorded that he killed 7 large full grown Bears in one week, with his Tomahawk—two of which at the same time most furiously attacked and wounded him, but such was the prowess of this Chieftain that he conquered his enemies and brought their skins in triumph to his residence—what makes his fate more marvellous is, that he was accompanied by one of his tribe who he commanded not to stir or interfere in the combat till called and such was the coolness of his attendant that he lighted his pipe and smoked during the sanguinary struggle. About 100 years ago the then King of France who heard of the warlike disposition of Thoma the I, engaged him in his service by presents of large value, amongst them were a seal and pipe of exquisite workmanship, and [the King] placed much confidence in the tribe under his command for assistance in the wars of that period.

The remains of Thoma the II were interred after remaining in *state* for 4 days, in the Royal Cemetry [*sic*] allotted to his race on the Island in the Bras D'Or lake which supports the Chapel built under his auspices, and exclusively the property of the Indians. The procession was conducted with great precision—the greater part of the tribe having assembled to take the last view of their chief, with grief silently but strongly depicted in their countenances, chanted a Requiem to the departed soul in a solemn strain characteristic of the Religious ceremonies, of those once warlike aborigines.

The body having been closed in its narrow shell, made out of a solid trunk of hemlock, was removed to the sea side and laid across two canoes lashed together, which were paddled by eight Indians, these were headed by twelve of his principal officers, in three canoes, attended by six young squaws who sung a funeral hymn in their native tongue; immediately after, followed his eldest son, bearing the tomahawk, spear, and gun of his deceased Father; the various branches of his family in succession and order formed a curious sight to such as never witnessed the manners of this harmless people. Several canoes of the tribe closed the scene, their inmates joined the chorus of the youthful songstresses who feelingly painted the virtues and deeds of their departed leader.

The succession is not hereditary, but left to the voice of that part of the tribe over whom the late Chief had controul [*sic*], and they usually elect at their annual meeting which takes place on the anniversary of their Saint's day the 25th [26] July—a period devoted to forming contracts of marriage and festivities which are generally attended by the tribes from the Neighbouring Islands, who during the period regularly attend the daily worship in the Chapel, attended by the Roman Catholic Clergyman of their parish to whom they pay marked respect.

Many difficulties of the preceding year are settled by their Pastor, who always unites the partners that had formed contracts of marriage—a joyful and innocent feast crowns the whole, and at the time of separation pledges of faith are renewed by the different tribes [bands] who had assembled.

Previous to Thoma the II's death, he left the charge of his people to his son-in-law, Francis Gregoire, in whose care he deposited the Ensigns of Royalty, charging him to act as their supreme till the choice is made and a Chief *Legally* chosen to whom he shall deliver all the Royal property— it is said by some that a wish was expressed by the late chief to have his Brother Christmas Thoma chosen as his successor, but it appears the family of the Gogoos will lay claim to the Throne—they once held Dominion prior to Thoma the I, but for some reasons were supplanted by the Thoma family who owe their rise to the voice of the tribe.

This Island contains 125 families of Indians or about 450 men, women and children.

The Cape-Bretonian. Sydney, 28 January 1834. In *The Colonial Patriot.* Pictou, N.S., 18 February 1834.

Canoe Trip from Dartmouth, N.S., to St. John, N.B., made by two Indians in a canoe in a single day, about 1831-5. Probably about 200 miles. This extraordinary canoe-trip was made by: Noel Jeddore [Isidore, son of Ned Isidore and grandson of We'jitu], who was born at St. Mary's Forks, Guysborough County, possibly about 1806, and who died at Windsor, N.S., about 36 years ago (say about 1890), aged 84 years. [The second man was] Handley Squegun [André Skwiqn]. Squegun is Micmac for Hole-In-Ice in which eels, etc., are caught. [He] was born and bred at Morris's Lake, east of Dartmouth. Not known when he died. In later years he had only one arm [the Indian Agent Report for 1855 says he had lost a leg, not an arm]. Both men were very powerful men, and in their prime then, say about 25 years of age, which would date it about 1831 or say it was as late as 1835. Both [were] about the same age. Lone Cloud heard the story from Noel Jeddore himself and also from old Ned Knowlen [Nowlan] (part Indian) of Dartmouth. They undertook the trip because they heard it had been accomplished by other Indians in the past.

Very early in the morning, about first week of July, when days are long, these two young Indians, Noel Jeddore and Handley Squegun, left Dartmouth in a birchbark Micmac canoe. Paddled through Dartmouth Lakes, and Grand Lake, and down Shubenacadie River to Milford where the Fundy tides come to. The hardest part of the paddling was from Dartmouth to Milford. At Milford they got the tide just flowing out the river swiftly, and rapidly went down to Maitland, at Mouth of river Shubenacadie. With the strong outflowing tide they very easily paddled down Minas Basin to near Blomidon, and across to Advocate Harbour. Then coasted westward to Cape Chignecto. Then, the tide still running outward, they crossed Chignecto Bay near the Three Sisters, to the New Brunswick shore westward of Point Wolf. Then as the tide began to come in, they proceeded westward along the N.B. shore, hugging close to the shore and taking advantage of the backwash eddied there which lessened the effect of the returning tide. That night they got into St. John Harbour, N.B., the trip being accomplished in a single day.

Jeremiah Bartlett Alexis [alias Jerry Lonecloud] to Harry Piers, 28 June 1926. Unpublished notes, Nova Scotia Museum Printed Matter File.

1836

The gypsum in the vicinity of Windsor [N.S.], abounds in those conical or inverted funnel shaped cavities.... In one of these caverns about ten or fifteen years since, the bones of a human being, supposed from the relics of arrows found with them, to have been those of one of the aboriginal inhabitants, were discovered in opening a gypsum quarry. It is presumed that this unfortunate individual, while pursuing his favorite occupation of the chase, was precipitated to the bottom of this frightful dungeon, and being confined by its inclined walls, was unable to reach its summit and regain the light. Thus incarcerated, he perished. His bones are preserved in the library of King's College, at Windsor, where they were politely shewed us, by the acting Vice President, Rev. Wm. King, who related to us the above story of their origin.

Charles T. Jackson and Francis Alger. "A Description of the Mineralogy and Geology of a Part of Nova Scotia." In *The American Journal of Science*. 1836, Vol. X:146-147.

Speaking of the wit of the Indians, we may give an instance, which was long a standing joke of Pictonians against their neighbors in Colchester. Some Indians being after geese in spring, shot one which fell on the ice. Seeing that it could not escape, they did not go for it at once, when some persons coming along in a sleigh picked it up. The Indians, however, came up and claimed it. The others refused to give it up, saying that they had shot it. "Where you from?" said an Indian. "From Truro," was the reply. "Sartin bleeve so; Pictou man no shoot dead goose."

George Patterson. *History of the County of Pictou, Nova Scotia.* 1972:191.

1837

The petition of Francis Paul, Chief of the Micmac Indians ... sheweth: that he and his family consisting of six persons reside at Shubenaccadie, and that the tribe are to meet there on Christmas Day at the Chapel there to worship God; that he has nothing to feed the people but a few potatoes and that if some relief be not afforded to them by You they will starve, and therefore your petitioner humbly prays relief in this presents. Francis Paul, his mark.

Public Archives of Nova Scotia, Halifax. MG15, Vol. 3, #49. 23 December 1837.

ca 1840

I remember well being in camp at the end of a beaver hunting expedition, on the Rossignol Lakes, at a picturesque spot called the Sedgewich, the Indian name for the 'run-out' of a lake. It was a grassy promontory, with a growth of white oak, 'an oak opening,' as it is termed. It was also an old Indian burying-place, and the graves of the old folk were still discernible, sometimes headed by a piece of rock, and all overgrown with roses and wild creepers. I don't know that our Indians quite liked our camping there. They seemed taciturn and subdued, but the evening fire thawed their reticence, and with the pipe after supper, we soon got talking about old times, and the old people, and of course Glooskcap came on the programme of the evening.... Of a nobler character than the Hiawatha legends of the Mohawks, the mythical tales of these sons of the forests would fill volumes. One discovers with wonder and surprise what a storehouse of the wild poetry of the woods is the mind of the Indian.

Campbell Hardy. "In Evangeline's Land." Unpublished MS, *ca* 1910. Nova Scotia Museum Printed Matter File.

Micmac hunter with fish spear, musket and paddle. Lithograph by Robert Petley, 1837.

Another [Pictou County Micmac], usually known as Beetle John [possibly "Bateau John"; the names Beato, Batteaux, Boittow, Poito, etc. appear in nineteenth-century census records], is especially worthy of notice, as having been the owner of a shallop. It was built on the Big Island of Merigomish, in a small cove at the head of the French channel, and for some time he traded in her.

George Patterson. *History of the County of Pictou, Nova Scotia.* 1972:191.

1840

It ought not to be forgotten or omitted, that the Nova Scotia Philanthropic Society have assumed a kind of conventional guardianship of Indian rights. In their anniversary of the landing of Governor Cornwallis, and the settlement of Halifax—observed by them every 8th of June—the Indians take a part in their procession; the last time that I saw the old chief [Louis-Benjamin Peminuit Paul] was on one of these annual festivals [probably the marriage of Queen Victoria; see next entry for 1840]; he was seated with his squaw in a gentleman's carriage, decked with evergreens; they were covered with ornaments peculiar to their race, dressed in royal Indian style, maintaining the peculiar gravity of demeanour for which they are so remarkable. Thus they headed the procession, followed by their tribe, and at the close of the day's entertainment they were regaled with plenty of substantial fare, the tables being spread in the grand parade, concluding the repast with the usual dance.
Charles Churchill. *Memorials of Missionary Life in Nova Scotia.* 1845:188-189.

One of the Micmacs, not long since, entering a tavern, in one of the country towns, to purchase some spirits, for which ten shillings were demanded, double the retail Halifax price, the [Micmac] expostulated on the extravagant price asked; the landlord endeavoured to justify it by explaining the expense of conveyance, the loss of interest, &c., and illustrated his remarks by saying that, "it was as expensive to keep a hogshead of rum as a milch cow." The Indian humorously replied, "maybe drinks as much water," alluding to its adulteration, "but certain no eat so much hay."
R. Montgomery Martin. *A History of Nova Scotia and Cape Breton.* 1837: 20.
[This story was first published in Haliburton (1829). George Patterson says that the Micmac Lulan, of Pictou County, was the wit in the case.]

1840

THE QUEEN'S MARRIAGE

Officers and wardens of the [Philanthropic] Society, with badges and wands, profusely decorated with blue and white ribbons, and May flowers ... Indians with badges, ribbons, flowers, and "Indian ornaments"—Indian boys, with bows and arrows, and badges—Squaws (female Indians) with their picturesque costume, of high peaked caps, and many coloured spensers, overlaid with beads, bugles and various ornaments; nearly every Squaw carrying or leading a "papoose"; the band of the 23rd; an Indian Chief [Louis-Benjamin Peminuit Paul], a venerable looking patriarch, aged 78 years—in a carriage, the horse decorated with blue and white ribbons.... The procession moved along Hollis street, past Hon. M. Tobin's and to Government House.... (The squaws fell out of march soon after leaving Government House.) At the extremity of Water Street the procession entered the Dock Yard; it made the circuit of the yard, the artillery fired a salute, three cheers were given, and the march was re-commenced through Dutch Town.

On the Parade, tables were spread—the Societies formed at each side, and their Indian guests sat down to a repast. This consisted in an abundance of fish, fish pies, bread, butter, cheese, cake, and porter. (The day being Friday, and the Indians of the R. Catholic persuasion, meat was not provided....) Thomas Forrester, Esq., President of the Philanthropic Society ... presented a scarf to the old Chief. The Indians did justice to the catering of their friends, and after dinner, an Indian dance concluded the proceedings.... That the marriage of our young Queen, to the Prince who was the choice of her heart—should thus meet such enthusiastic echoes, so far from the seat of Empire, is an interesting and delightful feature of the times.

The Novascotian. Halifax, 7 May 1840.

About the last of March or the first of April [one winter], the Indians had very few provisions—there was no game or fish. A big storm came. [Peter Ginnish's] grandfather heard a crow flying toward him. It came close to him, then cawed and cawed. He noticed it appeared to be greasy, and was wiping and cleaning its bill on its feathers. It cawed and cawed, then flew off to one end of Portage Island. He told his father about the crow. They went out with another man, put on their snowshoes, and crossed on the ice to the island. Something had come ashore. When they arrived at the place, they found it to be something large, like a ship, and black. It was a big whale. They found a big whale! There was seven inches of fat in addition to the meaty part. The men returned, each with a big load. Next morning a man went on snowshoes to Richibucto, one to Red Bank, one to Shippigan, and even to Bathurst and Restigouche, to take the news. From all these settlements the Indians came and hauled away pieces of the whale—every piece of it. They left only the bones. The Indians are never stingy. They are like a crow. It is never stingy. When a crow finds provisions, it brings the news to the Indians. It came to tell the people at Burnt Church about the whale which it had found at Portage Island.

Peter Ginnish to Wilson D. Wallis, 1911. In *The Micmac Indians of Eastern Canada,* by Wilson D. and Ruth Sawtell Wallis. 1955:432.

1841

LOST, by an Indian, Near the Province Building, a SILK PURSE, containing four five pound Notes, and four one pound Province Notes, a 7 1/2d and one penny. Whoever has found the same and will leave it at the Morning Herald Office, shall be suitably rewarded. January 13.

The Morning Herald. Halifax, 15 January 1841.

To the Queen

Madame: I am Paussamigh Pemmeenauweet [Benjamin Peminuit], and am called by the White Man Louis-Benjamin Pominout. I am the Chief of my People the Micmac Tribe of Indians in your Province of Nova Scotia and I was recognized and declared to be the Chief by our good Friend Sir John Cope Sherbrooke in the White Man's fashion Twenty Five Years ago; I have yet the Paper which he gave me.

Sorry to hear that the King is dead. Am glad to hear that we have a good Queen whose Father I saw in this Country. He loved the Indians.

I cannot cross the great Lake to talk to you for my Canoe is too small, and I am old and weak. I cannot look upon you for my eyes not see so far. You cannot hear my voice across the Great Waters. I therefore send this Wampum and Paper talk to tell the Queen I am in trouble. My people are in trouble. I have seen upwards of a Thousand Moons. When I was young I had plenty: now I am old, poor and sickly too. My people are poor. No Hunting Grounds—No Beaver—no Otter—no nothing. Indians poor—poor for ever. No Store—no Chest—no Clothes. All these Woods once ours. Our Fathers possessed them all. Now we cannot cut a Tree to warm our Wigwam in Winter unless the White Man please. The Micmacs now receive no presents, but one small Blanket for a whole family. The Governor is a good man but he cannot help us now. We look to you the Queen. The White Wampum tell that we hope in you. Pity your poor Indians in Nova Scotia.

White Man has taken all that was ours. He has plenty of everything here. But we are told that the White Man has sent to you for more. No wonder that I should speak for myself and my people.

The man that takes this talk over the great Water will tell you what we want to be done for us. Let us not perish. Your Indian Children love you, and will fight for you against all your enemies.

My Head and my Heart shall go to One above for you.

Pausauhmigh Pemmeenauweet, Chief of the Micmac Tribe of Indians in Nova Scotia. His mark +.

Louis-Benjamin Peminuit Paul to Queen Victoria, received by the Colonial Office, London, 25 January 1841. Colonial Office Archives 217/179, ff. 406-8. Photographs of this document published in *Micmacs and Colonists*, by L.F.S. Upton. 1979:188-192.

1841

An Account of the Indians within the County of Richmond, as taken on the 26th July 1841, at the Indian Chapel Bras dor Lake, being the Anniversary of Saint Ann's day.

Michael Dennie, 73, Chief; Mary, 62. Both becoming infirm. Planted 18 bushels of Potatoes, could have planted 30 Bushels if he had seed, has no cattle, raised 10 tons hay.

Joseph Nevin, widower, 80, very poor, very infirm, nearly blind.

Marie Joseph Basque, widow, 60, very poor, infirm and blind.

Magdelaine Basque, widow, 67, very poor, infirm and blind.

Susan Christopher, widow, 60, very poor, infirm, nearly blind.

Tharesa Jacque [Therese Jacques], widow, 70, very poor, infirm, not blind.

Alic Ambroise, 12, an orphan.

Charlotte Gogo [Googoo], 10, an orphan with a broken back, and can with difficulty walk.

Thomas Julian, 45; Mary, 40. Poor, man and woman able in body, children healthy, raised three tons of hay, planted no potatoes for want of seed.

Paul Andrew, 40; Ann, 30. Man & children healthy & strong, woman in delicate health, has one pig, 2 acres of land chopped and burnt ready to plant, planted [?] bushels, would have planted more, no seed.

John Knockwood, 70; Mary Ann, 64. Both sickly, planted only 6 bushels for want of seed.

Peter Scotchman, widower, 70.

William Lafford, 24; Mary, 33. The man lame in knee.

Peter Ambroise, 69; Anastasia, 60. Very infirm, can provide 2 tons hay.

Paul Francis, 48; Frances, 46.

Peter Antoine, 50; Anastasia, 40.

Francis Scotchman, 25; Mary, 20.

Martin Knockwood, 44; Mary, 36.

John Knockwood, 28; Christy, 27.

Joseph Louis, 66; Angelique, 53. Man and woman feeble, family helpless.

Paul Joe, 27; Louisa, 24.

Joseph Prosper, 33; Charlotte, 34. One girl 10 years of age broken back.

Francis Toney, 25; Betsey, 19.

Joseph Fraser, 28; Anastatia, 44. One boy 18 years of age very sickly.

Louis Tousay [Toussaint], 28; Bridget, 16.

Noel Julian, 47; Ann, 47.

Frank Matthew, 23; Mary, 17. Just arrived from Bay St. George, intends residing here, anxious to farm.

Thomas Nevin, 28; Angelique, 55. The woman an object of great commiseration.

Julian Basque, 53; Frances, 37.

Noel Gremo [Cremo], 39; Mary, 28. The woman lame; one boy 4 years old lame.

Peter Francis, 25; Margaret, 25.

Matthew Morris, 50; Anastasia, 30.

Joseph Moose, 25; Louisa, 22.

Francis Grigoir [Gregoire], 61; Magdalaine, 59.

Stephen Moose, 25; Mary, 20.

Joseph Francis, 28; Mary, 30.

Julian Googo [Googoo], 20; Ursule, 19.

Louis Cooko [Googoo], 24; St. Appolus [?], 28. The woman strong, the man has met with an accident and broke his back, unfit for hard labour.

Francis Nevin, 63; Angelique, 60.

Francis Doucet, 32.

Nancy Harney [Herney], widow, 37.

Joseph Muse [Mius, Meuse, Muese], 26; Mary, 21

John Michael, 56; Ann, 37.

Noel Basque, 27; Mary, 21.

John Lobster, 28; Oursule, 21.

Richard Baptiste, 21; Mary Ann, 19.

Noel Dennis, 42; Mary, 29.

Julian Paul, 37, Mary, 35.

Michael Joe, 30; Mary, 26.

Andrew Joe, 22; Susan, 22.

Joseph Cooko, 31; Mary, 20.
Francis Cooko, 28; Ann, 16.
Noel Lobster, 30; Mary Ann, 22.
Ann Jacko, widow, 40.
Frank Joe, 24; Mary Ann, 20.
Alic Scotchman, 40; Mary, 30.
Beloney Dennis, 32; Eliza, 28.
Peter Moose, 70; Francis, 65. The man very infirm, the woman blind—
the five children they keep are Orphans & very destitute. ['Moose'
possibly derives from 'Mius,' although it may be a nickname.]
Public Archives of Nova Scotia, Halifax. MG15, Vol. 3, #65.

The Indians have a story that a huge animal once raised its head out of the water of the Middle Barrasoi of Aspy Bay, near Cape North, and so terrified them, that it was long before any would venture thither again.
R. Montgomery Martin. *A History of Nova Scotia and Cape Breton.* 1827:101.

1842
12 December: The Commandant [Alphonse-Joseph Desrousseaux, *chef de la colonie*] advised the Department that the chief of a band from the west of Newfoundland, known as "King Michel Agathe," who came to Saint-Pierre with more than one hundred people of his tribe, at the beginning of this month, to make their annual devotions, was lost with all his people and goods, in a squall, while returning home.
Emile Sasco and Joseph Lehuenen. *Éphémérides des Iles St.-Pierre et Miquelon* 1970:12. Translated for this publication by Margaret Anne Hamelin.

1842
In one house [at Bear River] a man was cutting up a tanned hide, which was that of a Moose—in another, a Squaw was frying dough nuts and making pumpkin pies, while a second sat beside working quill boxes.
Joseph Howe. "Indian Journal." Public Archives of Nova Scotia, Halifax. MG432, 1842:102.

Left Truro to visit this tract of land [the Hants County Reservation] on the 11th of May, taking with me the Chief, Francis Paul, and Peter Thomas. In passing the Grand Lake, Shubenacadie, the Chief enquired if I had ever heard of whales being in fresh water. I answered, no. He said his grandfather had often told him and others that there was, at one

time, a whale in the Grand Lake. That he was there for some time, but at last stretched himself across the foot of the lake, above the river, and died there. I expressed my doubts of the truth of this story, but Francis declared it "sartin true," said it was always believed by his contemporaries, and that he had often seen some of the bones himself. In mentioning this story to Shultz he informed me that very large bones of some unknown fish or animal had been found at the foot of the lake.

Joseph Howe. "Indian Journal." Public Archives of Nova Scotia, Halifax. MG432, 1842:62.

[Shultz owned an inn on Shubenacadie Grand Lake; Howe often stayed there on his travels.]

1842

Baptised 7 January 1842: Noel Peter, of Joseph Peter and Sally Luxy [Alexis].

Baptised 13 March 1842: John Jeremy, of John Jeremy and Sally Tony [Antoine], aged 9 weeks.

Baptised 18 December 1842: Joseph Charles, of Francis Charles and Molley [Marie] Peter.

Baptised 18 December 1842: Molley Gload [Marie Claude], of Francis Gload and Fanny Lapier [Sapier, Xavier?].

Nova Scotian Baptismal Registries: St Gregory's, Liverpool, and St Jerome's, Caledonia, N.S. Extracted by Blake Conrad, 1983.

"Well, all right. The children who them were born in the time, they always had—had some—some 'nitial or 'nother, to repint the day the child was born. Maybe induring the summer, or maybe induring the fall, or springtime or wintertime. But more so they would form selection, they would form selection more dearly in summer; when the berries—'cording to berries and 'cording to blossom, and all so forth. And they was so glad when the child was born, 'specially especially a boy. They had manys to thanks, to give the child—to give the child this great living into this world, and to the great service into the—into the world effect. And of course, they took this to be the greatest of their doings.

So—so they would gather up different things, such as—such as a hide or skin of any garment that the boy would ... would wear. And others— and anothers would be makin'—makin' [cradle]boards. Well then, they'd go to work, and leave this—this crib aside of a tree, and then they was more sure to be not in danger for—for any reptiles or mosquitos or any other bug to trouble—to trouble the child. An' that's the way 'e 'ad moved when they would move from that place; they would go to work and put this child on their back and travel for miles, where there was a great hunting ground or sum' like that for their livin'. Just whatever 'bundance the woods, the forests, gave them. That's the 'bundance they had; and that's the 'bundance they had b'leeved—in that time.

Well now then, when this was all over, well then, they'd go to work—they'd go to work and notify each other, which them lived handy, to have a leetle pow-wow—about the—about this child 'bout they were giving him a great thanks and great wishes.... And the great wishes for his life, and all and they all—different things: all, all their real—realities they had gived him.

And so therefore they all were exsembled in the place where the child was, well they go to work and now we had give'm all those wishes, great wishes what we had carried and what we had—now we had showen all these wishes to this child and now then we better give'm more things, more thanks of his great life—great 'nority, and all so forth.

Well, now then, we better go to work now and we must have a leetle pow-wow, to make a little infantry dance around the child. The child would be right in the centre, and the dance would be circling around the child, three or four different times, three, four different times. And that's the way they give these full thanks of this child, and after they give all those great wishes. [He sings.]

Chief William Paul to Dr Helen Creighton. Taped interview, Shubenacadie, N.S., 1944. Transcribed by R.H. Whitehead from the original tape in Dr Creighton's possession.

[Chief William Paul did not speak English very well, but his great oratorical style comes through particularly clearly in this taped interview.]

1843

I learned on enquiry from many elderly people, who stated themselves to be childless, that they had had from 8 to 12 Children each, who had died in infancy from Measles, Whooping Cough, Scarlet Fever, Croup, Typhus, Small Pox, and a variety of other Diseases, to which Children are subject. The Infants are much exposed by the wandering habits of their parents, who rely almost entirely upon their own modes of treatment with roots and herbs, which are quite useless and ineffective in the majority of cases. During my visit to the Miramichi the Children were suffering dreadfully from Dysentery, and while at Burnt Church Point a death occurred almost daily.

Moses Perley. In *Legislative Assembly of Nova Scotia Journals.* 1843, Appendix 49:127.

1844

On the demise of their aged chief [Louis-Benjamin Peminuit Paul, Shubenacadie], a dispute arose about the succession, two candidates having claimed that distinction. Instead of raising the war cry, and testing the right by force of might, it was agreed to lay their respective claims before the Catholic Bishop resident in Halifax. The aisles of the chapel were trodden by the moccasins of the tribes; the claims were severally preferred in the house of their worship; the decision was made before the altar; the interference of the Bishop was satisfactory; the right of the decision was unquestioned, being received with unqualified submission; the newly elected chief [Francis Paul, brother of the former chief] was then invested with the insignia of office; homage was tendered to him by every Indian present; and a procession was afterwards formed, which wended its way to Government House, when the whole party presented their chief; tendered their respects to their "great mother's" representative, and concluded their visit to the Governor, Lord Falkland, with the native dance.

Charles Churchill. *Memorials of Missionary Life in Nova Scotia.* 1845:188.

1844

For several years Goreham Paul and his family lived in a framed house, but having let his place during a visit which he paid to his wife's relations, in New Brunswick, the house got out of repair—his stock was destroyed—and his farm much injured. On his return he abandoned the house, which has been turned into a barn, and has since resided in a wigwam near to it. His habitation was more spacious than Indian camps generally are, having an entrance at each end. To my surprise, I found a white girl living in the camp. On enquiring into her history, it appeared that her father was an Irishman, and her mother a Scotchwoman, who, from intemperance, or other causes, had neglected or abandoned her in infancy. Goreham, having no children, was induced to take her. [See a similar story of Madeline Hickey, adopted by Toney and Sally Paul, in the entry for 1827.] She had been brought up as his own, and although subsequently visited by her mother, refused to abandon those to whom she owed everything but existence.... A kick from a horse about a year ago, had injured her jaw, and changed the expression of her mouth, but she had been very good looking, and seemed healthy and cheerful. She spoke both Indian and English fluently, and her manner and expression of countenance was singular, interesting, but often painful. One could not but regret that a young creature, who might have been the honoured mistress of the best farm house in the neighborhood, had her parents done their duty, was the mere tenant at will of an Indian's wigwam.... Within the humble wigwams upon which we look with so much contempt, there may often be found the higher feelings of benevolence and steadfast fidelity, which, in the dwellings of our own race, are sometimes wanting. Mary Ann Paul (her former name I do not know), is now about 22, still unmarried, probably hesitating between her pale face and tawny admirers, but bears the reputation of being a good girl, and very dutiful to her parents.

Joseph Howe. In *Legislative Assembly of Nova Scotia Journals*. 1844, Appendix 50:122-123.

Governor Muise [Governor-Chief James Mius] brought his wife here on a handsled. She was bashful, and would come to our house and sit behind the stove and smoke her T.D. pipe (white clay). They were nice people.

Muise was a great friend of my father, and they were the same age. He was a member of parliament at Halifax, and used to go up there. The other men thought they would have some fun with him when he sat down to his first formal dinner. But when the courses came on he watched how they did, and he'd eat a little of each course just as they did, and when they got through and the next course came on, he'd do the same as the others. He was telling my father about it afterwards, and thinking of all the good food that went off the table, and he said, "George, if I'd a had that home in my camp, wouldn't I have scoffed it (cleared it up)."

When he came home he tried to have his wife do the same as the waiters did in Halifax; that is, take the food on and off. He had the same number of courses, but it was all the same food.

He was an educated Indian, born and brought up here and he went to school here. That would be over one hundred years ago (1837). [There may be some confusion here between James Mius, Sr, and James Mius, Jr.] When old Mrs. Richard Clarke was alive he always went there to see her and always dressed well in clothes that were given him and when he went to Halifax, he was fitted out with a suit made at the tailor's.

Anonymous [probably collected by Dr Helen Creighton]. "Legends, Bear River, Annapolis County, English, August 1937." Nova Scotia Museum Printed Matter File.

1844

Early in the spring, two Indians from Queen's County had visited me in Halifax, representing their anxiety to settle and become Farmers, if they could get land. The more intelligent, John Jeremy, informed me that he had selected a spot on the Fairy Lake, but was afraid to improve or build, until he was assured that he would not be disturbed. It was to visit this man, and some others, who, it appeared, had joined him in founding a Settlement, that led me to the Fairy Lake....

After rowing a mile, we turned a jutting point, and found ourselves in front of Jeremy's clearing, and were sufficiently uncomfortable to rejoice in the evidences of occupancy afforded by the smoke. He was from home, having gone through to Annapolis for nails. His Squaw received us hospitably, although some of her children were ill. A message dispatched to the neighboring camps, brought half a dozen swarthy men, of various ages and sizes, and a kettle of Moose meat. This was soon cut up into small pieces and fried in Carriboo fat, and with good potatoes, and a cup of tea, enabled us to refresh ourselves, and resist the effects of wet clothing....

Jeremy's family consisted of his wife Sally [Toney], and 6 children. His oldest daughter, Molly Oceola [Marie Ursule], is married to Jem Lewis, who was away. The other settlers on the Lake were—Joe Peter, wife [Sally Alexis] and child; Francis Charles, wife [Marie Peter], and 5 children; Francis Meuse, wife, and 5 children; Abraham Peter, wife, and child; John Pictou, and wife; Peter Glode (or Piel), wife, and two children; and Lewis Alexis, from Shelburne, and another Indian, who were anxious to join the Settlement....

I thought it best, in order to encourage and reward [Jeremy for his efforts to date], to give an example to his neighbours, and a character of permanence to the settlement—to go to the extent of the liberality authorized by the Act, and build him a house.

Joseph Howe. In *Legislative Assembly of Nova Scotia Journals.* 1844, Appendix 50:123-125.

In the early days when Greenfield at the foot of Pon Hook Lake was first being settled, the Indians possessed an old burying ground there which the newcomers desired as a site for a mill yard. The Indians made strong objections and appealed to the Local Government. Joseph Howe, who was then a member of the Government, went to Greenfield in order to conciliate the Indians and make the matter right with them concerning the supposed desecration of their burying ground.... The chief Cobbeyall [Gabriel],... a man of splendid physique and dignified bearing, was spokesman for the assembled Indians [who] sat in a circle, and Mr. Howe stood in the centre. He made a lengthy address using all his powers of persuasion to convince them that it would be expedient and even necessary for them to give up their ground to the service of the white man, and that no desecration of the graves of their ancestors was intended. The Indians sat sphynx like until he had finished. Then Cobbeyall arose, and with great deliberation and emphasis said: "Howe, I believe you lie."

Nova Scotian and Weekly Chronicle. Halifax, 10 July 1903:8, col. 5.

1844

I have been much interested with two Indians during the past year—one named John Stephens, a Shoemaker, living in Newport, and who supports himself, a wife and three children, by his trade. He was neatly dressed, spoke English fluently, asked for nothing for himself, and seemed only solicitous for the welfare of his people. Another, Michel, a youth reared and educated by Père Vincent [de Paul], at Tracadie, appeared very intelligent and ingenious —he spoke English, French and Micmac fluently, was an excellent Carpenter and Turner, and had built the waggon in which the Père and himself rode to Town.

Jospeh Howe. In *Legislative Assembly of Nova Scotia Journals.* 1844, Appendix 50:126.

Micmac Indian "Dr." Jerry Lone Cloud: Jerry Bartlett [Alexis], now known as "Doctor" Jerry Lone Cloud, Micmac Indian of Nova Scotia, was born at Belfast, Maine, USA, on 4 July 1846 (the same day the *City of Richmond* ran ashore there). His parents were Nova Scotian Micmac Indians (with mixture of French blood). When 13 years of age (about 1859) he came to Nova Scotia where he remained for 20 years (till about 1879), when he returned to the United States again and was there for 7 or 8 years (till about 1886), when he finally returned to Nova Scotia. Used to sell plant remedies throughout the country and also hair restorer, etc. Lately lived at Enfield. In 1923 lived in a house at Old Chapel, Mumford Road, Halifax. Micmac name [pronounced] Helsalmah. Jerry Bartlett was the son of Abram Bartlett Alexis. The Micmac surname Alexis, spelled variously Luxcey, Luxy, Lexy and Luxie, was often dropped by both father and son, who used the last name Bartlett. Abram Bartlett was from Ohio, Shelburne County, N.S., the son of a "full-blooded" Micmac man named Bartlett Alexis and a "full-blooded" Frenchwoman. Abram married Mary Ann Phillips, the only daughter of Tom Phillips, himself the son of a Micmac man and a French woman. Tom Phillips was a well-known man, who lived at the foot of Ponhook Lake, Hants County, N.S., where he had a sort of half-way house.

Jeremiah Bartlett Alexis [alias Jerry Lonecloud] to Harry Piers, 11 June 1914. Nova Scotia Museum Printed Matter File.

[See entry for 1854, for a second birthdate story for Lonecloud. As previously noted, Jerry Lonecloud and Nova Scotia Museum curator Harry Piers spelled "Lonecloud" as one word or two. I have chosen to spell it as one.]

1846

The better days of the Indians have long gone by. They are only the ghost of what they were—few in number, and poor in circumstances. They are the mere fragment of nations which have passed away. Once they were the powerful lords of the soil; now they are a few beggarly chiefs. The approach of the white man, and the march of improvement, have sealed their doom, and compelled them to fly from mountain to mountain, to seek a resting place; but they seldom find it till they cross the dark waters and reach the city of their father's sepulchres, where they sleep securely in their green savannahs, far beyond the reach of the intruder.

Their existence is incompatible with a state of civilization. The peaceful labours of the plough are nearly as fatal to them as the hostile rage of the camp. They cannot live when the wild animals are frightened away, and their hunting grounds are destroyed. Some of our old settlers still remember when the Moose Deer were as plenty on the river as the tame cattle. Francis Cope, the famous Indian hunter, has glided down the stream with sixty Moose skins in his canoe, on his way to Halifax. Now we seldom see a Moose or an Indian.

Rev. John Sprott, Musquodoboit, N.S., 1 February 1846. From *The Wigtownshire Free Press*, Scotland; quoted in *The Novascotian*, Halifax, 6 April 1846:110.

An Indian applied to a storekeeper to sell him a small article on credit, but he refused it. The Indian knew that the storekeeper had been lately appointed a captain of the militia. He sat down with his dogs before the door, and named them all captains. The storekeeper observed, "Your dogs are all captains." "Yes," said he, "all puppies are nowadays made captains."

Anonymous Micmac man. In Rev. John Sprott, Musquodoboit, N.S., 1 February 1846. From *The Wigtownshire Free Press*, Scotland; quoted in *The Novascotian*, Halifax, 6 April 1846:110.

1846

Last year my wife, on her way to Halifax, lost a fine muff, which I had brought her from Scotland. Next day, in town, an Indian came to her son George, and told him that he had found his mother's muff on the road, and he had left it for her at the inn where she stopped, and she would get it on her return. "But," said George, "how did you know me?" "Know you! I knew you since you were the height of a robin. Did not I carry Mrs. Sprott in my canoe when you were a baby?"

Rev. John Sprott, Musquodoboit, N.S., 1 February 1846. From *The Wigtownshire Free Press*, Scotland; quoted in *The Novascotian*, Halifax, 6 April 1846:110.

A farmer in one of the lower towns scolded an Indian for resting on his premises, and injuring his trees. The Indian coolly replied, "If you raise a calf or a cabbage you may call it your own, but you can have no claim to that tree (pointing to a tree five hundred years old). That tree was planted by the Great Spirit for the Red man before you and your fathers escaped from your murky shells and crossed the great waters. Is that your brook? Catch it if you can; it runs away from you. It runs past your house, it runs past everybody's house, and never stops till it reaches the sea. We never injure your pigs nor cows; but the other day your men frightened a bear, and prevented him from going into my trap."

Anonymous Micmac man. In Rev. John Sprott, Musquodoboit, N.S., 1 February 1846. From *The Wigtownshire Free Press*, Scotland; quoted in *The Novascotian*, Halifax, 6 April 1846:110.

1846

Isodore [Ned Isidore, also called Jeddore, son of We'jitu] the chief of Musquodoboit, died lately, and his ten sons had all crossed the dark lake and gone to the pleasant mountain before him. This venerable old hemlock, through whose branches the storms of ninety years had whistled, often visited me, kissed my hand and called me his father.... He had been a thirsty soul in his younger years, and when he got a glass of rum too much, a dream of dominion came over his mind, and he still claimed the sovereignty of the soil, for the land of Musquodoboit, he said, belonged to him, and we were all intruders. I visited his camp a few minutes after [one] son died. They were all on their knees, engaged in prayer and praise. To see these untutored children of the wilderness bowing before the Great Spirit, and crying for mercy, affected me more powerfully than to have seen all the worshippers of the most splendid Cathedral on their knees. They are all Roman Catholics, and so highly devotional in their way, and their little boys will not touch a meal of victuals without first making the sign of the cross. They would not hunt on the Sabbath, unless they were hungry. Their women are modest....

I have often in my long journeys met with strolling parties of the red skins, with their long knives and fire-arms in their hands, but never felt the least apprehension of danger. If I missed my way I would seek in no better guide than an Indian. I could sleep in their camps as soundly as I could do in your house.... You call them savages—they are not savages—they are Nature's gentlemen....

Rev. John Sprott, Musquodoboit, N.S., 1 February 1846. From *The Wigtownshire Free Press*, Scotland; quoted in *The Novascotian*, Halifax, 6 April 1846:110.

[Sprott later wrote of Ned Isidore, "After the commencement of the temperance movement I withheld from the old chief the usual beverage and told him that the great Spirit was displeased at his children for drinking *fire water*. He admitted that too much was not good, but I never could make him understand the benefit of temperance societies." (*The Novascotian*, Halifax, 30 June 1851.)]

1847

Average number of children in each family only 3.

Abraham Gesner. In *Legislative Assembly of Nova Scotia Journals*. 1848, Appendix 24:111.

1847

It has been supposed by some writers that the savage tribes of North America had no means of recording events. The wampum belt was generally applied to the different parts of a speech, or the different articles of a treaty; and on great occasions, when these belts were brought forth, individuals were found who, from memory or tradition, could explain each section of the precious girdle: but, besides this mode of record, the Micmacs and Melicetes [Maliseets] had pictorial representations of certain events, and communicated information through the medium of hieroglyphics. Rocks and trees in conspicuous situations have had figures cut or engraved upon them, which convey to the Indian traveller in concise terms the knowledge necessary for his safety and comfort.

During his geological survey of the Province, the Writer, with two companions and three Indians, were much embarrassed in not being able to discover in the wilderness an old Indian portage between the head waters of the St. Croix and Eel River Lake. From this difficulty they were relieved by observing some rude hieroglyphics marked upon an old cedar-tree. The representations were that of an Indian carrying a canoe, and the direction of the figures corresponding exactly with that of the portage path, which had been obscured by grass and fallen leaves. A hunter with his gun levelled at two deer, indicated that those animals were plentiful: this, and other information conveyed in a similar manner, was found to be correct.

In another instance, when the same party was descending Eel River, and their lives were in jeopardy on the brink of a fall, a large drawing of two Indians, with their heels uppermost and their canoes capsized, was seen executed in durable black ink upon a broad piece of cedar, secured to a post: this warning was immediately understood, and a landing was effected before the canoes and the whole party were plunged down the cataract.

Abraham Gesner. *New Brunswick with Notes for Emigrants.* 1847:111-112.

1847

I have the honour to report to his Excellency Sir John Harvey the History, Symptoms, Nature and treatment of the disease [locally called "Indian Fever," possibly typhus], which has been so destructive amongst the Indians in the neighborhood of Dartmouth as far as could be ascertained from our own observations and the information received from the more intelligent of the Indians. Early in the summer 1846 an Indian from St. John's died at "Petite." Soon after Joe Stephens, located at Tufts Cove—about a mile from Dartmouth—was seized with a Similar disease & died. A number of the Natives were successively attacked & died having had no medicine administered save the decoction of some astringent barks, which certainly hastened the fatal termination.

The first proper medical assistance rendered was by Dr. Richardson, 60th Riffles [*sic*], in the case of Mrs. Williams, who altho' in the last stages, was rescued from an exceedingly perilous state. The disease lurked amongst them (now & then one being carried off) till the month of January, when it assumed a most alarming appearance, the whole race in this district having been threatened with annihilation. Horror-stricken, those who were well fled from the wigwams of the Sick. Despair & distress were pictured in the countenances of all and it was evident that fear was the chief exciting cause of the disease.

By the direction of his Excellency, the promptest means were resorted to. I consequently suggested the indispensable necessity of a temporary hospital, to which those who were ill might be carried and such as might subsequently be affected. (I may here state that the miserable wigwams in which they lived, imperatively demanded the removal of my patients for their safety. Currents of cold air constantly passed in on their backs, while a frying heat was in front. Nor were they guarded against rain, which prevented the possibility of giving suitable medicines with advantage.) In addition to the Hospital ... warm clothing and shoes were procured & such food as would enable them to bear up against the depressing influence of the disease. Before the Hospital could be erected and the other necessaries obtained, five died, [but] there were only two deaths in Hospital—one Joe Stephens Jr. became convalescent, visited Halifax (contrary to our order), and returned after four days when the most powerful stimulants were ineffective to rally his system....

Many [people] were treated at their camps and carefully watched. It is very curious that the virulence of the disease was commensurate with the confidence they placed in us and in their own hopes of recovery. The deaths taken from the Revd. Mr. Kennedy's Registry are as follows:

Previous to medical attendance: 25

Before the erection of Hospital: 5

In Hospital: 2

From the 11th of January to the 12th of February there were 77 cases treated....

Dr Edward Jennings to Sir Rupert George, Provincial Secretary, 16 February 1847. Public Archives of Nova Scotia, Halifax. MG15, Vol. 4, #19.

1847

Dartmouth, N.S. 19 January 1847. [To be paid to] John Ross, &c. for the Work and Materials at the Indian Hospital 3300 feet of Hemlag Lumber; 756 feet of Spruce Lumber; 17 days Carpenter Work; 5 days of my own inspection; 60 lb. of nails; 2 pair of hinges & two Pad Locks; John George for Haling Lumber; Hasps and Staples; For Drink for the Carpenters Without Wich they would not work So nier the Seek Indians. Public Archives of Nova Scotia, Halifax. MG15, Vol. 4, #26.

1847

Return of the Names, Ages, Diseases, duration and termination of Diseases of the Indians of the Micmac Tribe near Dartmouth:

Elizabeth Finall [Penall, from French Bernard], 97, Indian Fever, Cured
Henry Finall, 27, Indian Fever, Cured
Mary Finall, 21, Indian Fever, Cured
Eliza Finall, 6, Indian Fever, Died
Stephen Finall, 2, Indian Fever, Cured
Michael Allen, 19, Indian Fever, Cured
Sally Allen, 27, Indian Fever, Cured
Hannah Glode, Jr., 21, Indian Fever, Cured
Mrs. Edward Nolan [Margaret, daughter of Chief Francis Paul], 35,
    Phthisis Pulmon., Still under Treatment
Tom Glode, 60, Indian Fever, Cured
Hannah Glode, 76, Indian Fever, Cured
Simon Francis, 16, Indian Fever, Cured
Noel Glode, 7, Indian Fever, Cured
Joe Glode, 22, Indian Fever, Cured
Nancy Glode, 20, Indian Fever, Cured
Sally Paul, 6, Indian Fever, Died
Francis Glode, 2 1/2, Mesenteric Disease, Died
John Paul, 40, Indian Fever, Cured
Mary Ann Glode, 9, Indian Fever, Died
Peter Glode, 8, Indian Fever, Cured
Abraham Stephens, 8, Indian Fever, Cured
Isabel Stephens, 7, Indian Fever, Cured
Joe Paul, 9, Indian Fever, Cured
Alex Morris, 29, Indian Fever, Cured
John Morris, 28, Indian Fever, Cured

Indians at Salt House Head:
Mary Simon, 46, Nervous Excitement
Joe Simon, 17, Nervous Excitement
Ann Simon, 11
Noel Simon, 9
Mary Ann Simon, 5
Peter Simon, 15

Indians at Maitland Chapel:
James Paul [Jacques-Pierre Peminuit Paul], 38, Nervous Excitement

Sally Paul, 41, Indian Fever

John Paul, 18

Navy Paul, 12

Sam [possibly Benjamin] Paul, 8

Margaret Paul, 9

Tim Paul, 32, Nervous Excitement

Madelina Paul, 40 [80?], Nervous Excitement [widow of Louis-Benjamin Peminuit Paul and James Paul's mother]

Louis Lapidore [Labrador], 18, Nervous Excitement

Dr Edward Jennings, 15 February 1847. Public Archives of Nova Scotia, Halifax. MG15, Vol. 4, #25.

1847

I am candid in stating that few, if any, gentlemen in the medical department could have been found, equal to Dr. Richardson for such a responsible office. His perfect knowledge of the nature and treatment of every case was proved by the sequel. His gentlemanlike and kind manner inspired them with confidence, a matter of the greatest importance, in fact without his assistance and judicious suggestions so favourable an issue could not now be reported. His exertions never ceased, morning, noon & night, even at the sacrifice of his health....

Dr Edward Jennings to Sir Rupert George, Provincial Secretary, 15 February 1847. Public Archives of Nova Scotia, Halifax. MG15, Vol. 4, #16.

1847

In compliance with the directions of his Excellency, accompanied by Dr. Richardson, 60th Riffles [sic], who was particularly requested by the Indians, and at the Solicitation of Bishop Walsh, to make every exertion to check the progress of the disease at Schubenachedie which proved so fatal near Dartmouth, I visited the Indians at Indian Road, 42 miles from Halifax, Maitland, 57 miles, & Salt House head, 62 miles from Halifax. The route was attended with many difficulties. The first day we traveled 37 miles & remained the night at Schubenachedie village from whence next day we proceeded to the "Indian Road" where we partially inspected the Indians. The deep snow & steep hills caused our progress to be not only slow but dangerous. Dr. Richardson was thrown from the Sleigh while one of the horses was hanging on a precipice & by a hair breadth escaped death. From this we proceeded to Maitland and arrived after many trials at 7 1/2 Oclock P.M. Next day we visited Salt House head,

Bay of Fundy. My having had my knee sprained from a fall on the Ice retarded our progress in the woods a little. We returned however the same day to Schubenachedie village, thrice being under the necessity of conveying our Sleigh into the woods to allow oxen to pass. The following day we revisited the Indian road for two purposes: to rest our horses which were broken down by fatigue, & to perform an operation on an Indian [Christopher Paul] who was absent at our first visit. His lower jaw was completely ulcerated, several pieces of bone came off, & two teeth the chief exciting cause. On the fifth day ... both men & horses perfectly exhausted. The rain fell in torrents which continued until we returned next day to Dartmouth.

Dr Edward Jennings to Sir Rupert George, Provincial Secretary, 15 February 1847. Public Archives of Nova Scotia, Halifax. MG15, Vol. 4, #18.

1848

During the last three years the potatoes crop has been a failure. In the second year the crop of hay also was so deficient as to occasion, in the absence of the usual supply of potatoes, a great loss of livestock, and much additional distress from the scarcity of grain—a large proportion of that crop being consumed as provender for the cattle. In the last year the prevalence of unusually wet weather prevented, in a great measure, the saving of the hay that promised to be abundant; and the same weather caused extensive destruction in the grain crops after ripening. From the pressure of these accumulated failures in the crops, the Indians have been forced to desert their agricultural settlements, and disperse over the Country in search of subsistence.

E.M. Dodd and H.W. Crawley, In *Legislative Assembly of Nova Scotia Journals.* 12 February 1848, Appendix 36:143.

1848

County of Halifax. Inquisition. Anne Gloud. 4th Jan'y 1848.

An Inquisition indented, taken for our Sovereign Lady the QUEEN, at Halifax, in the County of Halifax, the Fourth Day of January ... before James Finlayson Gary, Esquire, Coroner of our said Lady the Queen, for the said County, on view of the body of Anne Gloud then and there lying dead upon the oath of ... [twelve] good and lawful men of the said County, duly chosen, and who being then and there duly sworn, and charged to inquire for our said Lady, the Queen, when, where, how, and after what manner, the said Anne Gloud came to her death, do upon their oath say, that the said Anne Gloud on the third day of January in the year aforesaid being an Indian squaw in a certain uninhabited house in Halifax aforesaid in the County aforesaid was found dead without any marks of violence appearing on her body but how or by what means the said Anne Gloud came to her death no evidence has appeared to the said Sworn.

Inquest on the body of Anne Gloud [Claude]. Public Archives of Nova Scotia, Halifax. RG41 "C," Vol. 22, 6A.

Joseph Cope of Dartmouth in the County aforesaid Indian Man on his oath deponeth:
I have seen the body of the Indian woman lying now in the Dead House here. I did not know her at first but now I know her quite well. She was an Indian Squaw named Ann Gloud. She {having once?} lived among the Indians but was mostly about the City. She was not a very good character. {It is very near?} a year since I last saw her alive. That was in Margarets Bay. I never saw her since till this morning. She used to drink hard and was {then?} and four times past in the Work House. I put her in to {?} to make her good but she was just the same when she came out. Joseph Cope, his mark.

Inquest on the body of Anne Gloud [Claude]. Public Archives of Nova Scotia, Halifax. RG41 "C," Vol. 22, 6A.

[Brackets indicate illegible words.]

1848
Thomas {?} of Halifax aforesaid County on his oath deponeth:
I live with the Honorable H. H. Cogswell. I went out to Mr. Cogswell's Farm yesterday afternoon about one o'clock. About two or three o'clock I took out a trunk and put it in the barn but passing the old house near to {St. Andrew's Cross?} I thought I would look in to see after the things inside. When I went to the place that I used to go in which was a large window with a door across partly {unstuck?}, I found it fast as usual and opening it and going in I found the deceased lying in some hay near the south side of the house with one side of her face up which was disfigured apparently eaten by rats. The body appeared to have been there some time. She was about into the cellar through which the deceased might have got, but it was very difficult. She might have easily unfastened the window and got in and afterward fastened it again. The window was not more than two feet from the ground as near as I can say. As soon as I could

I came to town and on my way after meeting Mr. Cogswell there we fell
in with a constable and gave notice of the deceased having been found.
The body was moved a little before sun down and brought to the Dead
House here. To the best of my recollection it is three weeks {?} since I have
been in that house. In the summer when at work out there I have seen two
squaws passing to and fro out there on the place.

Thomas {Deschamps?}.

Inquest on the body of Anne Gloud [Claude]. Public Archives of Nova Scotia, Halifax.
RG41 "C," Vol. 22, 6A.

[Brackets indicate illegible words.]

1848

The inhabitants in general are kind to the Indians; but the wigwam is
seldom visited except from curiosity, and little is known of the misery
existing there. The half famished mother with her squalid infant and
naked children, the emaciated bodies of the aged, and frightful distor-
tions of the infirm, with the unrelieved sufferings of the sick, concealed
in the forest beneath a few pieces of bark or a thin shelter of boughs, have
a real but almost an unknown existence. The novelty of the Indians'
condition has ceased to excite compassion, and by the gift of a piece of
bread the conscience of the provincial settler is satisfied.

Abraham Gesner. In *Legislative Assembly of Nova Scotia Journals.* 1848, Appendix 24:119.

1848

The Average number of Children to each family is now only 2 1/2.

Abraham Gesner. In *Legislative Assembly of Nova Scotia Journals.* 1848, Appendix 24:116.

> *They drove us from place to place*
> *Like wild beasts*
> *That was not just*

1848

Almost the whole Micmac population are now vagrants, who wander
from place to place, and door to door, seeking alms. The aged and infirm
are supplied with written briefs upon which they place much reliance.
They are clad in filthy rags. Necessity often compels them to consume
putrid and unwholesome food. The offal of the slaughterhouse is their
portion. Their camps or wigwams are seldom comfortable, and in winter,
at places where they are not permitted to cut wood, they suffer from the

cold. The sufferings of the sick and infirm surpass description, and from the lack of a humble degree of accommodation, almost every case of disease proves fatal. In almost every encampment are seen the crippled, the deaf, and blind, the helpless orphan, with individuals lingering in consumption, which spares neither young nor old. During my inquiries into the actual state of these people in June last, I found four orphan children who were unable to rise for the want of food—whole families were subsisting upon wild roots and eels, and the withered features of others told too plainly to be misunderstood, that they had nearly approached starvation.

Abraham Gesner. In *Legislative Assembly of Nova Scotia Journals*. 1848, Appendix 24:119.

1849

Stephen Charles, who I mentioned in my former report, with the aid of the bounties he received for his industry, has become independent. He has now a stock of horned cattle and a horse, his potatoes and grain have been reserved to supply seeds for the coming season. Goreham Paul still continues his agricultural labors. Francis Paul (Chief) has grown aged and infirm, and although he requires a little aid, he is useful in affording wise council to his people. To his brother Louis Paul I am indebted for the exercise of much shrewdness and energy in agricultural enterprise.

Abraham Gesner. In *Legislative Assembly of Nova Scotia Journals*. 1849, Appendix 36:338.

1849

Hon. G. R. Young asked leave to present a Petition from Peter Toney, Chief of the Indians at Merrigomish. The hon. gentleman stated that there were about thirty five families who resided there supporting themselves by farming and the making of Buckets; that in consequence of the failure of the crops, they had been reduced to a very destitute condition. He (Mr. Y.) was of opinion that we have never respected the claims of the Indians as we should—the people of the United States had given them many privileges which we have not. He had met with a venerable Indian some years ago, who, in the course of conversation, told him that the only right we possessed to the land of Nova Scotia, was the guns on our citadel.

The Acadian Recorder. Halifax, 10 February 1849.

1849

Our city has just been visited by the Chiefs of the Micmac Nation, who assembled last week for the purpose of applying to the Legislature for aid.

Their meeting was held in Dalhousie College, from whence, accompanied by Dr. Gesner, the commissioner for Indian Affairs, they proceeded to Government House, where their petition was presented to the Lieutenant Governor, who, we understand, received it in the kindest possible manner.

The appearance of the ten Chiefs and Captains, dressed in their gay and ancient costume, and decorated with medals received by the tribe from different ancestors of Her Majesty—in former times, when the Indians outnumbered the British inhabitants of the country—was at once novel and interesting. The admirable proportions and symmetry of these fine stalwart fellows are such as will bear a comparison with the inhabitants of any country. Among the number was old *Saagauch* Paul, the Chief of Shubenacadie, a truly venerable and respectable man, remarkable for his wisdom and sagacity. He is the *Winjeet Sagamore* (High Chief) of this people.

From the residence of the Lieutenant Governor the whole party proceeded to the House of Assembly and Council Chamber, where they were also received with much attention. The appearance of the representatives of the ancient Lords of the Soil, to urge their claims, recall to our minds the melancholy fact that the whole tribe is fast fading away, or, according to the striking expression of the petition, "like a withering leaf in a summer's sun." We trust, however, that their visit to the Authorities will be productive of much good to the remnant of the Micmacs....

The Acadian Recorder. Halifax, 24 February 1849.

To His Excellency John Harvey, K.C.R. and K.H.H., Lieut. Governor of Nova Scotia:
The Petition of the undersigned Chiefs and Captains of the Micmac Indians of Nova Scotia, for and on behalf of themselves and their tribe humbly showeth:

That a long time ago our fathers owned and occupied all the lands now called Nova Scotia, our people lived upon the sides of the rivers and were a great many. We were strong but you were stronger, and we were conquered.

Tired of a war that destroyed many of our people, almost ninety years ago our Chief made peace and buried the hatchet forever. When that peace was made, the English Governor promised us protection, as much land as we wanted, and the preservation of our fisheries and game. These we now very much want.

Before the white people came, we had plenty of wild roots, plenty of fish, and plenty of corn. The skins of the Moose and Carriboo were warm to our bodies, we had plenty of good land, we worshipped *"Kesoult"* the Great Spirit, we were free and we were happy.

Good and Honorable Governor, be not offended at what we say, for we wish to please you. But your people had not land enough, they came and killed many of our tribe and took from us our country. You have taken from us our lands and trees and have destroyed our game. The Moose yards of our fathers, where are they. Whitemen kill the moose and leave the meat in the woods. You have put ships and steamboats upon the waters and they scare away the fish. You have made dams across the rivers so that the Salmon cannot go up, and your laws will not permit us to spear them.

In old times our wigwams stood in the pleasant places along the sides of the rivers. These places are now taken from us, and we are told to go away. Upon our camping grounds you have built towns, and the graves of our fathers are broken by the plow and harrow. Even the ash and maple are growing scarce. We are told to cut no trees upon the farmer's ground, and the land you have given us is taken away every year.

Before you came we had no sickness, our old men were wise, and our young men were strong, now small pox, measles and fevers destroy our tribe. The rum sold them makes them drunk, and they perish, and they learn wickedness our old people never heard of.

Surely we obey your laws, your cattle are safe upon the hills and in the woods. When your children are lost do we not go to look for them?

The whole of our people in Nova Scotia is about 1500. Of that number 106 died in 1846, and the number of deaths is 1848 was, we believe, 94. We have never been in a worse condition than now. We suffer for clothes and for victuals. We cannot sell our baskets and other work, the times are so hard. Our old people and young children cannot live. The potatoes and wheat do not grow, and good people have nothing to give us. Where shall we go, what shall we do? Our nation is like a withering leaf in a summer's sun.

Some people say we are lazy, still we work. If you say we must go and hunt, we tell you again that to hunt is one thing and to find meat is another. They say catch fish, and we try. They say make baskets, we do but we cannot sell them. They say make farms, this is very good, but will you help us till we cut away the trees, and raise the crop? We cannot work without food. The potatoes and wheat we raised last year were killed by the poison wind. Help us and we will try again.

All your people say they wish to do us good, and they sometimes give, but give a beggar a dinner and he is a beggar still. We do not like to beg. As our game and fish are nearly gone and we cannot sell our articles, we have resolved to make farms, yet we cannot make farms without help. We will get our people to make farms, build houses and barns, raise grain, feed cattle and get knowledge. Some have begun already. What more can we say? We will ask our Mother the Queen to help us. We beg your Excellency to help us in our distress, and help us that we may at last be able to help ourselves. And your petitioners as in duty bound will ever pray. (Translated and written for us by our *Mal-waa-laa-weet* and Commissioner [Abraham Gesner] at Chebucto, the 8th day of February 1840.)

Pelancea Paul [François Paul], his mark A CROSS [Chief at Shubenacadie]

Colum Paul [Gorham Paul], his mark A PIPE [Captain at Shubenacadie]

Piel Toney [Pierre Antoine], his mark THE SUN

Louis Paul, his mark A HEART

Cobliel Bonus [Gabriel Boonis], his mark A TREE

Saagaach Meuse [James Mius], his mark AN ARROW [Chief at Bear River]

Louis Luxie [Louis Alexis], his mark THE MOON [Chief at Yarmouth?]

Sabatier Paul [Xavier? Paul], his mark A CANOE

Piel Morris [Pierre Maurice], his mark A PADDLE

Pelancca Paul [François Paul], his mark A SPEAR

The Acadian Recorder. Halifax, 24 February 1849.

1849

A number of Indians have lately come to Charlottetown from Shediac and Miramichi, among whom is a venerable old Chief named Joseph Nokut, who has been entertained and feasted by the Indians residing here. The feast was held at North River, near Mr. Jacob Dockendorf's, and I am told cost about £5. The old *Sakumou* took his dinner inside the camp, and the rest outside. He holds a commission, given by Louis XVI, King of the French, to his grandfather, with a large silver medal, the badge of his authority. They bring dismal intelligence respecting a fearful mortality lately among the Indians at a place called Napan, near Miramichi. In some cases, whole families were cut off: 34 died in all, and they are under the apprehension that they were poisoned, and that it was done intentionally by the whites. They are a good deal excited about it. I have just been questioning the old Chief respecting the affair. He says that on New Year's Day last, according to custom, that Indians went round, firing salutes, and wishing the people a happy New Year; that they received presents as usual, and among the rest a quantity of flour and butter; that those who ate of it, were immediately seized with sickness and died. Two young men fled and went as far as Amherst, where one of them was taken sick in the same way as the rest had been, and the other brought a doctor to him. The Indian died, and was examined by the doctor, who stated that he had taken poison. The other Indian immediately spread the intelligence among his comrades. The news was brought to this place, more than a month ago, by two Indians, who seem to have come over for that purpose.

The Novascotian. Halifax, 30 July 1849:243, col.3.

1849

Every effort has been made to encourage the Micmacs at *Kedgeumcoogic,* or Fairy Lake, in the County of Liverpool.... commenced by the Hon. Joseph Howe. The clearings have been enlarged, and the roads that approach the Lake improved; but the general calamity of the failure of the crops has checked the progress of the little colony, although not in a greater degree than is manifest in the settlements of the other inhabitants. Unfortunately sickness broke out among the children, which carried off a number, and produced much distress.

Abraham Gesner. In *Legislative Assembly of Nova Scotia Journals.* 1849, Appendix 36:337.

Kejimkujik:
Now Rev. Silas Rand, in his First Reading Book in the Micmac language (1875:91), states that the fourth lake on the Liverpool River, is Kejimkoojik, which he says means "swelled parts."

On questioning a very intelligent Micmac Indian (Jerry Lonecloud) here, from whom I get very many Micmac names, & who is a sort of specialist in that way & assists Rev. Father Pacifique in such things— regarding this name Kejimkoojik—he informed me that that was a name for the lake which is only used among the Micmac *men,* & that they never use it in their camps when girls or women are present. The other name—the true name—is one which at the moment of writing I have forgotten, but which has reference to the islands in the lake. Now the origin of the men's nickname Kejimkoojik, according to him, is this: the lake is a very large one, & quite a heavy sea is frequently met with on it. The Indians frequently had to cross it in their canoes, & to do so, with a stiff wind blowing, meant a long, heavy paddle. When they finally landed and got out of the canoe, after having long sat in it, and after the arduous work, they very often found that their "privates" were chapped and swollen. Thus the men among themselves gave the lake a sort of nickname, Kejimkoojik, which means "swelled or chapped private parts", or as Rand, being a clergyman, merely stated meant "swelled parts," without telling us what the parts were. Perhaps his Indian informant did not give him the necessary details.

I have verified this by asking other Indians about here, & they agree with the above explanation, & that they will not mention the name before young girls, etc. It is a nice name for a fashionable sporting club to have embossed on the top of its letter paper!!

Harry Piers, n.d. Unpublished notes, Nova Scotia Museum Printed Matter File.

[Kejimkujik is now the name of a national park administered by the Canadian Parks Service.]

ca 1850

In my former mission [before going to Cape Breton in 1862] an accident happened one winter to an Indian in the woods; and hearing of it, I went to see if I could be of service to him in any way. A heavy tree, which he or a comrade had been felling, came down upon his foot and crushed it dreadfully so as to render immediate amputation necessary to save his life. The surgeon had already been there with some neighboring white settlers, to make arrangements for the operation. As this could not be done in his wigwam they had provided a stove and other things to fit up a neighboring school house for the purpose. His resolution however or his want of confidence in the white man had failed him, and he had refused to comply.

On my way there I met the men returning, and learnt from them that the intention was abandoned, and that the doctor was reluctantly compelled to leave him to his fate. I determined however to see what could yet be done, and went on to the camp which was about two miles from the Parsonage, and about half a mile into the woods. I found him in his wigwam, with his squaw and papoose, lying upon his bed of spruce boughs, but exhibiting no indication whatever of suffering, though his pain was great.

His calm features would have led you to believe that nothing was the matter: his wife too preserved the same undisturbed composure of countenance. I tried to convince him how wrong he was in his determination and that death must inevitably be the result. He did not however think so; and imagined that certain herbs were to be found in the forest, which if applied would effect his cure: "Besides how should he be able to go into the woods to get ash for his tubs and buckets, if he were to lose his leg?" I told him I had seen cases where a wooden leg in some measure supplied the place of the natural limb. This seemed to arrest his attention; particularly when I told him the name of the person to whom I particularly alluded.

Still he could not make up his mind; and his wife contributed a good deal to his hesitation, as she had a decided dislike to go into a house built after the manner of the "white man." I told him however that no time was to be lost; and that death was certain unless he would submit to have his leg cut off. He at last turned away his face to the wall of his wigwam, crushing a small chip convulsively with his teeth, and was silent for a moment or two, whilst deliberating with himself. He then turned round suddenly and said: "Cut!"

I knew from the nature of the Indian that his mind was made up; and accordingly I had everything reversed. A swift Indian named "Lewis Paul" ... was sent off to the neighboring town for surgical instruments. The surgeon of the Village—a kind and skillful man—attended; the patient was removed to the school house; and by the same night, or the next morning, the operation was over. His wife, however, could not be induced to live in the school house, but pitched her wigwam outside, as she (in common with the rest of her tribe) looked upon it as a disgrace to live in a civilized house. He bore the operation with stoical fortitude. Although a Roman Catholic he did not object to my offering up a prayer for him after his removal to the school house.

Rev. Richard J. Uniacke. *Uniacke's Sketches of Cape Breton, 1862-1865*, edited by C. Bruce Fergusson. 1958:112-113.

[This was possibly Noel Jeddore, listed in the Indian Agent Report for 1855 as having only one leg. He is the only Indian so described.]

A chief's son died at Mosher River, east Halifax County, in maple sugar time. His people cut open [the] body, filled it with maple syrup, formed a sort of birch bark coffin & immersed [the] body in maple syrup, &

took the body so preserved in [a] canoe to his home in Cape Breton for burial. This was long ago, 2 or 3 generations ago. Lone Cloud was told this by Bill Rumley (now alive, over 50 years old); old Joe Paul also told him.

Jeremiah Bartlett Alexis [alias Jerry Lonecloud] to Harry Piers, 7 June 1913. Nova Scotia Museum Printed Matter File.

1851

No nation pays more attention to the remains of their ancestors—they wrap them with the choicest furs, and preserve them with affectionate veneration. Some years ago, a young Indian died very near me, when most of the men were from home on a hunting expedition. His family applied to us for assistance in burying their dead—at once we offered them linen, and boards to make a coffin, and the choice of our burial ground; they accepted the boards and the linen, but the ground was of no use, it was not consecrated. The poor creatures mustered what strength they could, and carried away the young man to the resting place of his ancestors, nearly 30 miles, and the melancholy train of that funeral would have made an impression on the stoutest hearts.

John Sprott. In *The Novascotian*. Halifax, 30 June 1851.

A Micmac Indian, Joe Pennawl [Bernard], who was always known as Joe Goose, was born at the Indian Reserve at Milton, near Liverpool, N.S., and later lived about Yarmouth, N.S. Once after being drunk he was hailed before Justice of the Peace Nathan Hilton. Joe was found guilty of drunkenness and fined. He paid the fine immediately and then asked Hilton for a receipt for the money. Hilton said it was not the custom to give a receipt, and asked Joe why he desired it. "Some day," said Joe, "Judge Hilton die. Then sometime poor Indian Joe die, and he go up to gates of Heaven, knock, and ask St. Peter to let him in. St. Peter say what's your name, and Indian say Joe Goose; St. Peter say can't let you in here Joe, you drunk once. Indian say, 'Oh, but I pay Judge Hilton for that.' 'Did you?' say St. Peter, 'let me see the receipt.' 'Me say Judge no give me receipt.' St. Peter say, 'You have to go get receipt from Judge Hilton,' and how could a poor Indian go all over Hell to find Judge Hilton!"

Jeremiah Bartlett Alexis [alias Jerry Lonecloud] to Harry Piers, 17 June 1919. Nova Scotia Museum Printed Matter File.

1852

[Joe Cope's] hatred of all white men who are not of the class of his employers, particularly the settlers in the interior, is intense, and is often productive of much amusement. In the winter of 1852, I was proceeding along a bush-path, with Joe and Jim [his son] dragging a hand sled, loaded with our camping apparatus, when we met a party of settlers, and their teams. One of them, calling Joe aside, asked him whether he had not cut some moose snares in that neighbourhood, the fall previous. "Sure I did, always when I see them." "Well, Joe," replied the settler, who, as I afterward heard, had set them himself, "they belonged to a friend of mine, and I guess if you stop about here, you'll get your camp set a-fire." Joe flared up immediately. "I tell you what it is, you rascal. I know you. If you, or any other same sort, come near camp, and try do anything, I shoot you, 'pon me soul, all same as one moose. There now, you mind, I take my oate I do it, you villain!"

I should not have been surprised at old Joe carrying his threat into execution. The previous fall, his son Jim had fired at some animal, I believe a bear, which had crept up to him and his father while calling moose at night. "What was it, Jeem?" asked old Joe, as the creature went crashing off through the bushes. "Man," said Jim, "he creep on us. What business he come to meddle with us? I see him standin' when I fire."
Campbell Hardy. *Sporting Adventures in the New World*. 1855, I:182-183.

When Joe [Cope] has occasion to enter the bar-room of a roadside inn, as is sometimes the case in travelling to and from the hunting-country, he sits down in a corner, very sulky, and seldom vouchsafes an answer to the numerous questions put to him by inquisitive Blue-noses. On one occasion he was returning with me to Halifax, after an unsuccessful moose hunt, and was particularly short to the settlers and teamsters in the bar-room of the twenty-seven mile house. "Well, now, tell how you'd act when you got fixed in a snow-storm and couldn't find the camp?" asked one of his persecutors. No answer from Joe, who drew volumes from his pipe, and spat with great emphasis on the floor. "I guess you couldn't fix a moose with that 'are shootin'-iron of yourn, at a hundred yards—could you now?" It was too much for poor Joe, who said: "Wat you want know for? You mind your own business, and I do mine. Spose I ask question 'bout hay, and all that sort, wat fool I look. And now you want know 'bout my business, you look like fool. You people always 'quiring and askin' foolish question which don't consarn you." And with that, he stalked out of the room.

Campbell Hardy. *Sporting Adventures in the New World.* 1855, I:183.

1852

Mr. John Campbell presented two petitions from Dr. James Forbes of Liverpool, for reimbursement for attendance on sick Indians—referred to the Sick Indian Committee.

Mr. Hall presented a novel petition, which created a good deal of interest and some merriment:

"To the Honble. the House of Assembly—

The Petition of Peter Paul Toney Babey [Babiere, Bobbei, Bobbeiei], Physician, Chemist, and Alchemist of the tribe of Indians in this Province, humbly sheweth—

That your petitioner [is] now upwards of fifty years old, and from his youth has turned his attention to the nature of plants, herbs, and the various roots of the country, possessing medicinal qualities—that while his brethren of the forest have been employed in hunting the moose, catching the otter, and trapping the beaver, he has turned his attention to scientific pursuits—that while the white men practise in their profession in minerals and various medicines calculated to destroy life—your petitioner has endeavoured to extract from the simple plants of the forest and the field those cordial medicines which renovate the system, give vigour to the limbs, alleviate pain, and have a tendency to prolong life—That your petitioner all his life has administered to the wants of his people in different parts of the Province without any remuneration, and has frequently relieved the white men who pretend to give any assistance to the poor Indian and receive compensation from your honorable house, and considers himself now in approaching old age, entitled to have his case considered. Your petitioner will appear in person before any committee that may be appointed. And your petitioner will ever pray. Peter Paul Toney Babey, Halifax, Feby 19, 1852."

Hon. Provincial Secretary would move that the Indian be standing physician to the house. (Laughter)

Mr. Marshall—That might do very well, provided we know what party he belongs to.

The Novascotian. Halifax, 1 March 1852:69.

Micmac Indian Guides, according to Joe C. Cope, Indian:
Joe Pennall of Gold River, was a good guide for fishing.

John Williams was a good all-round hunter, but was not as smart as Peter Joe Cope [Joe Cope's grand-uncle].

Peter Joe Cope, uncle of J.C. Cope's father, Peter Cope. According to J.C. Cope, "everybody" says he was better than John Williams as a hunter. He always lived at Sheet Harbour Road, and died at Sheet Harbour when about 75 years of age. He was an all-round hunter, a good caller of moose, a fast snow-shoer, and all that. Could get his moose anytime. Probably the smartest snowshoer that ever lived. Peter Joe Cope once stalked a black fox, when snow was on the ground, at Indian Point, in the morning of one day. The fox headed for the Chezzetcook barren, then turned and followed up the Musquodoboit River, crossed the river and worked around Meagher's Grant way, and finally circled back to about half a mile of where it had started, and there Peter Joe Cope shot it towards evening. It was said that he must have covered over 40 miles that day on snowshoes. That was quite a feat that was often spoken of. Peter Joe Cope was with Captain Chearnley as a guide back of Sheet Harbour.

Jim Paul, a very small man, was great for still-hunting moose (creeping). Peter Cope (J.C. Cope's father) said he did not think anyone could surpass Jim Paul as a still-hunter.

John Cope, Peter Joe Cope's brother, of Sheet Harbour Road: he came on Monday to the reserve at Indian Point, Ship Harbour Lake, and that day shot 10 (ten) moose. Went out to Musquodoboit settlement, and offered to get moose for two cents a pound for a white man at Musquodoboit, who would sell it. Cope went back to same woods and shot 15 more moose on Wednesday, Thursday, Friday and Saturday, and Saturday night he was paid off for the meat and on Sunday he went home to Sheet Harbour Road. Only man ever known to have shot 25 moose in one week, and he said he would have shot more. This was a long while ago. ["He told this to present Joe C. Cope, my informant; (John) Cope has been dead about 4 years now." (Harry Piers)]
Joseph C. Cope to Harry Piers, April 1926. Nova Scotia Museum Printed Matter File.

Captain William Chearnley's guide, among others, was Peter Cope, formerly of Sheet Harbour Road, and afterwards of the forks of Preston and Waverley Roads, Dartmouth, where he died at age of 97 years. He was the father of Joe C. Cope. Peter was Chearnley's guide for five seasons, but never went to Newfoundland with him. When Chearnley had given Frank Harvey [son of Lieutenant-Governor Sir John Harvey] a terrible thrashing c. 1846-1852, Chearnley immediately sent word to Peter Cope to come over to see him. The next morning after the affair, Chearnley left Halifax with Cope in a waggon. They went up Bedford Road, but in order to avoid military lookout parties, they took the Hammond's Plains Road from Bedford, and that night they arrived at Gold River, Lunenburg County, and went up the river. They did not know if Harvey would survive. Spent the time fishing on the river, out of sight. They left John, Chearnley's white servant man, to keep an eye on the course of events at Halifax. He only knew where Chearnley was. One day, this John, who was a great walker, walked in one day all the way from Halifax to Gold River, and took the news that Harvey was all right again. Chearnley then returned to Halifax.

Joseph C. Cope to Harry Piers, April 1926. Nova Scotia Museum Printed Matter File.

1853

I arrived [that September] at a bridge over the St. Croix River, which here makes its exit from the succession of large sheets of water known by the name of the St. Croix or Ponhook Lakes. Here lived the Indians of whom I was in search, not in camps, but in small neat log houses, situated in a cultivated patch cleared by them. The owner of one of the huts, an old Indian hunter as my driver informed me, was engaged in hoeing a patch of potatoes when we arrived. He acknowledged my verbose salutation by a slight inclination of the head, and throwing a potato at his dog, which was yelping most piteously at me, Tom Phillips, as the old Indian was called, sat down on a rock, and lighting his pipe, told me I might say what I wanted. The Indians are generally noted for the paucity of their words; but this old fellow was the most taciturn I ever met with. After informing him of my wish to go up the lakes for a day or two, to creep and call moose in the surrounding forest, I asked him whether there were many moose in the neighbourhood.

"I don't know, I sure," he replied, with a shrug of the shoulders.

"But surely there are moose around Long Lake?" said I, affecting to be acquainted with the locality, about which I had made enquiries at Windsor.

A grunt, and another shrug, and the old fellow, dropping the stick which he had been whittling, whilst listening to me, looked up, and slowly scanning my person and accoutrements, said, "You got provee-sion?" On my pointing to the bags which had been left on the road-side, he said, "You see that house? Christopher Paul live there. Go, speak to him." And picking up his bot of wood, he declined further conversation.

Christopher Paul was a fine-looking Indian, quite a contrast to old Tom in point of loquacity, and [he] introduced me formally to his squaw. "You like fresh trout, you like blueberry, gentlemens? Take chair, sit youself down," said Mrs. Christopher. Not being particular, and feeling hungry, I made a hearty meal. Mrs. Paul so overwhelmed me with attention, and the eldest son, a fine lad, about fifteen years old, com-menced such a scraping on an old violin, by way of increasing the entertainment, that I could not get out a word on the subject I wished. Having prevailed, at length, on the young Indian to hang up his fiddle, I informed Paul of the object of my visit. He jumped at my offer of taking him, and said that there were plenty of moose at some distance up the lakes, and that it was a very good time to go out. He described his neighbor, old Phillips, who would have to accompany us, as a worthy old man, a widower, and living all alone with his dog. He had been one of the smartest Indians in the province, and was still a good hunter. Tom Phillips had a tight little canoe, one of the prettiest models, and best goers I ever saw, which he and Paul had built between them during the previous summer. We found her launched and old Tom, ready for a start, standing beside her, holding the paddles.

Campbell Hardy. *Sporting Adventures in the New World.* 1855, I:129-130.
[The Nova Scotia Museum Library copy of this book has pencil notes in the margins of these two pages, in Curator Harry Piers' handwriting: "Tom Phillips was born at camping ground at foot Big Indian Lake, head of St. Margarets Bay, and died at Three-mile Plains, Windsor, about 45 years before 1919, and {there is} a stone to him at the Old Parish Burying Chapel at Windsor, the stone put up by Judge Haliburton. This Christopher Paul {was not the Judge Christopher Paul, brother of Jacques-Pierre Peminuit Paul but was the} brother of Frank 'Winick' {Caninic} of Vinegar Lake, Hubbards. This Christopher Paul came from the Reserve on Ingraham River."]

"Hallo! Joe, what on earth are you going to do with that salmon?"

"Why, Capting, Mrs. Cope [s]he [there is no gender distinction in Micmac third-person singular] say this morning, 'Mr. Cope, I very fond of salmon, 'spose you try and get a leetle bit for dinner today.' I tell him yes, and I see this very fine piece very cheap." He had paid a

Mid-nineteenth-century ferrotype of Molly Muise, Annapolis County, N.S.

pound currency for it. Mrs. Cope makes a little money by working designs on birch bark with porcupine quills. Quill work, as it is termed, fetches a high price in Halifax, where it is bought by travellers to Europe or the States. Joe said in my room one day, "Mrs. Cope he make a hundred a year by his work, and I make good deal by huntin'. S'pose 'bout a hundred a year too." Before he departed, however, he said, "Capting, I most shockin' hard up just now. You got dollar handy? Pon my word I pay you in few days."

Campbell Hardy. *Sporting Adventures in the New World.* 1855, I:184.

1853

The beaver is easily domesticated, and will evince the affection of a dog for its master. In the spring of 1853, an Indian brought me a tame beaver, which he had captured when quite young, in the neighbourhood of Lake Rossignol, in the western end of Nova Scotia; when he wished to leave it, the little animal shuffled after him, whining piteously, having reached him, scrambled up his clothes to his neck. The Indian afterwards sold it to a zealous naturalist residing about two miles from Halifax, at the head of the North-West Arm. Nothing would satisfy it for days afterwards, but nestling in the Indian's blanket, which he was obliged to leave for that purpose. Its owner fed it on bread and milk, with a few cabbage leaves and other esculent vegetables. The animal was perfectly tame, appeared pleased at being noticed, and answered to the name of "Cobeetch," the Indian for beaver.

Campbell Hardy. *Sporting Adventures in the New World.* 1855, I:56-57.

1854

A reserve being different to a grant, the Indian still has a good title to many throughout the province, but unfortunately these lands have not been selected with due caution by those appointed to perform that duty. They are chiefly barren, and spots removed from the sea coast. Many portions of these reserves have also the white men as occupants, and although I am making efforts to force them off, I am met with a passive resistance from the squatter that will require all the vigor of the government to eject.

A source of great annoyance to the Indian is the desecration of their ancient burial grounds. Upon the grant that I have instanced in St. Margaret's Bay, one of these are situated; for many years it was duly honored, but lately it has been ploughed up. This proceeding has become general throughout the province. The resting places for the dead for the most part were selected in spots free from rocks, and on a fertile peninsula. The Indians frequently speak to me on this matter; I should think it would not be difficult to enclose these places held sacred by the tribe....

It is well-known that until lately the tribe in this province could live well by hunting and furring, but the country getting fast settled, diminishes the chance of getting game in the forests. The mills on the rivers are fast destroying the fish that frequented the streams, and upon which they formerly lived for six months of the year. The white man is now as great an adept with the spear as the Indian. The scarcity of fur makes it of great value; the white man has turned his attention to trapping, and interferes sadly with this former source of wealth to the Indian....

William Chearnley, Indian Agent, to Joseph Howe, 4 March 1854. In *Legislative Assembly of Nova Scotia Journals*. 1854, Appendix 26:211-212.

Francis Noel, Indian at Francis Knowel's Neck [Francis Noel's Neck, named after him; this is also the derivation for what is now called Francis Nose Island], near Musquodoboit, Halifax County, N.S. His proper name was Et-hoo-bay-etsh or Et-hoo-bay-eech: "One of Twins." He always lived between Halifax and Cape Breton. He died at Francis Knowel's Neck.

Jeremiah Bartlett Alexis [alias Jerry Lonecloud] to Harry Piers, 27 July 1927. Nova Scotia Museum Printed Matter File.

[The correct Micmac orthography is *Tqope'j*, 'one of twins,' or *Tqope'jk*, 'twins.']

1855

The petition of the undersigned respectfully sheweth, that Madeline Christmas, a squaw, was some days since fearfully burnt whilst sleeping beside a fire in Guysborough, whence she was removed to the house of Samuel Bayard a coloured man in the neighborhood. That the Overseers of the Poor refuse to take charge of the said Madeline or render her any assistance. That besides food, medicine, &c., the attendance of one person is constantly required to dress the burns which are very extensive, and it is the opinion of the Medical Practicioner, who is attending the said Madeline that she may linger for several weeks. That the said Samuel Bayard is a very poor man, with a large family, and cannot possibly provide for her, and no other person can be found to take charge of her....

Public Archives of Nova Scotia, Halifax. MG15, Vol. 5, #47, 3 February 1855.
[This petition postdates the next one, dated 25 January, at which time Madelaine
Christmas was already dead; it may have simply been received later.]

1855

The petition of Samuel Bayard ... humbly sheweth, that during the night
of the twenty-ninth of November last, Madelaine Christmas, a squaw
now deceased, whilst staying for the night at the house of one Thomas
Dollards was dreadfully burnt about her arms and body in consequence
of her clothes having accidentally taken fire. That the said Madelaine on
the following morning whilst attempting to reach an Indian encampment staggered into petitioner's house and fell down completely exhausted, and unable to move. That your petitioner and his family
impelled by a sense of humanity immediately administered to her
necessities by dressing her burns and providing her with clothing. That
as there was no resident Indian Commissioner in the place, your
petitioner applied to the Overseers of the Poor, as well as some Indians
in the Neighbourhood—all of whom declined to take said squaw in
charge or provide a place for her. Your petitioner had therefore no other
alternative but either to thrust this unfortunate woman out of his house
to perish on the highway, or to keep her under his roof and do all in his
power to alleviate her sufferings, &c. This latter course your petitioner
followed although at great inconvenience and annoyance to himself and
family. That notwithstanding the means used for her recovery, the said
Madelaine Christmas lingered for sixteen days when she died.

Your petitioner therefore humbly prays that your Honorable House
will be pleased to grant him the Sum of Four pounds Seventeen Shillings
and Six Pence, being the amount of his charge for the aforesaid services:
To supporting and taking care of Madelaine Christmas ...

For 16 days   £4.00
For digging Grave   7.6
For Coffin   10.0

Public Archives of Nova Scotia, Halifax. MG15, Vol. 5, #44, 26 January 1855.

**Jeremiah Lone Cloud, Indian, was 12 years old on 4th July, the day of
the Portland, Maine, fire, which occurred on 4 July 1866. He therefore
must have been born 4 July 1854. He landed at Yarmouth [N.S.], two
years after that, namely in 1868.**

Jeremiah Bartlett Alexis [alias Jerry Lonecloud] to Harry Piers, August 1921. Nova
Scotia Museum Printed Matter File.

[Lonecloud had as many birthdates—see entry for 1846—as he had aliases, and Harry Piers, Nova Scotia Museum curator between 1900 and 1940, faithfully wrote down all of them. Lonecloud collected many Micmac artifacts and anecdotes for the Nova Scotia Museum before his death in 1930.]

1855
Indian List for the Year 1855

Matthew Silome [Jerome], Wife

Christian Joe

John Williams, Wife [Madeleine, daughter of Louis and Mary Morris Thomas], Children 4

Michael Thomas [son of Louis and Mary Morris Thomas], Wife, Children 3

Absolem [Absalom] Charles, Wife

Charlotte Morris [orphan niece adopted by Tom and Christian Morris]

Thomas Morris

Christian [Paul] Morris (Wife)

James Glode

James Paul Jr.

Michael Bass [Barss and Basque]

Old Mary [Morris] Thomas

Michael Allen, Wife, Children 1

James Paul, (Chief) [Jacques-Pierre Peminuit Paul]

Maloney [Stephen Maloney, said to be the son of Col. William Chearnley, the Indian Agent filing this report (Harry Piers, Unpublished notes, Nova Scotia Museum Printed Matter File)], Wife [Catherine Sack Maloney, daughter of Peter and Marie Antoinette Sack], Children 4

Prosper Noel, wife

Joseph Nolan [Knowlan, Nowlan], St. Mary's River; Wife, Children 3

Edward Nolan [Knowlan, Nowlan] Wife [Margaret Paul Nolan, daughter of Chief Francis Paul]

Peter Sack [Jacques], Wife [Marie Antoinette Thomas Sack, daughter of Mary Morris Thomas], Children 3

Peter Morris, Wife, Children 5, 2 grown boys, 2 grown girls. Grown boys' names: Benjamin Morris, John Morris. Grown girls' names: Ann and Jane

Matthew Thomas, Wife, Children 1

Charles Tony, Wife, Children 3

Peter Tony, Wife

Mrs. Luxy [Alexis], Children 3
James Tony, Wife, Children 3
Noel Jeddore (lost leg), Wife, Children 2
Prosper Paul, Wife, Children 2
John Tony
"Old" Madeline Paul [widow of Louis-Benjamin Peminuit Paul]
Thomas Noel
Mrs. Louis Cope (widow), Children 3

At Sheet Harbour Road
Peter Cope, Wife, Children 2
Joseph Paul, "Molly" Mrs. Paul
Francis Cope, "Molly"
John Cope ditto
Peter Francis, Wife "Molly, daughter", Children 1
John Morris

Tatamagouche
Noel Joe
Joseph Francis
Alexander Philips, Wife, 2 Grown Boys

Pictou
Peter Wilmot [died 1932 aged 106]
Joseph Philips, Wife, Children 3
Old Mrs. Silome [Jerome]
Madeline Philips
Francis Philips, Wife, Children 6

Chester and Gold River District
John Hammond, Wife, Children 3
John Pennall [Bernard], Wife, Children 2
Joseph Pennall [Bernard], Wife, Children 3-4
Old Mrs. Pennall [Bernard]
Catherine Pennall [Bernard], Francis Paul, husband, alias "Kininick"
John Newel [Noel], Wife, Children 1
Francis Labrador, Wife, Children 1
Thomas Pennall [Bernard], Wife, Children 1
James Pennall [Bernard], Wife, Children 1
Glode [Claude], Wife, Children 1

Christina Morris [*sic*]. Oil painting by William Gush, 1859. Mary Christian Paul Morris was born in 1814 and died in 1884 at Chocolate Lake, near Halifax.

Shubenacadie
Francis Paul (Old Chief), Wife, Children 2
Stephen Charles, Wife
John Jadis, Wife
Goram [Gorham] Paul, Wife
Thomas Philips, Wife, Children 2
Widow Charles, 2 Daughters
Oliver Paul [son of Jacques-Pierre Peminuit Paul]
John Lymins, Wife, Daughter, 3 Boys
Black Louis, Wife

Peter Gooley, Wife
Mary Anne (White Woman) [adopted daughter of Gorham Paul]
Peter Stephens, Wife
Louis Paul, Wife
Noel Paul, Wife

Kentville
Joseph Moore, Daughter
Thomas Newel [Noel], Wife
Lewis [Louis] Morris, Wife, Children 5
Newel [Noel] Jeremy, Wife, Children 1
Peter Paul, Wife
Molly Coap [Cope], husband

Chester
"Two" Hammond Girls
Widow Paul (Louis Paul), Children 5
Michael Paul, Wife, Children 3
Francis Paul, alias "Kininick" [Caninic], Children 2 [appears twice on
    this list]

Ship Harbour [first written Sheet Harbour, then corrected]
Joseph Paul, Wife, Children 5
James Paul, Wife
Francis Paul, Wife, Children 6
Peter Joe Cope, Wife, Children 1
"Young" Joseph Paul
Peter Paul (old)
Noel Paul, wife
Christopher Paul, Roland Paul
Louis Paul, Wife, Children 1
John Newel [Noel], Wife, Mother, Children 2
William Chearnley, Indian Agent. "Indian List for the Year 1855." Public Archives of
Nova Scotia, Halifax. MG15, Vol. 5, #69.

The Indian Peter Paul was baptised at the Tannery, Dartmouth. Next
Friday, the priest came to his house for a visit, and there was a pot on
the stove, with meat cooking in it.
    "Why are you eating meat on a Friday?" inquired the priest.
    "That is not meat," said Peter Paul. "It is fish."
    "I can see that it is meat," said the priest.

"No, Father," said Peter. "It was meat, but I sprinkled water and salt on it, and christened it fish."

Jeremiah Bartlett Alexis [alias Jerry Lonecloud] to Harry Piers, 2 October 1929. Nova Scotia Museum Printed Matter File.

1856

By His Excellency Major General Sir John Gaspard Le Marchant, Knight, Knight Commander of the Order of Saint Ferdinand, and of Charles the Third of Spain, Lieutenant Governor and Commander in Chief, in and over Her Majesty's Province of Nova Scotia and its Dependencies, &c. &c. &c. To James Paul [Jacques-Pierre Peminuit Paul] of Shubenacadie in the said Province. The Reverend Michael Hannan, having certified to me that you have been duly elected to be Chief of the Indians, in the Western Counties of the Province, according to the usages and customs of the Micmac Tribe of Indians, in the place of Francis Paul, who has resigned that office: and my confirmation of such an election being requested: I Do by these Presents approve ratify and Confirm the said James Paul as the lawful Chief of the Micmac Indians within the Western Counties of this Province. Given under my hand and seal at Arms at Halifax in the 20th year of the reign of Her Majesty Queen Victoria, September the 15th Anno Domini 1856.

Sir John Gaspard Le Marchant to James Paul, 15 September 1856. Original document in the Nova Scotia Museum Printed Matter File.

"Joe Goose" (the Indian Joe Pennall) and his wife were found dead alongside the road, close to an old church site, about 4 miles below Conquerall Bank, on the south side, near Bridgewater, Lunenburg County. They were buried in that churchyard [St. Peter's, West LaHave], being the first burial there.

Anonymous "Old Lunenburg woman, who had been at the funeral," to Harry Piers, n.d. Nova Scotia Museum Printed Matter File.

1858

Gravestone in the Roman Catholic Cemetery, Chester:

In Memory of Joseph Pennall, Indian, by William Chearnley, A.D. 1858.
Gone to Death's call is Indian Joe.
Moose, deer, rejoice
Here buried rests your deadliest foe.

Photographed by R.H. Whitehead, July 1987.

My father's name was Stephen Glode. He was born in the vicinity of Milton, Queens County, in 1845.... My grandfather on father's side was Francis Glode, born about 1820. He was nicknamed "Ugluss," an old Micmac word that I don't know the meaning of. My grandfather, with other Indians of that time, lived at the old camp ground at Cowie's Falls, on the Mersey River near Milton, Queens County.... When my father was in his teens, his parents decided to go to Montreal by the Indian canoe route. They cut birch bark and the proper wood, and during one winter they made a 20-foot canoe. In the spring they started. They went up the Mersey River to Lake Rossignol, then up the Shelburne River to Koofang Lake. There they carried across to Moose-hide Lake and went down the Sissiboo River to Weymouth. They crossed the Bay of Fundy and coasted up to St. John, then on up the St. John River to its headwaters. They carried their canoe over the portage to the Riviere du Loup, and followed that river down to the St. Lawrence. Then up the St. Lawrence past Quebec to Montreal.

They lived all winter outside Montreal with some other Indian people that lived there. I don't know what people they were. I have heard my father describe the wigwam his parents built, and how they banked it very deep with fir boughs to keep out the cold. They found the winter very severe, and in the next spring they returned home by the same route. I don't know how long it took. When they left Milton it was in the spring, and when they got to Montreal it was beginning cold weather. They lived on fish most of the way. There was plenty of trout and salmon in the rivers those days.

Samuel Freeman Glode to Thomas H. Raddall. Raddall Papers, Dalhousie Archives, Killam Library, Dalhousie University, Halifax.

1860

AN APPEAL FOR THE INDIANS: The Committee for procuring Sub-scriptions and managing the affairs of the Indians in the Reception of the Prince of Wales, beg to solicit the contributions of Nova Scotians. The Indians are entirely destitute of suitable National Costume, and without the means to purchase material to make it, and they have been refused any public grant. The Committee have, however, to thank the liberality of that portion of the community already appealed to, but the time before the Prince's arrival is too short to admit of their applying to all. The Indian encampment have been visited, the men mustered and enrolled, a certain portion of them provided with cloths, beads, &c, and their canoes are being numbered and got in order. The Chief [Jacques-Pierre

Peminuit Paul] of the tribe is now here awaiting the Prince's arrival, and endeavoring through the Committee to clothe as many of his men as means can be provided for.... James Whitman, Chairman of Committee, Somerset House, Prince Street.

The Halifax Reporter. Halifax, 26 July 1860:3, col. 3.

James Paul, James Peter Paul, we called him Sak Piel Saqmaw. Our grandfather, Isaac Sack, used to tell us stories about him. He had great strength, a great power. There was an apple tree in the field near his house at Shubenacadie, and the trunk was divided into two stems—a crotch—and these boys were playing there, trying to pull on the two pieces. Grandfather said Sak Piel Saqmaw came up to the tree—he used to walk with a cane—and he put his cane down and put his hands one in each side of the crotch and then he just ripped that whole big tree in half.

Max and Isaac Basque to R.H. Whitehead, July 1977, personal communication.

1860

James Paul, Chief of Mic-mac Indian Tribe, of Shubenacadie. Sir, I have been requested by His Grace the Duke of Newcastle to acknowledge the Address presented by you on behalf of the Micmac Indians, and to express to you the satisfaction it afforded the Prince of Wales to see so many of your Tribe present on the occasion of His Royal Highness's visit to this City and also to receive the expressions of loyalty and affection towards the Queen which your Address contains. His Royal Highness before leaving the Province was graciously pleased to place in my hands £50 Stg. to be distributed among the Indians present on this occasion of His landing, which sum I have requested Captain Chearnley the Indian Commissioner to distribute. (Sgd) Mulgrave. Government House, Halifax, N.S. 6 August 1860.

Mulgrave to James Paul, 6 August 1860. Nova Scotia Museum Printed Matter File.

In Pictou Landing, they were trying to move a little house on rollers, logs, down the road. And it got stuck. Sak Piel Saqmaw said, "Wait a minute"—he was coming up the road—and everybody just stopped and moved away, and he went to the house, and lifted up his cane and touched it. That's all. He just touched it, and then said, "Now." And the house just moved along for the men as easy as anything.

Max and Isaac Basque to R.H. Whitehead, July 1977, personal communication.

1860

THE INDIANS: The fifty pounds sterling presented by His Royal Highness, the Prince of Wales, to the Mic-Mac Indians, were presented at noon to-day, in the orderly room of the "Chebucto Grays", by Capt. Chearnley and Mr. Whitman. A large number of ladies and gentlemen were present, and were much gratified by the appearance of the "children of the Forest", attired as they were in all the finery in which they delight. An address was presented on this occasion, and a peace pipe was smoked, though not, it is said, after the most approved style of the Indians of former days.

The Halifax Reporter. Halifax, 11 August 1860:2, col. 2.

1860

Temperance Hall, By Particular Desire, Monday Evening, August 30, THE WIZARD JACOBS! Has been solicited to give An Entertainment For the Express Amusement of THE MICMAC TRIBE OF INDIANS. The doors will be open at Six o'clock, and the performances will commence precisely at Seven and terminate at Nine o'clock, to give time for the tribe to return in the Dartmouth Boat [to their camp at Tufts Cove]. To the curious this will be a particularly interesting sight, as there is no doubt that the wonders of the Wizard Jacobs, witnessed by these children of the Forest for the first time, will have an extraordinary effect upon them. The Tribe is admitted Free, whilst the Public will be charged at the usual rates: Reserved Seats, 75 cents; Parquette, 50 cents; Gallery, 25 cents.

The Halifax Reporter. Halifax, 11 August 1860:2, col. 6.

ca 1860

John Andrew Chisholm of Margaree Forks gave me a note on Micmac burial customs. An Indian once stopped at their house and asked his grandmother if he might stay the night (date: c.1860). He had a big bag which he left on the porch, and she poked at it out of curiosity without learning what was in it. In the morning she asked the Indian. "That my grandfather," he said. "He want to be buried in Mabou. He not too heavy. I take out him guts."

John Erskine. "Micmac Notes, 1958." Unpublished MS, Nova Scotia Museum Printed Matter File. 1958:15.

1861

Francis Paul, chief of Micmac Indians, died at Dartmouth, N.S., on 18th May 1861. It was the wish of the tribe and his family to take his remains to Shubenacadie for burial.

"Vide letter of Captain William Chearnley, paper no. 128, vol. 431 of Public Records of Nova Scotia." Harry Piers. Unpublished notes, Nova Scotia Museum Printed Matter File.

[Chearnley's letter is now in the Public Archives of Nova Scotia, Halifax.]

1863

Kejimkujik: There was one lot set off to John Jeremy (Indian), and a small house was put up for him by Government. He began very well, but soon died; his family moved off.

Whitman Freeman. In *Legislative Assembly of Nova Scotia Journals.* 16 January 1863, Appendix 16:6.

Chief Jacques-Pierre Peminuit Paul (third from left), also called James Peter Paul, shortly after his election as chief, 1857; flanked by his brother Christopher (second from left) and his adopted son, John Noel (fourth from left).

Many years ago a friend of the writer, and also a friend of an Indian who accompanied him, chanced to be encamped for the night on an island in a lake that lies far from the haunts of men in the western border of Queens County. The Indian was a man of middle life. When the fire was kindled and supper was done he told his companion that he had not been on that place since he was a small lad, when he landed there one afternoon with his father and mother and younger brother, who was taken sick in the night and before morning was gone forever. The next day his father made a grave and fashioned a bark coffin, and the dead child was pillowed on moss, the grave covered with flat stones, and left to the care of Him who marks the sparrow's fall. While he told the story of this great tragedy his emotions choked him to almost inaudible speech. The next morning the Indian led the way to a low hilltop that overlooked the lake, and after several adjustments of himself with old trees and rocks on the main shore, he said, "We buried him here." And he was right. Covered deep under leaves were the stones, and a ring of smooth, pretty pebbles from the beach encircled the small grave. They had been placed tenderly there by hands that could not see their work for tears, and this untutored Indian wept, after all the lapse of years, for the lost playmate of his boyhood.

Robert McLeod. *Markland, or Nova Scotia*. 1902:171.

ca 1863

The first light snow had just fallen after two or three piercingly cold and frosty days towards the close of November, when our party, consisting of us two and our attendant Indian, the faithful John Williams (than whom a more artful hunter or more agreeable companion in camp never stepped in moccasin), arrived at the little town of Windsor, at the head of the basin of Minas, whence embarking in a small schooner, we were to cross to the opposite side to hunt the cariboo in the neighborhood of Parsboro'....

Our road lay through a valley, skirted by the lofty wooded slopes of the Cobequids. These hills are the great stronghold of the cariboo, and his last resort in Nova Scotia.... We stopped the sleigh opposite a group of Indian bark wigwams, which stood a short distance from the road.... followed the track which led up to them, and entered the largest. The head of the family, who sat upon a spread cariboo-skin of gigantic proportions, was one of the finest old Indians I ever saw.... an old man of nearly eighty winters was this aged chief, yet erect, and with little to mark his age save the grizzly hue pervading the long hair which streamed over his broad shoulders, and half concealed the faded epaulets of red scalloped cloth and bead-work. A necklace of beads hung round his bare expansive chest. His voice, as he welcomed us, and beckoned us to the post of honour opposite to the fire and furthest from the door, though soft and melodious, was deep-toned and most impressive. Williams, our Indian, greeted and was greeted enthusiastically; he had found an old friend, the protector of his youth, in whose hunting camps he had learnt all his science; the old squaw, too, was his aunt, whom he had not seen for many years.

The chief was engaged in dressing fox-skins; he had shot no less than twenty-three within the week or two preceeding, and whilst we were in camp a couple of traders arrived, and treated with him for the purchase of the whole, offering two dollars a-piece for the red foxes, and five or six for the silver or cross-fox, of which there were three very good specimens in the camp.

The old man told us of the curious method he used in obtaining his fox-skins. He would go off alone into the moonlit forest, to the edge of some little barren, which the foxes often cross, or hunt round its edges at night. Here he would lie down and wait patiently until the dark form of a fox appeared in the open. A little shrill squeak, produced by the lips applied to the thumbs of the closed hands, and the fox would at once gallop up with the utmost boldness, and meet his fate through the Indian's gun.

Campbell Hardy. *Forest Life in Acadie.* 1869:140-143.

Dr. Lone Cloud says that about 50 years ago, when he was a boy, squaw Polly Williams, then an old woman, of Great Lake, Pubnico, sister of John Williams, told him various things in [secret?]. Among them said (almost forgot about it), that the Micmacs in old times used to make cloth made of threads made from brown hair, & used a stone twirling thing such as this [plummet] for twisting the threads. Does not know how it was woven. This cloth was used for the special purpose of being finally put round a couple who were being married by the chief (who performed such ceremonies). The chief always had such a cloth which he retained for this use. Sometimes well-off couples had their own, which they retained & would pass on to their children when they were married afterwards.

Jeremiah Bartlett Alexis [alias Jerry Lonecloud] to Harry Piers, 3 February 1912. Nova Scotia Museum Printed Matter File.

1865

LOST, on Saturday morning, in Brunswick Street, 5 Small Worked Baskets, belonging to a SQUAW. Any person having the same will oblige by leaving them at this office.

The Acadian Recorder. Halifax, 7 July 1865:3, col. 1.

ca 1865

Once, about a couple of years before [1867, Jerry Bartlett Lonecloud] saved 2 of John Darby's sons. Jerry Bartlett, and two Darby sons, and another man, were in a canoe off Digby town, and were capsized. Swam for some distance, and Bartlett saved the two boys, one 13 and another 15 years, but the man was drowned. This man was John Darby's first wife's brother. Bartlett received considerable praise for this.

Jeremiah Bartlett Alexis [alias Jerry Lonecloud] to Harry Piers, 8 February 1919. Nova Scotia Museum Printed Matter File.

My name, Peter Paul; eighty-five years old last Christmas. People say, that was 1779, the year of American Independence, and now, I just so old as the American Constitution. Me little shaky, some say that government shaky too. My Father's name Joseph Paul, he die when ninety-nine years and six months old; he die thirty years ago [born *ca* 1734]. My mother's name Madeline Paul; die when seventy-four years old; twenty-seven years ago. I had five brother and four sister; three brother and two sister die; two brother and two sister living. I just twenty two years when married; my wife's name Jennie [Lulan] Paul; she die three years ago; seventy years old. I had nine children, four living, five dead. I believe me oldest Micmac man. I was born at West River (some great people born there). When little boy, live Antigonish and Little Harbor ... Pictou small town; New Glasgow two or three houses. That time Mortimer dig coal at Mines, haul coal in carts, put'em in scow, take'em to Loading Ground and put'em in vessel.

That time everything plenty; salmon, trout, eels, good many kinds fish. Plenty Moose, Carriboo, Bear, Beaver, Otter, Martin, Foxes, Wildcat and good many more. My father have'em coat—inside beaver, outside otter. That time plenty fresh fish in summer and dry'em for winter ... white men that time ... cut down woods ... spear'em salmon ... all gone now. Everything eat'em up make country cold—make rivers small; build saw mills, sawdust and milldam send all fish away. That time plenty codfish, white man set line scare'em all. White man burn up all wood for staves, baskets, everything scarce now. That time, great many Micmacs; white people learn'em to drink … many bad things … and great many die; not many Micmacs now. One time this Micmac country, our country; now white people say this their country, take'em from Indian and never pay'em. Indian speak'em 'bout that good many times.

Some white men very good; Edward Mortimer very kind to Indian—give'em flour, pork, and good many things to poor people. Squire Pagan very good man—Squire Pagan and Edward Mortimer married to two sisters. One Minister very good man, call'em Doctor McGregor; old Lulan and Mr. McGregor almost same two brothers. John McKay at Narrows, Robert's father, good man, he almost same one brother to old Lulan; John McKay and old Lulan make first road to St. Mary's; me very small boy that time. Mr. Carmichael call'em one vessel Lulan for my father-in-law. Squire Matheson, too, very good man; very well acquainted with my father—give my father plenty work; very good man to me too, always when meet'em, put hand in pocket and give me something.

One old man live at Middle River, call'em Deacan [Deacon?] Marshall, and my father live at West River, all same two brother. All old men gone now; my friends most all gone too. If old man come back, wouldn't know this country; nothing same now; vessels sail about, steamboat make water dirty, and scare'em fish; Railroad and steam engine make noise; everything noise, bustle, all change—this not Micmac country—Micmac country very quiet, no bustle; their Rivers make gentle murmur; trees sigh like young woman; everything beautiful. My father and mother Roman Catholic, me Roman Catholic too, most all Micmac Roman Catholic. Believe not much difference if believe in Jesus Christ and do good; all same in heaven.

Now, me old man, can't work—soon die, then white people miss old Peter—good many people very kind, now I thank them all—white man you got my country; keep'em good, be kind to poor Indian—he have no country now—call'em stranger here.

Me very well pleased if white man make this country large—take'em Miramichi, St. Johns, Ressigouche, Prince Edward Island, and Nova Scotia, and put'em all together. Me not want Canada; too far away— I don't know'em very well, though I stay there four years. Some people not very good there, and Mohawk stay there—leave'em out.

Me think something wrong with white man's Council. When

Micmac used to have Council, *old* men speak and tell'em young men what to do—and young men listen and do what old men tell'em; white man change that too: now *young* men speak'em, and old men listen; that's reason so many different kinds speak'em. Believe more better, Micmac Council.

Me not like all trees cut down—better have some woods. White man should plant trees now, because take'em away old trees. White man should keep some woods for Indian, some place....

I want all Micmac to be good people (me never did take anything from white people), now never steal—tell truth—don't get drunk—mind where bad people go, and where good people go, too.

This the first time ever I trouble Printer, I believe last time. Soon say Peter Paul dead. Good bye.

Peter Paul, his mark +.

Dr George Patterson Collection, Scrapbook No. 5, newspaper clipping: "Biography of Peter Paul—Written February 16th, 1865, From His Own Statement—By an Amanuensis." Public Archives of Nova Scotia, Halifax. Published in *First People, First Voices,* by Penny Petrone. 1983:54-56.

ca 1866

I strolled back to my look-out, and being tired, I suppose I "slept upon sentry." I was awakened by a shot, closely followed by another, again two more in quick succession. Now I knew that our party was alone in those deep woods, and that Peter [Cope] had carried my smooth bore, for which I had handed him only four bullets.... [Peter had shot a sow bear, and one of her cubs. The other remained in a tree, but for how long?] Peter had no more bullets, so what was to be done? Well, his first attempt to kill young "mooin" was with the stopper, or rather charger of the powder horn, which he rammed down into the right-hand barrel. This was a failure and a miss. "Mooin" still clasped the tree in desperation. Reflection made Peter search his pockets, when therein he found a halfpenny.... He sat down; and underneath the tree where the poor victim clung, aided by the butt-end of the gun, which bears the well-indented marks to this day, he doubled up that copper, drove it down over the powder in the left-hand barrel, fired, and brought down the bear from its perch. He had broken its near thigh—a frightful fracture; but, falling with three legs to work on, it took to the bush at a great pace. Scarcely a match at any time in point of speed for this agile young Indian, it was soon overtaken, and he had succeeded in beating it almost to fragments with a stick which he had snatched up in the wild chase, when I arrived to see him hauling it out from the thicket in which he had captured it.... That day we feasted gloriously at dinner-time on the roasted ribs of young bears, one of which had been shot with a halfpenny. "The Old Hunter" [William Chearnley]. In *Forest Life in Acadie,* by Campbell Hardy. 1869:362-363.

When Jerry Bartlett (Lone cloud) was about 17 or 18 years old (born about 1850 or 51), say about 1867, after Christmas probably, when Savary was running election, he went as camp boy with William Gilpin of Digby, with Governor [Chief] Jim Meuse (then about 44 years), Malti Pictou (who still lives, in 1919), and Johnny Peters (old Indian) as guides, and Jim Gorman as portager, and a cook also. Gilpin shot a doe caribou at Boundary Lake (west of Boundary Rock), in Shelburne Co., back end. [They] cleaned the carcass, and Gilpin offered Bartlett $5.00 to carry out the caribou to Clarks. $5.00 a good deal in those days, & Bartlett accepted. He carried it from Boundary Lake to Clarks at Lake Jolly (18 miles); and for $2.00 more, from Clarks to Morgan's, 4 miles from Bear River (total 26 miles), on his back. Then the carcass was taken on a team. Bartlett then walked with Jim Meuse from Morgan's by a short cut to Digby (about 14 miles). The caribou when weighed, without insides, weighed 100 lbs. on scales at Digby, head and small horns, & feet. They reached Digby on the night of the election day when Savary was elected. They reached Cornwall's tavern at Digby. (Gilpin had no business, lived on his money, sportsman, and had a big house with sporting trophies. Related to Dr. Edward Gilpin. He married a Smith.)

Once, when at Lunenburg, at Tichman's Lake about 30 years ago, [Jerry Lonecloud] carried two men together, one on each side of him [hanging onto his hair?]; two men, one 240 lbs, and other 236 lbs, both [named?] Captain Geldert (brothers).

Jeremiah Bartlett Alexis [alias Jerry Lonecloud] to Harry Piers, 8 February 1919. Nova Scotia Museum Printed Matter File.

ca 1866

[At my camp on Lake Mooin (the lake of the bear), Liscombe River, in company with Peter (Cope), and the boy Stephen, as my Indian hunters].... I was up very early.... I smoked, then called, and was at once answered by what was in my opinion the moose of the previous evening.

Micmac guides and sportsmen relaxing after a moose hunt. Wood engraving, *The Graphic*, London, 29 June 1878.

On he came dashingly—no signs of fear about his note. I roused up Peter.... The moose presently came in view. He was crippled in his gait, almost dead lame in the off fore leg. He carried just what I wanted, an A 1 pair of antlers. I shot him, and am persuaded he was not more than ten yards from me at the time.... All the noise (my shot having been fired absolutely over the head of my other camp follower, the boy Stephen) had failed to arouse the slumbering son of the forest. There he lay until I hauled off his blanket, when he appeared quite annoyed at the close proximity of the antlered monarch.
"The Old Hunter" [William Chearnley]. In *Forest Life in Acadie*, by Campbell Hardy. 1869:361.

I also faintly remember the great agitation the Confederation of the Provinces of Canada brought upon Indians. To most of them, it spelled a complete loss of every Right and privilege they enjoyed. For a false

Rumor got among them, That at the event that the so-called Confederation became a fact, the Indians in Nova Scotia would be deprived of all their former Treaty Rights (pretty darn near that now). Powwows or Council Meetings were held at Shubenacadie Reserve and at the Preston Road Indian settlement and other Reserves, in an endeavor to find out if that Rumor really came from the Headquarters in England in [other?] words. From the Queen Victoria.

I remember the last General Pow-wow held at Peter Cope's house at the fork of the Preston and Guysboro Roads (which is still standing). The Captains or Council Men were, the Grand Chief James Paul [Jacques-Pierre Peminuit Paul], John Noel [his adopted son], Joe Glode, Peter Cope, old Lewis Paul, Christopher Paul, and one Council Man from Pictou, Gabriel Niggiachoo. In that Pow-wow two captains were selected to go over to England: John Noel and Peter Cope. (The only two who could express their ideas in the English Language better than the Rest.)

A day was decided upon when these two Captains would embark on their important mission. Everything apparently moved along satisfactorily for some time. Funds were collected to defray these Captains' expenses. The necessary Indian Costumes or clothing suitable to be worn in presence of the Highest authorities in England were (furnished) made by the greatest Bead worker women. Mrs. Prosper Paul made Peter Cope's great Coat and I think old Mary Thomas [his mother-in-law] made John Noel's; of course other women assisted, however.

Before the time appointed came, everything was OK. A short Council meeting was held again at the Preston Road settlement, every Council Man attended, but one most important man, John Noel, who showed a white Feather, one day before the Inman Line steamer was due to leave Halifax for England. So Peter Cope had to Paddle his own Canoe alone to England. If I remember right I think he went over on the Inman Line steamer, *City Cork,* and came back on the *City New York.*

However, he was over to England to the Colonial office, where he met Dr. Tupper and Joseph Howe, who, it appears, were also over there on the same Business, the Confederation. The above-named Gentlemen introduced Cope to the Authorities of the Colonial Office, and assisted him, regarding his mission, where Cope was informed that as long as any Indian remained a True Ward of the English Government, so long His Treaty Rights would be respected and adhered to, to Hunt, Fish and Camp wherever and whenever He likes. No Bye Law can ever alter or change His Treaty Rights and Privileges. Indian's status as a "ward" is his only Protection and I am afraid some Magistrates and Judges don't know that. Peter Cope came back on the same Boat with Dr. Tupper and Howe. He said They were the Two Best Friends on the Steamer.

"Joe C. Cope, Indian," to Harry Piers, 9 February 1926. Nova Scotia Museum Printed Matter File.

The death of a well-known and responsible Indian named Peter Paul has been going the rounds of the Provincial Press, and very naturally, he objects to being removed from this mundane sphere before his time. He wishes the paleface to understand that he is still in the land of the living and desires to make the fact public in his own peculiar style as follows:

Francis Hadley [André] Camp, Indian Cove, Friday after storm, this year

To all white men:
Me hear 'em one Higlishman, Glasgow, tell me dead, cause me 88 years old and 'spectable Indian. That no reason. All dead men not 88 years old—some not 88 years, long dead—some more than 88 yet 'live. Suppose 'em man 'spectable, that no reason he dead. White man tell Peter Paul dead, tell too soon. Me not believe me dead.
Peter Paul, 5 February 1867.

Peter Paul. Quoted in *The Pictou Book,* by George MacLaren. 1954: 257-258.
[MacLaren adds a note to say that Peter Paul died 20 March 1867, at the East River. This same pre-death obituary error happened in the nineteenth century to a Lunenburg stage-coach driver who is reported to have said, "I knew it was a lie the moment I read it."]

ca 1867
Old Joe Cope, the Indian hunter, is still to the fore; his little legs, in shape resembling the curved handle of pliers, carry him after the moose nearly as trustily as ever. Perhaps his sight and hearing are failing him, and he generally hunts in company with his son Jem [Jim] as an assistant; and Jem, being a lusty young Indian, does most of the work in "backing out" the moose-meat from the woods. "Joe," said I, on meeting the pair one

Jim Glode, Micmac hunter and guide, Shubenacadie, N.S., St Anne's Day, about 1891.

morning late in September, a few falls ago, at the country-market at Halifax, where they were selling a large quantity of moose-meat, Joe's eyes beaming with ferocious satisfaction as he pocketed the dollars by a ready sale. "Joe, I think I must come and look at your castle, at Indian Lake; they say you have exchanged your camp for a two-storey frame-house, and are the squire of the settlement. Do you think you have left a moose or two in your preserves?"

"Well, Capten, I very glad to see you always when you come along my way. I most too old, though, to hunt with gentlemen—can't see very well."

"We will make out somehow, Joe; and Jem there will help you through, if you come to a stand-still."

"Oh, never fear," replied Mr. Cope (he always speaks of himself as Mr. Cope), laughing; "that Jem, he don't know nothing; I guess I more able to put him through yet." And so we closed the bargain; to wit, that we should have a day or two's hunting together in what Joe fully regarded as his own preserves and private property—the woods around Indian Lake, distant twenty miles from Halifax. What would the old Indians, at the close of the last century, have said, if told that in a short time a stagecoach would ply through their broad hunting-grounds between the Atlantic and the Bay of Fundy? Think of the astonishment of Mr. Cope and his comrades of the present age, perhaps just stealing on a bull-moose, when they first heard the yell of the [train] engine and rattle of the car-wheels! This march has been accomplished; the old Windsor coach, with its teams of four, after having flourished for nearly half a century, has succumbed to the iron-horse, and the discordant sounds of passing trains re-echo through the neighboring woods, to the no small disgust of Mr. Cope.... Joe said that in the country we were going to hunt, every train might be distinctly heard as it passed; "and yet," said he, "the poor brutes of moose don't seem to mind it much; they know it can't hurt them."
Campbell Hardy. *Forest Life in Acadie*. 1869:89-93.

Isabel, a well-known old Micmac Indian "doctor" woman (skilled in use of herbs and other remedies), was buried in old Indian burial ground on a little island, said to be the only island there, at head of tide in Country Harbour, Guysborough County, N.S. Hers was the last burial in that burial ground. This Isabel was no doubt the old Indian woman "Isabel", whom the late John Noel, Micmac chief, told me

[Harry Piers] used once to live at Chain Lakes (on the northern side between the upper and lower lakes, I believe), near Halifax, and that the Indians called Chain Lakes "Isabel's Lakes".

Jeremiah Bartlett Alexis [alias Jerry Lonecloud] to Harry Piers, n.d. Nova Scotia Museum Printed Matter File.

Isabel, Indian doctoress, who lived near Chain Lakes, Northwest Arm, Halifax: Isabel Dodo was the full name of the Isabel the Indian who was a doctoress and lived near Chain Lakes, Northwest Arm, Halifax County. Her family belonged to St. Mary's. She was buried in an island in the river, by Saulsman's between Upper Country Harbour and Cross Roads.

Jeremiah Bartlett Alexis [alias Jerry Lonecloud] to Harry Piers, 22 July 1927. Nova Scotia Museum Printed Matter File.

ca 1867

Presently the canoe was signalled, and, going down to the water's edge, I embarked, and in a few minutes stood before Joe [Cope's] castle. It was a substantial frame-house, evidently built by some settler who had a notion of making his fortune by the aid of a small stream which flowed into the lake close by, and over which stood a saw-mill. An old barn was attached, and from its rafters hung moose-hides of all sizes, ages, and in all stages of decomposition; horns, legs, and hoofs; porcupines deprived of their quills, which are used for ornamental work by the women; and, in fact, a very similar collection, only on a grander scale, to that what is often displayed on the outside of a gamekeeper's barn in England.

A rush of lean, hungry-looking curs was made through the door as Joe opened it to welcome me. "Walk in, Capten—ah, you brute of dog, *Koogimook!* Mrs. Cope from home, visiting his friends at Windsor. Perhaps you take some dinner along with me and Jem before we start up lake?"

... The interior of Cope Castle was not very sweet, nor were its contents arranged in a very orderly manner—this latter fact to be accounted for, perhaps, by the absence of the lady. Portions of moose were strewed everywhere; potatoes were heaped in various corners, and nothing seemed to have any certain place of rest allotted to it. Smoke-dried Eels were suspended from the rafters, in company with strings of moose-fat and dried cakes of concrete blueberries and apples. Joe had, however, some idea of the ornamental, for parts of the *Illustrated News* and *Punch* divided the walls with a number of gaudy pictures of saints and martyrs.

Campbell Hardy. *Forest Life in Acadie.* 1869:91-93.

ca 1867

Indian Lake is a beautiful sheet of water, nearly ten miles in length, and, proportionally, very narrow—perhaps half a mile in its general breadth. Rolling hills, steep and covered with heavy fir and hemlock wood, bounded its western shore; those on the opposite side showing large openings of dreary burnt country. The maple-bushes, skirting the water, were tinged with their brightest autumnal glow; and in the calm water, in coves and nooks, on the windward side of the lake, the reflections were very beautiful....

"Ah! here is the Halfway rock, what the old Indians call the Grand-mother," said Joe, steering the canoe so as to pass close alongside a line of rocks which stood out in fantastic outlines from the water close to the western shore of the lake. "Here is the Grandmother, we must give him [her; there is no gender distinction in Micmac third-person singular] something, or we have no luck."

To the rocks in question are attached a superstitious attribute of having the power of influencing the good or bad fortune of the hunter. They are supposed to be the enchanted form of some genius of the forest; and few Indians, on a hunting mission up the lake, care to pass them without first propitiating the spirit of the rocks by depositing a small offering of a piece of money, tobacco, or biscuit.

"That will do, Capten; anything a'most will do," said Joe, as one cut off a small piece of tobacco, and another threw a small piece of biscuit or a potato on to the rock. "Now you wouldn't b'lieve, Capten, that when you come back you find that all gone. I give you my word that's true; we always find what we leave gone." Whereupon Joe commenced a series of illustrative yarns, showing the dangers of omitting to visit "the Grand-mother", and how Indians, who had passed her, had shot themselves in the woods, or had broken their legs between rocks, or had violent pains attack them shortly after passing the rock, and on returning, and making the presents, had immediately recovered.... [They proceed to spend the day hunting.]

Late that night our canoe glided through the dark waters of the lake towards the settlement. The massive head and antlers [of our moose kill] were with us.

"Ah, Grandmother," said Joe, as we passed the indistinct outlines of the spirit rocks, "you very good to us this time anyhow; very much we thank you, Grandmother."

"It's a pity, Joe," I observed, "that we have not time to see whether our offerings of yesterday are gone or not; but mind, when you go up the lake again to-morrow to bring out the meat, you don't forget your Grandmother, for I really think she has been most kind to us."

Campbell Hardy. *Forest Life in Acadie.* 1869:101-103.

[Hardy added a note: "Since this was written, poor Joe has for ever left the hunting grounds of Acadie, having shot his last moose but a few weeks before he rested from a life of singular adventure and toil. *Requiescat in pace.*"]

The last stone pipe made by a Micmac Indian, according to Jerry Lone Cloud, was made by the late Johnny Peters, Micmac Indian, of Bear River, at Bear River, Digby County, for the late William Gilpin, of Digby, N.S. It was made from stone from Meteghan, Digby County, and was shaped, at Gilpin's suggestion, as a caribou head. Lone Cloud saw it [*ca* 1873], among various relics Wm. Gilpin then had. Does not know how many years before that it had been made. Johnny Peters died about 1897.

Jeremiah Bartlett Alexis [alias Jerry Lonecloud] to Harry Piers, 22 January 1918. Nova Scotia Museum Printed Matter File.

When Prince Arthur visited Nova Scotia in 1869, he was taken hunting near Caledonia. His Micmac guides were John Williams, Louis Noel, and old Peter Joe Cope, with John Jadis acting as camp boy. The prince was accompanied into the woods by officers in dress swords, and a band. "Who in hell going to kill moose with this noise going on?" said old Peter Cope. They were in the woods for three weeks, and didn't kill so much as a rabbit.

Jeremiah Bartlett Alexis [alias Jerry Lonecloud] to Harry Piers, 1 February 1926. Nova Scotia Museum Printed Matter File.

In 1870, as I remember, there camped at the fork of the Preston and Guysboro Roads, Twenty-seven Micmac Indian Families; and seven at Tufts Cove, Bedford Basin. The names of the Preston Road Indians were, Peter Cope, Peter Sack, Lewis Sack, Noel Lewis, Stephen John, Peter Glode, Joe Glode, Frank J. Paul, Lewis Philips, Mike Allen, Lewis B. Brooks [Louis Benjamin Brooks], Tom Brooks, Lewis Basque, Peter Francis, John Stephen, Noel Dennis, Ben Morris, John Morris, John

Caninic, Noel Paul, Abram Paul, John Bradley. At Tufts Cove: Chas.
Toney, Tom Toney, Frank Toney, Frank Paul, Oliver Paul [son of
Jacques-Pierre Peminuit Paul], Prosper Noel, and old Alex. Philips.
Joseph C. Cope to Harry Piers, 9 February 1926. "A Short History of the Mic Mac
Indians in Halifax Co. Nova Scotia Since Confederation." Nova Scotia Museum Printed
Matter File.

1879

Conne River, Newfoundland:

There was quite a settlement in those parts, consisting of a small saw-mill
and house adjoining inhabited by the white man who ran the mill, and
of two or three families of Indians, all rejoicing in the name of Joe. The
head of the tribe was old Abraham Joe, a fine specimen of his race, an
active upright man, standing about six feet two inches in his moccasins,
and broad and strong in proportion. He had spent nearly all his life in
Newfoundland, and knew the interior of the island better than any man
living....

The sole representatives of the Joe tribe left at home on the evening of
our arrival were an old woman and two girls of about eighteen or
twenty.... On inquiry, we found that most of the family had gone off
some days before to the copper mines, to solemnise the wedding of a
couple of fond and youthful Joes, and were expected home that night.
About midnight they returned; two large whale-boats full of them, rather
noisy and very jovial. The unfortunate but loving Joes had not succeeded
in getting married, as the priest, who was expected to arrive by the
coasting steamer, had failed to put in an appearance; but nowise
discouraged by this untoward event, the party had consumed the
wedding breakfast, wisely deciding that the ceremony might keep, but
the viands would not. The bride and bridegroom bore their disappoint-
ment with a philosophical composure to be found only among people
who attach no value whatever to time. In answer to our condolence they
replied, "Oh, no matter; mebbe he come next steamer, mebbe in two,
three months, mebbe not come till next year," and dismissed the subject
as though it were a matter of no importance whatever to them.
Earl of Dunraven. *Canadian Nights.* 1914:206-214.

Poor Old Abraham Joe was very unhappy about the state of things in
Newfoundland. Too much civilization was destroying the island, in his
estimation. "Yes, sir," he said to me one day, "things is very different

Micmac family posing before a spruce-bark wigwam near Halifax, 1873.

from what they used to be. Lord! I mind the times when a man might travel from one end of the island to the other and never see nobody nowheres. Beavers were plenty then, and there was a good price for fur too; now there ain't no price, and beavers and otters ain't plenty like they used to be. Those d—d lumbermen be come up the rivers and scare the game. Why, there ain't a bay scarcely anywheres without one, mebbe even two liviers ['live here,' a year-round settler] in it."

Abraham Joe to Dunraven. In *Canadian Nights,* by the Earl of Dunraven. 1914:211-212.

1879

INDIAN FUNERAL: A somewhat unusual sight was seen yesterday afternoon, viz., an Indian funeral. The cortege started from a camp near the North-West Arm and proceeded into the city and to the cemetery of the Holy Cross. The coffin was slung by cords to a pole carried on the shoulders of two men, and was covered by a white pall. One or two men and about a dozen squaws followed the coffin, walking in Indian file. The women all had their hair tied up with white ribbon [because] the deceased was a minor.

The Morning Chronicle. Halifax, 26 August 1879:3, col.6.

I have seen and heard some curious things.... I was hunting once with two gentlemen near Rocky River. We were all sitting in the camp; winter time, sir; pretty late, about bedtime. The gentlemen were drinking their grog, and we was smoking and talking, when we heard someone walking, coming up to the camp. "Holloa!" says one of the gentlemen, "who can this be at this time of night?" Well, sir, we stopped talking and we all heard the man walk up to the door. My soul, sir, we could hear his moccasins crunching on the hard snow quite plain. He walked up to the door, but did not open it, did not speak, did not knock. So, after a little, one of us looked out—*nobody there;* nobody there at all, sir. Next morning there was not a track on the snow—not a track—and no snow fell in the night. Well, sir, we stayed there a fortnight, and most every night we would hear a man in moccasins walk up to the door and stop; and if we looked, there was no one there, and he left no tracks in the snow. What was it, do you think, sir?

John Williams to Dunraven. In *Canadian Nights,* by the Earl of Dunraven. 1914:264.

1879

Sometimes we would meet a Joe striding over some barren or crossing a lake in his canoe; occasionally a Joe would drop into our camp, miles away from anywhere, unprovided with boat, canoe, provisions or baggage of any kind, and furnished only with a pipe, tobacco, a rusty gun, and some powder and lead. He would sit down quietly by the fire and chat a little and smoke a little, and after a while accept, with apparent insouciance, an invitation to eat and drink, and after consuming enough food for three men and swallowing a few quarts of tea, would say, "Well, I suppose I shall be going now. Adieu, gentlemen, adieu. Yes, I guess I was pretty hungry; most starved, I expect. How am I going to cross the lake?

Oh, that's all right; we—that's old Peter John Joe's son, and I—got a canoe a little way off; mebbe one, two, three, four miles; I'll cross in her, I reckon. Expect likely I'll see you again by and by—I shall be coming out again about the end of this month." "Well, good-bye," said we, "but where are you going to? Not trapping, evidently, because you have got no traps." "Yes, I'm a going a trapping, that's so. Not far—mebbe two or three days back in the woods—beaver pretty plenty there; left my traps there last fall—no, let me see, fall before last, I guess." "But what are you going to live on all the time?" "Oh, I got plenty grub, no fear; not much tea, though," (showing a little parcel of the fragrant herb knotted up in a corner of his dirty blanket) "and no sweetening: mebbe you could spare a little tea and sugar, eh? No! ah well, all the same, never mind, suppose my tea give out, perhaps make some spruce tea. You see young John Joe, he got a *cache* yonder, away off just across the blue ridge, about one day or one day and a half, or mebbe two days' journey, plenty flour there; and young Peter John Joe and Old John Peter Joe, they *cached* their cooking-pots on the little stream there, near the north end of big blueberry pond. See you again soon. Adieu!" and after a few words in Micmac to our Indians, this particular Joe would walk off, to be seen no more till he reappeared after some time with half a canoe load of beaver skins, or perhaps to turn up quite unexpectedly in the course of a day or two, in company with some other Joe whom he had come across promiscuous-like in the woods. Over this small community and large territory old Abraham Joe ruled after the manner of a feudal lord, settling all little disputes and parcelling out the country into hunting-grounds for each individual member of his family.

Earl of Dunraven. *Canadian Nights*. 1914:206-214.

When I was five we moved from wigwam into log cabin, over at the Point where they made maple sugar. The logs of the cabin were chinked with moss. Canvas door. Steven Paul, a man with a crooked back, had a mink trap. One day he set it in the doorway of the cabin. We children so 'fraid of it. That how I 'member when we moved into the cabin. I 'member, too, how hard this cabin floor was, we [were] used to boughs. 'Member too when they brought in the stove. They told us, "Now, children, don't move, this cow will jump at you." Called it a little black heifer, would not go near it, so 'fraid, didn't use it for a fortnight.

Isabelle Googoo Morris to Elsie Clews Parsons, Chapel Island, N.S., 26 July 1923. "Micmac Folklore," by Elsie Clews Parsons. In *Journal of American Folklore*. 1925, 38:98-99.

1879

I remember going over to old [Abraham] Joe's tent one morning for something or other, and finding a little French boy that he had with him lying outside by the dead sodden ashes of the fire, in a most uncomfortable attitude, leaning on his elbow with his head supported by his hand, drenched of course to the skin through his tattered clothing, and shivering with cold, but sleeping soundly all the same. "Why, Joe," I said, "what a shame to keep that miserable little boy out in the cold and wet all night." "Oh," he replied, "he don't mind; he hard, hard all the same as one d——d dog: do him good."

Earl of Dunraven. *Canadian Nights*. 1914:217-218.

1880

Old John Williams, the Indian, beaming with smiles, shakes hands, and says, "My soul and body, sir, I am glad to see you back again.... How have you been, sir? Pretty smart, I hope." "Oh, first-rate, thank you, John; and how are you, and how did you get through the winter, and how is the farm getting on?" "Pretty well, sir. I killed a fine fat cow moose last December, that kept me in meat most all winter; farm is getting on splendid. I was just cutting my oats when I got your telegram, and dropped the scythe right there in the swarth, and left."

Earl of Dunraven. *Canadian Nights*. 1914:247-248.

1880

The absence of schools has been a serious privation. Very few persons can even read, not one can be regarded as a scholar. The earlier missionaries had invented a system of hieroglyphics, which they subsequently gathered into a volume, and handed to the first converts. By the good offices of a religious foreign society, a reprint was made a few years ago, and many copies of this later edition are now in circulation.... This, I need not say, is the poor Micmac's greatest treasure on earth; father has explained to son, and son to grandson, this simple record, through two hundred and seventy consecutive years. Each Sunday evening, the head of the family with profound reverence, takes "the book" into his hand, deciphers it from beginning to end, and then with great earnestness, impresses what he considers its most important truths on the minds of his by no means inattentive hearers. Yet there are many drawbacks to this mode of teaching. The volumes are hieroglyphic. Their perusal imparts no conception of a written alphabet, of arithmetic, of secular history, of current events, or of literature properly so-called. The world that lies outside of personal observation is unknown to the ordinary Micmac.

R. MacDonald, Pictou, N.S., to the Department of Indian Affairs, 1 October 1880. In *Dominion of Canada Parliament Sessional Papers.* 1881:45-46.

Fathers, we are poor
Do not forsake us.
Remember the promises
Your Fathers made to ours.

1880

I found the year ending 30th June, 1880, one of the hardest I have ever known. The low price of furs, and also porpoise oil, I suppose, had something to do in making the times hard, as hunting and killing porpoise are the two principal industries that the Indians of my agency engage in, and when the price of oil and fur are good, there are many that can really make a good living; but as the Indians never lay by a dollar they are sure to be in trouble at the first approach of hard times. I had an unusually large number of aged and helpless to care for last winter. The way I managed this was to allow a certain amount weekly to families that would board them; by this means I managed to do a great deal of good; these old people always are very grateful for help when it is so much needed; quite a number of them died during the winter.

John Harlow, Bear River, N.S., to the Department of Indian Affairs, 11 September 1880. In *Dominion of Canada Parliament Sessional Papers.* 1881: 40.

1880

My attention was called to one very sad case about the middle and coldest part of the year. The family in question lives in Bridgewater, beside four other camps. When I arrived at the spot, I found the father and mother in the last stages of consumption, without fire, food or clothing. They told me they had been in that state for three days and nights. I can safely say they were the coldest days and nights of the whole winter. By means of speedy aid from the Department, together with the help solicited from kind, charitable friends, I was soon able to administer amply to their wants [but] both have since become victims to this disease.

E.J. McCarthy, Chester, N.S., to the Department of Indian Affairs, 22 September 1880. In *Dominion of Canada Parliament Sessional Papers.* 1881:41-42.

1881

The Dominion Exhibition, 21-30 September 1881
Class 24, Indian Work, exhibitors' list:
Jacob Brooks, Maccan, Cumberland County, Ladies' Chip Hat
Mary Gooley, Ladies Work Boxes
Nancy Jades [Jadis], Shubenacadie, Ladies Work Boxes
Stephen Maloney, Dartmouth, N.S.
Dennis Newal [Noel], Antigonish, Indian Work Baskets
Mrs. John Newal, Shubenacadie, Indian Work Baskets
Mary Newal, Shubenacadie, Indian Work Baskets
Sarah Paul, Truro, N.S., Indian Work Baskets
Isaac Sack, Shubenacadie, Indian Work Baskets
Classified Alphabetical List of Exhibitors and Exhibits, Dominion Exhibition of 1881.
1881:45.

1881

Some years since Stephen Knockwood, jun., worked upon the railroad, earned and laid by his wages until he accumulated eighty dollars, with which he purchased four acres of land. He has since built quite a respectable house and barn, and has become possessed of a pair of steers. He applied to me for seed to plant his land, and thinking it my duty to encourage him I purchased the seed for him to plant about one and one-quarter of an acre. He has a wife and six children. He has left them to take care of his home, while he himself has gone porpoise hunting for the summer; but his land is poor, he having paid three times its value for it.
J.E. Beckwith, Cornwallis, N.S., to the Department of Indian Affairs, 23 July 1881. In *Dominion of Canada Parliament Sessional Papers.* 1882:24-26.

1882

In 1877 our Indian population was 74, this year's statement shows 106.... One family returned from Massachusetts after an absence of eight years, the husband and wife dying within a half-hour of each other, leaving three helpless children to be cared for.... There have been three heads of families taken away during the year and two children among our own Indians proper, and but three births, but several children have come in by adoption.
J.E. Beckwith, Cornwallis, N.S., to the Department of Indian Affairs, 26 July 1882. In *Dominion of Canada Parliament Sessional Papers.* 1883:24.

1883

GOLD has recently been discovered in the vicinity of Bridgewater. A few of the Indians have fared very well by the stroke of good luck, two especially, John and Lewis Labrador, the original discoverers. Their proprietary rights have been acknowledged and recorded, and now the old time blanket is contemptuously discarded to be succeeded by high coloured dry-goods.

Thomas J. Butler, Caledonia, N.S., to the Department of Indian Affairs, 28 August 1883. In *Dominion of Canada Parliament Sessional Papers*. 1884:37-38.

1883

All these families are temperate, quiet, peaceable and industrious, yet sickness is making its ravages amongst them. There are three families owning private property. Foremost among them stands Stephen Knockwood, the first Indian here about to own a fine horse and riding waggon and good harness, also a fair farm waggon and other agricultural implements. Another of these, Isaiah Pictou, is a good cooper, making barrels for sale. The third, Joe Brooks, a quiet peaceable man, farms on a small scale. These three families are comparatively comfortable, yet death has been making inroads on two of them.

J.E. Beckwith, Cornwallis, N.S., to the Department of Indian Affairs, 12 August 1883. In *Dominion of Canada Parliament Sessional Papers*. 1884:36-37.

1884

Death has carried off, within the past two months, Mr. Peter Gload, of Grafton, and his wife, Hannah. Gload was a man of an industrious nature, and had made a very comfortable home for himself and family. He was the only self-supporting Indian in the County. Bad neighbours have since frightened their only daughter from the homestead, in order, I am told, that the practice of stealing timber may the more easily be carried on.

Thomas J. Butler, Caledonia, N.S., to the Department of Indian Affairs, 25 August 1884. In *Dominion of Canada Parliament Sessional Papers*. 1885: 41-42.

1884

Death has stricken down two of the most notable men among them, father and son—I mean the two Pauls. I placed more confidence in Joseph Paul than any other man among them. I entrusted the management of the Indian or Government land entirely to him and was guided much by his judgment. They will be much missed here.... Some six weeks since, I received information of an outrage committed upon two peaceable, inoffensive families, by two drunken roughs breaking into their camp in the night, beating the men, the women fleeing into the woods, in their fright, for safety. They then set fire to their camp, after breaking and destroying everything valuable. This occured about eighteen miles from here. I immediately wrote to a prominent magistrate in that neighborhood, asking him to take notice of the affair and bring the offenders to justice. I have since learned that with the help of Father Holden they have compromised the affair with money; but it should have been a criminal matter.

J.E. Beckwith, Kentville, N.S., to the Department of Indian Affairs, 17 July 1884. In *Dominion of Canada Parliament Sessional Papers.* 1885:41.

Jerry Lonecloud, Indian, was at Niagara Falls when he was about 6 or 7 years of age. Was again at Niagara Falls in 1885, and went by train from there to New York to see General U. S. Grant's funeral which took place on 8 August 1885.

Jeremiah Bartlett Alexis [alias Jerry Lonecloud] to Harry Piers, n.d. Nova Scotia Museum Printed Matter File.

1886

Mrs. Joseph Glode also has an acre of land, which I presume, belongs to the Government, and the whole of which she cultivates, but, for want of proper cultivation, she does not obtain much return. She is the same patient, persevering, industrious woman that she ever was within the past ten years. I have known her to nurse and bury her husband, her son, her two daughters and a grandson, and never saw her shed a tear but upon one occasion, when she called upon me to enable her to get something from the doctor to ease the pain and hacking cough, when a tear came forth unbidden, but turning for a moment, as if ashamed, she became herself again.

J.E. Beckwith, Kentville, N.S., to the Department of Indian Affairs, 10 August 1886. In *Dominion of Canada Parliament Sessional Papers.* 1887:37.

1886

Stephen Knockwood Jr stands above all the rest as an industrious, enterprizing and ambitious man. Not content with the four acres of land and house and barn which he always owned as private property, he has within the last year purchased fifty acres of land further up the river, and, although owing for the most of it, if his health continues for a few years, I think he will pay for it.

J.E. Beckwith, Kentville, N.S., to the Department of Indian Affairs, 10 August 1886. In *Dominion of Canada Parliament Sessional Papers.* 1887:37.

"Stephen Knockwood Junior had a farm house at what is now Aldershot; he sold the land for Aldershot to the government. This land used to be called Knockwood Hill, which at one time was known as Hungry Hill by Kentville residents. Stephen Knockwood Jr. died in 1934, aged 104 years, and is buried in Kentville. He had only sons: John, Spurgeon, William, Benjamin, and Joseph. Spurgeon Knockwood still lives at New Ross Reserve."(Henry Knockwood to R.H. Whitehead, 1984)

About the last of November or first of December of about 1887, Abram Paul, Indian, tracked in a little snow some bears to their den, about 1/4 mile north of the head of north end of Lake Major, beyond Dartmouth, Hx. Co. He was alone. Found an opening, down which he went, and then a sort of long cavity, horizontal, about 15 ft. long, with the bears' den at its extremity. Crawled in with some birch bark, which he lighted for a torch. Saw bears in the den, and he then started shooting at them and killed 3. He thought he had shot them all, but it afterwards was proved that there were 4 in all, an old she-bear and her three cubs of the previous spring. It was one of the young ones which was left. He crawled out of the den. The next day a crowd of men from Cow Bay went back to the bears' den with him, with ropes, etc., to drag out the dead bears. Old Frank Brooks, Indian, was one of them. They lowered Abram Paul into the hole with rope. While tying the rope to [the] head of one of the dead bears, Abram felt something touch his shoulder, and immediately knew that a live bear was still in there. Called for a gun. He crawled out, and got a gun, and went in the den again, alone. Then the outsiders heard the report of the gun, and he had shot the fourth one. It was considered very brave of Paul. The bears were all over a year old—a mother, and her three cubs which had been with the mother all the previous summer and were going to winter with her in the den. It was one of the cubs which was the last one shot.

"Vide Joe C. Cope, Indian, aged 67 years." Joseph C. Cope to Harry Piers, 16 April 1926. Nova Scotia Museum Printed Matter File.

ca 1890

Jim Penall [Bernard] was his name.... His family name was, in his native language, Agdamoncton. He came of a family at one time numerous, and he still had brothers and sisters, many in the Gold River [Lunenburg

County, N.S.] district. When I saw him first he was marching at the head of a little detachment that moved, Indian file, along the highway—first Jim, "Indian Jim", as some called him, tall and graceful; then his wife, with a papoose hurdled on her back in an old shawl, with its arms clinging to her and its head swaying to the mother's step ... and then in the rear a little girl and a little boy, straying off now and again to look for daisies in the grass.... I then sought for a reason why I should go to visit him. I did not wish to appear intrusive by going without a reason, and was glad when I discovered that there was a need at home for a basket. I made the ordering of it my excuse for calling.... Jim's wigwam was not large, but it was clean.... It boasted some modern conveniences in the midst of its barbarous furnishings, notably a camp-chest which served as a chair for his visitors, and two windows, one on each side of the lodge, each consisting of one pane of glass eight inches by ten, set with tacks in the birch bark. As I sat on the camp-chest and held converse with this citizen of the wildwood, his wife and children sat on the floor in dutiful silence. She had been once, no doubt, a beauty, and traces of her comeliness still lingered in her eyes and feminine features. The children looked healthful and vigorous, but the baby in its cot of twisted withes was evidently sick. An Esquimaux dog, upon which the owner looked with unconcealed tenderness and admiration, was playing among the bushes at the entrance to the tent. He came in once, but was not permitted to remain. He possessed a peculiarly villainous face, and when Jim turned him out he remarked half-apologetically, "He's a half of a wolf, sir." After the shape and dimensions of the basket had been agreed upon and the time of its delivery arranged, I left.

The next time I came that way I called. There was no sign of a basket or of basket-making. A blight had fallen on the family. Jim was taciturn and gloomy. The baby was gone. The poor little thing had died, and he had carried its body in his arms to the consecrated ground and laid it in the grave himself, while his wife repeated over it such parts of the burial service as she could. The burial-place was miles away, and there was no priest to perform the service; he came only occasionally. A few days later I came that way again, and found the wigwam deserted. A robin sat on the ridge-pole piping a mournful song, and the crickets chirped among the chinks of the bark. Nobody knew where the Indian family had gone. Doubtless the sad memories which clung to the spot where his babe had died, had proven too much for Jim and caused his departure; but where he now had pitched his moving tent I was unable to learn. I was sorry to lose all traces of him so suddenly, now that I was becoming acquainted.

But one day, some months later, I overtook a strange procession upon the road; a cart with two wheels and no springs, drawn by a very lean horse, and seated in the cart with their arms about each other to keep from falling out, five Indian women, and the driver my old friend Jim. Several Indian men were walking along. As I approached them, I was busy trying to divine the meaning of the strange demonstration. An idea occurred. There had been some excitement in the town from which they were coming, over the opening of a new railroad. So when I came near, I accosted them.

"Been over to see the railroad, Jim?"

"My brother is dead, sir."

It was a funeral. Consumption was doing its work with the poor fellow himself. His cheeks were hollow. His eyes were sunken and bright.... The

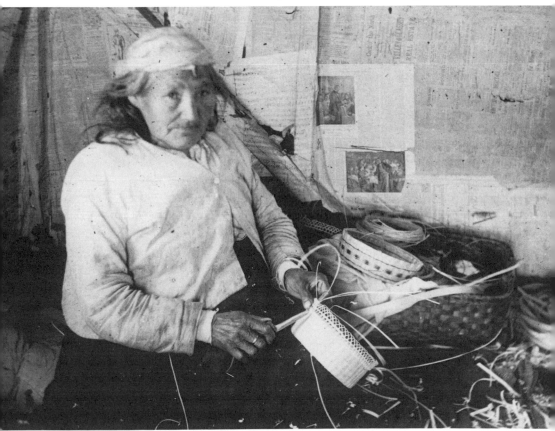

A Micmac basket-maker, nineteenth century, Queens County, N.S.

next I heard of him he was dead. He had gone to his babe and his brother. According to the light he had, he was a believer. *Requiescat in pace.*
Luther Roth. *Acadie and the Acadians.* 1891:57-61.

The son of a white man who had been adopted in infancy by a Micmac couple, had later married a French girl, and had left the reserve, gave an account of these Indians:

"When my father's adoptive parents were very old and feeble, he brought them to our house to live; but they could not accept our ways. They would not sit at a table to eat, but squatted cross-legged on the ground, a piece of skin spread out in front of them as a table. We gave them a bed, but they removed the mattress and the covers and slept on the floor. Such things as pies, custards, and sweets they did not care for, and they did not like bread unless it was cooked in the coals, without the use of a vessel. They craved the flesh of wild animals. In the fall, when this craving was strongest, they were in such a state of dejection and drooping spirits that, if you did not know them, you would think they were sick. Whenever I killed a rabbit, squirrel, or porcupine for them, they were delighted, and the meat lasted them three or four days. They insisted, however, on having the meat put on spits and cooked on a grate or roasted over a fire. This was about 1890."
Anonymous. In *The Micmac Indians of Eastern Canada,* by Wilson D. and Ruth Sawtell Wallis. 1955:5.

1891
And when consumption and bad rum have undermined his constitution and broken down his strength, he quietly stretches himself on his bed of spruce boughs on the floor of his damp, unwholesome dwelling, coughs up his life-blood, and dies. His neighbors gather from far and near, drink more bad rum to his memory, and then bear his body to its last long home in the consecrated ground. Is he better off than he was of old? God knows. It does not look so. And if he be worse now than then, somebody must be to blame.
Luther Roth. *Acadie and the Acadians.* 1891:52.

John Williams died about [1893], at the Indian Settlement near Shubenacadie.
Harry Piers, n.d. Unpublished notes, Nova Scotia Museum Printed Matter File.

1893

In August, 1893, two Indians, Louis Pictou and Peter Muise, started in a canoe up the Bay Shore for white maple. After passing Green Point the water was quite smooth and Pictou seized his gun to shoot a loon that was near by. Muise continued paddling, when on looking behind him he saw a shark coming towards the canoe. Pictou, who had his gun already loaded, fired full into the body of the shark, not, however, before this huge fish had bitten a piece out of the canoe over a foot wide and two feet long. The bark was not bitten through, but being of a brittle nature was literally torn off. The ribs also were destroyed for some feet. The two Indians were soon struggling in the water, the canoe going over and over like a log. Muise grasped hold of one end and told Pictou to do the same, but he was so far gone that falling backward he went down for the last time. Muise continued calling for help and paddling with one hand for the shore which he had nearly reached when help came. Pictou's body was afterwards found very near where he went down. The verdict of the Jury after viewing the body was this—"That Louis Pictou, Indian, age thirty-eight, came to his death by accidental drowning on the seventh of August, 1893, caused by injury to his canoe from a huge shark thrusting its nose clear through it, making a hole fifteen inches across and causing it to upset and fill."

Lennie D. Wade. *Curious Glimpses of Digby County.* [1907]:n.p.

Jacques-Pierre Peminuit Paul, called James Peter Paul or Sah Piel Saqmaw:

He lived at Windsor, once a year he came down this way [Lequille]. Our father here knew him. He was a *bu'owin* [*puoin*]. He could twist a clay pipe around his hat, he could squeeze a large bowl, china or clay, into a small one, then make it big again. Once he stopped a windmill, grabbed hold of one of the wings. The mill owner begged him to let his mill run again, and gave him milk and cheese.... Once a man from Sydney built a dam on the river at Windsor. They couldn't get any fish. Sah Biel [*sic*] asked the man to make a way for the fish. No, he couldn't be bothered. So Sah Biel got seven men. One he sent down under the apron of the dam, one to the key log, to hitch a rope (one inch rope), and drive in a peevie. On one side of the dam he drove down a pointed stick, another on top of the dam. They pulled out the key log, they didn't have to pull hard. There is no dam yet on the river. No dam can

stay there, bridges, yes, but no dam, any dam would be flooded away.
Lucy Pictou to Elsie Clews Parsons. "Micmac Folklore," by Elsie Clews Parsons. In
Journal of American Folklore. 1925, 38:92-93.

My grandfather, Isaac Sack, he was visitin' down at old James Paul's
place, and James Paul he had a—well, it was more likely a caribou hide,
because there was no deer here then—he had this bit of a moose hide,
and that was his bed, near the stove. He had this old Waterloo stove,
very like old William Paul at Shubenacadie, and that was his favorite
spot—there'd be room between the stove and the wall. That's where
he'd sit in this spot, so he could put in the wood, now and again. There
was no central heat then, and none of the houses was even finished,
they's just a frame house. Well, he said this old gent was asittin' by the
stove, and he said that the old lady had made us all a cup of tea. Said,
"We was all drinkin' tea, and after a while, the old lady made the
rounds, another round, another cup of tea." They really drank strong
tea, no sugar or milk. He said the old man passed out his cup too: "Give
me a little more tea." And he said the old lady just go to give him a little
more tea, and she pulled the teapot away, saying, "Ah, yes, our old
father's gone crazy again."
   "Our father", you know, that's a great name amongst us; instead of
sayin', "Uncle", or "Old Man", they'd say, "Our Father"....
   But the old man had squeezed his cup [china cup], you could see his
finger-marks all round. She pulled the teapot away from him, put it
back on the stove. The old man just laughed, "Oh, I'll straighten it up
here." He straightened it up as if it were made out of [wet] clay, and the
old lady said, "That's more like it, now I'll pour you a cup of tea."
   He had squeezed it up on the old lady; "Our father's gone crazy
again."
   My grandfather Isaac Sack, well, that's the way it happened, he said.
And some said, you must have had, well, a hallucination.... But he said
no. Grandfather said, "No, I wasn't the only one seen it, everybody seen
it; just that he done so many weird things it didn't surprise nobody.
Didn't surprise *me* any." He said just a matter of fact that things like
that happened.
   Like him stretching his clay pipe round his hat. He stretched his clay
pipe round his hat! He'd no way to carry it, 'fraid he'd break it, so he
stretched his clay pipe round his hat. That's goin' beyond belief. Then
he straightened it up! Mass hallucination is right. Or else I spose they'd

think up who can tell the weirdest tale about old James Paul, Sak Piel Pol. James Peter Paul.

Course there'd be all kinda tales, I know when I was younger, people that can remember him, and one of the other tales is this windmill somewheres near Dartmouth; this man had a windmill for grinding grain. A big windmill and has a main shaft that come right down to turn the main grindstone. And he (my grandfather, that was Grandfather Sack, you see) said, "We used to ride round this main shaft, like, grab it and ride round. And old James Peter Paul, he grabbed that and the whole thing stopped. And the miller come in, goin', 'What are you fellows doin'?' And they said this old gent grabbed that pole. Miller said, 'He can't stop it, take more than the old man to do it.' The old man said, 'All I did was do THIS,' and it stopped it again. The miller said, 'Don't do it any more, you've stopped the whole mill.'"

'Nother one of them weird tales.

Max Basque to R.H. Whitehead and Ronald Caplan, Halifax, 9 March 1984. "A Visit with Max Basque, Whycocomagh." In *Cape Breton's Magazine*. 1989, No. 51:15-29. [Jacques-Pierre Peminuit Paul adopted his second wife's son, John Noel. Noel in turn adopted *his* second wife's son, Isaac Sack, the grandfather of Max Basque.]

Martin Sack, for thirty years counsellor of the Shubenacadie Reserve ... was very factual and added no hearsay. When he was a boy, his maternal grandfather (his father was dead), took the family up the Stewiacke River where there were then few farms, and they pitched their wigwam with some other families. In the morning his mother called to him: "Martin, make up the fire!" He put on his coat, tied his cap under his chin, put on his mittens and began to blow up the fire which had died down to embers. A very small fire kept the wigwam warm. When the fire had burned awhile, his mother rose, took buckwheat meal, added water, and kneaded a cake which she placed among the embers, covering it also with a few embers. There were only a few burned spots, and it was very good with butter. The time would come when she would say: "Puppa, food running out." Then the grandfather would get up, cut a big chunk of cake, fill the centre with butter, roll it in his handkerchief and tie this around his waist for his dinner, and would go out. He would not be gone long. He would come back with the tongue, the liver and the fat from inside the moose, as much as he could carry. Then a man would go from every wigwam and would take from the carcass as much as he could carry. After that the grandfather would take the rest to sell at the store and would buy needed things such as flour. Sometimes the men went up to the bog to hunt caribou. One man said, "Why don't we move the camps up to the bog where the caribou are?" But they never did.

Martin Sack to John Erskine. In "Micmac Notes: 1958," by John Erskine. Unpublished MS, Nova Scotia Museum Printed Matter File. 1958:15.

THE
TWENTIETH
CENTURY
1900 TO 1960 A.D.

THE FIRST HALF OF THE TWENTIETH CENTURY subjected the Micmac to a variety of upheavals: two world wars, the Great Depression, the Halifax Explosion of 1917, residential schools, and the centralization of numerous small reserves into "manageable" federal nightmares. Tuberculosis was still a major killer. The early twentieth century was a painful experience, as Micmac life was forced more into line with the mainstream "European" culture. A strong sense of family, however, and a strong sense of the ironies and humour of life saw the People through it all.

1900

I began my visit to Cape Breton with a piece of good luck. The first Indian I met was John Googoo, once a guide, and now just back from hospital. He was not one of the very knowledgeable Indians, but he was friendly and very helpful. In his youth [*ca* 1900] he had belonged to the band of four families which had travelled the area Whycocomagh/Lake Ainslie/ Mabou/Port Hood, and he remembered having dug arrowheads at a camp near Little Narrows.... According to John Googoo, [an eighteenth-century camp there] had become uninhabitable some forty years ago because of ghosts.... Googoo told me also why there were no oysters to be found there. He and a friend had been gathering oysters nearby when some white oyster-fishers drove them away. The friend then suggested: "Let's take the oysters out of the bay." So they hung oysters on grasses from the gunwales of their canoe and trailed them in the water out towards Little Narrows. The oysters took the hint, and now they have all moved out there.

John Erskine. "Micmac Notes: 1958." Unpublished MS, Nova Scotia Museum Printed Matter File. 1958:15.

Grandfather Isaac Sack's father was Peter Sack. They were hunting, and Isaac was only a boy. They were going through the woods, and Isaac, my grandfather, was walking ahead. He said first thing his father stopped him real quick. He said, "Wait a minute, boy," and Great-Grandfather started looking and smelling. "Something is telling me to stop. Something is wrong here." So he looked around, said, "Something just told me to stop." Finally he started looking around on the ground and he got a stick, started tapping the ground, and WHAM, a bear trap! It snapped right on the stick and chopped it in half. When they came home, he told the rest about it, he said, "Pure luck, something told me to stop. I got the notion to stop, and for a long while I couldn't make up my mind why I should stop. I thought I should start tapping, and it was a bear trap." He said, "Just where I had stopped. If we had gone any farther, it'd have grabbed the boy."

Max Basque to R.H. Whitehead, July 1978, personal communication. Max Basque to R.H. Whitehead and Ronald Caplan, 9 March 1984. In *Cape Breton's Magazine*. No. 51, 1989:23-24.

Once when out with a brother hunter, Tom Isaacs by name, an otter was stolen from Tom's steel trap by a bear; made evident by the tell-tale track. Tom swore a terrible revenge, for an otter was worth about $12. Wandering afterward on a neighbouring barren, he came quietly upon a bear feeding on berries. "Where's my otter?" thundered Tom. The bear jumped aside nearly twenty feet, and failing a satisfactory answer, was shot dead by Tom.

Arthur P. Silver. *Farm, Cottage, Camp and Canoe in Maritime Canada.* n.d. [*ca* 1907]:234.

Old woman Sallie, who now [1912] lives at Pictou, and is said to be one hundred years old—she is the head of four generations—went on the train to New Glasgow. The conductor, a stickler for fares, would not permit her to stay on the train, for she did not have enough money. She got off. A little farther on, the train ran off the track. Later, it again went off the track. While they were putting the engine on the track, after this second mishap, the conductor lost a finger. He felt that something was wrong, and said to old Sallie, "Mother, get on and go inside." After this the superintendent at Moncton told the conductor, "Whenever an Indian wants to go, take him whether he has the fare or not."

Anonymous. In *The Micmac Indians of Eastern Canada,* by Wilson D. Wallis and Ruth Sawtell Wallis. 1955:389.

1912

Peter Paul (called "Big Peter Paul" to distinguish him from Peter Paul, a Cape Breton Indian who lives near the Brewery at Dartmouth) was elected Chief of the Micmac Indians of Halifax, Lunenburg, Kings, Hants, Colchester & Cumberland Counties, at a small gathering of Indians held for the purpose at Spring Brook Reserve, near Shubenacadie, Hants County, on Saturday, 27 July 1912. At the same meeting John MacDonald was elected a captain. On the morning of Saturday, 15 March 1913, Chief Peter Paul, accompanied by Captain John MacDonald, Captains Lone Cloud (Jerry Bartlett) and Martin Saac ['Sak,' Micmac spelling of 'Jacques'; now rendered into English as 'Sack,' 'Sock,' or 'Sark'], (the latter a nephew of Isaac Saac, the last a step-son of late Chief John Noel), came to Halifax and went to Archbishop McCarthy's residence on Dresden Row, where at 10 o'clock, he and the rest of the company kneeling, received His Grace's blessing, was invested with the gilt medallion of the Pope which the late Chief Noel had worn, was exhorted to perform his duties as chief in an upright, faithful manner, and to attend the services of the Roman Catholic Church and to tell his beads regularly even when unable to attend chapel, etc. Candles were lighted during this ceremony. Then the Archbishop shook hands with the party. The silver medal of George III was not given to the chief on this occasion.

The party came to the museum at 10:24 o'c. and the new chief was introduced to me. None of them were in the native uniform, merely old homespun clothes, the chief with an umbrella. Chief Peter Paul, who succeeds Chief John Noel, was born at Indian Reserve, Shubenacadie, on 10 May 1850, and will be 60 [*sic*] years of age on 10 May 1913. He is a son of Christopher Paul. At 25 years of age (1875) Peter Paul was made

Left to right: Father Pacifique, Big Peter Paul, Catherine Sack Maloney, Judge Christopher Paul, and Mary Jeremy Jadis (seated), Shubenacadie, N.S., St Anne's Day, *ca* 1905.

a captain for Chief James Paul of Shubenacadie (stepfather of Chief John Noel), and was afterwards first captain for Chief John Noel.

Harry Piers, 15 March 1913. Unpublished notes, Nova Scotia Museum Printed Matter File.

1912

Chief Big Peter Paul only held office for a while. He began to totter after this.

Harry Piers, n.d. Unpublished notes, Nova Scotia Museum Printed Matter File.

1913

Parchments (Commissions) and old stone beads [wampum belts], formerly in possession of Chief James Paul [Jacques-Pierre Peminuit Paul] of Shubenacadie (stepfather of Chief John Noel) when Chief James Paul died [1895] Rev. Father W.F. Young, now of Yarmouth, but then of Shubenacadie or Enfield, it is said, got them, and Chief Peter Paul and Dr. Lone Cloud think he must still have them, and the chief would like to get them back for the tribe. They ask me to try to get them for them.

Harry Piers, 12 April 1913. Unpublished notes, Nova Scotia Museum Printed Matter File.

Mr. Piers, Dear Sir, We got an answer from the Indian Department regarding the five counties an electing a chief. Now as far as I can remember an my father knowledge we have Been going to Shubnacadie reserve every Sant an [St Anne's Day] and every holiday and we have laid out money on that chapel helped in every respect in keeping it up an we have voted at every election. Now we don't feel like to Be chucked out after all this trouble not only us But the Band of Indians in this five counties. So would it Be adviseable to wright a pitision in regards of this and get some respected gentlemens to Sigin it to Be fact if it would Please give the chief you opeanion and do what you can. and oblige John L. McDonald. PS I am working and cant leave my job or I would be to Pleased to go an see you.

John L. McDonald to Harry Piers, July 1913. Nova Scotia Museum Printed Matter File.

1915

The death occurred at Indian Reserve, Shubenacadie, on Thursday last (11th March 1915) of Mary Noel, widow of the late Chief John Noel of the Micmac Indians, at the venerable age of about 93 years. She was universally respected by both white men and Indians, to the latter of whom she was always known as Marl-nan-ette [this was her baptismal name, Marie Antoinette], and was lovingly spoken of among the tribe as "our old great mother." She had been a Thomas, and her grandfather [Paul Morris] set mink traps on the site where Halifax now stands. She had been twice married, her first husband being a Sack, by whom she had a son Isaac who is now a captain in the tribe. She will be buried today at Indian Reserve.

Harry Piers MS, 13 March 1915. Unpublished notes, Nova Scotia Museum Printed Matter File.

[Marie Antoinette, born 16 October 1822, was the daughter of Mary Morris Thomas and her second husband, Louis Thomas; her maternal grandfather was Paul Morris, and her paternal grandfather, the English deserter Thomas mentioned in entries for 1749 and 1758. Her brother Michael Thomas married Mary Jerome, and her sister Madelaine Thomas married John Williams. She herself married Peter Sack (Jacques), and had Francis, b. 1840, Louis, b. 1845, Catherine, b. 1849, Martin, and Isaac, b. 1855. After the death of her first husband, she married in March 1870 Chief John Noel, himself a widower, and the adopted son of Chief James Paul. She had no children by John Noel, who predeceased her on 20 May 1911. A skirt made for Marie Antoinette Thomas Sack Noel by her mother, Mary Morris Thomas, is in the collections of the Nova Scotia Museum.]

1916

The death occurred this morning, 24 February 1916, at Tufts Cove, Dartmouth, at a very advanced age, of a well-known Indian and guide, Andrew Paul, who was familiar to Halifax sportsmen of the past generation. He was born at Whycocomagh, Cape Breton Island, but had lived near Dartmouth for about 75 years. At the time the Prince of Wales was in Halifax about 1860, he was one of the captains of his section of the tribe, and with the then Chief James Paul and other sub-chiefs, in full Indian costumes, was presented to the Prince. The Paul family has always been a very prominent one among the Micmacs and Peter Paul is now Chief at Shubenacadie. Andrew was a good hunter, and in the past acted as guide for many of our sportsmen. His tall, very erect figure and grey head was well-known in the Halifax market on Saturdays.

Harry Piers, 24 February 1916. Unpublished notes, Nova Scotia Museum Printed Matter File.

1916

James Glode of Kejimkoojee, Liverpool River, N.S., a member of the old well-known Micmac family of Glode [Claude], and a captain in the tribe of Halifax county and vicinity, yesterday enlisted as a private in the 219th Battalion of the Highland Brigade now being raised for overseas service. This is the first Micmac Indian to take up arms for his King and country in the present war and no doubt his example will be followed by many others of his tribe.

Harry Piers, 11 March 1916. Unpublished notes, Nova Scotia Museum Printed Matter File.

1916
The Micmac Indians are showing their loyalty by joining the corps for overseas service. Four brothers of the Glode family of Kejimkoojie, Queens Co., N.S., have enlisted, James and Peter in the 219th Highland Battalion, and Sam and Stephen in the 64th. They are sons of the late Stephen Glode, formerly chief of the tribe for Queens County (he died about 17 years ago). Another Micmac who has enlisted in the 219th is Moses Paul, son of Joe Paul of Mossman's Grant, Lunenburg Co., who is a member of a branch of the Paul family which has so long been chiefs of part of the tribe.

Harry Piers, 18 March 1916. Unpublished notes, Nova Scotia Museum Printed Matter File.

I worked with another Indian from Milton, named John Francis. The weather was hot and it was hard work. One day, after John and me had felled a big hemlock, we stuck our axes in the stump and sat down for a rest. We were tired of the whole job, really. We knew about the war overseas, and we knew the Canadian army was paying $1.10 a day, besides your clothes and grub. So John said to me, "Sam, let's go to the war. It can't be no worse than this."

Samuel Freeman Gloade to Thomas Raddall. In *Cape Breton's Magazine*. 1984, No. 35:11. Excerpted from the Raddall Papers, Dalhousie Archives, Killam Library, Dalhousie University, Halifax.

Chief Aleck Moose, Indian Reservation, Pictou Landing, Pictou County, N.S.;

Chief Isaac Paul, Indian Reservation, Newville, Cumberland County, N.S.;

Chief John Nockwed, Indian Reservation, Kentville, Kings County, N.S.;

Chief Silbye Pictou, Indian Reservation, General's Bridge, Annapolis Royal, N.S.;

Captain Tom Glode, Indian Reservation, Truro, N.S.;
Tom Labrador, Indian Reservation, Bridgewater, Lunenburg County, N.S.

This is to inform you that a Grand Meeting of the Micmac Tribe of the District comprised in Halifax, Lunenburg, Kings, Hants, Colchester, Cumberland, and Queens Counties, will be held at the Chapel at Indian Reservation, Spring Brook, Shubenacadie, N.S., on Tuesday afternoon, the 22nd August 1916, for the purpose of electing a permanent Grand Chief for the said seven counties of Halifax, Lunenburg, Kings, Hants, Colchester, Cumberland, and Queens. Please take notice and inform the members of the Tribe in your county.

Jeremiah Bartlett Alexis [alias Jerry Lonecloud] to Chiefs, Shubenacadie, N.S., 15 August 1916. Nova Scotia Museum Printed Matter File.

Enfield, N.S. 5 Dec. 1916
To The Secretary, Department of Indian Affairs, Ottawa
Sir: The Micmac Indians of Halifax and Hants County, Nova Scotia, of whom Peter Paul of Shubenacadie is head chief, and myself, John Denney Paul, of Enfield, sub-chief for Halifax County, desire to send a delegation to Ottawa in order to renew certain old treaties which said delegation will bring with it, and to discuss other matters. Will you therefore state what date would be convenient for such a delegation to arrive at Ottawa, and oblige.
Your obedient servant, John Denny Paul, Chief for Halifax County.

John Denny Paul to the Department of Indian Affairs, 5 December 1916. Nova Scotia Museum Printed Matter File.

Tufts Cove, Dartmouth, N.S. 9 April 1917.
To the Secretary, Department of Indian Affairs, Ottawa.
Sir, By petition to you dated 20th March of this year, certain Indians of Tufts Cove, Elmsdale & Enfield, N.S., requested that moneys coming to them for sale of timber on Indian lands at Ship Harbour, Halifax County, be applied to the erection of dwelling-houses for them at the Indian Reservation at Spring Brook near Shubenacadie, N.S., to which place they wish to move this spring in order to begin to cultivate the soil there. No reply has been received to that petition and meantime the season is rapidly passing, and the cost of provisions being much higher, which will bring distress to many of the Indian families, particularly those at Tufts Cove. Four families at Tufts Cove, namely the families of Frank Brooks, Joe Brooks, Jim Brooks & Jerry Lone

Cloud, desire to locate at Shubenacadie as soon as possible, or else the season will be too late to plant.... We also beg that speedy consideration be given to our petition of the 20th March, and that it is not allowed to lie undealt with until it is too late to be of material assistance. I have the honour to be, Sir, Your obedient servant, Jerry Lone cloud.

Jeremiah Bartlett Alexis [alias Jerry Lonecloud] to the Department of Indian Affairs, 9 April 1917. MS in Harry Piers' handwriting [he may have drafted the letter]. Nova Scotia Museum Printed Matter File.

[Jerry Lonecloud and Nova Scotia Musuem curator Harry Piers spelled "Lonecloud" as one word or two. I have chosen to spell it as one.]

1917

A number of Indians left the woods and the rivers and went to fight for King and country in the Great War. They fought valiantly and distinguished themselves on the field. "I was in the 6th Indianeer's Battalion," said an Indian to me. "No, it wasn't an Indian battalion. We made tunnels and that sort o' thing—indianeering. I was wounded at Vimy Ridge in 1917."

Clara Dennis. *More about Nova Scotia.* 1935:410.

Secretary, Department of Indian Affairs, Ottawa.
Sir, Since time out of mind, members of the Micmac Tribe have camped on ground near Tufts Cove, a little north of the Brewery, on the east side of Halifax Harbour, where there is also situated an Indian school House. This camping land is claimed by Mr. Farrell of Halifax, and notice has been given the Indians to remove within two weeks. The Indians claim that although this land is not a reservation, yet they have surely rights there by long occupation, even if it be regarded only in the light of what is termed squatter's rights. We claim that we should not therefore be pressed to leave; and that if we do leave, it should be by mutual arrangement between the Indians and Mr. Farrell, and by the payment of money in order that we relinquish our rights. Some of the Indians are willing to remove, while others of the older families hold to what they consider to be their rights, and desire compensation if they leave the place. We desire that your Department will promptly render us assistance and protection in this matter, as we are unable to do much by ourselves without due backing from the Department. I have the honour to be, Sir, Your obedient servant, Jerry Lone Cloud.
Tufts Cove, Dartmouth, N.S.

Jeremiah Bartlett Alexis [alias Jerry Lonecloud] to the Department of Indian Affairs, 27

November 1917. MS in Harry Piers' handwriting [he may have drafted the letter]. Nova Scotia Museum Printed Matter File.

[Lonecloud's petitions of 9 April, 27 November, 5 December and others to the department were apparently fruitless; the people were not assisted to move from Tufts Cove, and on 6 December 1917, 10 days after this last petition was sent off, the ships *Imo* and *Mont Blanc* collided in Halifax Harbour, before the entrance to the Narrows, opposite Tufts Cove. The *Mont Blanc* was loaded with ammunition and explosives, and the resulting explosion completely destroyed the Indian camp at Tufts Cove, along with much of northern Halifax and Dartmouth.]

Micmac Indians and the Halifax Disaster of 6 December 1917

Jerry Lone Cloud on 31 December 1917 gave me the following particulars as to how the Micmac Indians at the little settlement just north of the Brewery, near Tufts Cove, north Dartmouth, suffered as a result of the terrible explosion of 6 December 1917. This little settlement was directly opposite the place where the explosion took place. Many of the Indians had gone down near the shore to see the steamer on fire, & were there when the explosion occurred. Pieces of iron were hurled about them. The settlement consisted of seven (7) shanties in the spruce woods there. These shanties were destroyed. There were 21 Indians in the settlement, of whom 9 were instantly killed or afterwards died from injuries received, and 12 escaped but mostly badly injured.

The following Indians were either killed directly or else later died from injuries received:

Frank Brooks, the well known oar-maker, an old man aged 71 years.
Mrs. William Nevins, aged about 73 years; burnt to death.
Mrs. William Paul, aged about 37 years.
Janet Glode, aged about 32 years, belonged to Milton, Queens County, N.S.
Rosie, daughter of Jerry Lone Cloud (Bartlett), aged 30 years.
Hannah, daughter of Jerry Lone Cloud (Bartlett), aged 15 years.
Only son of Isaac Saac [*sic;* Isaac Paul], aged about 15 years.
Ben Labrador, aged about 13 years; burnt to death (burnt up). He was a son of Louis Labrador of Milton, Queens Co., N.S.
Richard Nevin's baby.

Six of the Indian victims of the disaster were buried in one grave in the Roman Catholic cemetery at Dartmouth, on Thursday, 20th

December, the Rev. Father Underwood officiating, and a large number of Indians following the remains.

Rosie, daughter of Jerry Lone Cloud, had been pinned beneath timbers, but not instantly killed. She asked that she might see a priest. She died later.

Jeremiah Bartlett Alexis, also known as Jerry Lonecloud.

The Relief Committee is building houses for the surviving Indians near the school-house adjoining the late settlement. They have received food, clothing and shelter from the Dartmouth Committee.

Jerry Lone Cloud was at Kentville, N.S., at time of explosion, but he immediately returned on a relief train, and reached Dartmouth that evening by walking all the way from Windsor Junction. His wife was also absent, in south-eastern New Brunswick. Lone Cloud himself is at present quartered at 145 Upper Water Street, Halifax.

The Indians greatly regret the death of their school teacher (a white man) named George F. Richardson of Halifax, who was apparently instantly killed by the explosion on the Halifax side, probably when about to proceed to Dartmouth by the Hanover Street ferry-boat. He had done good work at the Indian school at Tufts Cove, and was also a pianist of considerable skill (was the pianist of the King Edward Theatre, Halifax).

Jeremiah Bartlett Alexis [alias Jerry Lonecloud] to Harry Piers, 31 December 1917. Nova Scotia Museum Printed Matter File.

1917

Tufts Cove, Dartmouth, N.S.

You spoke about the Indians. I was brought up with them, we lived right alongside of them. I understand they were all killed except the Nevan family. I don't know if they were. I knew the Nevans, and I know it's Nevan Avenue now, going down there. They were the only ones that were left. They got them a place there, and they stayed there until they all got grown up. I went to school with them. I remember them, they lived in these teepees, with mud floors. A ring of stones around, where they had their fire. Smoke came out through the top of the roof there. I used to go in there and watch the old ladies making baskets, and things like that. We played with them, and went to school with the kids.

They were right close [to the Narrows where the explosion happened] there, and maybe they were all out watching the fire. They were right on the bank, right opposite the boat, a little further up than the Brewery property. They had a nice place. The Indian Village. There were quite a few of them there, as I remember. We used to go down—it was all spruce wood—they were down right on the shore. There was quite a collection of teepees, covered with birch bark, or any old piece of stuff likely to be found on the shore. As I remember, it was mostly birch bark, because in those times there wouldn't be much on the shore, because there wasn't much as far as the wood goes, because you gathered it up as fast as you could. I believe that most of them were killed. The only one I know of that was left was the Nevan family. Very nice fellow, he worked at the Armament until he died.

Leighton Dillman to Janet Kitz, October 1982, personal communication. Courtesy Janet Kitz.

1917

The Nevin family came to Tufts Cove about 1912. They had a respectable wooden house, rectangular, with a verandah. Mr. Nevin used to sit out on the verandah playing his violin to amuse himself. My father used to take us to visit the Chief—a Prosper, he was, who had a wooden shanty and a wigwam. In the winter, the Prospers lived in the wigwam, I think. We used to go swimming at the beach there on Sundays, and eat supper with them.

Ian Forsythe to R.H. Whitehead, 3 November 1982, personal communication.

Mrs. Oscar North, Hair-dresser
Arlington, Mass.
Dear Sophie,
I know you must of heard of the terrible explosion which occurred in Halifax Harbour on 6th December, which destroyed a large part of Halifax, and entirely wiped out the Indian encampment which was directly opposite to it. Two of my children, Rosie and Hannah, who you will remember, were killed and all my things destroyed, but I escaped as I was in another part of the province. I wonder if you and some of your good friends would be willing to assist me at this very hard period in my life? Any aid you may be able to give will be very greatly appreciated by and do much good to,
Yours truly,
Jerry Lone Cloud
145 Upper Water Street, Halifax

Jeremiah Bartlett Alexis [alias Jerry Lonecloud] to Mrs Oscar North. Draft or copy of a letter in Harry Piers' hand, possibly written for him by Harry Piers, n.d. Nova Scotia Museum Printed Matter File.

1918

Ben Morris, a very aged and well-known Micmac Indian, died at Three-Mile Plains, near Windsor, N.S., on 19 February 1918, aged 95 years. He was born about 1823 at Shag Bay near Halifax. The correct name of his family was Mollise, which has been corrupted by white men to Morris [actually, it was originally the French 'Maurice,' which becomes 'Moli's' in Micmac, and 'Morris' in English]. His father, Sebmolie [Sosep-Mali or Joseph-Marie?] Mollise, and grandfather, had camped for very many years at the outlet of Morris's Lake, near Dartmouth, the lake being named after this Indian family. It is said that the family also had rights on what is now McNab's Island. Ben lived for fifty or sixty years at Shag Bay, and hunted and fished in the vicinity of Nine-Mile River where game was then plentiful. He then lived at Dartmouth for a few years (4 or 5 years), and while there became totally blind, and was led about by one of his children, he being a familiar figure about the town. From Dartmouth he moved to his son's place at Three-Mile Plains, Windsor, where he resided until his death at an extreme old age. A nephew of his is serving his king in the overseas forces.

Harry Piers, n.d. Unpublished notes, Nova Scotia Museum Printed Matter File.

No. 470813 Private Abram Paul
25th Battalion (formerly 64th), Canadians
c/o Army Post Office
London, England
Dear Nephew Gabe,
We are very sorry to hear that you have been in hospital suffering with shell shock, and hope that you are now better and able to be about, as they tell us you were admitted to hospital in 18 November.

I suppose you have heard of the very bad explosion which took place at Richmond, Halifax, on 6 December, when two steamers collided and one blew up killing nearly 2,000 people about Richmond and Dartmouth. The Indian settlement at Tufts Cove was destroyed and several Indians killed. My daughters, Rosie and Hannah, were killed. My daughter Mary Anne died three weeks after you went across. You will be sorry to learn that Kathy Francis and her baby died last fall. Her father and mother are also dead.

As you know I am the one who is your nearest relative, and if you could see your way to be able to assist me in any way, I would be very glad.

Let us know from time to time how you are getting along, as we would like to know of your welfare.
With best wishes, your aunt, (Mrs. Lone Cloud), Tufts Cove.

Elizabeth Paul to Abram Paul, 25 February 1918. Rough draft or copy of a letter in Harry

Piers' hand, possibly written by Piers at her request. Nova Scotia Museum Printed Matter File.

[The author, Elizabeth Paul, was a Maliseet Indian from New Brunswick who married Jeremiah Bartlett Alexis (alias Jerry Lonecloud) but used her own name, Paul; she later separated from him.]

1918

The death occurred on 12th April, at the Micmac Indian reservation, Church Island, Whycocomagh, of John Denney, Chief of the Micmac Tribe of the Island of Cape Breton. His jurisdiction in the tribe embraced the whole of that island. He was seventy-four years of age, a native of Whycocomaugh, and had been chief for about forty years. The chieftainship of Cape Breton, although [by] election as on the mainland of Nova Scotia, yet has always within the memory of man been in the Denney family, and the deceased had succeeded his father, also John Denney, in that office. It is the intention of his tribe to give him a largely attended funeral.

Harry Piers, n.d. Unpublished notes, Nova Scotia Museum Printed Matter File.

T.D. McLean, Esq. Asst. Deputy and Secretary, Department of Indian Affairs, Ottawa.

Sir, For about the last six or seven years I have received from the Indian Department, the sum of Two Dollars ($2.00) a week, as being over 60 years of age, with a family, and my eyesight bad. My age is now 69 years (will be seventy in next July). On applying for this weekly allowance on last Thursday (25 April), I was informed that there was no money for me, and that there would be none for the future, being told that Mr. Dan Chisholm, Indian Agent for Halifax County, had telephoned instructions to that effect. I beg to respectfully protest against this, and beg that you will be so good as to consider the matter and to give instructions that my grant be continued, as I much need it at my age, and have lost two daughters killed in the recent explosion who had assisted in supporting the family.

Jeremiah Bartlett Alexis [alias Jerry Lonecloud] to T.D. McLean, 27 April 1918. MS in Harry Piers' handwriting [he may have drafted the letter]. Nova Scotia Museum Printed Matter File.

By this time [1918] I was a corporal, and one morning the sergeant left me in charge of the section working in the tunnel.... We knew the Germans were tunnelling. We had a man with a listening outfit. On this particular day, all of a sudden he said, "Say, the Germans have stopped working." We stopped for a while ourselves, wondering what that meant. Nothing happened. Finally we went on with the work. I was sitting on a ledge in the tunnel, watching the men timbering up behind the diggers at the "face." All of a sudden everything went black. I felt like somebody had hit me on the head with a big club. I don't know how long I sat there like that.

Samuel Freeman Gloade to Thomas H. Raddall. In *Cape Breton's Magazine*. 1984, No. 35:11. Excerpted from the Raddall Papers, Dalhousie Archives, Killam Library, Dalhousie University, Halifax.

1918

The death occurred at Stewarts, Upper Musquodoboit, on 31st August, of an old and well-known Indian, John Cope, at the age of 71 years, he having been born at Beaver Dam, Halifax County, in April 1847, son of old Mollie Cope who is said to have been 113 years of age when she passed away about 13 years ago. The original Micmac name of the family was not Cope, but Bolmoltie, which means "a clear space." [Bernie Francis thinks "Bolmoltie" was originally French 'Paul Martin.'] John Cope had considerable fame as a hunter, at least judging by the number of moose he shot, and acted as guide for various Halifax sportsmen some thirty years ago. He used to hunt back of Beaver Dam and Moose Head [?] with Captain C. Lestrange, who was formerly well-known here. One winter, probably forty years ago, Cope by himself killed eighteen moose, according to his own admission, although the claim has been erroneously made that the number was seventy. The meat of these he sold to the Fifteen-Mile Stream gold camp, which was then in active operation. He was then camping at Indian Rips at the head of Hunting [?] Lake on Liscomb River. He was a big man, of unprepossessing appearance, but a genuine Indian in all respects.

Jeremiah Bartlett Alexis [alias Jerry Lonecloud] to Harry Piers, 6 September 1918. Nova Scotia Museum Printed Matter File.

When I came to my senses I was wet with sweat and my ears were singing like a steam whistle was inside them. Our candles had gone out. I could hear some men stirring, but nobody spoke till I did.... The officer had left an electric torch in the tunnel, and I fumbled around and found it. When I switched it on, I could see that the tunnel had collapsed behind us and in front of us. We were in a kind of cave. Some of the men said, "What are we going to do?" I said, "Get out of this as quick as we can." I figured the only chance was to dig up to the surface. It couldn't be far. So I took a pick and began to tear a hole in the roof of our cave. The others didn't offer to help, they just watched me, dull-like. They had all been coal miners and they couldn't think of anything but that 80-foot shaft straight down before the tunnel began. It's something to be an Indian after all. You look at a piece of country and it's like a picture in your mind. I remembered the long dip of the ground between our front line trench and the Germans. I kept picking away. The air got worse and worse. I had to force myself to work but I was desperate and I was strong. I don't know how long it took. Hours and hours. And I can't remember how far up I had to dig. That blue clay wasn't so hard up there towards the surface, and after a time I could dig through turf and there was daylight and a rush of cold air. You could breathe good then. I called out to the men below to light a candle and they lit one and it burnt all right. I widened the hole in the surface a bit, and scrambled down to the others. I said, "That hole is in no-man's-land, where the Germans can shoot any head that shows. We will have to wait till dark, and then slip out one by one, and make our way back to our own lines."

Samuel Freeman Gloade to Thomas H. Raddall. In *Cape Breton's Magazine.* 1984, No. 35:11. Excerpted from the Raddall Papers, Dalhousie Archives, Killam Library, Dalhousie University, Halifax.

1918

So deadly was the constant fire of the Hun snipers that it was certain death for any of the Allies entrenched to pop their head above the parapet for even a second. Stephen Toney [was positioned] some distance down the line, and upon the solicitation of an officer who knew of the Indian's powers as a sniper, the General sent for him. It was not long after that the keen eye of the Nyanza Micmac discerned a suspicious object in a tree fully one thousand yards distant, and he told the officers so. The latter immediately trained their powerful field glasses on the tree but assured the Indian there was nobody on it. "Spose you watch," coolly replied Toney, and taking a careful bead, pulled the trigger. Instantly dropped the dead body of a sniper, and the astonished officers and men were raptured in their applause.

On that occasion the General saw seven German snipers bite the dust, and particularly for this did the Nyanza Micmac earn the coveted V.C.

Shortly after, Toney was gassed, and when the doctors thought he was fit for the trenches he was sent back. However, his eyesight became impaired, and he was sent home on furlough, and is at present with his mother in Pictou County.

The Echo. Halifax, 18 November 1918.

1918

Considering Millbrook's tiny population earlier in the century, her record on enlistment in the armed forces in wartime was a most commendable one. Roll of honour 1914-1918: John Abram, John Brooks, John Cope Sr., John Cope Jr., John Doyle, killed in action; Andrew Francis, James Francis, James A. Gloade, died of wounds; James Muise, Louis J. Newell, Denis Paul, Joseph Louis Pictou, John Smith.

Douglas Ormond. *The Roman Catholic Church in Cobequid, Acadie, etc.* 1979:214-215.

You wanted to know the names of two or three of the oldest Micmac residents on [the Elmsdale, N.S.] Reserve, I beg to say that the following are such names: Elewie [Louis] Doodoo, who died 38 years ago, his age unknown, but died from old age; also his brother, Newell Doodoo, who died two or three years ago, at the age of 84 years; also Joe Howe (Jeremy) who has been living there since he was 14 years of age, and is now about 74 years old, and has been living there ever since he went there as a boy. It is claimed that their fathers before them also lived there....

Martin Sack to H.L. Bury, Department of Indian Affairs, 18 January 1919. Nova Scotia Museum Printed Matter File.

Chief Garble Hood [known as Gabe, Abe, Abram], River Hibbert, Cumberland County, N.S.; Charles Francis, Cambridge, King's County; Chief William Paul, Dorchester, N.B.: Please attend a meeting which will be held at the Indian Reservation, Spring Brook, Shubenacadie, N.S., on Saturday, 26th July 1919, for the election of a Grand Chief for the Six Counties. Jerry Lonecloud, 11 July 1919.

—N.B.: Meeting failed. Tried to get another meeting on Sunday, 21 September 1919, at Chapel, Indian Reservation, Shubenacadie, to elect a Head Chief [Big Peter Paul]...but this meeting also failed.

Jeremiah Bartlett Alexis [alias Jerry Lonecloud] to Harry Piers, n.d. Nova Scotia Museum Printed Matter File.

1920

Pygmy Sperm Whale, Specimen Taken at Herring Cove, Halifax County, N.S.

On 17th January, 1920, when Jeremiah Gray and other men were cutting out ice to prevent it carrying away the wharves, in case of storm, in Herring Cove ... they chanced to come upon the body of a small-sized whale. The animal was eight and a half feet long, and it was lying dead just beneath the ice.... On showing the head of this whale to a very well-informed Micmac Indian, Jeremiah Lone-cloud (*alias* Bartlett), he examined it carefully and stated that he had never seen the species before, but from descriptions given him to two very old Indians, Noel Jeddore, who is now dead, and Soolian (William) Bill [William Prosper], he felt sure it must be what was known by the Indian name *Ded-men-ak-paj-jet,* a name which means 'Blunt-head' fish. Noel Jeddore had been born at Melrose, St. Mary's, N.S., and died about twenty years ago, aged 84 years, and old Soolian Bill had formerly belonged to Cape Breton Island and now lives on the Truro reservation, aged about 97 years.

Noel Jeddore told Lone-cloud that about fifty years ago, say about 1870, he and other Indians were encamped on a small island called by the Indians *Up-quaw-we-kunk,* or 'Bark-camp Island,' off West Medford, on the south side of the entrance to Pereau Creek, in Minas Basin, Kings Co., N.S., when a school of about a dozen cetaceans became stranded on a mudflat there. The Indians examined them and got some of the flesh for food, and he said that the cooked back-fin was much relished by them. The animals were about 12 or 15 feet long, coloured black, and had a small dorsal-fin. Such cetaceans had never before or afterwards been seen by Jeddore and his companions, but he had heard from other older Indians that such animals had occurred years previously, and that they had been called by the Micmacs *Ded-men-ak-paj-jet,* from the blunt appearance of their head. This word resembles an old Micmac name applied to another rare cetacean ["true" sperm whale] which once occurred here: *Ded-men-ak-part,* which means 'head cut off squarely,' not merely 'blunt head'....

Old Soolian Bill very recently told Lone-cloud that he also had seen the cetacean which they call *Ded-men-ak-paj-jet,* and said it occurred in the same season when the others were taken off West Medford. About fifty years or more ago, he states, a number of sea animals of the kind seen at West Medford came ashore in a "gut" of water near the Indian reservation at Whycocomagh, St. Patrick's Channel, Bras d'Or Lakes, Cape Breton Island. Bill and other Indians examined and cut up the animals and obtained much oil from the blubber; and one which they opened contained a foetus. They also called the animal *Ded-men-ak-paj-jet*, agreed it was the same species as that taken in the Minas Basin, and that it was extremely rare, but that old Indians told them it had been taken years before. It also had a dorsal-fin…. (*It may be mentioned that at the same time that these cetaceans came ashore at Whycocomagh, two very large whales—Micmac *Bootup*, name for any large whale—came in at the same place and one ran ashore and was killed by the Indians with a scythe-blade on the end of a pole. Soolian Bill saw it, and he said it made a great commotion with its very long fins, so that one had to be careful in approaching it…. Probably it was the Humpback Whale….)

Harry Piers. "Accidental Occurrence of the Pygmy Sperm Whale (*Kogia breviceps*) on the Coast of Nova Scotia; an Extension of Its Known Range; With Remarks on the Probability of the Former Presence in These Waters of the True Sperm Whale (*Physeter macrocephalus*)." Read 9 February 1920. In *Proceedings and Transactions of the Nova Scotia Institute of Science*. 1920:Vol. XV, 8: 95-114.

1920

Two old Indians died of influenza on last Thursday, 4th March 1920, at the new Indian reservation at Truro, N.S. They were Delair, widow of Soolian (William) Soowa, whose age was 82 years, and Louis Jeekouse who had reached the great age of 89 years. The latter was the father of Mrs. Joe Cope, whose husband is a well-known educated Indian of Enfield, but lately of Lunenburg. (Soowa, an old Indian name meaning 'He takes out what he brought in.' Jeekouse, an old Indian name meaning, 'Listen!')

Harry Piers, n.d. Unpublished notes, Nova Scotia Museum Printed Matter File.

[Jeekouse, now spelled *kjiku's*, actually means 'great moon' or 'great month'; this is December, the Christmas month, and the common Micmac surnames Noel, Christmas and Kjiku's were sometimes used interchangeably in the historical documentation.]

My ancestors camped on this Mersey River. I myself lived in wigwams until I was about thirteen. Then we built a little house like white people…. My ancestors got their livin' outa the woods and rivers and at one time all I done was hunt and fish, but the way they got the law now is slack time for us Indians. They 'pinted fish warden, tryin' to ketch everybody. One see me fishin' one day long time ago. I just dip fine salmon from river when I see him. He see me with the salmon, so I know he ketch me. I chucks the salmon up over the dam! "Hey! What you doin'?" he hollered. I say, "I'm just helpin' salmon over the dam." Fish warden walk away: he don't bother me no more. I go down to the river and dip me another salmon—of course that long time ago now.

Anonymous Micmac man to Clara Dennis. In *More about Nova Scotia*, by Clara Dennis. 1935:409.

Micmac Indian Guides (Good), According to Chief Isaac Sack:
John Williams was the best. Lord Dunraven used to send some money each year to John Williams.

John Noel [Cope], with a crippled hand. He lived at Beaver Dam, Halifax County. Been dead about 4 years, say about 1917. They said he [on one hunting trip had] killed 70 moose, but he said it was only 18.

Joe Paul, Beaver Dam. Husband of Mollie Cope [her second husband]. Died about 10 years ago, say about 1910.

Francis (Frank) Cope. Beaver Dam. Son of Mollie Cope, by her first husband, Francis. He died about 7 years ago, say about 1914.

Jim Glode, of Bear River, Annapolis County. He is still living, aged about 90 years or more, and stone blind. He and John Williams were out with Lord Dunraven when he was hunting in Nova Scotia about 1876. Glode then went to the Rocky Mountains with Dunraven. [Piers notes that this was an error, and that Glode had gone to the west of Canada with the Honourable Charles Alexander and his brother, and to the Rocky Mountains: "The Alexanders came out here for about 25 summers. John Williams and Jim Glode also went hunting with Prince Arthur when he was here in 1869, but they got nothing."]

Joe Brooks, used to live at Truro, but now living at Stillwater. Is an old man now. Used to make good oars.

(Campbell Hardy considered John Williams and Joe Cope to be very fine Indian guides. Also Ned Nolan, the Pauls of Ship Harbour, the Glodes of Annapolis, and Joe Penaul [Bernard, Penall] of Chester ["Joe Goose"] are all capital {?} in the woods. All ask the regular charge of $1.00 a day in the woods.)

Isaac Sack to Harry Piers, 26 February 1921. Nova Scotia Museum Printed Matter File. "Isaac Sack was born near Dartmouth, where the Truro Road branches from Preston Road, the son of Peter [and Marie Antoinette Thomas] Sack. He (Isaac) was born on 15 June 1855, and was 65 years old on 15 June 1920. In June 1917, he was elected Grand

Chief of the Micmac [being the adopted son of former Grand Chief John Noel, who had married his widowed mother, Marie Antoinette Thomas Sack.] He lives at the Shubenacadie Reservation." (Harry Piers)

[Isaac Sack died in November 1930.]

Micmac Indian Hunters and Guides of the Old Days: According to Lewie Newell McDonald of Enfield, N.S.

Peter Joe Cope, Beaver Dam, Sheet Harbour, Halifax County. Dead.

Frank Cope, of Beaver Dam, Sheet Harbour, Halifax County. Dead.

John Newell Cope, of Beaver Dam, Sheet Harbour, Halifax County. Dead.

Lewie Newell, of Red Bridge, Dartmouth, and afterwards of Cole Harbour Indian settlement, where he died, Halifax County, N.S. His father lived to be about 95 years of age. He was of the old stock of Indian hunters, and trained most of the Indians in hunting. He was the adopted father of Lewie Newell McDonald, a white child, born 14 March 1856, and adopted by Lewie Newell when a few hours old, and was well brought up by them. Lewie Newell and his adopted white son hunted with Captain Lestrange about 1860 [?]; with Captain Chearnley, when Lewie Newell McDonald was about 12 years of age, say about 1868; with Captain Campbell Hardy, prior to 1867 when Hardy left North America; Lieutenant Dashwood, about 1867; Lord Dunraven, about 1874. They were first in Newfoundland with Dunraven, and then in Nova Scotia with him; and with the Honourable Charles Alexander, say about 1879-1880.

John Williams, Indian Reserve, Shubenacadie. Dead.

Peter Joe Cope, one of the best moose callers in the province at that time. He lived at Red Bridge, Dartmouth. Dead.

Stephen Maloney, Indian Reserve, Shubenacadie. Dead.

Peter Wilmot, Indian, now living near Truro, very old. Formerly of Pictou. Very old man now; now about 88 years old. (Last year, 1920, at moose-calling time, he got a moose near Sunnybrae, Pictou County, according to Jerry Lonecloud.)

Sandy Cope, son of Frank Cope of Beaver Dam, Sheet Harbour. Now alive at Truro, N.S., about 65 years of age.

Lewie Newell [Louis Noel] McDonald, born 14 March 1856, and brought up by Lewie Newell, Indian, and his wife. Although a white man, he says he was well and kindly brought up by them, and he has always lived with Indians, and would not take up the life of a white man.

He says he was about, as camp helper, with his foster father, with the gentlemen hunters mentioned above. He is also a good hunter himself. Was with his foster father with Dunraven in Newfoundland. Was out with Chearnley, with his foster father, when but 12 years of age. He says Dashwood hunted all about Nova Scotia, and that he was a good sportsman. L.N. McDonald once borrowed a fast but cranky[?] birch bark canoe from Harry Piers, about 1893, for a regatta on Dartmouth Lakes, and won easily; his crew were himself, John Denney (Peter Paul's brother), and Tom (L.N. McDonald's son).

Jim Paul of Ship Harbour. One of the best of the old hunters.

John Dennis, of Pomket, Antigonish County. (A little fellow, great hunter, according to Lonecloud.)

Jim Glode of Bear River and about Shubenacadie. He is old and blind now.

Louis Noel McDonald to Harry Piers, 28 April 1921. Nova Scotia Museum Printed Matter File.

Mattio Salome, or Seloom [Jerome], Micmac Indian hunter and guide, is said to have had 7 wives. He used to camp at Squaw Point, on west side of Ladle Lake, West Branch of the Liscombe River, Guysborough County, and also at Sloane's Lake [Salome's Lake], about eight and a half miles SSW of Upper Caledonia, Guysborough County. It is said that he killed a wife at each of these places. After the death of each wife he abandoned his camping places at the lakes. His wife at Salome's Lake was found in the water after the ice broke up, and she was buried on the island in the lake.

When he would be seen with a new wife, someone would ask him, "Hullo, Mattio, what's become of your old Mollie?" and he would reply, "Mollie may be die."

He was a rather ugly man in appearance, but was a good hunter.

Jeremiah Bartlett Alexis [alias Jerry Lonecloud] to Harry Piers, 23 December 1921. Nova Scotia Museum Printed Matter File.

That was 1920.... And that's when they started paving the first road that was ever paved, I guess, in Nova Scotia—from Bedford to Halifax. And of course there was a lot of hand labour and pick-and-shovel work. And finally by the end of the summer ... there were about 60 camps— wigwams and shanties—up near the lakes there. I know my Uncle Henry [Sack] came there not too long after we arrived there. I suppose the word spread there was lots of work, 1920. And he was a foreman on the road where there were all these Indians that were working there. A lot of them were from Cape Breton—Eskasoni and Wagmatcook, Nyanza—and it seems to me not too many from Whycocomagh. But there were a few: Charlie Poulette and William Poulette. And then some Goulds. But I know there were lots of Indians there.

Max Basque to R.H. Whitehead and Ronald Caplan, 9 March 1984. In *Cape Breton's Magazine.* 1989, No. 51:17.

Oh, as I might mention, 1920 we moved to Whycocomagh for a little while. And there was quite a crew raking oysters at Little Narrows.... there were 4 camps there—my uncle Gabriel's [Gabriel Sylliboy, half-brother to Max Basque's father] wigwam, tarpaper wigwam, and my father's. And Levi Poulette—he died only a few years ago. And Levi Poulette's parents, they were really old people. They weren't there to rake, they just wanted to be there with the crowd. They were raking oysters. They got two dollars a barrel, delivered at the wharf.... And my father used to rake all day. I remember he used to get up awful early in the morning.... And we'd have to put in long days if we wanted to get that barrel—rake all day for that barrel. And then row it across to where the little wharf is now.... And I remember the man kicking because one of the barrels—oh, several times—"Oh, you've got to get more in there." Cause they were short about that much. They had to be right level, for that two dollars.

Max Basque to R.H. Whitehead and Ronald Caplan, 9 March 1984. In *Cape Breton's Magazine.* 1989, No. 51:18-19.

ca 1910-1920

"I remember about the Indians coming," said Mary Wentzell, who spent the first 90 years of her life in Indian Point [Lunenburg County]. Her father, Captain Jeffrey Hyson, retired from fishing to open the first store in the community. "The Indians came from the reserve in Gold River by canoe to trade salmon for tobacco and molasses. That was summer barter. The salmon was never weighed. It was just a swap.... they wouldn't do business with my mother. If my father wasn't there they'd sit on the flagstone walk smoking clay pipes until he came home." Although the Micmac had been converted to Catholicism, they kept their old ways, said Mrs. Wentzell. Food would appear on unmarked graves in the cemetery. "They brought food for gifts to their spirits," she said. "But no one ever saw them bring it. They were very illusive [*sic*]."

Mary Wentzell to Jennifer James. "Micmac Legacy in Lunenburg County." *The Bridgewater Bulletin*. Bridgewater, N.S., 24 May 1989.

Matteo Glode and Jim Glode, cousins, were with Lord Dunraven at Dunraven's Bay, Queen's County, in 1876. Matteo was a good hunter, short little fellow. Matteo died at Pubnico Head, N.S.

Old Joe Paul, called "Old Mollie Joe," now dead. Died a very old man about 15 years ago. Had only one eye. Was with Lord Dunraven at Hunting Lake, Liscombe River, Guysborough County. He had a camp at Dreadnaught Dam, Liscombe River, to the east of Hunting Lake, Halifax County. The coals of his camp are yet to be seen. Lost his eye while out with Dunraven at that place. Had a large spruce tree on Lookout Hill, from which Molly [*sic*] Joe would look out for caribou. (Called Mollie Joe because he was old Mollie Cope's second husband.)

Matteo Jeremy, one of the finest hunters of his district. Camped for years at Fairy Lake, Queens County. Lived alone. Before he died, he came out to the settlement. Now dead. The Kejimkoojik club used to hoist a flag for him to come across with his canoe [to fetch them].

Abram Toney, good hunter, was found dead alongside the road, at Canaan River, near Tusket, Yarmouth County.

Will Carthy was a good hunter as well. He was found drowned in Great Lake, Pubnico, the same day as Toney was found dead.

Jeremiah Bartlett Alexis [alias Jerry Lonecloud] to Harry Piers, 29 April 1921. Nova Scotia Museum Printed Matter File.

Matteo Salome once killed 2 or 3 bears in Halifax County, not far from the Hants County boundary. The bounty on bears was $8.00 in Hants, and only $4.00 in Halifax. Matteo therefore took them to Windsor. Was asked in what county they were killed. He replied, "What do Bear know about County?" The story about him having killed his wives was probably not true.

Louis Noel McDonald to Harry Piers, 28 April 1921. Nova Scotia Museum Printed Matter File.

1921
Chief William Paul, son of Joseph Paul of the Peminuit Paul line, was born 19 July 1858 at South Cambridge, Massachusetts. He was elected chief at Shubenacadie, N.S., on 26 July 1921.

Harry Piers, n.d. Unpublished notes, Nova Scotia Museum Printed Matter File.

Micmac Hunter Abram ("Gabe") Hood, born 1853, died 1922:
"Gabe" (Abram) Hood, whose surname was really Jeremy, was born at
General's Bridge, Annapolis, N.S., in 1853. He was the son of old
Stephen Hood, of General's Bridge, who as a young man went to live
at Amherst, N.S., and lived there about 50 years, and who was also a
good hunter. [Stephen Hood was possibly a Penobscot who immi-
grated to Nova Scotia.]

"Gabe" Hood lived at River Philip, N.S., for about 30 years, and died
there, of paralysis, after about a couple of years illness, on Sunday, 12
February 1922. He was one of the best of Indian hunters, a great
"caller", and always to be depended upon. He went out ... with hunting
parties, many of them Americans, and used to hunt back of Parrsbor-
ough [sic]. Had hunted in Newfoundland with parties, for caribou. He
thoroughly knew the Malicite language as well as the Micmac. Big
Peter Paul of Shubenacadie, and the Chief at Truro, with others
attended his funeral.

Jeremiah Bartlett Alexis [alias Jerry Lonecloud] to Harry Piers, 21 February 1922. Nova
Scotia Museum Printed Matter File.

1922
"Abe" Hood, the great Micmac hunter, trapper and guide, has passed
over to the far-off hunting ground, says the Amherst *Daily News*. He was
one of the greatest hunters and moosecallers in the Maritime Provinces.
For years he accompanied General Dashwood in his many hunting
expeditions.

The Evening Echo. Halifax, 24 February 1922.
[Richard Lawes Dashwood was at Saint John, N.B., with the 15th Regt of Foot, about
1862 to 1868.]

I asked Dad one time, because we liked Millview, "Why did we leave
Millview?" He said, "Because they were going to put you boys in St.
Patrick's Home because you fellows weren't going to school." He says,
"We couldn't send you to school in Bedford.... The people in Bedford,
they said they didn't want you. Some bigshots from Halifax that live in
Bedford, they said, 'I won't let my children go to school with no Indian
kids.'" I guess they were the big money-makers for that school. But they
wouldn't have no more to do with that school if these Indian children
went to school. "So," he said, "we had to come back to Shubenacadie."
So we came to Shubenacadie. And we farmed.

320

Max Basque to R.H. Whitehead and Ronald Caplan, 9 March 1984. In *Cape Breton's Magazine.* 1989, No. 51: 25-26.

Micmac Indian John Jadis, born possibly about 1827 ... of Shubenacadie Reservation, N.S., is now (1923) about 96 years old, and has lived to see 4 generations of his descendents. He is a half-breed, his father having been an Englishman named Jadis, who lived over at or near Windsor, N.S. His mother was the daughter of the Indian Gorham Paul, of Shubenacadie.

John Jadis's first wife [Catherine] was the daughter of old Lewie [Louis] Morris of Shubenacadie. This Lewie Morris was one of the very best canoe paddlers in Nova Scotia, and used to successfully contend in canoe races, having as the rest of his crew, his brothers John Morris and Ben Morris. John Jadis had several children by his first wife. One daughter is the wife of Lewie Newell MacDonald, another is the wife of Isaac Cope, and another is the wife of Joe Cope.

John Jadis's second wife had been Mrs. [Mary Jeremy] Thomas, widow of Michael Thomas. He had no children by his second wife.

Louis Noel McDonald to Harry Piers, 20 November 1923. Nova Scotia Museum Printed Matter File.

1922

I remember an ancient Indian, a Micmac, whom we encountered on a bridge. There he stood, a bronze statue, with a profile like a medallion, his white drooping mustache giving him the appearance of a dignified walrus. We paused to speak with him; but only a few monosyllables issued from his trembling old lips: "Squaw dead. Children all married. Eighty-six year old. Sick now." (His great hand went to his chest, and his beautiful eyes turned heavenward.) About a mile back in the country, over the hills, there is a government reservation, with good shacks, where those of his tribe who are left make a living acting as guides, hunting and fishing.... His name was Matthew Pictou, he said. "Oh yes, very lonely now. Me so old." He did not mind in the least being sketched, as we feared he would, but I knew that life was about over for him when he turned away, after the picture was made, without even glancing at what the Artist had done. Perhaps the sight was fading from those dark eyes, and in his curious vanity he did not wish us to know it. We watched him vanish down the road, and once he turned and feebly waved to us; but I had the sense of his definite wish to be alone. We were aliens, after all, and

had little meaning for him. I wonder what he thought of all day long, as he wandered from his people and looked down into the water.
C.H. Towne. *Ambling Through Acadia.* 1923:100-101.

William Prosper, a very aged Micmac Indian, who was well-known as Soolian [Micmac for 'William'] Bill, died at the Truro Indian Reservation, Nova Scotia, about 3rd April, at the very great age, it is claimed, of one hundred and one years. He was born at Bay of Islands, Newfoundland, about 1822, as it is claimed; and he had many traditions of the old Beothuk Indians of Newfoundland which became extinct between 1810 and 1825. About 1848 he came to Whycocomagh, Cape Breton Island, and about 1860 came to Halifax and attended the welcome which the Indian representatives gave the Prince of Wales in that year and received some of the bounty money which the Prince distributed among the Tribe. He was first camped on a hill near Farrell's Pond, Dartmouth Lake, and later on the side of the stream where Greenvale School now is. He was a very prominent figure in the Halifax market, always standing in front of Walsh's hardware shop. About 1880 he moved to the Indian Reservation at Truro, Colchester County, and made his headquarters there ever since, though after coming to Halifax. For several years his health has been failing, although his mind was comparatively good. He was a man with many fine qualities and was a great favourite with all who came into contact with him, and these will have pleasant recollections of the good-hearted old Indian. He was a big man, tall, and straight as an arrow even in his old age. He was an expert cooper in his time, but did not excel as a hunter. He had a wonderful fund of tradition, and was appealed to for information regarding the old days, and the old customs of his tribe. He contributed quite a large sum of his savings to help build the chapel on the Truro reserve. None of his children survive him.
Jeremiah Bartlett Alexis [alias Jerry Lonecloud] to Harry Piers [who then wrote this obituary], 7 April 1923. Nova Scotia Museum Printed Matter File.

Mr. Lone Cloud says, "I remember Newell [Noel] Jeddore (descendant of Ned Jeddore, from whom Jeddore, N.S., is named). I helped buried [*sic*] him; he paid me $4.00 for digging his grave before he died. He died from old age, 84 when he died. (Newell Jeddore died about 25 years ago [1898].) Newell Jeddore said that in his time the Micmac Indians numbered over 70,000 Indians in Nova Scotia." Now Mr. Lone Cloud says there are not 7,000 Micmac Indians in Nova Scotia. "Newell

Micmac and Scottish settlers re-enact the 1773 arrival of the *Hector* at Pictou, N.S., 1923.

Jeddore said yellow fever carried many off; they died on their feet. Then small pock [*sic*] took off a good many. Consumption is now taking them off.... In the olden times there was nearly always a pigeon pair (4: 2 boys & 2 girls) in every family. Now this is all gone.... Furthermore, our wives don't like to be called after their husbands.... They don't like to get into white ways."

Jeremiah Bartlett Alexis [alias Jerry Lonecloud] to Clara Dennis. Public Archives of Nova Scotia, Halifax. Clara Dennis Collection, Scrapbook #1, 1923, rear of book. [Lonecloud's wife, Elizabeth Paul, refused to use her husband's surname.]

Enfield, Hants County, N.S. Jan'y 21, 1924
Mr. H. Piers. Dear Sir:
I am sending you my first attempt in Old Indian Story writing, as I promised you. I am sure it will require lots of patching up. You attend to that. In my next, I am going to send you the names of old Indians, as I remember them, who lived in Halifax County, Hants, Kings & Colchester in 1870. Chiefs and all the council men and their doings [see entries for 1867, 1870] and also the Indians of today, 1924. I'll call in again the next time I go to Halifax. Yours truly, J.C. Cope, Indian.

Joseph C. Cope to Harry Piers, 21 January 1924. Nova Scotia Museum Printed Matter File.

Jerry Lonecloud, Micmac, says that the making of birchbark canoes is now practically a thing of the past. The big birch trees from which large sheets of bark could be obtained are all gone. The last canoe which Lonecloud saw built, and the last one he knows of, was built about 1911 (about three years before the beginning of the Great War) by Matteo Jeremy at or close to New Grafton, about 2 or 3 miles from Fairy Lake (part of Kejimkujik Lake), northwest part of Queens County, N.S.

The only Micmac Indians in Nova Scotia that Lonecloud knows who could now build a birchbark canoe are Jim Glode of Shubenacadie, who is blind and probably about 100 years old (exact age is not known); he came from near Kejimkujik way, Queens County. [The second is] Peter Paul of Truro, who is about 54 years old, and was born at Morris's Lake, near Dartmouth, N.S., a brother of the Paul [John Denney Paul] who made the scale model of a Micmac canoe which is in the Provincial Museum.

Lonecloud says he has assisted at making canoes, and knows how they are built, but he does not now know such essentials as the measurements of the various parts, which were done by fingers, elbow lengths, etc. These correct measurements are hard to remember. A canoe for the woods, for hunting and going up streams and portaging was about 16 ft long. A seashore canoe was about 18 to 19 ft. long.

Harry Piers, 1 December 1924. Unpublished notes, Nova Scotia Museum Printed Matter File.

A Short Unwritten Indian History About Awiskookak, the Mohawk Indian Spies, by Joe C. Cope, Micmac Indian, Enfield, N.S.

Now, what would we do if some very powerful nation drove us out of our beloved Country [as the Micmac, according to this account, drove the Mohawk from the Maritimes]? Would we not do our dirtiest? If we could. To make its newly acquired Country as unpleasant as possible? Now, that is just what Mohawk Indians tried their best to do, to Micmacs. [Chief Jacques-Pierre Peminuit] Paul says only on too many occasions they succeeded. The Mohawks swore eternal vengeance upon Micmacs, but luckily, the appearance of Black Robed White Man and His Religion put an end to that bad piece of Business, as far as killing and scalping was concerned.

But the sworn vengeance upon Micmac Indians was not to be so easily forgotten. For about two hundred years after these two Tribes of Indians were converted to Christianity, Mohawk Indian spies, some say 100 Men, of course divided into parties of 6 or 7, all picked Men, would come down to Nova Scotia every summer, as soon as the leaves and other green stuff grew large enough to hide in. Then and only then the Micmacs had good reason to be a little cautious in their Movements. These Men visited every Indian village from Yarmouth to Cape North in Cape Breton. They were very annoying, like Night Hawks, disappear during the day, and at dusk they would let themselves [be] known by throwing stones at the camps, imitating the warble of birds, hoot of an owl, and start every dog in a village Barking. But many a time they were more than well paid for their sport.

The first few hundred years these spies were very cruel. Murdering innocent women and children, setting fires to all the Micmacs best hunting grounds. [This was the practice of the Mohawk Ranger companies, brought in by the English in the eighteenth century to exterminate the Micmac.] Paul says that all the old Barrens, all through this country are the works of Mohawks. But since the Christianity came in vogue, although it did not prevent them from Making their annual visits as usual, these spies became more lenient, as civilization grew and spreaded finally. About seventy five years ago they gave up the Idea. As a bad job. One squaw shot three of them along the shore of Bras D'Or Lake; another is buried at Chapel Island, Potlotek, C.B. [Cape Breton Island].

But old man Noel Lewis, a well-known Indian around Dartmouth, years ago had the worst experience with these spies. While [he was] camping near Antigonish, one of these Mohawks crept In to his camp while they were asleep, and snatched a one-year-old baby boy from his mother's arms and made off with him. But the cries of [the] child awakened the parents. Old Noel said, "I jumped up, grabbed my gun, and made after them as fast as my legs would let me. I heard the Child's cries, and followed it. As I had nothing to hinder my speed, I soon overtook them. When they saw I was within about twenty yards behind, they dropped the boy, and I thanked them with two big loads of buck shot as they disappeared in darkness. Them fellows did not bother me any more that summer. On a second occasion, about five years after, they did not make another attempt to kidnap any of my children. But they lured my hunting dog to follow them. My dog was lost for a week. When it returned, it was clean shaven from its nose to the tip of its tail, and painted in all the colors of a Rain-Bow."

A whole Book could be written about these spies. But strange thing about them. They never molested the white people, and were very little known by them.

"Glooscap the second, J.C. Cope." Joseph C. Cope to Harry Piers, 21 January 1924. Nova Scotia Museum Printed Matter File.

Mr. H. Piers, Dear sir: Your letter and one of your Micmac Indian Books came to hand safely. Many Thanks. In regard to Micmac Indians who lived in Halifax County in 1870, is somewhat puzzling. As mostly all Indians belonging to Shubenacadie and all along the line generally spent their summer months either at Dartmouth Lake Indian camping grounds or at Tufts Cove. But I'll do my best to place every one of them in their own respective Counties, &c.

Since I sent you the other paper I have been working on a new Invention in shape of a Rat Trap. A Wholesale Killer. A Trap that will destroy from one Rat to 1000 at night. I'll have one made in week's time, ready for a test. Enfield station House is full of them. I'll test it there first. If it works all right I'll show it to you.

Yours truly, J.C. Cope.

Joseph C. Cope to Harry Piers, 31 January 1924. Nova Scotia Museum Printed Matter File.

And then I went hunting. I really loved hunting.... I shot a moose on the first day of the season; I was 14. I shot 3 that fall ... but not an ounce of that went to waste. Even though we had no deep freeze or refrigerators. And moose meat won't salt very well.... my mother fried a lot of it, and put it in this 5-gallon creamery crock, and lots of fat. Put fried, and put it there with fat. And then after it was full, cover it with some weight. And it'll keep. Cause it's all cooked and in fat; you just take a bit of it out.

I shot one the first day of the season. I had no license, I was only 14. And then I wounded another one 3 weeks after. And I went back home and my uncle Henry Sack, he used to hunt moose but he didn't get good money for it. And I told him about wounding this moose with a great big set of horns. And we followed next day, tracked it across to Sandy Desert. I always think of that—boy, he was a real woodsman. He never even slowed down, tracking that moose, and I couldn't even see the tracks. And ... he said, "I'll track the moose. You keep an eye out." We got into the woods and he was saying, "Well, the next time we come to a creek or something, we'll have lunch." First thing I looked, and there's a moose. And he saw it about that time and he just pointed. And me, I was only 14. I up and shot it. And the moose dropped, just more or less turned. My Uncle Henry got mad; he said, "You son-of-a-gun, you shot a cow moose." And sure enough … it wasn't the moose we were after, it was a different moose.…

And next day, me and my mother and father went to where this moose was. And a 24-pound bag of flour—almost filled it up with the fat from the insides of this cow moose. Oh, it was really fat. About 20th of October.… And quite a few of the men-folks—Thomas McDonald and the Maloneys—packed it out. We had a horse and wagon, and we took the back road for it, brought it out.

Max Basque to R.H. Whitehead and Ronald Caplan, 9 March 1984. In *Cape Breton's Magazine*, 1989, No. 51:26-27.

[In an earlier interview with R.H. Whitehead, Max Basque had said that he was the last boy at Shubenacadie to be given a feast upon the killing of his first moose.]

Rough Notes of Proceedings of the Sylliboy Case of 1928:
Port Hood, C.B., July 4/28
King & Sylyboy [King *vs* Gabriel Silliboy]
Mr. MacLennan KC for prosecution
Mr. Joseph MacDonald & Mr. John MacKenzie for defense

Joe Christmas called: (John Gould sworn as interpreter)
Sworn: Exd. by Mr. MacKenzie: Live at Sydney, Nova Scotia. Am 74 years of age. Chief of Micmac Sydney Band, North Sydney Band, Ass't Deputy Chief to Grand Chief. Grand Chief then [was] John Denys. He is dead now. Accused is Grand Chief now. When Chief, I had to make rules for tribe. Made myself familiar with traditional rights of tribe. While I was chief made rules for people not to disturb other people's rights. Told them they must not hunt when fur not fit, but that they could at any other time. For example, when muskrats had little ones, must not kill them. When fur was fit, they cd. dry and sell it, they could hunt. I am a Micmac and was chief for six years. Became chief in 1909. Heard that according to treaty we had right to hunt & fish at any time. I cannot read. Heard it from our grandfathers. Heard that King of England made treaty with Micmacs, with the whole tribe. (Objected to.) Remember hearing that goods were given—blankets—under treaty. (Objected to.) About 65 years ago. In the fall before Christmas. Big coats and old fashioned guns & powder horns also. And some hide

to make moccasins. And some food. In the spring potatoes & {?} some for seed. Tobacco too. And some spears for spearing eels. Where people had little farms they got oats. These goods distributed every six months. Where people hunting they were supplied with powder shot & guns. My grandfather got word from Halifax 62 or 63 years ago and his brother. They and another man went to Halifax. One Campbell was Member and sent for us. Looking to get school for Micmac children. After two years got school. They were representing Cape Breton Micmacs. Gov't at Halifax at same time surveyed all Indian Reservations. They had been surveyed before but white people were interfering and that was one of reasons for going to Halifax. They got new survey. From my earliest recollections no one ever interfered with our rights to hunt and fish at any time. About 65 years ago with my father when he got goods to distribute. At that time only one Indian agent in Cape Breton. Old Judge Dodd's father. Goods obtained from him. Dodds told people goods came from Government.

Xd [examined by] Mr. Maclennan: Living in Sydney since in 1875. Previous to that in Escasconi [*sic*] County of Cape Breton. Never lived at Whycocomagh. I did not hunt. Never killed a muskrat a fox or deer. No knowledge of hunting or trapping. Never saw my people hunting. Have seen them coming from woods. I did Indian work making baskets & handles tubs etc. When I was a boy used to fish around shore.

Reexd Mr. Mackenzie: Have seen my people coming in with fur animals. Know they went hunting and trapping.

Gabriel Sylyboy called: Sworn: Exd. Mr. MacDonald: Accused. Live at Whycocomagh on Indian Reservation there. I am Grand Chief Micmacs of Nova Scotia. All Nova Scotia as well as Cape Breton. Start to go trapping on Halloween. For last 34 years. Get few muskrats then. Did not kill fox. Found fox dead in an old snare. Killed the muskrats whose pelts were found. Am a Micmac Indian of Nova Scotia tribe. Never interfered with in my hunting before. Heard of some Indians on other side of Truro being interfered with a year ago. Since I was boy heard that Indians got from King free hunting and fishing at all times. Still believe Treaty good. When officer took pelts I told him I had treaty. He sd he knew nothing about that. I sd. let me go and I'll show you copy of treaty. I sd. if I wanted to I cd. prevent him taking furs but as he didn't know about Treaty I wd let him take furs. Under Treaty get from Gov't blankets and flour and some shoes & long coats. Still get them. Haven't got any for a year. From Mr. Boyd Indian Superintendent River Bourgoise. Where there is no game in hard months {?} get order for $10.00 for goods in store. In Spring, get seeds. Gov't put up & maintain schools on every reservation. Putting up Home at Shubenacadie. All by virtue of Treaty. In Treaty promised to teach us. Did not know nor believe I was breaking any law in taking muskrats when I did.

Xd Mr. Maclennan: Grand chief elected for life. Have about six subchiefs under me. I am a sort of king among Indians. Had been hunting four days at Askillou [Askilton?] before skins taken. Killed 14 all told. Meat good. Skin will dry on stretcher in a half a day. Indians honest lawabiding since Treaty. Don't know who set snare in which fox taken. Too early for fox. Fur of fox no good but fur of muskrat good. Took fox out of snare & threw it on one side. Old man with me skinned it. Skin with muskrats in my tent. Found fox second day I was trapping. Indian Reservation on South bounded by land of Donald Allan Mc{guirc?}. Runs a mile & a half back. Includes Indian Island Southern boundary of Reservation about 16 or 20 miles from where I was hunting. Told officer that I had treaty with King and that I had right to furs. Have not got furs back. Never killed a kitten [a baby muskrat] yet. Killed these with gun. Setting dead falls too.
Rexd Mr. MacDonald: Used every bit of flesh of muskrat for food.

Andrew Alek called: Sworn: Exd. Mr. Mackenzie: Live on Indian Reserve near St. Peters. Born there & lived there all my life. I am 78 years old. Mostly fishing. All kinds of fish. Am a Micmac. Micmacs had right to fish all they cd. eat or sell at all seasons of year. Remember getting gifts from Gov't. When I was 10 years old father had a team. No one else had a team. At first went to Sydney for blankets. Father & mother & each child got blanket. Went with my father to Sydney for blankets. Got them from Dodd. Knew him when I saw him. Got coats as well and hide for moccasins. And flour Indian meal gun powder shot. In Spring wd. get seed. Potatoes oats corn and turnip. Nobody ever interfered with our fishing and hunting.

Xd. Mr. Maclennan: No school our reservation when I was a boy. Am not a hunter. Have often seen others go hunting.

Andrew Bernard called: Sworn: Exd. Mr. MacDonald: Am 78 years of age. Born at Nyanza, Victoria Co. on Indian Reservation. Bro't up at Little Bras d'or. About 20 Indian {illegible} lived there. They moved to reservation at North Sydney. [My] Father [was named] Francis Bernard. He was a Captain a sub Chief of Micmacs in Cape Breton. Am a Micmac. Remained at North Sydney 40 or so years. For 14 years of that time trimmed coal. About 21 years ago returned to Reservation at Whycocomagh. Farming. Receive aid from Mr. Boyd Indian Agent and Father Maclennan of Glendale also Agent. Receive $8.00 a month not cash but order for goods. Remember my father receiving flour coats gun powder & shots fish spears. From Mr. Dodd in Sydney. Old man Dodd of all. After his death from Dr. Cameron Indian Agent at Christmas Id. [Island]. Micmacs can fish or shoot any thing they want all year round. Father told me that. Got right from King.

Francis Gould called: Sworn: Exd. Mr. MacKenzie: Live at Escasoni. 74 years of age. Remember my grandfather going to Sydney & getting blankets long coat corn (3 bushels) gun powder flour sometimes seed corn beads for moccasins. He told me he got these from the King. Under the Treaty. We promised to keep Treaty & got these things in return. That is what my grandfather told me.

Mr. MacDonald tenders original volume Nova Scotia Archives Certified Copy of Treaty with Micmacs 1727 (2) Pages 672 *et seq* more especially p. 682....

Ben E. Christmas called: Sworn. Exd. Mr. Mackenzie: Live on new Indian Reserve Sydney. Chief of that band nearly six years. Two of chiefs whose signature appears on Treaty [of 1752] was Andrew Hadley Martin [André Martin; André is 'Antle' in Micmac, often corrupted further into 'Hadley' by English speakers, who then compound it as 'Andrew Hadley']. He came from Nyanza Victoria Co. And Gabriel Martin. He came from Escasoni. Indians believe Treaty still in force. Nothing ever pd. Indians for cancellation or revoking of treaty. Treaty never revoked so far as they are concerned. Still believe they have rights of hunting and fishing at all times.

Inverness County Court. King *vs* Sylyboy. Minutes 1928. Public Archives of Nova Scotia, Halifax. Courtesy Bruce Wildsmith.

John and Malti Francis were brothers, they had no women and they lived together in the little house where John lives now. I was tenting alone in a little field I had from my father, in the woods by the road to Caledonia [*ca* 1928]. I was building the little house I have now. It is about a mile up the road from John and Malti's house.

One day John came to me. He looked pretty serious. He said, "Something is the matter with Malti. He is acting funny. I don't like it. You better come." So I went down to their house. Malti was sitting inside, by the door. He wouldn't say anything. He just sat and stared. His eyes were queer. I never saw a man's eyes like that. It made you scared to look at them. I said, "Malti, are you sick, or what is the matter?" He didn't answer.

By and by he got up and took some cups and plates off the shelf and threw them on the floor so they broke. Then he sat down again. I said, "If you keep on doing that you won't have anything to eat off." He didn't say anything. I went outside with John. John said, "Last night he said, very quiet, that he was going to kill me. He got the rifle and pointed it at me. So the first time he wasn't looking I hid all the cartridges and I hid the shotgun too. This morning I woke up and he was standing in the middle of the floor with the rifle. He had found a shotgun shell somewhere, and he was trying to push it into the breech of the rifle. It wouldn't go, but he kept working at it and working at it, till he got it all crushed down in the breech. He pointed the rifle at me then. But of course it would not fire. But I got scared then. I hid the axe and the knives and came up to get you. You know what I think? I think Malti is *eloowawea*." That is the Injun word for crazy.

I didn't know what to do about that. I thought it was none of my business so I went back to my work. That afternoon John, and Andrew Francis, who lived across the road from John and Malti, took some grub and a canoe and went away up the river. They stayed up there. They were scared. Andrew's wife came to me. She was scared. She said, "You got to do something about Malti, Sam. He's bad." I said I didn't know what to do. I said, "You better send Little Chief down and tell Mr. Brown." Little Chief was Malti's boy. John used to call him that for fun. Mr. Cecil Brown lived in Milton. He was Indian Agent then.

He came up and talked to Malti a little. Malti wouldn't talk. Mr. Brown came up to my tent. He said, "You better go down and stay with Malti tonight, Sam. He is dangerous. You go down and keep him quiet somehow till morning. In the morning I will get a car and we will send Malti to the crazy hospital in Dartmouth."

So along towards dark I went down to spend the night with Malti. He wouldn't talk to me. He sat at the table. There was a loaf of bread and he would break off pieces and chew them. Then he made a sweep with his arm and knocked the loaf and the pieces of bread off the table on to the floor. I said, "You better go to bed, Malti." So he got into bed. I lit the kerosene lamp and stood it on the table. It was near the bed and I could watch him. I sat on the floor across the room, in the corner, with my back against the wall, and watched Malti.

He had covered himself all up with the blanket. But every once in a while he would lift a corner of the blanket ... slowly ... slowly ... and stare out at me. His eyes were awful wild. So I tried to keep awake, but in the middle of the night I went to sleep. I woke up sudden. The house was dark. Malti had put the lamp out. I thought he was there in the dark, coming for me. I lit a match, quick. The bed was empty. The door was open. He was gone.

Samuel Freeman Gloade to Thomas H. Raddall, 1944. Raddall Papers, Dalhousie Archives, Killam Library, Dalhousie University, Halifax.

Malti was my brother. He hunted and fished like all us Injuns, but he was a good worker, too. He would work in lumber mills, and went lumbering and river-driving. Malti was a quiet man, didn't say much. He went to the war in 1915, in the 112th Battalion. When that was broken up in England he went into the Forestry Corps.... When Malti come home from war he married an Indian woman and they had a baby, that is the boy Joe, the one I call Chief.... Malti worked along steady and saved a little money. Then his woman died and he felt bad. He felt bad a long time. He spent his money, too; most of it anyhow.

He and Chief came to live in this place with me. Malti slept on a bunk downstairs and Chief and I slept overhead. There was nothing down-stairs but the bunk and a stove and a bench and a table and a shaving-horse, like you see now. Malti was 'sponsible for the wood; he got all the firewood and the wood for making baskets and axe-handles and all that. I was 'sponsible for the grub. I got money guiding sports and sometimes I would work a little somewhere. So would Malti. He was a little bigger than me and could work harder.

All of a sudden I begun to notice something funny about Malti. It was the year they begun to build the dam at Big Falls (1929). Malti was getting wood for winter. He would cut it in the woods and carry it home on his back. All of a sudden Malti begun to carry bigger and bigger logs on his back. It was all green birch and maple and sometimes oak and that is very heavy stuff to lug if you have to lug it far. Well, Malti begun to bring home great big sticks of maple and oak on his back. I saw him bring home a piece of oak that must weigh two hundred pounds. I said to myself, Malti is getting very strong.

Then Malti took a notion to dig a little ditch to drain the water away from under the house. He dug it a way and then there was a couple of big boulders that would weigh maybe two hundred, maybe four hundred pounds, I don't know. Come over and see them. Look! There they are, just where he put 'em. That's some rock, eh? You couldn't lift that one, eh? Nor could I. Nor could anybody I know.

But Malti did. I looked out one morning and there he was. He had dug a hole round that big boulder, and he stood 'bout knee-deep in that hole and he was tugging at the stone. I called out the window, "Leave it alone a while and I will cut a pry and we will pry it out." Malti didn't let on he heard me. He just stopped and grabbed hold of that rock and swung it up out of the hole. By gracious I never saw anything like that. Then he began to roll the rock towards the woods. Whenever it come up against another rock, Malti would just stoop quick and pick it up and drop it on the other side. I said to myself, By gracious there is something queer about this. And all this time he didn't say anything, just kept looking straight ahead of him. I said to Chief, "Malti must think he's the strongest man in the world all of a sudden."

That night, in the middle of the night, I woke up and heard Malti working downstairs by the stove. Chief woke up too. I looked down the hole where the ladder is and saw Malti mixing flour to make bread. I said, "Malti, we got lots of bread." He looked up then, and his eyes was awful queer. He said, "I ain't mixing this for you." He had the lamp lit and after a while he put the pan in the oven and went over to the bench. We had a dog, a little pup. The pup was laying on the floor by Malti's feet. Chief went back to bed. So did I.

All of a sudden we heard the pup give a queer sound, a little yelp like, not very loud. We looked down through the hole. Malti had a stick of hardwood, a piece of firewood, and he was pounding the dog on the head. The dog was dead already but Malti went on pounding and pounding till the dog's head was all mush and the blood running over the floor.

I looked at Chief and Chief looked at me. We didn't say anything but we were scared. All the rest of the night we watched Malti through the hole. He just sat on the bench looking down at the dog, and every once in a while he would open his mouth and let out a bark, just like a dog.

As soon as it come daylight we went down the ladder and set about making breakfast, just like nothing had happened. Malti didn't say anything. But he come and ate his breakfast just like usual. He ate good, I mean. After breakfast Chief and me sat talking and watching Malti out of the corner of our eye. Chief was only a boy then, about 9 or 10 year old.

By and by Malti got up and took his knife—his Injun knife, I mean, the kind we called crooked-knife. He felt himself through the shirt ... here, where the heart is ... and he took the knife in his right hand and begun making little jabs at that place, just little swings, not enough force to push the knife through the shirt, but just like he was trying the place and the swing, getting ready for a good jab....

I got scared then and went up the road for Sam Glode. Sam came down but he couldn't do anything with Malti. So I went across the road where my brother Andrew lives and told him. We were scared, by gracious. So I said, "Let's go moose hunting," and me and Andrew took a canoe and went up the river. When we come back Sam and some men were taking Malti away in a car. That's all I know. You will have to ask Sam about the rest. I never saw Malti again.

That's the way it was. Malti begun to get awful strong, then his eyes went funny, then he beat the dog to death. Then I knowed he was crazy.
John Francis to Thomas H. Raddall, 1944. Raddall Papers, Dalhousie Archives, Killam Library, Dalhousie University, Halifax.

A few years after that I had to go to Halifax for something and I went across to Dartmouth to see Malti. One of the attendants took me to a little room. Malti was in there, lying on a couch, by himself. He was clean and dressed nice. He opened his eyes and looked at me, blank-like.

I said, "Malti, do you know me?"

He said, "Yes, you're Sam Glode." And he shut his eyes again.

I didn't know what to say. I said, "How do you feel, Malti?"

He said, "I'm all right."

I tried to think of something to say. I said, "Malti, do you ever think of your people and the woods and everything?"

That was the wrong thing to say, but I didn't know. He opened his eyes very wide, and I saw that queer look come in them. His eyes was on fire like a cat's. He said, very loud, "No, I never want to think of those god-damn people nor the woods nor any god-damn thing."

I thought he would jump at me. So did the attendant, I guess, because he took Malti by the arm and hustled him out of the room quick. So I come home then. That was the last time I ever see Malti. I guess he's living yet, up there. But, you know, he must be very crazy if he don't think sometimes of his people, and the woods, and everything.

Samuel Freeman Gloade to Thomas H. Raddall, 1944. Raddall Papers, Dalhousie Archives, Killam Library, Dalhousie University, Halifax.

[Raddall adds a note to say that Malti lived to be an old man; he died at the mental hospital at Cole Harbour in the autumn of 1956. His body was shipped to Liverpool and buried by Father Delaney. John Francis died in 1947, and Sam Gloade in 1957.]

1930

Micmac Indian Jeremiah [Bartlett Alexis] Lone Cloud died at Halifax, April 1930.

Note in Harry Piers' handwriting, on the outside of an envelope. Unpublished notes, Nova Scotia Museum Printed Matter File.

1932

Truro, July 27—Four witnesses testified in the police court today at the preliminary hearing of Stephen Glode, an Indian of the Truro reservation charged with setting fire to a summer cottage at Shortt's Lake. He was remanded until Thursday. W.P. King, local insurance adjustor, Joseph Julian, Indian, Henry Sack and Alex Cope and McIsaac [Isaac] Sack gave evidence. It was stated in evidence that Glode had stated he was paid for firing the cottage.

The Halifax Herald. Halifax, 28 July 1932:2.

1932

INDIAN MISSION WILL NOT BE HELD

Sydney, 27 July—for the first time in nearly 200 years there will be no "Indian Mission" at Chapel Island in the Bras d'Or Lakes this August. The economic situation has hit the people, explained Gabriel Silliboy, grand chief of the Micmacs, after a conference with Benjamin Christmas, Chief of Membertou Reserve, John Gould and other leading chiefs....

The Halifax Herald. Halifax, 28 July 1932:2.

1932

MISSION IS GREAT SUCCESS

St. Peter's, Aug. 1—Giving vigorous denial to the many stories circulated that the Indian Mission had been called off this season for the first time in 200 years, representatives of the Micmacs arriving in town today declared the present Mission one of the most successful ever held. It began on Wednesday, July 27, and the closing ceremonies will take place August 3. The Indian Mission Sunday celebration was carried out with all the beautiful ritual and color proper to the festival. Rev. Leo J. Keats, PP, St. Peter's, at the request of His Excellency Bishop Morrison, who did all possible to accommodate Grand Chief Sylliboy, conducted the Mission. Four or five spiritual exercises were held each day, and the white people were kind enough to stay away from Chapel Island so as not to disturb the Indians in prayer.

"Depression has not hit our people very much," said one of the Micmacs. "We are getting more Government relief than ever before, but the depression hit the white people so hard they have no money to come by steamer and car to our Mission. Think perhaps that is better, as many do not come to pray...."

Since a half-century the Mission has been conducted by the Red Island's parish priest, until 1931 when the Bishop asked Father Keats of St. Peter's to take charge. His first act was to ban the whites as intruders....

The Halifax Herald. Halifax, 2 August 1932:3.

1932
Truro, Oct. 16—Peter Wilmot, ex-Micmac chief at the Indian reservation here, who is in poor health, is much pleased over a letter he received from Premier Harrington as follows: "I am informed that you have reached your 108th birthday during the past summer and that you are probably the oldest person in Nova Scotia. I congratulate you upon attaining this age."

The Halifax Herald. Halifax, 27 October 1932:3.

1932
Peter Wilmot, ex-Micmac Chief, died at the home of his son, Charles Wilmot, at the Indian Reservation, Truro, at 11 o'clock last night [27 December 1932]. His death was wholly due to old age, he having no organic disease. His church record[s] reporting his baptism are said to bear out his claim that he was 106 years old. He was born [baptised] at Pictou Landing, according to this, on [St Anne's Day] July 26, 1826.

Harry Piers, 28 December 1932. Unpublished notes, Nova Scotia Museum Printed Matter File.

1932
"I wonder if there are people still living in Halifax who can recall the notorious Cape Breton Indian, who was well known throughout eastern

Peter Wilmot, former chief at Pictou Landing, N.S., shortly after his 106th birthday, 26 July 1932. He died several months later.

Nova Scotia a half century ago under the nickname 'Too Late Squeak'um'"
writes S.A. MacDonald, New York. "And the story of how he received
that name is a strange and a sordid one. When the cholera epidemic
struck Halifax about 65 or 70 years ago, so virulent was the plague and
so fearful were the inhabitants of contamination that only prisoners and
ne'er-do-wells could be induced to work at burying the dead. And so
gruesome and dangerous was the task that even these men were paid for
their services, the sum fixed being, I think, a shilling a head. Among those
pressed into service to dispose of the dead was Gabriel, then a police
character and the story goes that one day while engaged in putting a
supposed corpse under the grounds, the dead suddenly came to life and
protested his interment. Being unwilling to lose his shilling when he had
it partly earned, Gabriel promptly finished his helpless victim with a blow
over the head, at the same time uttering the classic remark that stuck to
him through the remainder of his life: 'Too late squeak'um!'"

S.A. MacDonald, quoted in *The Halifax Herald*. Halifax, 3 December 1932:7.

[This story is apparently a fabrication, as the next entry may show.]

1932

Miss Mary C. MacKenzie, writing from Baddeck, gives another version
of the "Squeak'um" story as follows: "Many Cape Bretoners other than
myself were doubtless astonished to read "Home History from Abroad"
in the shape of a legend of "Too Late Squeak'um" from the pen of S.A.
MacDonald, New York, formerly of Cape Breton.... That you may be
assured of the extreme absurdity of Mr. MacDonald's story, we append
the legend as we know it, in the Island home of law-abiding "Too Late
Squeak'um", a legend decidedly more in keeping with Micmac character.

The hero was not Gabriel, but Joe. Hundreds of American tourists, as
well as Nova Scotians, have seen and talked with Old Joe in front of his
little roadside house in Nyanza Reservation, and many of them will regret
to learn that he passed away two years ago, at the old age of one hundred
and eleven (111).

Well, Joe in his youth, like many another son of the countryside,
enjoyed drinking eggs. The method followed was a slick opening of the
end of a raw egg, a deft up-tipping, and one luscious swallow! At one of
these occasional snacks, Joe heard a despairing "Cheep-cheep!" from
somewhere in the region of his palate. It was as he wiped the back of an
appreciative hand across a satisfied smile, that he uttered the well-known
words, "Too Late Squeak'um!"

Mary MacDonald, quoted in *The Halifax Herald*. Halifax, 10 December 1932:7.

1933

Dear Mr. Piers,

Today I saw Alex Cope of the Indian Reserve in re the old Flint Lock gun I sent you. He is a man of 50 years and says the Gun was used by his Father Alex or more commonly [known] as Sandy Cope who died 1930 aged 76 years and also by his Grandfather the Late Frank Cope who died in 1915 aged 86. This Frank Cope was a son of that well known old woman "Old Molly Cope" who died I think died about 1900 at the great age of 104. I well remember stories of Her when I was a child told by my Grandfather who knew her well. For many years she made a business of catching Bear Cubs when very young and raising them until Partly grown & taking them to Halifax used to sell them at fancy Prices to Officers in the Garrison, at that time Bears were Prized as Pets or Novelties. This Molly Cope was said to have belonged to a Pioneer White Family somewhere in N.B. or Cumb[erland] Co. and Stolen by Indians when Very Young after she grew up she went back to Visit her parents but only for a short time, when she returned to the Indians. You might find out more about her History from Miss Clara Dennis of the Halifax Herald, who wrote an article re her for the Herald not very long ago....

Howard Cruikshank to Harry Piers, 5 February 1933. Nova Scotia Museum Printed Matter File.

1933

Dear Mr. Piers,

I saw Aleck Cope yesterday and he says old Molly Cope's husband's name was Francis Cope, who was drowned from a Canoe near Indian Point, Ship Harbour Lake [now Lake Charlotte, Halifax County]. He was subject to weak spells or Perhaps Fits, & fell from canoe while in Company with an Indian boy, & drowned. This man was a direct descendent of the Major Jean Baptiste Cope who was first to Sign a Peace Treaty with the English, although he was at one time very bitter against them, but after signing the Peace Treaty had a great influence in bringing over other Indians to sign. Aleck says there is a missing link in their family History that he cannot find, between this Major Jean Baptiste Cope & his Great Grandfather Francis, but says he knows for certain they are the direct descendents. He tells me that Dr. Jerry Lone Cloud, who you well knew, had a book with much historical matter in it Pertaining to the old treaty, Laws, & some of their Family records, but he loaned the book to some American & never got it back. I wonder what became of the old Treaty written on Beaver Parchment which "Lone Cloud" showed me on a visit to my Place not more than a year before he died. Now if you wish to write Aleck Cope, "The Reserve", Truro, in re to any thing, I am sure you will receive any information that he has or can get. You will find him very intelligent, a graduate of Truro Academy I think, and have found him a good Friend of over 24 years experience.

Yours very truly, Howard S. Cruikshank.

Howard Cruikshank to Harry Piers, 28 February 1933. Nova Scotia Museum Printed Matter File.

[Cruikshank was a taxidermist who often collected artifacts, specimens and information for the Nova Scotia Museum during Piers' term as curator.]

1933

Bear River, July 25—Shades of the days when Indians alone roved Nova Scotia's forests were seen at the Indian reservation here today by 300 people.... Presenting a series of ceremonial [sic], members of the reservation revived all the old Micmac customs of their forefathers, the function beginning in the morning and lasting throughout the day.... It was a colourful scene, with chiefs in the feathered head dress of their tribe, and braves dancing and whooping as they carried out the famous war and snake dances. Their renditions of the hymns taught them by the missionaries and the other songs which they gave in unison were impressive features, with the Micmacs gathered around the camp fires.... the committee in charge comprised Louis Peters, John Pictou and John McEwan. John Paul, chief of the Micmacs in the western section of the Province was in charge of the ceremonial order, while an interesting figure was Honorary Chief John Malti, oldest Micmac in the district....

The Halifax Herald. Halifax, 26 July 1933:3.

I spent New Year's Eve in Dunkirk [in the Merchant Marine, 1939]. There was a ship hit one of them magnetic mines.... I forget the name of the ship, but it hit—blew up—struck something. And when the smoke drifted away, it was almost a calm night. And all this black smoke. And we had lots of iron we were bringing from Belgium ... it looked like a big iron bridge, and I think the other ship had the same thing. But when the smoke cleared, the ship had already sunk. And I remember there was another fireman standing by me. He said, "That's what'd happen to us if we ever hit one of them things." It went down fast.

Max Basque to R.H. Whitehead and Ronald Caplan, 9 March 1984. In *Cape Breton's Magazine.* 1989, No. 52:56.

I was going to get married when I was on the cable ship, *John W. MacKay*. I had a girl friend in England. 1940. I said, "If I ever get back to Canada, I'll get a job on a tugboat or cable ship." I said, "I'll get you to come over." And I used to write letters to her. And, I'd write. Well, at that time there was no air mail. Took months.... And I'd mark Number 1 letter, Number 2 letter, Number 3 letter. Every week or two I'd write. And the last letter I got from her, she wrote around the 28th of December, 1940. And I kept writing.... She got killed on the first big air raid in Hull. I was shipmates with her father, Ben Wadden. And there were three of them home: Mrs. Wadden, and Mary my girl friend, and Elizabeth—she was about 13. And the first big air raid in Hull, they cleaned up the works. Never.... that was the end of that.

Max Basque to R H Whitehead and Ronald Caplan, 9 March 1984. In *Cape Breton's Magazine*. 1989, No. 51:17.

[In an earlier interview with R.H. Whitehead, Max Basque said that he had gone to the Waddens' street hoping to find Mary, but there was absolutely nothing left of any of the houses.]

The Navy recruiting officer looked at me. He said, "Are you an Indian?" I said, "Yes, sir." "Sorry, we don't take Indians in the Navy. But," he said, "you're not a full-blooded Indian." "No, I'm not," I said. "I don't think there's any full-blooded Indians east of Winnipeg!" I said. "But on the books I'm an Indian. Here's my border-crossing card." You know, we used to carry those cards, that I'm an Indian, this and that. Didn't have any pictures, like. "Well," he said, "you've got a French name: B-a-s-q-u-e. We'll sign you as a Frenchman." I said, "No, you won't ... that's not a French name, anyway. It's Basque—it's from northern Spain." "Well," he said, "we'll sign you as a Basque." I said, "No. On the books, I was born on an Indian reservation and I've always gone as an Indian all my life.... Disown my own race, just to get into the Navy? I'm a Canadian, even if I am an Indian. Same as you are. I don't know who you are, but you're a Canadian first." He said yes. I said, "I'm a Canadian too. I was born here in Canada." "Well, I don't make the rules," he said. "They make them up in Ottawa."

Max Basque to R.H. Whitehead and Ronald Caplan, 9 March 1984. In *Cape Breton's Magazine*. 1989, No. 52:58.

1945

With the death some few years ago of "Chief Lone Cloud", there was removed, perhaps the one Micmac who was easily recognizable to all

Haligonians. He was "Chief Medicine Man" of the Nova Scotia Micmacs. With his graying hair, tied in neat little pigtails, and with gay ribbons woven into the end of the braids, he was generally to be seen for a few days of each week wandering about the streets of the city.

In his role of Chief Medicine man, and quite a power in the tribe, he was in possession of a number of priceless historic documents, treaties with the white men, representatives of the British Crown, that extended back to the earliest days of the founding of the settlement on the shores of this harbour. They were thrust into an inside pocket of his coat, and bound with a long piece of string. Friends of the old Micmac tried to impress upon him the dangers which he took of losing the interesting documents. The late Harry Piers [d. 1940], curator of the Nova Scotia Provincial Museum, argued with him in vain to allow them to be taken for safe keeping. "Lone Cloud" was adamant. They were not to part from the custody of the Chief Medicine man.

Then he learned his lesson. He made his way to the office of the *Halifax Mail* one day, where he was a seasonal visitor.... On this occasion ... he had a tale of woe. The precious papers had become lost. A story on the mishap appeared in the press, and in quick time came a call from a station in the Musquodoboits. They had been found on a seat in the waiting room, where "Lone Cloud" had apparently stretched out for a sleep while waiting for a train, and getting up, had not noticed the treaties had slipped from his pocket. Then it was that he finally agreed the precious documents should be placed in care of the museum. [No such documents were ever put into the keeping of the Nova Scotia Museum.]
William C. Borrett. *Down East.* 1945:44-45.

1945
Recently a fortunate visit was made to the Market Building in Halifax. There was found John Marr, a soft spoken, intelligent young Micmac Indian. John, at the age of thirty years, is the Grand Chief of the Indian Reservation at Shubenacadie. Chief Marr is an interesting talker ... he went to the ninth grade in school. His studies were carried out at the Catholic High School at East Angus, Quebec....

Today there are about 160 Indians on the reservation.... But under the plans now made for centralization of Indians on the mainland of Nova Scotia, he expects that upwards of 2,000 people of his race may be congregated there. He will then be the Grand Chief over that number, he says. Despite his comparative youth for the responsibilities that will be his, his appearance suggests that he will be well able to cope with any duties that may fall to him.

William C. Borrett. *Down East*. 1945:42.

And then [1946] I got back on another ship, the *Lake Nipigon*. And we went to China. The second engineer was from Herring Cove.... And before we got to Shanghai, there was a Canadian ship coming out. And Sparks, the radio operator, brought a bulletin down, put it on the bulletin board. He said, "We got warning from that Canadian ship not to let your boys to go ashore alone, cause some boys got killed...." Yeah, that was in Shanghai, too. They were gathering bodies from Shanghai. The Communists—Mao Tse-Tung's outfit was about 100 miles north of Shanghai, fall of '46. They were gathering anywhere from 100, 200 corpses—bodies off the streets.... I saw a truck coming, just like any old truck. Throwing those bodies on top of this cart, the cart of this truck. I asked a Chinaman who was working aboard.... "Where are they taking all these bodies they pick up?" He said, "They take them to a fertilizer factory." And he named the place. He just got that far, and a sort of a foreman, he spoke real fast to him in Chinese. And this fellow changed his story—"Oh, I don't know. I think they go out and burn them."

Max Basque to R.H. Whitehead and Ronald Caplan, 9 March 1984. In *Cape Breton's Magazine*. 1989, No. 52:62-63.

1947

One of our best known and most popular Indian guides and hunters passed away at the Bridgewater Hospital on the night of February 15th, John Noel Francis, familiarly known as John. He was a son of Stephen and Kate Francis, and was born in the little Micmac Village at Two Mile Hill, near Potanoc, in the year 1874. In John's boyhood the Micmac people were still numerous in Queens County.... At the age of eleven John began to make the summer journeys to the coast, sometimes with his parents, usually with an elderly Micmac couple named Luxi [Alexis]. Their favourite camping spot was just outside the town of Lunenburg, near Second Peninsula where the brook from Dares Lake enters the sea. There they stayed all summer making baskets, mast-hoops, etc., which old Luxi and young John sold in the town. Each autumn they went back to Potanoc in time for the moose-hunting season. These journeys were performed on foot, with the family possessions on a small cart pulled by a big St. Bernard dog....

In 1915, at the age of 41, John enlisted in the Canadian Army, went overseas and served in France in the 25th Nova Scotia Battalion. His skill at stalking and shooting soon won him a post as a battalion sniper, and he had many adventures between the lines. Finally, while carrying rations up to the front line one night, he was thrown down and half buried by a German shell, which exploded almost alongside him. The rest of the fatigue party failed to find him in the dark and gave him up for dead. John lay unconscious until daylight and then managed to extricate himself. He made his way to the battalion lines and reported for duty. He remained at his post for several days before a medical officer noticed that he was suffering from shell-shock and ordered him to the rear for treatment....

After many months in hospitals in England and France he was sent back to Canada and finally was discharged from the army.... He decided to try some of the ancient remedies of his own people. He brewed various barks and roots and eventually in the peace and solitude of his small home on Two Mile Hill he recovered.... by the sale of axe-handles, baskets, lobster traps and other products of his knife and shaving-horse, and his services as a paid guide with sportsmen in the Queens County woods, he supported himself comfortably the rest of his days.... When people were lost in the woods John was always ready to turn out, at any hour, to lead a search party, and would never take pay for his services.

The Advance. Liverpool, N.S., 20 February 1947.

ca 1957

[Angus Googoo took me to an archaeological site] south of the road between Nyanza and the turn-off to Little Narrows.... Angus dug up a large chip of black rhyolite and told me that he was going to put it under his pillow to see if the ghost would come for it. He made the mistake of confiding in his father. When Angus was out, John [Sabattis Googoo] bored a hole through the floor and fastened a wire to Angus' blanket. Angus went to bed, perhaps thinking of that chip under his pillow, and in the dark his blanket suddenly began to slide off his bed. He bolted for the stairs, and rushed down, "panting and sweating big drops." John Googoo still rocks with laughter as he recalls the joke.

John Erskine. Unpublished MS, collated by Michael Deal. Nova Scotia Museum Library.

1957

Next time you are down Sable River way on the South Shore stop off at Steve Labrador's home and ask him to tell you about the eagle that flew off with his saw horse or the pet trout he owned one time that used to follow him around the woods.... it seems that one morning Steve was doing some work outside in the yard. One of the chickens was walking around when all of a sudden a lightning big eagle swooped down. "That chicken didn't have much time to move, but he ducked under a pile of lumber. The eagle was diving so fast it just latched onto my saw horse and flew off. There was the chicken sitting making fun of him." A couple of weeks later Steve was visiting a neighbor, Bob Lloyd, who lives a short distance away through the woods. The first thing Steve saw was the saw horse in Bob's yard.

"Where did you get the saw horse, Bob?"

"I found it on top of that hill, it was in the clear. I brought it home and used it a couple of times."

"It's mine," explained Steve. "An eagle flew off with it the other day, and that hill must have been the first place he stopped to eat."

"This pet trout," continued Steve, "I caught one trip when I was up the Sable River with a friend. We were camping on Governor's Island and had a good catch, but one was only four inches long. I was sorry I brought it home, it was so small. It seemed to have a little life, so I dropped it in the well. Bless my soul if it didn't get right perky in that water. He stayed in the well about two years and grew oh! oh! about so big, maybe nine inches. The next summer I was cleaning the well and took the trout out and put it in a wash tub. I was just a kid then, and when the job was done, forgot all about the trout. It must have been a couple of days later that Mom said she wanted the tub to wash. So I dumped out the water. Two days later she says to me, 'Look, that trout is still out there in the grass. Why don't you kill it?'

"I went out, and there he was in the tall grass, having a time. I brought him in the house and put the trout in a box behind the stove, and he stayed there all winter. The next spring I went back in the woods to cut some fire wood. I had one back load cut, brought it out, and went back for another load. I looked back, and there was the trout crawling over a log that crossed the brook. The poor little fellow was wiggling and coming along fine when he slipped and fell in the water. So I thought I'll cut another back load, and when I come out, I'll pick the trout up and carry him home in my pocket. But when I came out again the trout was

floating in the water, and belly up. He had drowned."
Steve Labrador to Roy K. Cooke. *The Chronicle-Herald*, quoted in *The Advance*.
Liverpool, N.S., 31 December 1957.

Grandfather [Isaac Sack] really could tell some great stories.... Everything would be quiet, be ready to go to bed. Over at Grandfather's place. And somebody'd say—well, it's a signal for somebody to tell a story: "*Ke'skw a.*" Which means something like 'Once upon a time.' Everything just went quiet. *Ke'skw a.* That means that somebody would tell a story. And Grandfather would tell—I wish to goodness I'd marked some of them down, or remembered. All the weird stories about the Badger [Ki'kwa'ju, the Wolverine] and about the Rabbit. And even about the Frog and the Wild Geese. About the Wild Geese and the Turtle....

Oh, stories like that. God! I can remember some of them, but I could never begin to tell that the way he used to tell them. He'd make that story last all evening, till we'd go to sleep, me and my brothers.... Or sometimes, when he'd see we were getting too sleepy—"I will tell you about it next time...."

Oh, tales.... No wonder they could tell stories, because there was no radio, no gramophone, or no nothing in the evenings, when it got dark. Might keep the home fires, keep the bonfire going, inside a camp. If it was outside, good enough—outside. Sitting all around it. And there would be nobody say anything. And then somebody would say, "*Ke'skw a. Ke'skw a.*"
Max Basque to R.H. Whitehead and Ronald Caplan, 9 March 1984. In *Cape Breton's Magazine*. 1989, No. 52:65.

BIBLIOGRAPHY

PUBLISHED MATERIAL

The Acadian Recorder. Halifax, N.S., 10 February 1849, 24 February 1849, 7 July 1865, 4 August 1883.

The Advance. Liverpool, N.S., 20 February 1947, 31 December 1957.

A General Description of Nova Scotia. Halifax: Royal Acadian School, 1825.

Akins, Thomas. *History of Halifax City.* Halifax: Nova Scotia Historical Society, 1895. 2d ed. Belleville: Mika Publishing, 1973.

———, ed. *Selections from the Public Documents of the Province of Nova Scotia.* Halifax: Charles Annand, 1869.

Archer, Gabriel. "The Relation of Captain Gosnold's Voyage to the North Part of Virginia, 1602." In *Collections of the Massachusetts Historical Society,* Vol. III, Third Series. 1843:73.

Bezanson, Rev. W.B. *Stories of Acadia.* Dartmouth: privately published, 1924.

Birch, Thomas. *Court and Times of Charles I.* Vol. II. Edited by R.F. Williams. London: Henry Colburn, 1848.

Borrett, William C. *Down East.* Halifax: Imperial Publishing Co., 1945.

The Bridgewater Bulletin. Bridgewater, N.S., 24 May 1989.

Brown, Richard. *History of the Island of Cape Breton.* London: Sampson Low Son & Marston, 1869.

Burrage, H.S., ed. *Early English and French Voyages.* New York: Charles Scribner's Sons, 1906.

Campbell, J.R. *A History of Yarmouth, Nova Scotia.* Saint John: Macmillan, 1876.

Campbell, Patrick. *Travels in North America.* Edited by W.F. Ganong. Toronto: The Champlain Society, 1968.

The Cape-Bretonian. Sydney, N.S., 25 January 1834, 28 January 1834. In *The Colonial Patriot.* Pictou, N.S., 18 February 1834.

Champlain, Samuel. *The Works of Samuel de Champlain.* 2d ed. Edited by H.H. Langton and W.F. Ganong. Toronto: Champlain Society, 1971, I-VI.

Churchill, Charles. *Memorials of Missionary Life in Nova Scotia, etc.* London: Mason, Hamilton, Adams, 1845.

Clarkson, John. *Clarkson's Mission to America, 1791-1792.* Edited by C. Bruce Fergusson. Halifax: Public Archives of Nova Scotia, 1971.

Classified Alphabetical List of Exhibitors and Exhibits, Dominion Exhibition of 1881. Halifax: Halifax Herald, 1881.

The Colonial Patriot. Pictou, N.S., 22 February 1828, 21 May 1828, 18 February 1834.

Cormack, William. "Narrative of a Journey Across the Island of Newfoundland in 1822." In *The Beothucks or Red Indians*, by J.P. Howley. Cambridge: Cambridge University Press, 1915.

Dalhousie, Ninth Earl of (George Ramsay). *The Dalhousie Journals*. Edited by Marjory Whitelaw. Ottawa: Oberon, 1978. Vols. I-III.

Dennis, Clara. *Down in Nova Scotia*. Toronto: Ryerson Press, 1934.

———. *More about Nova Scotia*. Toronto: Ryerson Press, n.d.

Denys, Nicolas. *The Description and Natural History of the Coasts of North America (Acadia)*. Translated and edited by W.F. Ganong. Toronto: Champlain Society, 1908.

Department of Indian Affairs. "Annual Report of the Department of Indian Affairs." In *Dominion of Canada Parliament Sessional Papers*. Ottawa: MacLean & Rogers, 1881-1887.

Dickason, Olive P. "Sea Raiders of Acadia." In *Tawow, Canadian Indian Cultural Magazine*, Vol. 5, No. 2. 1976:11.

Dièreville, Sieur de. *Relation of the Voyage to Port Royal in Acadia*. 2d ed. Edited by J.S. Webster. Toronto: Champlain Society, 1968.

Dunraven, Earl of. *Canadian Nights*. London: Smith, Elder & Co., 1914.

The Echo. Halifax, N.S., 18 November 1918.

The Evening Echo. Halifax, N.S., 24 February 1922.

Fergusson, C. Bruce, ed. *Minutes of His Majesty's Council at Annapolis Royal, 1736-1749*. Halifax: Public Archives of Nova Scotia, 1967.

Floyer, Matthew. *Captain Matthew Floyer's Survey Report: Journal of the March by the River Shubenaccadia*. Halifax: Public Archives of Nova Scotia, 1958.

Foreman, Carolyn Thomas. *Indians Abroad: 1493-1938*. Oklahoma City: University of Oklahoma Press, 1943.

Frame, Elizabeth. *Descriptive Sketches of Nova Scotia*. Halifax: A & W MacKinlay, 1864.

Gesner, Abraham. *New Brunswick with Notes for Emigrants*. London: Simmons & Ward, 1847.

Gyles, John. *Memoires of Odd Adventures, Strange Deliverances, etc.* Cincinnati: privately published, 1869.

Hale, Robert. "Journal of an Expedition to Nova Scotia, 1731." In *Report of the Board of Trustees of the Public Archives of Nova Scotia for the Year 1968*. Appendix B. Halifax: Public Archives of Nova Scotia, 1968.

Haliburton, Thomas Chandler. *An Historical and Statistical Account of Nova Scotia*. Halifax: Joseph Howe, 1829.

The Halifax Herald. Halifax, N.S., 28 July 1932, 2 August 1932, 27 October 1932, 3 December 1932, 10 December 1932, 26 July 1933.

The Halifax Journal. Halifax, N.S., 27 December 1824.

The Halifax Reporter. Halifax, N.S., 26 July 1860, 11 August 1860.

Hardy, Campbell. *Sporting Adventures in the New World*. 2 vols. London: Hurst and Blackett, 1855.

————. *Forest Life in Acadie.* New York: D. Appleton & Co., 1869.

Holland, Samuel. "Letter from Samuel Holland Esqr. surveyor Genl. of the northern district of America, to the Secry., dated Novr. 24, 1765." In *Holland's Description of Cape Breton Island and Other Documents.* Edited by D.C. Harvey. Publication No. 2. Halifax: Public Archives of Nova Scotia, 1935.

Insh, G.P. *Scottish Colonial Schemes: 1620-1686.* Glasgow: n.p., 1922.

Jackson, Charles T., and Francis Alger. "A Description of the Mineralogy and Geology of Nova Scotia." In *The American Journal of Science.* 1836, Vol. X:146-147.

Knox, John. The *Journal of Captain John Knox: An Historical Journal of the Campaigns in North America.* 3 vols. Edited by A.G. Doughty. Toronto: The Champlain Society, 1914.

Chancels de Lagrange. "Voyage Made to Isle Royale or Cape Breton Island in Canada in 1716 Aboard the Frigate *Atalante* Commanded by M. de Courbon St. Leger." In *Revue d'Histoire de l'Amérique Française.* Vol. XIII, No. 3, Décembre 1959:427-432.

Lanctot, Gustave. *Documents Relating to Currency, Exchange and Finance in Nova Scotia ... 1675-1758.* Ottawa: Public Archives of Canada, King's Printer, 1933.

Lawson, Mrs William. *History of the Townships of Dartmouth, Preston and Lawrencetown.* Halifax: Morton & Co., 1893.

LeClercq, Chrestien. *New Relation of Gaspesia.* 2d ed. Translated and edited by W.F. Ganong. Toronto: The Champlain Society, 1968.

Leland, Charles. *The Algonquian Legends of New England.* New York: Houghton Mifflin, 1884. 2d ed. Detroit: Singing Tree Press, 1968.

Lescarbot, Marc. *History of New France.* 2d ed. Toronto: Champlain Society, 1968. Vols. I-III.

————. "The Defeat of the Armouchiquois Savages by Chief Membertou and his Savage Allies, in New France, in the Month of July, 1607." Translated by Thomas H. Goetz. In "Membertou's Raid on the Chouacoet 'Almouchiquois'— The Micmac Sack of Saco in 1607," by Alvin H. Morrison. National Museum of Man Ethnology Service, Mercury Series Paper No. 23, Sixth Algonquian Conference. 1974:159-162.

MacLaren, George. *The Pictou Book.* New Glasgow, N.S.: Hector Publishing, 1954.

MacMechan, Archibald, ed. *A Calendar of Two Letter-Books and One Commission-Book in the Possession of the Government of Nova Scotia, 1713-1741.* Halifax: Public Archives of Nova Scotia, n.d. [1900].

Maillard, Pierre Antoine Simon. *An Account of the Customs and Manners of the Mikmakis and Maricheets, Savage Nations, Now Dependant on the Government at Cape Breton.* London: S. Hooper & A. Marely, 1758.

————. "Lettre à Madame de Drucourt," n.d. [*ca* 1750] In *Les Soirées Canadiennes.* Québec: Brousseau Frères, 1863. Translated for this publication by Margaret Anne Hamelin.

————. "Abbé Maillard à Abbé du Fau, 18 October 1749, Archives du Séminaire de Québec." See *Micmacs and Colonists*, by L.F.S. Upton. Vancouver: University of British Columbia Press, 1979.

Marsden, Joshua. *The narrative of a mission to Nova Scotia, New Brunswick, etc.…* [1800]. 2d ed. London: J. Kershaw, 1827.

Martin, John Patrick. *Our Storied Harbor, the Haven of Halifax.* Halifax: Department of Tourists and Travel, 1948.

Martin, R. Montgomery. *A History of Nova Scotia and Cape Breton.* London: Whittaker & Co., 1837.

"Max Basque, Whycocomagh—Conclusion." In *Cape Breton's Magazine.* 1989, No. 52:53-65.

McLeod, Robert. *Markland, or Nova Scotia.* Chicago: Markland Publishing, 1902.

More, James F. *The History of Queens County, N.S.* Halifax: Nova Scotia Printing Co., 1873.

The Morning Chronicle. Halifax, N.S., 26 August 1879.

The Morning Herald. Halifax, N.S., 15 January 1841.

Morse, William Inglis. *Acadiensia Nova.* Vols. I-II. London: Bernard Quaritch, 1935.

The Novascotian. Halifax, N.S., 7 May 1840, 6 April 1846, 30 July 1849, 30 June 1851, 1 March 1852.

The Novascotian or Colonial Herald. Halifax, N.S., 10 August 1825.

Nova Scotian and Weekly Chronicle. Halifax, N.S., 10 July 1903.

Ormond, Douglas. *The Roman Catholic Church in Cobequid, Acadie, etc.* Truro: n.p., 1979.

Parsons, Elsie Clews. "Micmac Folklore." In *Journal of American Folklore.* 1925, Vol. 38:55-133.

Patterson, George. *History of the County of Pictou, Nova Scotia.* 1st ed., 1877. 2d ed. Belleville, Ont.: Mika Studios, 1972.

Petrone, Penny, ed. *First People, First Voices.* Toronto, University of Toronto Press, 1983.

Quinn, David B. "The Voyage of Etienne Bellenger to the Maritimes in 1583: A New Document." In *Canadian Historical Review,* XLIII. 1962.

Rand, Silas T. *Legends of the Micmacs.* New York: Longmans, Green & Co., 1894.

Ribault, Jean-Yves. *Les Iles Saint-Pierre et Miquelon.* Saint-Pierre: Imprimerie au Gouvernement Saint-Pierre, 1968. Translated for this publication by Scott Robson.

Roth, Luther. *Acadie and the Acadians.* Philadelphia: Lutheran Publishing Society, 1890.

Sasco, Emile and Joseph Lehuenen. *Ephémérides des Iles St-Pierre et Miquelon.* Saint-Pierre: Imprimerie au Gouvernement Saint-Pierre, 1970. Translated for this publication by Margaret Anne Hamelin.

Seccombe, Rev. John. "The Diary of Rev. John Seccombe." In *Report of the Board of Trustees of the Public Archives of Nova Scotia for the Year 1959.* Appendix B:20-37. Halifax: Public Archives of Nova Scotia, 1959.

Seume, Johan. *Mein Leben.* Stuttgart: Philipp Reclam Jun., 1961. Translated for this publication by Horst Deppe and Brigitte Beckershaus Petersmann.

Silver, Arthur P. *Farm, Cottage, Camp and Canoe in Maritime Canada.* London: G. Routledge & Sons, n.d. [1907].

Smethurst, Gamaliel. *A Narrative of an Extraordinary Escape out of the Hands of the Indians in the Gulph of St. Lawrence.* London: privately printed, 1774.

Surette, L.L., "The Abbe Jean Mande Sigogne, from 1763 to 1844." *Collections of the N.S. Historical Society,* Vol. 25. Halifax: N.S. Historical Society, 1942.

Thomas, John. "Diary of John Thomas." In *Journals of Beausejour.* Edited by John Clarence Webster. Halifax: Public Archives of Nova Scotia, 1937.

Thwaites, R.G. ed. *Jesuit Relations and Allied Documents.* 73 vols. Cleveland: Burrows Brothers, 1896-1901.

Towne, C.H. *Ambling Through Acadia.* Toronto: Goodchild, 1923.

Uniacke, Rev. Richard J. *Uniacke's Sketches of Cape Breton, 1862-1865.* Edited by C. Bruce Fergusson. Halifax: Public Archives of Nova Scotia, Nova Scotia Series, 1958.

Upton, L.F.S. *Micmacs and Colonists.* Vancouver: University of British Columbia Press, 1979.

Vincent de Paul, Père. *Memoir of Father Vincent.* Translated by A.M. Pope. Charlottetown: Coombes, 1886.

"A Visit with Max Basque, Whycocomagh." In *Cape Breton's Magazine.* 1989, No. 51:15-29.

Wade, Lennie D. *Curious Glimpses of Digby County.* Digby, N.S.: Courier Press, n.d. [1907?]

Wallis, Wilson D., and Ruth Sawtell Wallis. *The Micmac Indians of Eastern Canada.* Minneapolis: The University of Minnesota, 1955.

Webster, John Clarence. *Acadia at the End of the Seventeenth Century.* 2d ed. Saint John: New Brunswick Museum, 1934.

———, ed. *Journals of Beausejour.* Halifax: Public Archives of Nova Scotia, 1937b.

———. *Thomas Pichon, the Spy of Beausejour.* Halifax: Public Archives of Nova Scotia, 1937a.

West, John. *A Journal of a Mission to the Indians of the British Provinces of New Brunswick and Nova Scotia, etc.* London: Seely, 1827.

UNPUBLISHED MANUSCRIPTS

Dalhousie Archives, Killam Library, Dalhousie University, Halifax, N.S.

Francis, John, to Thomas H. Raddall, Two Mile Hill, Milton, N.S., 1944. Raddall Papers.

Gloade, Samuel Freeman, to Thomas H. Raddall, Two Mile Hill, Milton, N.S., 1944. Raddall Papers. Excerpts from this interview were published in *Cape Breton's Magazine.* 1984, No. 35.

Paul, Chief William Benoit, to Thomas H. Raddall, Broad Cove, N.S., August 1933. Raddall Papers.

Raddall MS, Thomas H. Raddall Papers.

Province of Nova Scotia
Legislative Library, Province House, Halifax:
Legislative Assembly of Nova Scotia Journals. 2 April 1800.

Chearnley, William, to Joseph Howe, 4 March 1854. In *Legislative Assembly of Nova Scotia Journals*. 1854, Appendix 26:211-212.

Dodd, E.M., and H.W. Crawley. In *Legislative Assembly of Nova Scotia Journals*. 12 February 1848, Appendix 36.

Gesner, Abraham. In *Legislative Assembly of Nova Scotia Journals*. 1848, Appendix 24; 1849, Appendix 36.

Freeman, Whitman. In *Legislative Assembly of Nova Scotia Journals*. 16 January 1863, Appendix 16:6.

Howe, Joseph. In *Legislative Assembly of Nova Scotia Journals*. 1844, Appendix 50.

Perley, Moses. In *Legislative Assembly of Nova Scotia Journals*. 1843, Appendix 49.

Nova Scotia Museum, Halifax

Anonymous. "Legends, Bear River, Annapolis County, English, August 1937." Unpublished MS, probably collected by Dr Helen Creighton. Printed Matter File.

Anonymous woman to Harry Piers, n.d. Unpublished notes, Printed Matter File.

Bartlett Alexis, Jeremiah [alias Jerry Lonecloud, Jerry Bartlett, Jerry Luxie]. Personal communication to Harry Piers. 3 February 1912, 7 June 1913, 11 June 1914, 20 December 1915, 17 July 1916, 24 July 1916, 17 September 1917, 31 December 1917, 22 January 1918, 6 September 1918, 8 February 1919, 17 June 1919, 29 April 1921, August 1921, 23 December 1921, 11 August 1922, 21 February 1922, 1 February 1926, 28 June 1926, 22 July 1927, 27 July 1929, 16 September 1929, 2 October 1929. Unpublished notes, Printed Matter File.

———, to Nova Scotia Chiefs. Shubenacadie, N.S., 15 August 1916. Rough draft of letter, Printed Matter File.

———, to the Department of Indian Affairs, 9 April 1917, 27 November 1917. Printed Matter File.

———, to T.D. MacLean, 27 April 1918. Printed Matter File.

———, to Mrs Oscar North, n.d. [1918]. Printed Matter File.

Coape Sherbrooke, Sir John, to Louis Benjamin Pominout, 28 April 1814. Original parchment document 31.24.

Cope, Joseph C. [?] to Harry Piers. 14 January 1914, 31 January 1924, 9 February 1926, April 1926, 16 April 1926, [?] 1926. Unpublished notes, Printed Matter File.

———. Letter to Harry Piers, 21 January 1924. Printed Matter File.

———. "A Short History of the Mic Mac Indians in Halifax Co. Nova Scotia Since Confederation." Unpublished MS, 9 February 1926. Printed Matter File.

Cruikshank, Howard, to Harry Piers, 5 February, 28 February 1933. Printed Matter File.

Erskine, John. "Micmac Notes: 1958." Unpublished MS, Printed Matter File.

———. Unpublished MS, collated by Michael Deal. Nova Scotia Museum Library.

Gaspard Le Marchant, Sir John, to James Paul, 15 September 1856. Printed Matter File.

Hardy, Campbell. In "Evangeline's Land." Unpublished MS, *ca* 1910. Printed Matter File.

McDonald, John L., to Harry Piers, July 1913. Printed Matter File.

McDonald, Louis Noel, to Harry Piers, 28 April 1921, 28 November 1923. Printed Matter File.

Morris, Ben, to Jeremiah Bartlett Alexis, personal communication to Harry Piers, 20 December 1915. Unpublished notes, Printed Matter File.

Mulgrave to James Paul, 6 August 1860. Printed Matter File.

Noel, Chief John, personal communication to Harry Piers, n.d. Unpublished notes, Printed Matter File.

Pacifique, Père J., Restigouche, Québec, to Harry Piers, June 1911. Printed Matter File.

Paul, Elizabeth, to Abram Paul, 25 February 1918. Printed Matter File.

Paul, John Denny, to the Department of Indian Affairs, 5 December 1916. Printed Matter File.

Sack, Isaac, to Harry Piers, 26 February 1921. Printed Matter File.

Sack, Martin, to John Erskine. In "Micmac Notes: 1958," by John Erskine. Unpublished MS, Printed Matter File.

————, to H.L. Bury, Department of Indian Affairs, 18 January 1919. Printed Matter File.

Wood, Thomas. "Rev. Thomas Wood to Rev. Dr. Burton of the Society for the Propagation of the Gospel in Foreign Parts. The Society for the Propagation of the Gospel in Foreign Parts, Lambeth, Letter B.25; Nova Scotia 1760 to 1786." Handwritten copy, H. Piers' handwriting, Printed Matter File.

Whitehead, Ruth Holmes. "The Kwetejk Wars." MS adapted from *Legends of the Micmacs*, by Silas T. Rand. New York: Longmans, Green & Co., 1894.

Public Archives of Nova Scotia, Halifax

Bartlett Alexis, Jeremiah [alias Jerry Lonecloud] to Clara Dennis. Clara Dennis Collection, Scrapbook #1, 1923.

Casteel, Anthony. "Anthony Casteel's Journal." British Museum, Brown MSS, Add. 19073, f.ll, No. 23. Copy in Public Archives of Nova Scotia, Halifax, RG1, #23.

Chearnley, William. "Indian List for the Year 1855." MG15, Vol. 5, #69.

Colonial Office 217, Vol. 54.

Deschamps, Isaac. MG1, Vol 258, Item 8:8, 20, 21.

Hopson, Peregrine Thomas, to the Right Honourable the Earl of Holdernesse, 10 October 1752. CO 217, Vol. 40, p. 371.

Howe, Joseph. "Indian Journal." MG432, 1842.

Inverness County Court. King *vs* Sylyboy. Minutes, 1928.

Jennings, Dr Edward, to Sir Rupert George, 15 February 1847. MG15, Vol. 4, #16.

————, to Sir Rupert George, 15 February 1847. MG15, Vol. 4, #18.

————, to Sir Rupert George, 16 February 1847. MG15, Vol. 4, #19.

————. 15 February 1847. MG15, Vol. 4, #25.

Morris to Lord Cornwallis. Prefixed to Anthony Casteel's Journal. British Museum, Brown MSS, Add. 19073, f.ll, No. 23. Copy in Public Archives of Nova Scotia, RG1, #23.

MG15, Vol. 3, #49. 23 December 1837.

MG15, Vol. 3, #65.

MG15, Vol. 4, #19.

MG15, Vol. 4, #26.

MG15, Vol. 5, #44, 26 January 1855.

MG15, Vol. 5, #47, 3 February 1855.

Nova Scotian Baptismal Registries: St Gregory's, Liverpool, and St Jerome's, Caledonia, N.S.

Paul, Peter. "Biography of Peter Paul—Written February 16th, 1865, From His Own Statement—By an Amanuensis." Dr George Patterson Collection, Scrapbook No. 5, newspaper clipping.

RG1, Vol. 37, #14. "Ceremonials at Concluding a Peace with the several Districts of the General Mickmack Nation of Indians in His Majesty's Province of Nova Scotia and a Copy of the Treaty. 25 June 1761."

RG1, Vol. 430, #23.5, 17 December 1783.

RG1, Vol. 319:315. Extract, Council Minutes, 9 March 1790.

RG1, Vol. 430, #57. William Barss's Account, n.d., ca 1801.

RG1, Vol. 430, #62, 19 March 1801. Edited for this publication by R.H. Whitehead.

RG1, Vol. 430, #77. Jon. Crane's Account, n.d, ca 1800-1801.

RG1, Vol. 430, #109. William Nixon's Account, n.d.

RG1, Vol. 430, #146, 1808-1809.

RG1, Vol. 146, 2 January 1826.

RG41 "C," Vol. 22, 6A. Inquest on the body of Anne Gloud [Claude].

Private Collection

Bain, Bethiah Brown. Document in Bethiah Bain Family Bible.

Province of Prince Edward Island

Alguimou, Louis Francis, and Piel Jacques, Oliver Thoma, Peter Tony, Michael Mitchell. In *Legislative Assembly of Prince Edward Island Journals*, 1832:11.

National Archives of Canada, Ottawa

Prevost to Minister. Louisbourg, 12 May 1753. MG1, Archives des Colonies, Série C 11 B, Correspondance général, Vol. 33, 159 ff.

Prevost to Minister. Isle Royale, 17 June 1753. MG1, Archives des Colonies, Série C 11 B, Correspondance général, Vol. 33.

Admiralty Records, London, U.K.

Thompson, Captain Samuel, HMS *Lark*, to Philip Stevens, secretary to the Lords of the Admiralty, 16 April 1764. Admiralty Records 1/2590, #4.

Newberry Library, Chicago, Illinois
LaChasse, Père Pierre. "General Census Made in the Month of November 1708, of the Indians of Acadia who reside on the East Coast." Ayer MS 751. Excerpts translated by R.H. Whitehead and Bernie Francis.

INFORMANTS
Basque, Max, to R.H. Whitehead, personal communication 1976, 1977, 1984, 1990.
————, to R.H. Whitehead and Ronald Caplan, taped interview, March 1984.
————, and Isaac Basque to R.H. Whitehead, personal communication, July 1977.
Dillman, Leighton, to Janet Kitz, October 1982, personal communication. Courtesy Janet Kitz.
Forsythe, Ian, to R.H. Whitehead, 3 November 1982, personal communication.
Knockwood, Henry, to R.H. Whitehead, personal communication, 1984.
Letson, Ella Marguerite, to Blake Conrad, Port Medway, Nova Scotia. Taped interview, 4 April 1983. Courtesy Blake Conrad.
Paul, Chief William, to Dr Helen Creighton. Taped interview, Shubenacadie, N.S., 1944. Transcribed by R.H. Whitehead from the original tape in Dr Creighton's possession. Courtesy Dr Helen Creighton. Tape now in the Public Archives of Nova Scotia.

ACKNOWLEDGEMENTS

I WOULD LIKE TO EXPRESS MY APPRECIATION, ONCE again, to Dr Marie Elwood of the Nova Scotia Museum, for encouraging me to write this book. Scott Robson proofread the rough draft, and has provided numerous sources over the past fifteen years, as have many other staff members of the museum. Publications committee chairman John Hennigar-Shuh was instrumental in overseeing the book's completion. I am grateful to Dorothy Blythe and Nancy Robb—thanks for the computer—at Nimbus and to Kathy Kaulbach, the book's designer, for all their help.

Putting together such a collection would have been infinitely more difficult without the generosity of Dr H.F. McGee, Jr, of Saint Mary's University, who permitted me to make use of his extensive personal library of Micmac sources. Rob Ferguson, Birgitta Linderoth Wallace, and many other Canadian Parks Service staff in Nova Scotia, particularly at the Fortress of Louisbourg, have provided important material over the years. Jonathan King in Great Britain and Harald Prins and Bruce J. Bourque in Maine have contributed many "finds" of documents, as have Charles Martijn in Québec and Ed Tompkins, Ralph Pastore and Ingeborg Marshall in Newfoundland. Claudia Haagen did some of the preliminary newspaper surveys in 1978. Janet Kitz, Blake Conrad, and the late Dr Helen Creighton all very kindly allowed me to use entries from oral histories which they had collected from non-Micmac sources.

Bernie Francis provided translations of Micmac words and help with Micmac nomenclature.

Dr Thomas H. Raddall graciously gave permission to use excerpts from his unpublished papers, now in the Dalhousie

Archives. I would also like to take this opportunity to thank the Champlain Society, Toronto, for making so many seventeenth-century sources available in English, and for allowing researchers to quote from them liberally.

Most especial gratitude is due to the many Micmac informants whose contributions of oral histories, over the centuries, has made this book so much less one-sided. My particular appreciation goes to Max Basque, to the late Isaac Basque, and to Henry Knockwood, as well as to Richard McEwan, Sarah Denny, and Rita Joe. Dr Peter Christmas of the Micmac Association of Cultural Studies kindly vetted the manuscript, and wrote the foreword.

Finally, I owe a debt of the heart to my family—Sarah Whitehead, Satya Ramen, and Peter Hull—for all their support. This project has been fifteen years in coming to fruition. I thank everyone for their patience, and hope that the book may be of use for many more years to come.

INDEX